D1070753

Designing
INSTRUCTION

Designing
INSTRUCTION

Making Best Practices Work in Standards-Based Classrooms

Judith K. March   Karen H. Peters

CORWIN PRESS
A SAGE Publications Company
Thousand Oaks, CA 91320

For information:

Corwin Press
A Sage Publications Company
2455 Teller Road
Thousand Oaks, California 91320
www.corwinpress.com

Sage Publications Ltd.
1 Oliver's Yard
55 City Road
London EC1Y 1SP
United Kingdom

Sage Publications India Pvt. Ltd.
B 1/I 1 Mohan Cooperative Industrial Area
Mathura Road, New Delhi 110 044
India

Sage Publications Asia-Pacific Pte. Ltd.
33 Pekin Street #02-01
Far East Square
Singapore 048763

Printed in the United States of America.

Library of Congress Cataloging-in-Publication Data

March, Judith K.
Designing instruction : making best practices work in standards-based classrooms / Judith K. March, Karen H. Peters.
        p. cm.
Includes bibliographical references and index.
ISBN 978-1-4129-3884-6 (cloth)
ISBN 978-1-4129-3885-3 (pbk.)
    1. Curriculum planning—United States. 2. Education—Standards—United States. 3. Educational change—United States. I. Peters, Karen H. II. Title.
LB2806.15.M365 2007
379.1'550973—dc22

2006101259

This book is printed on acid-free paper.

07 08 09 10 11 10 9 8 7 6 5 4 3 2 1

Acquisitions Editor:	Allyson P. Sharp
Editorial Assistant:	Mary Dang
Copy Editor:	Ani Ayvazian
Typesetter:	C&M Digitals (P) Ltd.
Proofreader:	Theresa Kay
Indexer:	Sheila Bodell
Cover Designer:	Rose Storey

Contents

Acknowledgments

We gratefully acknowledge the hundreds of districts with which we have worked over the years. In particular, we wish to thank the thousands of teachers who never get enough credit for being subjected to one reform process after another, including ours. We learned something from every one of them, and it is their work that has made this book possible.

We greatly appreciate the contributions of the following reviewers:

Deborah Alexander-Davis
2004 Tennessee Principal of the Year
Adjunct Professor
Tennessee Technological University & Tusculum College
Kingston, TN

Sandra E. Archer
NBCT
Volusia County Schools
Ormond Beach, FL

Nancy Marie Borie Betler
Full-time Mentor, NBCT
Instructional Excellence Department, Charlotte Mecklenburg Schools
Charlotte, NC

Linda C. Diaz
Program Specialist for Professional Development
Monroe County School District
Key West, FL

Arthur Ellis
Director of Curriculum and Instruction
Peoria School District 150
Peoria, IL

Cindy Miller
Program/Project Coordinator
University of North Texas
Denton, TX

Helane Smith Miller
Assistant Principal
Woodrow Wilson High School
Washington, DC

Sara E. Spruce
Professor of Education
Olivet Nazarene University
Bourbonnais, IL

Barbara W. Weaver
Teacher, Instructional Leader
Thomas Eaton Fundamental Middle School
Hampton, VA

About the Authors

 **Judith K. March**, PhD, is currently a Senior Consultant for EdFOCUS Initiative, Stow, Ohio. EdFOCUS is a nonprofit agency of dedicated education professionals who provide customized consultation, data management, and training services in school reform. Dr. March is a retired professor from Kent State University and is currently an adjunct member of the graduate faculty of Ashland University. Her special areas of focus are (a) standards-based curriculum redesign; (b) the Best Practices research for classroom instruction; (c) assessment and accountability, including the construction of diagnostic and benchmark tests; (d) long-term and short-range planning; (e) capacity-building for continual improvement, featuring Collaborative Observation; (f) data-based decision making; and (g) compliance with No Child Left Behind (NCLB).

March has worked in school reform for over two decades, providing services to nearly 50 school districts in Canada, California, Florida, Indiana, Minnesota, New Jersey, and Ohio. Her work has included urban, suburban, and rural districts. She and the other EdFOCUS consultants are currently working with federally funded Comprehensive School Reform projects in Minneapolis and Hamilton Township, New Jersey. They are also designated providers for Ohio's newest school reform initiative: regional assistance teams working through Educational Service Centers. March and colleague Karen H. Peters have been contracted by the Battelle-for-Kids Division of the Battelle Institute to work in with various research initiatives with Value-Added. Dr. March is also a consultant for Harcourt Assessment, Inc.

An experienced educator, March has taught high school English, Speech, and Drama and served as an Assistant Principal for a large high school. She has also been a Curriculum Supervisor, the Director of Curriculum, and the Assistant Superintendent for an Educational Service Center. She was Director of Developmental Education at Ashland University and Associate Professor at Ashland University and served on the graduate faculty at Kent State University. While at Kent State, March and Peters operated an outreach center for school reform, and these experiences compelled them to develop the *Instructional Design* process to integrate standards-based reform with the Best Practices research to deliver and assess classroom instruction. In addition, March and Peters are developing a Diagnostic and Mastery Testing process to help teachers determine students' entry levels and pinpoint their precise learning needs and then to assess their year-end mastery to determine the extent of growth.

With Peters, March has coauthored a variety of articles on educational reform, staff development, instructional design, and collaborative supervision. Through Phi Delta Kappa International, they published a book about the role of curriculum in school reform titled *Developing High-Performance Schools: Instructional Redesign for the Learner-Centered Classroom.* In addition, the two coauthored *Collaborative Observation: Putting Classroom Instruction at the Center of School Reform,* published by Corwin Press. March earned her bachelor's and master of arts degrees from the Bowling Green State University and her doctorate in Curriculum and Instruction from the University of Toledo.

Karen H. Peters, PhD, is currently a Senior Consultant for EdFOCUS Initiative in Stow, Ohio. EdFOCUS is a non-profit agency of dedicated education professionals who provide customized consultation, data management, and training services in school reform. Dr. Peters is a retired professor from Kent State University and is currently an adjunct member of the graduate faculty of Ashland University. Her special areas of focus are (a) standards-based curriculum redesign; (b) the Best Practices research for classroom instruction; (c) assessment and accountability, including the development of diagnostic and mastery tests; (d) the training and development of principals; (e) capacity-building for continual improvement, featuring Collaborative Observation; (f) data-based decision making; and (g) compliance with No Child Left Behind (NCLB).

Peters has worked in school reform for over two decades, providing services to nearly 50 school districts in Canada, California, Florida, Indiana, Minnesota, New Jersey, and Ohio. Her work has included urban, suburban, and rural districts. She and the other EdFOCUS consultants are currently working with federally funded Comprehensive School Reform projects in Minneapolis and Hamilton Township, New Jersey. They are also designated providers for Ohio's newest school reform initiative: regional assistance teams working through Educational Service Centers. Peters and colleague Judith K. March have been contracted by the Battelle-for-Kids Division of the Battelle Institute to work with them on the Value-Added research initiative. Dr. Peters is also a consultant for Harcourt Assessment, Inc.

An experienced educator, Peters has taught at the elementary- and middle-school levels in Ohio and Florida, focusing on math and science. She has served as an Elementary Principal and has been a Curriculum Supervisor and the Director of Curriculum for an Educational Service Center. She also served as a member of the graduate faculty of Kent State University. While at Kent State, Peters and March operated an outreach Center for school reform, and these experiences compelled them to develop the **Instructional Design** process to integrate standards-based reform with the Best Practices research to deliver and assess classroom instruction. In addition, Peters and March are developing a Diagnostic and Mastery Testing process to help teachers determine students' entry levels and pinpoint their precise learning needs and then to assess their year-end mastery to determine the extent of growth.

With March, Peters has coauthored a variety of articles on educational reform, staff development, instructional design, and collaborative supervision. Through Phi Delta Kappa International, they published a book about the role of curriculum in school reform titled *Developing High-Performance Schools: Instructional Redesign for the Learner-Centered Classroom.* In addition, the two coauthored *Collaborative Observation: Putting Classroom Instruction at the Center of School Reform*, published by Corwin Press. Peters earned her bachelor's degree at the University of South Florida, her master's from Youngstown State University, and her doctorate in Educational Administration from Kent State University.

Introduction

OUR JOURNEY THROUGH SCHOOL REFORM ■

As veterans of school reform, we can't remember when schools *weren't* being reformed! The two of us have spent over 25 years each in various sorts of school improvement efforts, first to increase student achievement in our own districts and then attempting to be of assistance to others as professors, researchers, and onsite providers. With the release of "A Nation at Risk" in 1983, the pursuit of educational reform became a matter of public concern. The country suddenly felt itself vulnerable due to the mediocre quality of its schools, and education reform was thrust into national prominence. By 1990, every bookstore had a prominent display rack with the latest in school reform, documenting the urgency, describing various models of reform, and announcing what other countries were doing. Soon thereafter, a spate of books came out lamenting the failure of most school reform efforts; despite the flurry of activity, schools continued to operate much the same as before, and student performance was still below par. Fast-forward to 2007, and not much has changed.

On a less conspicuous rack were books about curriculum and instructional delivery, physically and intellectually separate from school reform as if the two were totally disconnected. This was unfortunate, since what happens in classrooms determines the quality of a school and is largely responsible for reforms that succeed or fail. Test scores don't improve because a new set of academic standards are in place, or a new mission is adopted, or students are grouped heterogeneously. Education had yet to acknowledge what medicine, the automobile industry, and even government had long since discovered: Each part of the enterprise operates in conjunction with all of the others and change in any one element affects the entire system. Ironically, the very institution charged with teaching children to understand the interrelatedness of things had not applied systemic thinking to its own reform. "School reform" and "classroom instruction" are still in separate racks, an uncanny symbolism for what had become two parallel and sometimes competing fronts to restore America's confidence in its schools.

Now in the first decade of the twenty-first century, the effects of this split persist. One set of districts adopts prominent models of comprehensive school reform, reinvents their infrastructure, and yet fails to see a difference in student performance. They bring together school and community

1

to articulate a vision and a set of beliefs, redeploy district resources for greater efficiency, and increase graduation requirements. But there is never any real change in classroom instruction.

Another set of districts purchases beautifully packaged instructional materials with scripted delivery strategies, and they attempt to plunk these into an infrastructure that is essentially unchanged. Their building administrators behave as usual, assuming that classroom instruction is the sole issue. Teachers feel no ownership for the new materials; someone else wrote them, and there is really no need for a personal investment. In neither set of districts is the school reform effort a success, essentially because it is incomplete. We feel that the reform of the infrastructure and the reform of classroom instruction should be integrated into the same project as a seamless whole.

■ ENTER *INSTRUCTIONAL DESIGN*

By the mid-1990s, we had been working with various school reform initiatives in dozens of school districts. Whether dealing with the social and political challenges facing the urban schools, helping suburban schools satisfy the demands of increasingly frustrated parents/guardians, or assisting small rural districts collaborate with each other to maximize their resources, we saw the same lack of attention to the teaching-learning process in the context of the other reform activities. We found that teachers were basically relying on adopted textbooks in much the same way they always had, trusting that publishers certainly knew better than the classroom professional what was best. Many innovative teaching practices were being attempted, but they were isolated here and there with no real consistency. Professional development activities were largely "sit-and-gets" with a prominent speaker who spent more time criticizing current practices and belaboring the obvious need for reform than offering specific, practical suggestions to make things better.

Administrators were being challenged to exercise "instructional leadership" but were never involved in the reform of classroom instruction itself; they were not specifically trained to exercise leadership during a reform process. Most distressing of all were the districts that used an annual succession of new reform initiatives as an excuse to keep starting over. This meant no consistency, no longevity, and no accountability. These multiple switches and shifts prevented any sort of continuity or quality control in classrooms, resulting in what has become known in the vernacular as the "flavor-of-the-month" or the "strategy-de-jour" approach. Trying to help those districts get a handle on reform was like herding cats.

What made us think we could do any better? As members of the graduate faculty at Kent State University in northeast Ohio, we had an opportunity to respond. In 1995, we launched the *Instructional Design* process. It was not a curriculum and not a set of canned teaching strategies; there were already hundreds of both. What we created was a series of professional development activities to help teams of teachers and administrators identify essential curricular outcomes as measurable performances (called *Performance Indicators*) and then devise planning, delivery, and assessment strategies (with materials) to implement the new curriculum and to monitor its success. Our premise was that whether the district selected a commercial curriculum-instructional program or developed their own, they needed a process to fully integrate that program into the deep culture of each building as part of the daily routine. Concurrent with classroom improvements, the infrastructure of each school had to be adjusted to support and sustain these reforms, which includes the direct involvement of the principal. Parents/guardians needed to become more fully integrated in the academic program, and the community needed to become aware that it was no longer "business as usual." Working with so many different types of schools gave us varied settings in which to pilot and field-test the process, to have it externally evaluated, and to publish our findings (see Appendix A). The results were promising, and we have continued to modify and improve the *Instructional Design* process. Every client district provides another contribution.

Instructional Design is the subject of our three books and numerous articles (referenced in the bibliography) and is being utilized in several urban, suburban, and rural districts around the country. With each project, we continue to validate the process and learn something new to share with the next group of teachers. We are proud of our many successes and admit to having made our share of mistakes. We gladly share both, since what we learned from these "uh-ohs" has helped make our process that much stronger.

THE PURPOSE OF THIS BOOK ■

Our purpose in writing this book is simple: to provide practitioners the kind of book we wish we'd had 20 years ago when we started out in school reform. It addresses what happens in classrooms as the heart of school reform but always within the context of the building infrastructure to facilitate the enacted classroom reforms and to sustain them once they are in place. Successful school reform is the inseparable union of the teaching-learning process and the infrastructure, and one cannot exist without the other. We attempt to present a doable and research-based process for improving student achievement through classroom instruction within the context of a supportive infrastructure. We also offer several capacity-building strategies to strengthen the reforms as they are enacted and to sustain them once they are in place. To be practical, such a book has to meet three criteria: (a) it must be written by practitioners, (b) it must be well-grounded in research, and (c) it must be written in a conversational mode.

1. **It must be written by and for practitioners**, just like the people who will use it. Those responsible for school reform need to read stories and see examples from people who have been working "in the trenches" and not just watching from the safety of the podium. The suggestions offered should be relevant for every setting, from urban districts facing the maximum levels of scrutiny to the least remarkable township school still struggling to get two subgroups to make Adequate Yearly Progress (AYP).

2. **It must be well grounded in research** and reflect current developments in school reform. The most trustworthy advice on school reform comes from authors who gladly attribute their ideas to those whose work they are using. In fact, there is no higher compliment to the scholars and researchers of education reform than to be cited in the credits for successful reform efforts. For the reader's convenience, we have available on request an annotated review of the research cited in each chapter.

3. **It must be written in a conversational mode.** Today's practitioner has neither the time nor the patience to wade through pedantic discourse just to find the subject of the sentence. So this book departs from conventional exposition. It is an attempt to talk with, not down to, the modern school reformer. We make no apologies for an occasional contraction, nor for the use of second person as "you." Every so often, there is even an occasional *bird-walk*, or an aside that attempts to highlight observations and lessons we've learned. These appear in a box and are designated with a [. . . ✒].

In trying to provide the kind of book we wish we'd had, we have endeavored to keep things simple, but not simplistic; we respect the complexity of school reform and fully acknowledge there are no quick fixes. We have attempted to achieve a tone of collaborative problem solving to offer what we've observed and to encourage the reader to reflect on his or her own experience. The anecdotes and examples included are from actual school districts where we have worked, and the sample materials were actually developed by teachers and/or are those that have been validated in actual training.

■ THE FIVE PARTS

Part I: The *Instructional Design* Process

Chapter 1 describes the eight core elements of school reform most frequently found in the research as associated with improved student achievement. It details how the features of *Instructional Design* interface with those core elements and how together they focus on the primary locus of school reform, the classroom. It also provides an aerial view of the *Instructional Design* process, including (a) standards-based curriculum and (b) the integration of the Best Practices techniques into the delivery and assessment of classroom instruction.

Chapter 2 addresses *Performance Indicators*, or the translation of content standards into the academic performances required of students. These indicators are developed by teams of teachers in the context of the district curriculum, and they are adopted by the Board as the official achievement targets of the district.

Part II: Planning

Chapter 3 looks at *Curriculum Mapping*, or the development of yearlong calendars showing when each of the *Performance Indicators* is to be taught. The *Indicators* are assigned to content units, and some *Indicators* reappear several times across the year. The *Map* is an informal "contract" between the district and its community to ensure that the adopted *Performance Indicators* will be implemented in every classroom.

Chapter 4 is devoted to *Unit Planning:* Rationale and Format. The *Unit Plan* is the format for delivering and assessing classroom instruction. It is based on the *Performance Indicators* and structured around the Best Practices, teacher-effects, and constructivist learning research. Chapter 4 provides the Rationale and Format and includes logistical considerations and issues related to the four-quadrant *Unit Planning* process.

Part III: Best Practices

Chapter 5 addresses Quadrants 1 and 2 of Unit Planning: Motivation and Information. These two quadrants comprise the INPUT half of the *Unit Plan,* and this chapter discusses the criteria for each quadrant, including examples. To help teachers include various levels of mental processing, Bloom's Taxonomy is discussed, including specific examples.

Chapter 6 extends Quadrant 2 by providing an in-depth examination of the Best Practices referred to as *Unit Planning:* Learning Constructs. These include Organizational Patterns, Summary, Note Taking, Vocabulary, Problem Analysis and Problem Solving, Graphic Organizers, Levels of Questioning, and Similarities and Differences.

Chapter 7 concludes Quadrant 2 with an in-depth description of the Best Practices referred to as *Unit Planning:* Delivery Strategies. It includes Lecture or Explanation, Demonstration, Guided Discussion, Inquiry, Learning Circles, the Socratic Seminar, and Action Research.

Part IV: Assessment

Chapter 8 addresses Quadrants 3 and 4 of the *Unit Planning:* Assessment and Culmination. These two quadrants comprise the OUTPUT half of the *Unit Plan* and address how to measure student mastery of the *Performance Indicators* on which the unit is built. This chapter discusses the criteria for each quadrant, including explanations and examples of how to devise valid paper-pencil assessments that simulate high-stakes tests and how to construct valid performance or authentic assessments, including scoring rubrics appropriate to the *Performance Indicators* of the *Unit Plan.*

Part V: Capacity-Building to Sustain Classroom Reforms

Chapter 9 addresses how best to fully integrate the enacted reforms into the deep structure of each school and throughout the district so that they become "the way business is done here." We offer five strategies to accomplish this formidable task, each of which should begin at the outset of the effort and gradually develop in strength throughout the process. The five strategies are the following: (a) various benchmarking processes to monitor student progress; (b) the use of data by teachers and administrators to inform classroom instruction; (c) the use of Building

Leadership Teams to plan, implement, and monitor the reform process; (d) specific Stewardship roles and responsibilities for administrators to lead and sustain the reform efforts; and (e) coaching on the Collaborative Observation process to help teachers work as partners to implement the enacted reforms.

■ WHO SHOULD BUY THIS BOOK

In our opinion, this book is equally useful for every stakeholder in the educational enterprise who genuinely cares whether research-based teaching and learning reforms are actually accomplished in America's schools and whether these reforms persist after the initial funding to put them in place is gone. It's a great resource for (a) *superintendents* who want a practical, user-friendly process to help them accomplish needed reforms in the district's curricular and instructional program; (b) *curriculum supervisors* charged with finding a reform process that is standards-based, utilizes the Best Practices research, and will work equally well with all four core subjects, PreK-12; (c) *professional developers* responsible for putting together workshops and training sessions that result in teachers devising course tools that ensure the implementation of standards-based and Best Practices reforms in every classroom; (d) *lead teachers* who are eager to find a classroom reform process moreover, it is not a deficit model but a continual growth process; moreover, it meets all the criteria set forth in the school reform research and yet includes teachers from the outset and is sensitive to their needs and priorities; and (e) *parents/guardians* who are tired of all the excuses and want assurance that there is a process available that their school can use to accomplish needed classroom reforms.

Notice: Portions of this book were first published in March, J., and Peters, K. *Developing High-Performance Schools: Instructional Redesign for Learner-Centered Classroom Reform.* Bloomington, Ind.: Phi Delta Kappa International, 1999. For the reader's convenience, an annotated review of the research cited in each chapter is available on request from the authors.

PART I

School Reform Is All About What Happens in the Classroom

1

Instructional Design as the Catalyst for Successful School Reform

We are surprised by the number of intelligent people who say, "Improving what goes on in the classroom is important, but it's only one of the many aspects of school reform." It's always tempting to reply, "What other aspect matters if what happens in the classroom isn't working?"

THE EIGHT CORE ELEMENTS OF SUCCESSFUL SCHOOL REFORM ■

In over two decades working with dozens of school districts, we have observed many attempts to achieve school improvement with varying degrees of success. In our experience, success has not come as much from strict adherence to any one reform model as using what works from one or even several models. What they all have in common is to build the Reform Plan around the curriculum and instructional program, put it in place, provide the resources and infrastructure to sustain it, and then stay with it.

We will briefly describe each of the eight core elements of successful school reform that the research continually cites and our experience has borne out. Our intent is to provide a nontechnical description of how to build school reform around classroom instruction. In other words, how might districts implement the complete package. Just as it would be a mistake to pursue school reform without attention to the classroom, it would be foolish to attempt classroom reform without the infrastructure to support it. That would be like attempting to serve a gourmet meal without the dishes and silverware to eat it, or to set an elegant table and forget to prepare the meal.

Before we begin these eight elements, we've added a ninth of our own: Patience. From the individual classroom teacher through the NCLB sheriffs, educators are afflicted with a common myopia about reform: If it doesn't produce immediate results, it must not be working. Ironically, these people understand the importance of waiting for seeds to grow, for interest to accrue, for relationships to mature, even for fine wine to age. But they seem unable to come to accept that student and staff performances are learned behaviors, the effects of several years of practice, which would take time to undo. One way to assuage this impatience for quick results is to build in impact checks as indicators of progress along the way, examining student and staff performance frequently as opposed to waiting until the end of a project year. By collecting various types of formative data, the staff can watch the steady progress of individual students and see themselves growing as well. Admittedly, Boards of Education and funding agencies like to see aggregate test scores and overall results, but with multiple indicators of progress and strategic disaggregations by subgroups and categories, these general, overall scores can be mined to reveal specific patterns of progress that can inform daily practice in every classroom while giving direction to the overall Reform Plan.

Core Element 1: Honest Self-Appraisal

Schools (or districts) that have achieved successful reforms began with a candid appraisal or needs assessment of their current status. For each school, they examined not only the effects of their efforts (i.e., student performance, gaps among subgroups, parent/guardian and community support, etc.) but also the root causes to which these can be attributed. Most of these causes are aspects of the operation over which they have some control, including what happens in classrooms, the day-to-day operation of the building, and the attitudes and beliefs that characterize each school's value system and form its deep culture. Some of the most common data points in the self-study or needs assessment do double duty as the Criteria for Success in the district (and school) Reform Plans:

♦ **current levels of academic achievement**, indicated by the district's high-stakes test results, disaggregated by NCLB subgroup (i.e., children with Special Needs, minority populations, English language learners, and children who are economically disadvantaged). Unfortunately, the overall test score alone (e.g., Math) and even the subtest scores (e.g., Measurement) are of little help to teachers without an indication of what skills and concepts students have or have not mastered (e.g., linear, capacity, weight). This deep-level analysis is typically not available with high-stakes test results but can be accomplished with the district's own standards-based assessments.

◆ areas highly correlated with academic achievement such as **discipline**, **attendance**, **parent/guardian involvement**, and the scheduling and **placement of students**

◆ the alignment of the district curriculum with what NCLB calls world-class **academic standards**, including the developmental flow achieved by strategic articulation among grade levels

◆ each school's **classroom practices** in the light of such accepted findings as the Best Practices, the "school-effects" research, and current theories about differentiation and constructivist learning

◆ current school reform **initiatives underway** and the distinction between those that *are* and are *not* having a positive effect on student performance and/or school effectiveness

◆ the **perceptions of key stakeholders**, including parents/guardians, staff, community, and older students, about the effectiveness of their school and its programs, how involved they are, how welcome they are made to feel, and the extent to which they find the school climate encouraging and conducive to learning.

Armed with the foregoing data, these schools or districts made honest and thoughtful distinctions about what was and was not working and discontinued programs and practices that were unhelpful and/or unnecessary. The leadership of these schools or districts paid particular attention to staff morale, validating the hard work and loyal service of every employee throughout the reform process. Special measures were taken to assure staff that the reform efforts were not as much about working harder as working smarter.

Core Element 2: Board Commitment

The impetus for school reform may have begun in the boardroom, the classroom, or the living room, but for reforms to succeed and persist, it requires the involvement and support of all three. But since the Board of Education is legally responsible for the district and accountable for its successes and failures, their support from the very outset is logical and mandatory. After all, they sign the checks. The Board's commitment is essential on at least two fronts:

◆ **to enact policies and procedures that give prominence to the reform process and integrate the reforms into the infrastructure of the district**. The mandates of NCLB require the Board of Education to adopt policies and procedures to ensure that every student makes Adequate Yearly Progress (AYP). To accomplish and sustain these procedures, the Board must establish supporting infrastructures and provide adequate human and monetary resources. These enactments affect the entire operation of the district, including, for example, the master schedule and assignment of students; the recruitment, development, and evaluation of staff; programs to provide supplemental services for academic and behavior needs; the purchase of materials and equipment; the adoption of a curriculum and a classroom delivery system; a program of assessments to monitor student progress; and parent/guardian involvement. Empowered by Board-adopted policies and procedures, the programs and practices set forth in each school's Reform Plan not only become "the way business is done here" but are fully integrated into that building's deep culture: part of the daily routine in every classroom, the topic of professional conversations, and the bulk of every faculty meeting agenda.

♦ **to expect and manage staff unease**. Like the warning bell when your car is too close to an object, the expression of constructive concern by staff is a positive aspect of reform. Heads-up decision makers learn to distinguish legitimate concern from that born of sloth, apathy, or an attempt to dodge accountability. The former springs from sincere individuals who believe that successful reform will benefit their students, themselves, and the community. Where reform has succeeded, the Board has successfully managed the "whine factor," keeping watchful tabs on legitimate concerns without acquiescing to pernicious complaints.

Core Element 3: A Narrow, Directed Focus

The surest ways to defeat any reform effort is to attempt too much in a given time frame, to go in too many directions at once, and to hopscotch from program to program, always starting over. Successful reform is guided by a carefully deliberated and strategic plan that focuses all of the district's energies on a limited number of targets and then stays the course. Naturally, the plan is carefully monitored and adjusted as needed, but all the activities stay between the lines, and the effort is seen through as planned. All the materials and any professional development requested must be directly connected to the plan, or they are not approved.

Core Element 4: Student Achievement Defined as More Than Test Scores

It is an unfortunate fact of life in school reform that the community, business leaders, many parents/guardians, most funding sources, and the media tend to reduce the quality of a district and each school to its high-stakes test scores. And while high-stakes test scores are an important political measure of a student's academic success, they are just one of many measures. Districts and schools who have achieved successful reform have made a point of going behind their test scores to provide a three-dimensional view of their students' performance. They have collected several other pieces of data that were useful to plan classroom instruction, to deal with at-risk students, and to provide differentiated instruction, including enrichment as well as remediation. A checklist of these data include the following: (a) **mastery of content standards** (as determined by teachers using valid criterion-referenced tests and performance assessments) to compare classroom mastery with that assessed by high-stakes tests, (b) **attendance,** to determine the correlation between achievement and presence, (c) **behavior** and the correlation between citizenship and academic success, and (d) **exit competencies** to reflect readiness for entry into a career or higher education.

Core Element 5: The Adoption of a Standards-Based Curriculum for All Students

Reforms that end with increased student achievement began with increased academic expectations. And these expectations are based on a robust curriculum in each subject that incorporates the state content standards. In terms of NCLB, mastery of these academic standards is expected by all students in each subgroup. Admittedly, even successful districts continue to struggle with persistent achievement gaps between subgroups, but a standards-based curriculum provides the lever by which that gap can be reduced. When the standards are translated into classroom-ready learning expectations, the Board should adopt them as the official achievement targets of the district. This step verifies the Board's resolve to take the standards seriously and to make them the basis of the district's comprehensive instructional program.

Core Element 6: A Process to Deliver and Assess Classroom Instruction

Although the standards-based curriculum is the bedrock of every successful reform initiative, it would have been useless until and unless it was implemented in every classroom. The accountability for its implementation rested with the classroom teachers and building principals. This implementation has not been left to chance. Rather, the Board and Superintendent put in place an organized system or game plan to ensure that the standards-based curriculum was used to deliver instruction and assess student mastery at each grade level.

Core Element 7: Continually Monitoring Student and Staff Performance

When student achievement has been fully assessed, it has been measured on three levels: (a) by **high-stakes test scores**, which is the gold standard for determining a district's effectiveness as per NCLB and public opinion; (b) **classroom unit tests** based on the cluster of standards on which the unit is based; and (c) standards-based **benchmark assessments** devised by the district to provide consistent and objective measures at key intervals. This multitiered assessment system provides the most thorough and valid means to monitor each student's performance and maximize his or her chances for academic success.

Essential to the monitoring aspect of school reform is the disaggregation of data into the NCLB subgroups. Moreover, the various data that determine student performance must be carefully and continually integrated to form a holistic and progressive picture of each child's mastery. Districts typically develop or purchase a software system to organize these data and to generate useful reports that are both summarized and disaggregated. Recently, many states have decided to use growth models to determine the extent of gain from one year to the next, the most popular of which is Value-Added analysis.

Core Element 8: Linking It All Together—Integrating the Reforms Into the School's Deep Culture

The most compelling feature of every successful school reform is that it is still there. It has become so ingrained into the daily routines and core operation of the district and each school that the staff cannot imagine doing things any other way. It is truly "the way things are done here." Such a transformation did not occur by accident, nor did it happen overnight. It was the result of strategic capacity-building among the staff that began at the outset of the reform process; it was specified in the Reform Plan and then carefully, deliberately nurtured throughout the process. Such capacity-building among the faculty, central office staff, and building administration is the link between the all-important classroom aspects of the reform and the infrastructure needed to implement and sustain it. In our experience, the most successful of such capacity-building programs include teacher leadership, specific roles and responsibilities of the building principal and other key administrators, and teachers providing each other with peer support and coaching. Without these strategic efforts to integrate the reforms into the deep culture of each school, practices tend to regress to their former state, or worse.

■ HOW DOES *INSTRUCTIONAL DESIGN* INTEGRATE WITH SUCCESSFUL SCHOOL REFORM?

Although there are multiple factors that affect student performance, the reform research continues to document what has always been commonsense: The single greatest determinant of student success or failure is what goes on in a district's classrooms. *Instructional Design* represents a combination of the published work on standards-based curriculum and the research on Best Practices teaching and testing strategies, strategically interspersed among the eight elements described above. This section provides an aerial view of the process as an introduction to the remaining chapters, each of which provides a close-up look at each component.

The Catalogue Description of *Instructional Design*

Instructional Design is a comprehensive, research-based process to increase student achievement and reduce the performance gaps among various subgroups of students. It is built around a standards-based curriculum and uses the Best Practices methods to deliver and assess classroom instruction. Through a series of professional development activities, teachers integrate the state content standards into the curriculum, produce course tools based on the Best Practices research to deliver the curriculum, and develop standards-based assessments to continually monitor student progress. Particular emphasis is given to constructivist learning strategies, differentiation for enrichment as well as remediation, and the provision of accommodations and modifications for students with Special Needs.

In contrast to many other approaches to classroom reform, *Instructional Design* is not a one-size-fits-all model. It is a process that takes its shape and substance from the unique features of the district and its schools and is strategically nested in the context of the district (and school) infrastructure to increase the likelihood it will succeed. Throughout each stage, there is a continual reaching back to link what happens in classrooms to the other aspects of district reform and to build capacity within each building and the district as a whole to sustain the classroom reforms once they are in place. It begins with the endorsement and support of the Board of Education, including their clear understanding that (a) the standards-based curriculum must be adopted as the official achievement targets of the district and (b) that Board policies and procedures (as well as corresponding procedures in each school) must be adopted to govern the processes and materials attendant to student performance, classroom instruction, assessment, parent/guardian involvement, and staff accountability.

Capacity-Building

As staff teams are developing the course tools for classroom reform, three capacity-building programs are concurrently underway. These are (a) training and support of Building Leadership Teams to provide a flow of continual, two-way communication among all teachers, (b) training of designated central office staff and each school principal in stewardship practices to facilitate the reforms throughout the district, and (c) training key teachers and administrators in the Lesson Study and Collaborative Observation process to provide every teacher with coaching and peer support to implement the classroom reforms. Throughout the *Instructional Design* process, the continual monitoring of student and staff performance informs the day-to-day practice of every teacher and administrator and provides a mirror by which the district (and each building) reflects the progress of the overall reform effort and makes adjustments as needed.

History

The *Instructional Design* process has been used in hundreds of districts and is continually updated with emerging research and enriched with the addition of actual classroom examples. The results of its implementation in several districts are displayed in Appendix A as data tables reflecting gains in student achievement. In addition to the increases in student achievement, the process has yielded impressive growth in the competence of teachers and administrators alike, documented by written feedback not only from participants but by third-party validations provided by staff working with participants.

Figure 1.1 is a graphic of the *Instructional Design* process. Below are general descriptions of each component, and in the remaining chapters of the book, each component is developed in greater detail. Annotated citations for the research supporting each component are available from the authors on request.

Figure 1.1 The *Instructional Design* Process

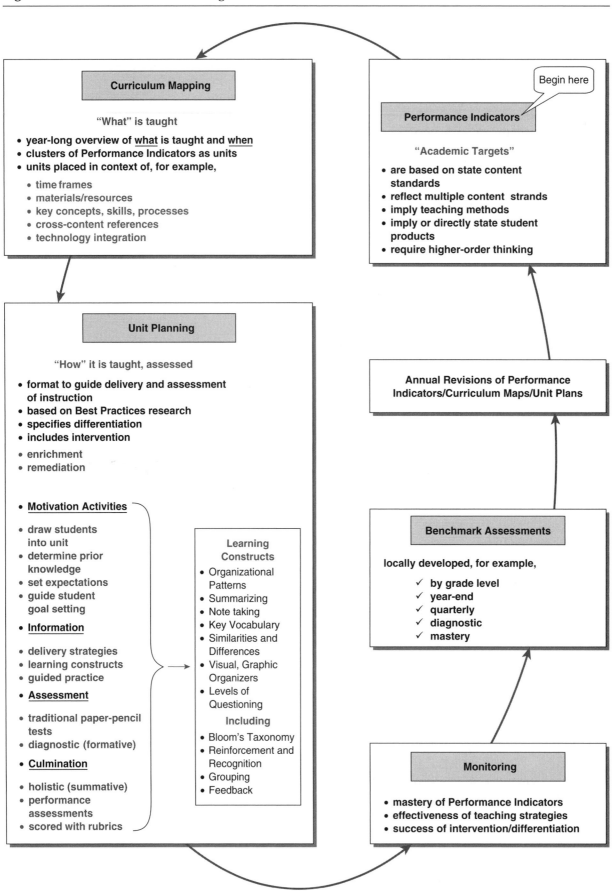

Components of *Instructional Design*

The Standards-Based Curriculum

Performance Indicators *(PIs).* The ***Instructional Design*** process begins with the end. That is, if the ultimate goal is that every student master world-class academic standards, the district must build such standards into its adopted curriculum. And by *standards*, we do not mean high-stakes test scores but the specific academic skills, knowledge, attitudes, and processes students are expected to demonstrate that, in turn, would allow them to do well on tests. Adopted by the Board of Education as the official achievement targets of the district, the standards drive everything else in the instructional program. These learning targets should be developed and approved by the staff and kept clearly in mind as they devise or select teaching and testing materials, purchase equipment, plan professional development, and report progress to parents/guardians.

As written, however, the state content standards are not classroom ready. If they are to be the basis of an authentic curriculum, the standards must be translated by teams of teachers into learning expectations that correspond to the most recent teaching-learning theories and that can be taught and tested using the methods set forth in the Best Practices research. These considerations require that the learning expectations or targets accomplish the following: (a) be focused on **output**, or the student's construction of meaning, rather than **inputs** (which characterized the curricula of the decades of the twentieth century); (b) integrate skill strands **within the subject** rather than teaching each strand in isolation (e.g., the Number Facts strand in Math should not be taught in isolation but combined with the Measurement or Geometry strands); (c) integrate learner outcomes **across subjects** to broaden the real-world context for students (e.g., election activities in Social Studies can be combined with Language Arts' focus on persuasive techniques); (d) expect students to use **higher-order thinking** and **problem-solving skills** to process information, causing a dramatic shift in the way teachers present the material and the way it will be assessed; and (e) provide for **differentiation** from the outset, acknowledging that students have different learning needs (this is not to expect less of some students but to provide alternate methods of learning and to adjust the time allotted).

The ***Instructional Design*** process helps district teams translate the content standards into *Performance Indicators* and circulate them among their colleagues as Critical Friends for input. A complete description of this process is included in Chapter 2.

Modifying Classroom Instruction

Curriculum Mapping. Although it is the critical first step, merely developing *Performance Indicators* is not synonymous with their actual integration into classroom instruction. Unless there are corresponding changes in classroom teaching and testing practices, the adoption of a standards-based curriculum is futile. That's as silly as purchasing new workout togs and a set of digital scales and then expecting to lose weight. Without an exercise program and a change of diet, nothing will change. Clearly, things must change in every classroom if the new learning targets are to be achieved by every student.

The second component of the **Instructional Design** process is *Curriculum Mapping*, the development of year-long plans to fully implement the *Performance Indicators* as the centerpiece of the curriculum in every classroom. Naturally, the *Indicators* cannot simply be taught in a list; they must be strategically clustered and sequenced across the school year within the context of other variables that affect student learning. We call this *Curriculum Mapping*. The clustering step brings together those indicators that relate to a common topic or theme, referred to as units. For example, a Social Studies unit on the Cold War might include *Performance Indicators* from the History, Economics, and Social Studies Skills and Methods strands. But appropriate cross-curricular connections might include references to specific fiction and nonfiction popular during the late 1950s and 1960s (Language Arts) as well as population tables displaying the relative military strength of the superpowers (Math).

The *Curriculum Maps* for each grade level (and/or subject) are best developed by the same team of teachers who devised the *Performance Indicators*. Although it is also prudent to expand the writing team to broaden staff involvement and assist with the workload, it is important for consistency and continuity to retain at least a critical mass of the core group who devised the indicators. As with the first draft of the *Indicators*, the first *Maps* are also circulated among other staff teaching at the same level (or course) to get their feedback. Some districts allow each teacher to devise his or her own *Curriculum Map*, but the majority prefer that teachers from the same grade level and subject operate from a common core *Map*. A complete description of this process is included in Chapter 3.

Unit Planning. If the *Curriculum Map* sets forth the *what* of classroom instruction, the *how* is guided by the *Unit Plan*. The **Instructional Design** *Unit Plan* uses a research-based format that helps teachers plan, deliver, and assess classroom instruction. It incorporates the Best Practices methods and relies on the principles of experiential and constructivist learning. Each unit is taken from the *Curriculum Map* and is circumscribed by the cluster of related *Performance Indicators* that address a particular theme or topic. The format is a simple four-part diagram that organizes the delivery and assessment activities for each unit into (a) those dealing with *Motivation*, (b) strategies and techniques that provide *Information*, (c) traditional *Assessments* using paper-pencil measures, and (d) *Culminating* activities that are performance or constructive assessments, evaluated with rubrics, the criteria for which are drawn from the *Performance Indicators*. Through their training, teachers learn how to select those learning constructs and delivery strategies that are most likely to help all students master the *Performance Indicators* around which a unit is built. More important, teachers are shown how to plan their units to include differentiation from the outset, building in options for remediation and enrichment as part of their instructional routines. Training is also provided in constructing valid formative and summative assessments strategies that are congruent with the teaching activities and also criterion-referenced to each unit's list of *Performance Indicators*.

Like the *Curriculum Maps*, the *Unit Plans* for each grade level (and/or subject) are best developed by at least a core group of the same teachers who devised the *Performance Indicators* and the maps. Because there are typically 10 to 12 *Unit Plans* across the school year, it is prudent to expand the writing team to broaden staff involvement and assist with the workload. As with the first draft of the other products, the *Unit Plans* are also circulated among the Critical Friends teaching at the same level (or course) to get their feedback. Teachers who work in grade-level and/or subject teams to jointly devise the *Unit Plans* not only maximize their talents and energies but experience enormous pedagogical growth while strengthening their collaborative bonds as a community of teacher learners. A complete description of the *Unit Planning* process and its various features is included in Chapters 4 through 8.

The most immediate results of the **Instructional Design** approach to *Unit Planning* are the documented improvements in classroom instruction. But a secondary feature, and the one that provides a direct connection between student test results and what happens in classrooms, is the link to student growth, using such models as Value-Added. In the analysis of each student's growth (or decline) from one school year to the next, an important feature to examine is what teaching methods were used. In particular, which strategies were used with students whose growth was either as expected or higher and which were used with students whose scores declined? Were there any differences in curriculum, personnel, leadership, or elements of the infrastructure in classrooms where students made satisfactory progress compared with those where students lost ground? More detail about Value-Added is provided in Chapter 9.

Monitoring/Benchmark Assessments. During the processes of developing *Performance Indicators*, *Curriculum Maps*, and *Unit Plans*, the discussion invariably turns to monitoring student mastery. Among the **Frequently Asked Questions** are the following: How will we know that students have mastered the *Performance Indicators*? How well do they have to do? What if they master the *Performance Indicators* in one unit but unmaster them in the next? What if some of us are hardnosed about what is mastery, and others are more lenient? How many opportunities should a student have to demonstrate mastery, and what if some of us give students only one chance and others allow multiple tries? Is mastery the same for all students, Special Education as well as general education? Are teachers the sole determiners of mastery, or is there a districtwide test of some sort? Is it possible that students do well on the high-stakes (NCLB) tests and not on their classroom mastery? Is the reverse possible?

The answers to these and other mastery questions can only be discovered by the district itself as it implements the **Instructional Design** process and begins to collect student performance data. Some districts decide that teacher-made or classroom assessments are adequate, particularly when the NCLB and other high-stakes tests are also in place. Some districts devise standards-based Diagnostic Tests and parallel Mastery Tests to bracket the school year. Other districts feel they need an objective, uniform set of measures to continually monitor students' mastery and nonmastery throughout the year. These are often called short-cycle assessments or benchmark assessments. There is fully as much research in favor of these interval assessments as opposed to them; advocates for either side can find support for their argument if they look. The one caution we attempt to keep in the foreground of the conversation is not to assess to the point that students use more in-school time being tested than being taught. If I'm trying to lose weight, most of my time at the gym needs to be burning calories, not standing on the scales.

One recommendation we make is to not decide until the *Unit Plans* are in place and the classroom assessments for the units have begun to gel. This will give decision makers a good indication of how valid the teacher-made tests are and how reliable the results will be. We suggest that throughout the piloting process, teachers and administrators discuss the various classroom assessments being used. It is crucial that the assessments used in each *Unit Plan* be labeled as to the *Performance Indicators* being measured. Later, the most effective classroom tests may be incorporated into the district's benchmark assessments or their Diagnostic Tests and/or Mastery Tests, if this is the direction taken. A complete description of the Monitoring and Benchmarking processes is included in Chapter 9.

Lessons Learned and Underlying Assumptions

Having implemented parts and all of **Instructional Design** with hundreds of schools, we have learned all sorts of valuable lessons that help to undergird the process, keeping it dynamic and responsive. Two of the most fundamental lessons serve as bookends for the others: the need for customization and the danger of being held hostage by the "test."

The Importance of Customization: Begin Where They Are

Services must be customized to each client's particular priorities. Although this may not be as cost-effective as the one-size-fits-all approach or trying to retrofit the district's needs into a rigidly prescriptive model, cutting corners here will result in certain failure. It is important to "take districts where they are and help them to move where they need to be." Although there are basic core principles of **Instructional Design**, adjustments can and should be made in time frames, training agendas, the format of classroom materials, the number of subjects taken on at once, and methods of capacity-building, all to fit the unique needs and circumstances of each client. Districts must establish, and stick to, a multiyear plan that involves doable steps each year rather than attempt too much at one time. Furthermore, districts are advised to begin building internal capacity from the outset so that they can support the process from within the district and be less dependent on outside consultants. Finally, it may be to a district's advantage to form a consortium with neighboring districts with the same needs not only to share expenses but also to exchange materials and services.

The Folly of "Teaching to the Test"

The Bird Walk below takes a closer look at this Test Paralysis phenomenon.

> [. . . 🖋] **Crippling School Reform With Test Paralysis.** Forced to comply with NCLB, most states have moved ahead to put in place high-stakes Tests that measure their adopted content standards. But unless and until their districts have actually integrated the standards into their taught curriculum, their only recourse

has been to take valuable instructional time to "prepare students for the Test." Totally intimidated by the fear of failure to make AYP, many districts seem to have ignored the necessity of integrating the new standards into their curriculum and of changing the way they teach and test. Instead, they do "whatever it takes" to raise high-stakes Test scores. It's a sort of "Test Paralysis," and unless a district snaps out of it, the quality of its curriculum and the effectiveness of its instruction will remain exactly as it was before.

In addition to losing 20 to 30 days of instruction to Test Prep, these districts have made the decision that the entire curriculum must be taught before the spring testing. Their teachers admit to putting all the fun, interactive lessons "after the Test." Furthermore, many of these districts single out the students who have not passed one or more parts of the Test and subject them to an even more intense level of drill-and-practice, wrongly assuming that giving these students a double or triple dose of what they didn't understand in the first place will ensure their passage the next time. This is unfortunate because these are the students who can least afford to miss regular classroom instruction.

If these districts read the research that has been conducted in districts whose students have taken either the TIMMS or the NAEP tests, they would discover that for both tests, students from classrooms emphasizing reasoning, critical thinking, and constructing meaning outperformed students from classes focused on the rote drill and practice of basic skills. While researchers acknowledge that students cannot perform higher-order thinking and processing without a strong foundation in the basic skills, they are careful to frame such basic skills as part of the means and definitely not the ends of learning. Please note that complete annotations of all works cited in the text are available, by chapter, from the authors on request.

Involve the Entire Staff

Another of the essential aspects of enduring school improvement is to be certain that each staff member has been involved in various stages and that there are strategic connections among the various components of the process that continually loop around to keep everyone informed and involved. Naturally, the planning and development stages are more likely to involve representative teams of staff, but successfully changing the culture of classroom practice involves every staff member in the implementation phase. If done correctly, *Instructional Design* includes a gradual but deliberate and strategic phase-in process that tiers or levels staff participation to include everyone. Figure 1.2 illustrates this tiering effect and references the pertinent chapters in the book. The role of teachers and administrators is described in Figure 1.3.

Quality Control

Although the qualities of creativity and initiative should be encouraged among the staff, teachers are not self-employed, and the Board of Education is legally responsible for assuring its community that the classroom practices in every building are valid, timely, and appropriate to students' needs. According to NCLB, every child is to receive a world-class curriculum taught by a highly qualified teacher. As the agents of the Board, the administrative team is responsible for seeing to it that the

Figure 1.2   The Suggested Tiers for Whole-Staff Involvement

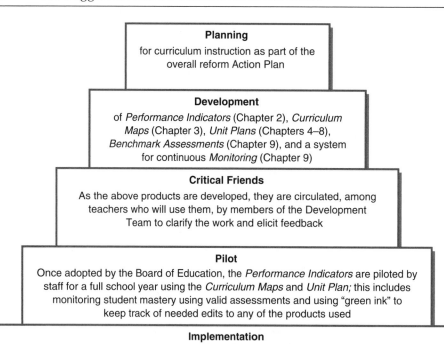

Planning
for curriculum instruction as part of the overall reform Action Plan

Development
of *Performance Indicators* (Chapter 2), *Curriculum Maps* (Chapter 3), *Unit Plans* (Chapters 4–8), *Benchmark Assessments* (Chapter 9), and a system for continuous *Monitoring* (Chapter 9)

Critical Friends
As the above products are developed, they are circulated, among teachers who will use them, by members of the Development Team to clarify the work and elicit feedback

Pilot
Once adopted by the Board of Education, the *Performance Indicators* are piloted by staff for a full school year using the *Curriculum Maps* and *Unit Plan;* this includes monitoring student mastery using valid assessments and using "green ink" to keep track of needed edits to any of the products used

Implementation
After the pilot is complete, revisions are made, the Board adopts the *Performance Indicators* as the official achievement targets of the district, and the *Maps, Units,* and assessments are placed on the building Web sites for ready access

adopted curriculum and instructional practices are followed and that teachers are provided the resources and training needed to do so. At each school, it is the responsibility of the Building Improvement or Leadership Team to maintain a vigilant watch that the provisions of the reform Action Plan are honored by all staff. Moreover, the Building Leadership Team must be certain that any changes in direction are consistent with the spirit and the letter of the state standards and reflective of the needs and priorities of the district.

The Annual Review Process

Given the enormous amount of work involved, the most unpopular aspect of school reform is that it is never done. Like cleaning the garage, it is best done each spring. If allowed to coast (even for a year or so), taking corrective measures is far more complicated than if reviewed annually. And the reforms enacted for curriculum and instruction are especially fragile in that they must be responsive to the needs of students, emerging trends in the research, and sometimes to the vagaries of funding. It is recommended that all the products and procedures associated with **Instructional Design** be examined each year in the light of student performance and district priorities. Any needed changes and adjustments can be made prior to the start of the next school year. The "green ink" is an uncomplicated but apt symbol of ongoing reflection and positive adjustment, and in our client districts, it has become an integral part of the culture of annual review and continuous improvement.

Figure 1.3   Specific Detail of Tiers for Whole-School Involvement

Planning

Teacher Role

- provide input with regard to logistics; for example,
  - development (e.g., meeting times, who might represent each grade level and subject)
  - the role of development teams with other teachers and the building administrator
  - the rollout of products to entire staff
  - meeting regularly to review progress and make adjustments
  - monitoring progress and updateing Plan at least annually
- communicating progress to staff

Administrator Role

- all central office administrators are involved with planning for Curricular and Instructional activities: each
  - participates in training
  - serves on one or more Development Teams
  - works with at least one building during Critical Friends, Pilot, and Implementation stages
- each principal will be involved with planning for all Curricular-Instructional activities

Development

Teacher Role

- represent each grade level in grade-band Teams (e.g., PreK–3 Math, Grades 4–8 Reading) to devise the products: *Performance Indicators, Curriculum Maps,* and *Unit Plans* for each subject
- maintain consistency by retaining the same membership throughout the process, e.g., the Team developing the *Performance Indicators* should also develop the *Curriculum Map, Unit Plans,* and Benchmark Assessments (or at least a critical mass should be retained each time)
- broaden the base of involvement by including additional teachers to develop the next product

Administrator Role

- at least one central office administrator is assigned to each subject area (e.g., K–12 Math)
- at least one building principal is assigned to a subject area grade-band Development Team (e.g., PreK–3 Math)

Critical Friends

Teacher Role

[members of the development Teams]

- share the draft materials among colleagues
- explain, clarify, and ask for input
- increase their own leadership capacity and strengthen trust relationships among staff

Administrator Role

[each building principal]

- coordinates the Critical Friends share-out (i.e., scheduling, preparation of materials, etc.)
- monitors the feedback
- works through any special needs or problems that may surface
- demonstrates awareness of and commitment to the Process

(Continued)

Figure 1.3 (Continued)

Pilot

Teacher Role

- pilot the products, and mark edits with "green pens" (Maps, Unit Plans, etc.) as they are used with students
- meet as grade level teams to
  - discuss the pilot efforts
  - compare "green ink"
  - exchange ideas about teaching and assessing student mastery
- review student work
  - discuss differentiation strategies

Administrator Role

[central office administrators]

- submit *Performance Indicators* to the Board for approval to pilot as the district achievement targets
- distribute pilot materials to each teacher involved
- work with at least one subject during pilot

[principals]

- schedule and attend team meetings where "green ink" and student mastery are discussed
- report progress on the pilot effort at least quarterly (Board, Superintendent)

Note: Some districts use the Pilot year to

a. devise or perfect a data management system to track student progress, enabling the staff to make more timely and accurate decisions about students' needs; and/or
b. develop benchmark or short-cycle assessments, Diagnostic Tests, and/or Mastery Tests.

Implementation
of materials and procedures, revised after Pilot, as the "official" program

Teacher Role

- use the "official" materials and procedures to deliver and assess classroom instruction
- continue to use the "green ink" to mark areas needing revision
- note more and less successful teaching techniques
- note where differentiation occurred and the results
- devote a portion of grade-level, team, or department meeting agendas to discussion of "green ink" and other implementation issues and concerns
- label paper-pencil tests and performance assessments with *Performance Indicator* code to indicate those measured
- monitor student mastery of the *Performance Indicators,* and use the information to make more timely and precise decisions about interventions, including enrichment
- share student progress data with parents to involve them in their children's development
- share student progress at grade-level meetings

Administrator Role

[central office administrators]

- report outcome of pilot issues to Board; recommend adjustments and revisions
- secure the Board's adoption of the final version of the *Performance Indicators* as the district achievement targets
- distribute materials for implementation
- determine formal means for monitoring student mastery
- devise Benchmark Assessments
- analyze high-stakes test results to make decisions about curricular and instructional practices in each classroom

[principals]

- facilitate the implementation in each building
- schedule and attend the "green ink" sessions
- collect paper-pencil and performance assessments and review them with teachers
- monitor each teacher's implementation efforts, providing assistance and support
- report progress about the implementation effort to the Superintendent at least quarterly and to the Board annually

THREE-YEAR TIME FRAME   ■

As is true of every school reform initiative currently appearing in the literature, the *Instructional Design* process takes between 24 and 36 months to complete, depending on the number of subject areas and grade levels involved. Thereafter, the products and processes are reviewed annually to make needed revisions and adjustments. Table 1.1 is a sample three-year plan involving two content areas, but there are any number of variations to accommodate the particular needs of the district. As we develop the components of *Instructional Design* in subsequent chapters, the time line will be filled appropriately.

Table 1.1   Sample Three-Year Time Frame for *Instructional Design* (Two Subject Areas)

		Year 1			Year 2			Year 3		
		Summer	*Fall*	*Winter/ Spring*	*Summer*	*Fall*	*Winter/ Spring*	*Summer*	*Fall*	*Winter/ Spring*
Two Subjects, PreK–12, for example, Reading and Math	*Performance Indicators (PIs)*	Develop, Pilot Critical Friends →			Revise, Implement →			Continue (annual → review)		
	Curriculum Maps	Develop, Pilot Critical Friends →			Revise, Implement →			Continue (annual → review)		
	Unit Plans				Develop, Pilot Critical Friends →			Revise, Implement →		
	Continuous Monitoring	Unofficially keep track of student mastery			Develop, Pilot Critical Friends →			Revise, Implement →		
	Benchmark Assessments	Collect classroom tests that measure the *Performance Indicators*			Develop, Pilot Critical Friends →			Revise, Implement →		

2

Performance Indicators

The Passkey to Standards-Based Curriculum

■ **WHAT'S IN THE NAME?**

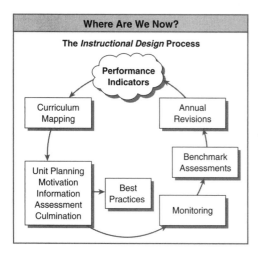

Where Are We Now?

The *Instructional Design* Process

Performance Indicators

Curriculum Mapping

Annual Revisions

Unit Planning
Motivation
Information
Assessment
Culmination

Best Practices

Benchmark Assessments

Monitoring

The *Instructional Design* process begins with its endpoint: what students are expected to master, or the indicators of successful academic performance. It is a list of what students are expected to do to demonstrate competence at each grade level in a subject. Unfortunately, test results have become surrogates for academic proficiency—and the lack thereof. But that's because we in the profession have been unable to otherwise document what students have learned to solve authentic problems and construct meaning for themselves. The *Instructional Design* process includes test results as a secondary or *indirect* measure of academic success. The primary or *direct* measures are the academic performances demonstrated by each child by the end of a grade level in each subject. We call these *Performance Indicators* (*PIs*). Prior to the standards-based movement, the district curriculum consisted of objectives or learning outcomes, an icon of the early 1970s and the behavioral or performance objectives movement. By the 1990s, the term *objective* connoted isolated skills and easily measured (but splintered) factoids or sets of narrow, easily measured competencies. In many cases, teachers tended to think of objectives as checklists for what they must teach rather than what students were expected to learn. While conceptualizing **Instructional Design** in the mid-1990s, we somehow landed on the term *Performance Indicators* and have continued to use it to represent those academic competencies or learning outcomes adopted by a Board of Education as the official achievement targets of the district. But the very foundation of the standards movement *is* combining isolated skills and fragments of disconnected knowledge into more holistic, contextual performances that demonstrate a student's ability to apply what has been learned to solve problems or construct meaning—not merely to pass a test.

THE CRITERIA FOR VALID ■
PERFORMANCE INDICATORS

Although they are related to the conventional objective in that they are verb phrases, *Performance Indicators* wrap together several skills or processes, place them into an authentic or life-related context, and are demonstrated with an observable product or process that reflects mastery. *Performance Indicators* ask students to construct meaning for themselves and apply what they have learned to a new or unfamiliar situation. For example, they might solve a life-related problem, perform a task, compose an original piece, or construct an object or model. The underlying assumption is that constructing meaning for oneself instills deep-level mastery of skills, concepts, knowledge, and attitudes. In so doing, a student owns and can continually access and adapt that deep-level mastery as needed to be a successful and productive citizen.

The basic structure of a *Performance Indicator* is best shown with examples that illustrate each component. Note, (a) the underscore indicates the cognitive demand of the content standard and underlying concept; (b) the box offers a real-world context in which students consider the issue, apply the skill, or solve a problem using a higher-order thinking; and (c) the **bold** designates a product that requires students to construct new meaning.

Grade 2 Science

Compare and contrast the different activities of the state's familiar animals during different seasons, and create a **four-column table to display** the findings.

Grade 3 Math

Count money and make change for single and multiple purchases using coins and bills to ten dollars; make purchases at a class department store or restaurant, and **draw pictures to represent the transactions**, including the money used and the change involved.

Grade 10 Social Studies

Determine the necessity for race and gender laws enacted during the twentieth century based on the abuses resulting from the Jim Crow laws and other discriminatory practices of the late nineteenth century; prepare a time line as a prewriting strategy, including significant events, implications, and any cause-effect relationships at play; **compose two editorials** to publish in the 1890s, one for a conservative and one for a liberal newspaper.

Grade 7 Language Arts

Analyze various themes that recur in fictional literature (e.g., tolerance, loyalty, good over evil); assemble passages from multiple genres that illustrate one such theme important to typical ninth graders, and develop **various levels of questions (and answers)** for classmates—at least three literal, two interpretive, and two evaluative—to guide their analysis of the pieces.

As illustrated in these few samples, *Performance Indicators* are carefully structured to give direction and substance to the curriculum. Below are listed the criteria for *Performance Indicators* drawn from the research on standards-based curriculum, process-product correlations, teacher effects, Best Practices, and constructivism. *Performance Indicators*

♦ are based on the **content standards**, preserving both the content and the cognitive demand of the standards and not a lower level that is easier to assess; for example, if the standard asks for "*analyze* the causes and effects of ___," the indicator cannot use "*identify* the causes of ___ " or "*match* the causes and effects of ___."

♦ are built around **real-world contexts** or lifelike applications to limit the use of worksheets or "naked" drills; the prefatory remarks in every standards booklet reminds districts that the concepts and skills in each standard are intended to be mastered in the context of real-life applications.

♦ result in a designated or implied **product** or a tangible object, model, composition, or problem-solving process that reflects mastery of the standard; this contrasts with a test item, where students respond to someone else's prompt; it reflects the student's own construction of meaning; while products may have similar attributes, each student's product is a unique expression of his or her own thinking.

♦ involve **higher-order processing skills** so that students are required to think beyond the literal or memory level, to think analytically and inferentially, and to use creative and critical problem solving that goes beyond what was discussed in the classroom.

♦ allow for **multiple means to complete the task**, providing an opportunity for students to select from several options or, ideally, to devise viable options of their own to demonstrate mastery.

♦ imply or state **the means for instruction** and **assessment**, reflective of Best Practices and primed for differentiation.

◆ reflect **integration** among strands **within the same subject**; for example, in Reading, the *Vocabulary*, *Comprehension*, and *Literary Analysis* strands are linked to analyze a passage for the author's message.

◆ make connections, as often as appropriate, **across subjects**; for example, in Math and Science, the *Data Analysis* strand in *Math* and the *Scientific Method* strand to record a month's precipitation to prevent students from developing the misperception that learning is compartmentalized and fragmented; this wrapping together of skills and concepts within and between subjects provides a more holistic, lifelike mastery experience, requiring students to reach beyond a single subject or strand for other skill sets and understandings to complete their tasks.

These criteria are useful as teams develop *Performance Indicators*. Three additional factors related to the district and building infrastructure provide for the deep-level integration of the *Performance Indicators* into the routine of every classroom. *Performance Indicators* are

◆ developed by the teachers who will use them; this is accomplished using grade-level teams of teachers, PreK–12 in each subject to achieve a developmental flow, maximize ownership, and provide a common ground of consensus; depending on the size of the district, not every teacher may develop the *Indicators* initially, but all teachers at a grade level serve as Critical Friends to react to them and provide input.

◆ adopted by the district Board of Education as the official achievement targets of the district and, as such, drive the entire curricular and instructional program, including the purchase of materials and equipment, the placement of students, the assessment of educational progress, what is reported to parents/guardians, the professional development for faculty and administrators, and so on.

◆ reviewed annually and adjusted according to student performance; *Performance Indicators* must remain dynamic, responsive to emerging trends and developments.

HOW THE STANDARDS ARE ORGANIZED ■

The prefatory material in most standards booklets acknowledges that the standards are not classroom ready as published and encourages districts to translate the standards into their own curriculum. It is further suggested that each district take measures to ensure the appropriate developmental articulation from grade to grade, an especially tricky task in states where the standards apply to grade range (e.g., 5–7) rather than an individual grade. In addition, NCLB requires that children with Special Needs be provided instruction in on-level standards, rather than the previous practice of working with standards at their academic levels. The need to translate content standards into the district curriculum has been widely supported in the research, and annotated citations are available from the authors on request. It is an opportunity for conscientious districts to achieve lasting curricular reforms rather than rely on a textbook or teacher-proof "scripted" course of study.

The very process of a district reviewing its own curriculum in the light of the content standards and developing *Performance Indicators* in the context of local curriculum priorities is instructive. In fact, it helps to bond teachers in the common pursuit of clarifying their expectations and finding ways to help students achieve mastery. This process provides an unprecedented opportunity for teachers to hold productive and thoughtful discourse about the skills and concepts that comprise course content and how the standards can best inform that district's courses of study.

We caution districts against purchasing a canned curriculum created by outsiders. Even the samples we use in this book and during our training aren't necessarily appropriate for every district. And while we're extending the caution about purchasing canned curricula, the same advice applies to canned assessments. The standards can no more be assessed in isolation than they can be taught one at a time. Beware of companies or consultants offering pools of test items that match every standard. Gluing test items together without regard for the context of the unit disconnects classroom instruction from the assessments, making them relatively unimportant. In essence, the unit is being held hostage by the test. The need for congruence among the intended learning outcomes, the teaching strategies, and the assessments is addressed more fully in Chapters 4 through 7.

Table 2.1 displays the major content and process skill strands used in most states to organize their content standards. Although each state has adopted its own set of content standards, there are considerable similarities among the major categories within each subject based on the national standards set forth by their respective professional associations.

The following shows the major headings and subheadings within each of the four core content areas for five states: (a) In Ohio, the labels are Standards → Benchmarks → Grade-Level Indicators; (b) in Minnesota, Strands → Substrands → Standards → Benchmarks; (c) in New Jersey, Standards → Strands → Cumulative Progress Indicators; (d) in Florida, Standards → Strands → Benchmarks → Grade-Level Expectations; and (e) in California, Standards → Strands → Focus Statements → followed by specific grade-level outcomes.

Just for convenience, we will use the term *Strand* to denote the major categories within a subject, such as in Math (Number Sense, Geometry, Algebra, etc.), and *Standard* to denote the specific performance expected of the student.

■ NOT CLASSROOM READY, BUT THAT'S OKAY

There are at least eight reasons that state content standards are not necessarily classroom ready as published. We have taken these reasons into account as we help teachers translate the standards into the *Performance*

Table 2.1   Strands and Substrands Found in Most State Content Standards

Math	English/Language Arts	Science	Social Studies
Number, Number Sense and Operations (i.e., Number Relations, Number Theory)	Reading	Earth and Space Science	History
	Phonics (or Word Analysis) Vocabulary	Life Science	People in Societies
	Comprehension (processes)	Physical Science	Geography
Measurement	Applications to Informational Text	Science and Technology	Economics
Geometry and Spatial Sense	Applications to Literary Text	Scientific Inquiry	Government
Algebra (i.e., Patterns, Functions, and Algebra)	Writing	Scientific Ways of Knowing	Citizenship Rights and Responsibilities
	The Writing Process		Social Studies Skills and Methods
Data Analysis and Probability	Writing Applications (products)		
Math Processes (often integrated into the content strands)	Writing Conventions (mechanics)		
	Research (often may be combined with Writing)		
	Oral and Written Communication		
	Visual or Media Literacy		

Indicators for each subject, PreK–12: (a) They are written in separate strands but meant to be taught in combined strands. (b) Many are written without a context or real-world application (instead, they make reference to the skills and concepts needed for mastery). (c) Many are too narrow and should be combined rather than taught separately. (d) Many are too dense to master all at once and should be pulled apart to teach and learn. (e) Most are written for one content area and lack any reference to cross-curricular connections. (f) Most do not include (nor imply) how they might be best assessed. (g) Most are listed only once but are intended to be taught in multiple contexts. (h) The grade placement of the standards may be at variance with the district's traditional (and preferred) placement of the corresponding content.

To demonstrate how these eight considerations affect a district's translation of the standards into its curriculum, we offer several illustrations in Table 2.2. Naturally, every district will have its own preferences for combining, separating, and integrating standards across subjects to reflect its unique needs and the priorities of the community it serves.

While many of the standards need to appear only once in the curriculum of a grade level, several others will take longer to master and may need to appear multiple times and in more than one *Performance Indicator.*

Table 2.2   Sample Standards Converted to Sample *Performance Indicators*

> 1. **The standards are written in separate strands but meant to be taught in combined strands.**
> 2. **Many standards are written without a context or real-world application.**

Sample Standards	Sample Performance Indicators

Math—Grade 3
 	
Strand: Number Sense and Operations
  Standard: 12. Add and subtract whole numbers with and without regrouping
  Standard: 13. Demonstrate fluency in multiplication facts through 10 and corresponding division facts
Strand: Patterns, Functions, and Algebra
  Standard: 7. Create tables to record, organize, and analyze data to discover patterns and rules
Strand: Data Analysis and Probabilities
  Standard: 3. Read, interpret, and construct bar graphs with intervals greater than one
	Collect and record data about temperature changes during the day for a week; organize the data into tables and then into bar graphs with intervals greater than 1; make appropriate computations to discover any patterns in the data

> 3. **Many are actually too narrow to be taught alone and should be combined** (some "narrows" also lack context, but the *Performance Indicator* can easily provide it).

Sample Standards	Sample Performance Indicators

Reading/Language Arts—Grade 3
 	
Strand: Writing Conventions
  Standards: 11. Use nouns, verbs, and adjectives correctly
    12. Use subjects and verbs [sic; predicates] that are in agreement
    13. Use irregular plural nouns
    14. Use nouns and pronouns that are in agreement
    15. Use past, present, and future verb tenses
	Evaluate a student composition for the correctness of the grammar; make revisions as needed for accuracy and to improve quality of the work

> 4. **Many are too dense to master all at once and should be pulled apart to teach and learn.**

Sample Standards	Sample Performance Indicators

Science—Grade 9
Strand: Physical Science
  Standard: 23
  Explain the change in motion (acceleration) of an object. Demonstrate that the acceleration is proportional to the net force acting on the object and inversely proportional to the mass of the object ($F_{net} = ma$. Note that weight is the gravitational force on a mass.)
	(1) Compare constant motion and accelerated (changing) motion by conducting trials with toy cars (e.g., battery powered and not battery-powered); collect data, graph the distance versus time for each motion, and explain orally or in writing how and why the graphs look different.
	
	(2) Design and conduct an investigation to demonstrate the qualitative relationships among force, mass, and acceleration (Newton's second law of motion) to show how a variation in one quantity might affect another quantity; record and graph data for all of the investigation trials; interpret the results, and predict how the results may impact a real-life event.

---

5. Most are written for one content area and lack any reference to cross-curricular connections.

Sample Standards	Sample Performance Indicators

Math—Grade 4
 	
Strand: Data Analysis and Probability
    Standard: 1. Create a plan for collecting data for a specific purpose
    2. Represent and interpret data using tables, bar graphs, line plots, and so on
    3. Interpret and construct Venn diagrams to sort and describe data
 	
Science—Grade 4
 	
Strand: Earth Science
    Standard: 5. Record weather information on a calendar or map and describe changes over a period of time (e.g., barometric pressure, temperature, precipitation symbols, and cloud conditions)
 	
Social Studies—Grade 4
 	
Strand: Geography
    Standard: 5. Describe and compare the landforms, climates, population, vegetation, and economic characteristics of places and regions in Ohio
	Compare the precipitation (rainfall and snowfall) across multiple months in two regions of North America, one of which is Ohio and the other in another region (e.g., Canada or Mexico); note and explain any shifts or changes across time that yield a pattern; use these data to compare and contrast the two regions, featuring the climate, vegetation, landforms, and the influence of the precipitation on the economies of both regions; note whether any of the changes across the months were significant enough to alter the lifestyles of the regions

---

6. Most do not include (nor imply) how they might be best assessed.

Sample Standards	Sample Performance Indicators

Reading/Language Arts—Grade 8
 	
Strand: Writing Process (PreWriting)
    Standard: 5. Use organizational strategies to plan writing
        [This wording ⇧ is so "open," it would be difficult to score any attempt as incorrect.]
	Devise a prewrite that reflects the organizational pattern appropriate to the prompt (e.g., compare-contrast; chronological sequence; cause-effect; etc.)
	    [The *Performance Indicator* gives enough shape and substance to the standard that students can tell exactly what is expected without being overly prescriptive and formulistic.]

---

7. Most standards are listed only once but are intended to be taught in multiple contexts and in conjunction with several strands.

---

8. The grade placement of the standards may be at variance with the district's traditional (and preferred) placement of the corresponding content.*

---

*This is what might be called an unfortunate "casualty of war." In some states, districts rated as "Excellent" are not required to adhere to some or all of the regulations and requirements set forth in the state-adopted standards. This is in deference to the fact that their students are likely to do well on

(Continued)

Table 2.2 (Continued)

any local, state level, or national tests. But districts who continue to struggle and are in "Academic Watch" or "Emergency" often face major shifts in placement to increase the likelihood their students will pass major tests. Here are a few examples from Ohio, but every state has similar issues:

- Prior to the standards, Ohio districts could offer American History in Grades 6, 7, and/or 8, if they chose. Now they are required to offer Ancient World History in 6th, World History in 7th, and American History in 8th.
- Before the new standards, American History was a Grade 11 staple; teaching American Literature at Grade 11 became the sensible complement. Now, American History is required at Grade 10, wreaking havoc with the venerable order of high school literature.
- Until the new standards, high schools needed to offer no physical science in Grades 9 or 10. Now, Physical Science must be addressed in Grade 9 and Life Science in Grade 10 because of their prominence on the Ohio High School Graduation Test.

In *Math,* for example, the standards dealing with the four basic operations, the math facts, and converting among decimals, percentages, and fractions may all appear several times and in several combinations, very likely in the *Measurement* strand, the *Geometry* strand, and the *Algebra* strand. In *Language Arts,* the standards dealing with the writing process and the writing conventions will reappear in several *Performance Indicators,* including the writing products, the *Research* strand, the *Oral Communication* strand, and in some states the *Visual Media* strand.

■ USING STANDARDS TO STRENGTHEN THE LEARNING CULTURE AND INCREASE EXPECTATIONS

The development of *Performance Indicators* by teachers is essential to standards-based reform, not only because the standards themselves are not classroom ready but also because they need to take root into the deep culture of the district. Teachers need to "fiddle" with the standards in the context of what they know about their students and the expectations of the community they represent. Without this direct involvement, there is no staff ownership; and without staff ownership, the reforms always belong to someone else and will not be taken seriously.

We have seen elaborate and expensive canned programs with every conceivable attachment and peripheral go ignored by teachers and principals alike. While many districts may resist taking the time to translate the standards into academic performance outcomes (or *Performance Indicators*), skipping this step to use someone else's work is a waste of time.

If carefully planned and strategically implemented, the translation process provides three dimensions of staff ownership and acculturation, all of which mutually reinforce the other like interconnecting vines on a garden trellis.

Local Norms and Needs, Stepped Up a Notch

The ultimate goal of translating content standards into *Performance Indicators* is to "raise the bar" on the level of academic performance expected of students in the district. In the shadow of NCLB, it is to make certain that all demographic subgroups and students with Special Needs experience comparable levels of academic success. In most states, the standards themselves represent the minimum level or academic floor of achievement, and districts are encouraged not to consider them as the ceiling.

With hundreds of effective translations already underway in many schools, it is not necessary for each district to start from scratch. But there is no substitute for a district growing its own curriculum, even if it decides to borrow some features from others. Teams of teachers need to make informed and thoughtful decisions about what to borrow, what to develop, and how then to weave the parts in to the unique tapestry that reflects *their* students and *into the* community. And these same teams should review the curriculum annually in the light of student performance to make needed adjustments and ensure its continued fit.

Controlling—Not Being Controlled by—the Standards

Although the standards were established to be helpful and to increase student achievement, they can become a weapon if misused. They can undermine the professionalism and effectiveness of a staff and threaten the academic success of all but the highest-ability students. Used inappropriately, the standards can be coercive and intimidating, and the critics of the standards movement are ready to pounce on any abuse with an "I told you so." But the best defense is to respect the opposition, and those who value the appropriate use of standards must be vigilant not to fall into the traps that the critics have articulated.

In developing their *Performance Indicators,* each district makes the determination about which standards to combine, which to divide, and which to integrate across strands and subjects. They then decide how to teach and how to assess these *Performance Indicators* at both the classroom level and across the entire district. With these decisions, and the rich professional discourse that leads to them, comes a positive, proactive type of control that makes the standards work for a district and its students, rather than the reverse.

It empowers the staff to maintain the wide angle in constant view, even while addressing the details. It also builds in them the capacity to honestly review their own teaching and testing each year in the light of student performance and to make adjustments if and as needed.

Accountability

Along with the autonomy to translate the standards into the district's own curriculum comes the responsibility of seeing to it that the curriculum is followed. Adopting the Performance Indicators as the official achievement targets of the district equips the Board of Education and administrative team with the means they need for quality control. They can hold themselves and their staff accountable for seeing to it that every student is provided the opportunity to master the curriculum in classrooms taught by highly qualified teachers. This "highly qualified" designation reflects the use of Best Practice techniques for planning and delivering instruction and for the formative and summative assessment of student learning. The *Performance Indicators* are also the basis of the district's Benchmark Assessments, the purchase of materials and equipment, the continual monitoring of student performance, and the professional development of all staff, including the central office team and building principals as well as the faculty.

From a staff perspective, all teachers should be held accountable for their part in seeing to it that every student is given the optimum chance to master the indicators, including intervention as needed. But in addition, central office staff should ensure that teachers are provided the training and resources necessary to fulfill these obligations. Moreover, building principals have the responsibility to facilitate the day-to-day implementation of the *Performance Indicators*, once they have been adopted as the basis of the instructional program.

■ THE PROCESS OF DEVELOPING *PERFORMANCE INDICATORS*

During the early stages of the school reform process, each school's Leadership Team will have devised a multiyear Action Plan to guide the various initiatives and activities. Among the reform goals will be the improvement of student achievement in one or more subject areas, necessitating the reform of the curriculum and the instructional delivery in the target subjects and grade levels. For each subject, at least one teacher per grade level should be selected for the developing Team. These work Teams should be divided into 3- or 4-year ranges (e.g., K–3; 4–6; 7–9; 10–12) to provide adequate time for each grade level to consider its own standards in relation to those of contiguous grades. Districts are encouraged to appoint at least one teacher to straddle two or more groups to ensure development between the groups, particularly if the effort is K–12.

Step 1: Getting an Aerial View

For each subject area, the Team should first be asked to identify the key concepts, skills, and themes that currently characterize the district curriculum for that subject and grade levels represented: Who typically does what? These items are listed on wall charts and set aside. Next, Team members examine the grade-level content standards and list the content and skills set forth in the standards. Most Teams quickly discover if there are any discrepancies in the two lists. Without prompting, the Teams typically discover that many of the standards are really not classroom ready, and they nearly always identify most of the eight considerations previously described. Typically, these discrepancies deal with placement of topics. For example, the focus on Life Science at Grade 3 may have moved to Grade 4; or American History, a tradition at Grade 11, may have shifted to Grade 10. Just as often, teachers discover gaps or topics missing from their current curriculum but mandated by the standards. Because the school year remains the same length, this necessitates that some long-time favorites or "sacred cows" may need to be sacrificed on the altar of compliance.

Step 2: What's a *Performance Indicator?*

When they compare the traditional textbook objectives to the state content standards, teachers on the developing Teams realize that the objectives are relatively isolated and address only portions of a standard. But with so many objectives in the text, the natural question becomes, How do we adapt these objectives to fit the standards? For all the reasons described in the previous section, the *Performance Indicator* is the ideal solution. Each one includes the content as well as the cognitive demand of the standard(s), and each leads to a tangible, measurable product that demonstrates mastery of the standard(s) in a realistic context. Once teachers see several samples of *Performance Indicators* and how each has been translated from one or more content standards, they are able to build their own checklist of attributes that characterize the *Performance Indicator*. Each (a) reflects an integration of strands rather than single strands (e.g., the Fraction standards from Number Theory are combined with some of the *Measurement* standards rather than appearing alone); (b) includes real-world contexts or lifelike applications (e.g., letters to the editor, planning a trip); (c) designates or implies a product that can be accomplished in multiple ways; (d) integrates several skills and concepts rather than one at a time; (e) requires higher-level thinking and processing to solve a problem, devise a product, or complete a task; (f) implies or states how it can best be taught and assessed; (g) allows for options and alternatives that enable differentiation (e.g., various modalities and intelligences are used, the potential for enrichment or remediation is clear, and accommodations or modifications can be applied); and (h) in some cases will illustrate interdisciplinary connections (e.g., how latitude and longitude relate to the seasons and conditions of climate [Social Studies and Science]).

Step 3: The Developmental Flow

It helps most developing Teams to see a sample PreK–12 Matrix of *Performance Indicators* listing all of the *Indicators* in the left-hand column, with a column for each grade level, PreK–12 (so labeled across the top), and check marks indicating the grade level(s) for each *Indicator.* This provides a scope and sequence of content and shows the developmental flow of student mastery from one grade to the next. Because each *Indicator* is clearly coded to the content standards, the district can assure itself that not only is every standard represented (some more than once), but there is a developmental articulation in the curriculum. In addition, there are strategic back laps in this flow to accommodate standards that appear at multiple grade levels. A sample Matrix is included in Appendix B.

Step 4: Translating the Standards Into *Performance Indicators*

Although they may prefer to reference a sample from another district, each district's development Team should review the content standards to determine (a) which are too narrow and are best combined, (b) which are overly dense and should be split, and (c) which are satisfactory as they are and need only the addition of context or a product. By using the rubric of criteria they derived from the samples, Teams can craft their own *Performance Indicators* for each grade level and subject targeted in the Action Plan.

Step 5: Grade-to-Grade Articulation and Individual Grade-Level Lists

As the teams work across several days, they should prepare drafts of their work showing the articulation of *Indicators* among grade levels (e.g., K–3); these drafts should be provided to the next grade-level band (e.g., 4–6) to use as a point of departure and continual reference for their work. Gradually, the Matrix unfolds, and teams can monitor the flow across grade levels. For convenience, but only after the developmental flow has been assured, the list of *Performance Indicators* for each grade level (or course) is generated separately for review by the other teachers who will be using them. The format we use with **Instructional Design** is shown in Table 2.3 on the following page, including an explanation of the various symbols and codes.

Step 6: Review by Critical Friends

In Chapter 1, Figure 1.2 is a graphic resembling a wedding cake; it displays how to tier the involvement of the entire staff in the **Instructional Design** process. The Critical Friends tier is one of the most important in the entire process since it provides the strategic link between the development teams and the other teachers at a grade level and/or subject who will be using the material. Of particular significance are the *Performance Indicators* since they will be adopted by the district Board of Education as the official achievement targets of the district. As such, they drive the district's instructional program. From these *Indicators* will come such course tools as the *Curriculum Maps*, the *Unit Plans*, and the various Assessments, not to mention the materials and equipment purchased by the district and the information on student progress communicated with parents/guardians. Clearly, the significance of the *Performance Indicators* cannot be overstated, and their development by a representative Team necessitates their review and acceptance by other teachers who will be using them.

This review typically yields important suggestions and edits to make the *Performance Indicators* more workable, to clarify the logic behind each, and to rectify any omissions. By the time they are submitted to the Board for final approval, the *Performance Indicators* bear the fingerprints of the entire staff, thus broadening the ownership and deepening the accountability for their mastery by all students.

Table 2.3 Cutaway of Grade-Level List of *Performance Indicators*

Tippecanoe Local Schools
Language Arts *Performance Indicators*
Grade 7—Abridged

Annotations (left/margin callouts):

- The four circles represent grading periods; darkened circles show when the indicator will be assessed
- The I, II, III numerals reflect the level of difficulty of each indicator **[Levels I, II, and III are explained later in the chapter]**
- The bold brackets show subcategories
- The bracketed **code** includes standards, for example, R = Reading 7 = grade level 2 = category 5 = standard Also indicates the integration of other strand, for example; this one ties in Communication [C.7.9]
- The **code** also indicates any designated state Benchmarks
- [… tie-in with Writing]
- The shaded rows indicate categories within the strand

I. READING		
B. Acquisition of Vocabulary		
○●●●	II	**[Affixes-Roots-Word Origins-Contextual Cues]** 23. Identify and use in speaking and writing words adopted into English from other languages that appear in fiction and nonfiction reading selections; keep a log of such words, and use in Oral Presentations. [R.7.2.5] Voc D [C.7.9]
○○●●	III	24. Apply knowledge of Greek, Latin, and Anglo-Saxon roots and affixes to unlock the meaning of difficult or technical words; record in reading journals/logs, and create an activity for fellow students (e.g., a board game, crossword puzzle, Web quest). [R.7.2.6] Voc D, E
●○○○	II	**[Overall Context, inclusive of all cues]** 33. Define the meaning of unknown words through context clues and the author's use of comparison/contrast, definition, restatement, and/or example; use a T-chart [or H-chart] that displays the word, the contextual definition, and the author's technique. [R.7.2.1] Voc A
○○○●	III	**[Analogies]** 53. Use analogies in the rewrite or verbal explication of a fiction or nonfiction passage to clarify the possible relationships among the ideas and concepts in the original passage (i.e., synonym:synonym, antonym:part-whole, object:function, etc.). [R.7.2.3] Voc B [W.7.2.6]
C. Reading Processes: Concepts of Print, Comprehension Strategies, and Self-Monitoring Strategies		
●○○○	I	**[Text Features]** 12. Utilize text features such as chapter titles, headings and subheadings, and parts of books including the index and table of contents, appendices, and online tools (e.g., search engines, online encyclopedias) to locate specific information or answer specific teacher-generated questions. [R.5.4.1] [R.6.4.1] [R.7.4.1] Info A, E [Rsrch 5.6; 6.8; 7.4; 8.3]
●●○○	II	**[Summarize]** 40. Summarize the information in fiction and nonfiction texts, using key ideas and supporting details in nonfiction and literary elements in fiction; reference gaps or contradictions, and display as an outline or text map. [R.7.3.4] Info A, C; Lit C, D, E
etc.	etc.	etc.

Note: As shown in the Three-Year Time frame (see Table 1.1), it is best if during the summer just preceding the Pilot year, the *Curriculum Mapping* component would have begun as a way to expedite the piloting process. The sample Three-Year Time Frame has been repeated at the end of this chapter, with the *Performance Indicator* step highlighted for easy reference.

Step 7: The Pilot—Pass Out the Green Pens

Once reviewed by the Critical Friends network and adopted by the Board, the *Performance Indicators* are ready to be piloted in all or selected classrooms throughout the district. The course tool for the Pilot is the *Curriculum Map*, a year-long calendar that shows how the *Performance Indicators* are clustered to form thematic or topical units and placed in an appropriate sequence. Many indicators are strategically repeated in additional units across the school year to provide students with multiple opportunities for mastery. As with the *Performance Indicators*, the *Curriculum Maps* are developed by representative Teams of teachers and circulated among Critical Friends for feedback and adjustments. Chapter 3 is devoted to the development of *Curriculum Maps*.

A distinctive feature of **Instructional Design** is the "green inking" process. As they pilot the indicators and the *Curriculum Maps*, teachers are encouraged to make correcting notes and edits with "green ink." Throughout the Pilot, the principal should arrange grade-level and department meetings to discuss the *Performance Indicators* and how they are working in the context of the *Curriculum Maps*: Are any of them more or less difficult for students? Are some more difficult to assess? Are the available materials and/or equipment inadequate for some? This information, along with the compilation of the "green ink," should be candidly and continually discussed as likely revisions for the next school year.

Step 8: Adoption and Implementation

With the conclusion of the Pilot, the *Performance Indicators* are revised as needed and presented to the Board for formal adoption as the official achievement targets of the district. The remaining chapters in the book detail the specific materials and procedures that are used in the piloting and implementation process, including the training that occurs and the products that are developed.

■ FREQUENTLY ASKED QUESTIONS AND RELATED ISSUES

When institutions make significant changes in the way they operate, all sorts of questions and uncertainties arise, even though the changes are productive and necessary. The same is true when a school district attempts to restructure its curriculum by integrating the state content standards and establishing performance expectations for its students. The most typical in our experience are described as follows:

❓ What About Gaps? What if the Standards Leave Out Important Skills or Concepts?

Although the content standards in most states have been carefully crafted to accomplish a developmental flow from one grade level to the next, Teams developing the indicators may discover gaps that need to be filled. For example, in Language Arts, *Figurative Language* may not be a standard until Grades 4 or 5, but the team may want to insert idioms into Grades 2 and 3. Or in Social Studies, the concept of *Latitude/Longitude* may not be a standard after Grade 7, but a team might decide to extend it through Grade 9.

❓ What About Indicators That Are Unlikely to Be Mastered the First Time They Are Addressed?

From the outset, Developing Teams can earmark certain *Performance Indicators* as needing to appear in more than one unit across the year. This is formally addressed in developing the *Curriculum Maps* to pilot the *Indicators*. These "toughies" are strategically placed in several units and in different contexts to provide students with multiple opportunities to master them.

❓ We Can Differentiate for the Can'ts, But What About the Won'ts?

With NCLB has come the mandate that students of all ability levels and prior achievement records will experience academic success. To this end, there has been an increased emphasis on the inclusion of students with Special Needs (rather than pullout) and the resulting focus on differentiating instruction in every classroom. But as hard as teachers try and despite an endless parade of differentiated opportunities to succeed, there will be students who do not succeed during a given school year. The *can'ts* of this group have tried their best and have taken advantage of every opportunity. And although they may not have succeeded to the level desired, they will have experienced some degree of mastery in some areas, and they will get the opportunity to work on many of their missed skills during the following year. By contrast, the *won'ts* of the group who did not succeed have a different set of issues that must be addressed, most of which are as much or more about attitude as academic need. And although they must be afforded every opportunity to succeed, care must be taken not to further enable them with overindulgence and thus perpetuate their refusals to try. Put another way, their decision to fail should not steal precious time and resources from the *can'ts* as well as from the mainstream students who are working as expected to achieve mastery. Teachers must be encouraged, and fully supported, not to be held hostage by *won'ts* and to keep their sights set on those who "want to" and "will."

❓ What About Cross-Content Integration? We Do a Lot of That.

Many elementary schools make a concerted effort to integrate the disciplines to help students see the broadest possible context for what they learn and to make viable links among the subjects. In middle schools using the community model, this practice is also encouraged. In a perfect world, teachers at every level would write interdisciplinary *Performance Indicators* wherever appropriate. This is indeed possible since the four core content areas have many parallel standards:

♦ Interpret various tables, charts, and graphs: In Science, collect information about recorded temperatures or precipitation to make viable predictions about subsequent temperatures and precipitation.

♦ Use primary and secondary sources to locate and cross-check information: In Social Studies, compare news accounts of the Normandy invasion with letters written by soldiers.

♦ Distinguish fact from opinion (or inference): In Science and/or Social Studies, to what extent could the losses from Hurricane Katrina have been prevented?

♦ Compare and contrast multiple writers' perceptions of the same topic or concept: In Social Studies, compare the description of President Clinton's impeachment written by a Democrat with that written by a Republican.

♦ Use graphic organizers to display relationships among and between ideas: Students write in every subject; this is one of the easiest ways to integrate content areas and promote logical thinking.

♦ Identify multiple means to solve a problem or resolve an issue (one *not* used in class): Math: another way to arrive at the same answer; Science: a way to help plants grow when there is no sunlight; Social Studies: a means of running an election without political parties; Language Arts: use figurative language to inform readers about a literal scientific or political issue.

♦ Make predictions about subsequent details or events, and verify or adjust using actual data: In Social Studies, use infant mortality data in developing countries and undeveloped countries in the context of prenatal diet and medical care to make viable predictions about population growth and decline.

❓ Like the Standards, Are Some of the *Performance Indicators* More or Less Difficult Than Others?

The preface to the content standards in most states contains an admonishment similar to the following: These content standards are promulgated to "challenge students to think at higher levels . . . to exercise their critical judgment . . . and to apply their creative ingenuity to solve problems."

The underlying assumption is that if students are to actually own a concept or skill-set, they must construct meaning for themselves and use their knowledge and skills to solve problems and develop an original product. To accommodate these loftier sentiments of higher-level thinking and the use of creative ingenuity, we have included a leveling aspect to the *Performance Indicator* process to help students proceed developmentally from basic knowledge through inferential thinking and on into independent construction. This provides an effective diagnostic trail to provide intervention as needed when mastery has not occurred.

Level I *Indicators* are basic skill-driven or knowledge level; students are expected to recall the information or to perform the skill when prompted by the teacher or text. Little reflection or interpretation is required. Typically, only one content standard is reflected in Level I indicators. And although they are essential to establishing adequate baseline knowledge, they should not be the majority of the *Indicators* in a course. Samples follow: (a) compute math facts to 18, and record in a pocket chart to use in solving word problems; (b) list the distinctions between animals that live on land and those that live on water, citing examples from the class terrarium; prepare as a pamphlet; (c) locate Tennessee and its contiguous states on a map; and (d) define the following types of figurative language: simile, metaphor, and so on, and prepare as a bookmark.

Level II *Indicators* are interpretive; students are expected to make viable inferences about or draw valid conclusions from the information provided. They react to prompts or problems posed by the teacher or text, similar to but not those covered in class. Students must apply a rule or procedure to reach a solution. Examples follow:

♦ Use the data in the class graph to make three inferences about the students, including a prediction about how the graph would be affected if some of the data were changed (e.g., another class were added, the same data were examined a year later or a year earlier); show the alternate graphs.

♦ Compare work done using carpenter tools based on simple machines with modern power tools using the production of furniture or guns in colonial times; display as a Then-And-Now poster that includes explanatory detail.

♦ Compare and contrast Nebraska with three contiguous states in terms of industrial base, economic conditions, demographics, landforms, and transportation systems; prepare a letter to a major industrial firm who plans to relocate to one or two of the four states.

♦ Interpret a poem in terms of its use of style, figurative language, and imagery to achieve a particular effect, citing specific examples; prepare as a lesson plan to help younger students understand the poem.

Even though students are working well above the memory or knowledge level, they are still operating within the material presented by the texts or teacher. Yet they are required to draw inferences and to solve problems they have not seen before by applying what they have learned in class. In many case, multiple standards are included in each Level II *Indicator.*

Level III *Indicators* are constructive level and involve high-end application. Students are expected to extend what they've learned beyond the classroom to solve a real-world problem, develop an original product or point of view, or create an interpretation unique to them. In essence, they construct their own meaning. Examples follow:

♦ Submit a proposal to redecorate an area (e.g., a student lounge to serve a specific grade level or number of homerooms). Include a scale drawing of the finished product; a list of the furniture, paint, and carpeting needed; and an estimate of the cost. Append all calculations, showing all of the work.

♦ Construct an apparatus made of simple machines and powered without fossil fuel that will accomplish a physical task (e.g., move an object, power a vehicle); include an annotated blueprint of the apparatus that includes the Laws of Motion and Conservation of Energy it demonstrates.

♦ Recommend a set of policies and procedures for a particular government body to solve a problem, taking into account prevailing economic and political constraints (e.g., how the city or village, having just laid off sanitation workers, can clean up the litter from public areas to keep residents from leaving and attract others to move in); prepare as a presentation to the Board, including visual aids and appropriate documentation.

♦ Critique a brief work of fiction (e.g., short story, play, or novel), including how each of its elements (i.e., characters, setting, plot detail, and conflicts) were developed by the author, featuring his or her style of writing and use of language to achieve the overall effect; decide how well the author succeeded, citing examples of what did and did not work well, and concluding with a series of specific recommendations to improve the piece.

Clearly, the Level III indicators represent the most cumulative and constructivist level of standards mastery. They typically involve several standards and often extend to other subjects. They are what many refer to as "project-based learning." But not every Level III is a huge project requiring several weeks and multiple external resources to complete. In many cases, they can be on-demand demonstrations, assuming students can have access to the resources they need. Since most Level III *Indicators* do not rely on students' memories but rather on their ability to use resources and make interpretations of information to solve a problem, students develop a deep-level understanding that they can reapply as needed in other contexts, without prompts.

Typically, developing Teams need not worry about the level of their *Performance Indicators* until after they are all developed. It is during the leveling process that teams often discover an oversupply of one level or another and then revisit the *Indicators* to achieve a more appropriate balance. This balancing step is far easier to accomplish when looking at all of the *Indicators* rather than one at a time.

❓ Aren't Some of These Indicators Best Accomplished as a Team?

Helping students function successfully as part of a team and mastering group processing and problem-solving skills are all important goals of schooling. With most project-based learning activities, the emphasis is placed on group work, and students clearly benefit from the experience. But the mastery of content standards, including performance on high-stakes tests, is an individual proposition. No amount of "works well with others" or holding up one corner of the wall mural created by the team is going to fulfill a single requirement for NCLB. None of the high-stakes tests that are currently used to judge a district's academic pedigree or decide whether a student meets AYP is a group measure. This includes not only the NCLB Achievement Tests at Grades 3 through 8 but also the traditional PSAT, ACT, and SAT tests at the district level, and the NAEP, PISA, and TIMSS tests for more national and global comparisons. If schools are not careful to provide students an adequate balance between group and individual accountability, it is the student who will lose in the end.

The need for each student to demonstrate his and her own mastery of each *Performance Indicator* in no way precludes rich and enabling group activities to prepare for this individual accountability. But some group activities are simply not assessments and need to be amended to provide for the individual assessment of each student:

♦ When the standards require each student to identify the various probabilities for a game of chance, the group's identification of such probabilities from a game they will create will not suffice; each student will need to explain or describe the various probabilities, including an example of each.

♦ When the standards require each student to write a story that includes specific elements, the class story does not document each student's mastery (even though it is an excellent way to learn the *how-to* of story-writing); each student must write his or her own story, including the specified elements.

♦ When the standards require each student to describe the connection between the water cycle and specific weather-related phenomena (e.g., tornadoes, floods, droughts, floods, forest fires, and hurricanes), a group-conducted experiment is not an adequate means to assess the individual student; each student must be able to write or tell the connection, including an illustration.

♦ When the standards require students to analyze how governments and other groups have used propaganda to influence public opinion and behavior, a team's role-play of propaganda techniques does not measure each student's mastery; each student must analyze an unfamiliar text passage containing propaganda techniques to identify the techniques and explain how they may influence the way people think.

❓ What is Mastery?

The issue of mastery typically surfaces during the development of *Performance Indicators*, but if not, it most certainly will during the Pilot. Teachers naturally want to be sure they know how to determine if and how well students successfully demonstrate what is expected in each *Performance* indicator. Although the final decisions about mastery cannot be made until the Pilot is well underway and teachers get a sense of how the *Indicators* work, questions about mastery arise throughout the process. And that's a good thing. Teachers and administrators—and parents/guardians, wherever possible—should give themselves time to think about what's at stake and problem-solve about possible scenarios.

It's the old adage that the best time to think about a decision is before you have to make it, and the worst time is when you have no choice. We have explored several of these issues below.

Most teachers realize that mastery cannot mean perfect or 100%. But there is always the debate about whether 75% (the gentleman's C) is good enough, or must it be 80%? Teachers cannot help themselves; their prior habits and predispositions gravitate their thinking to what they know: the traditional 90% = A, 80% = B, and so on. But that's a good place to begin, and they'll discover on their own that they may need to tweak their thinking to accommodate exceptions. They'll see that those *Indicators* best assessed with paper-pencil tests can be considered along more traditional lines. And as long as students have, say, five items that assess the same *Indicator*, the fact that they correctly answer four of the five is a comfortable level of mastery for most teachers.

But when the *indicator* involves products that are more holistic, the determination is not quite so clean. In those cases, the teacher may use a rubric or checklist of criteria. Two examples are shown:

♦ The "short story" may use a rubric that requires the following: (a) a compelling introduction; (b) at least three characters, each with distinct personalities and yet linked through the plot lines; (c) a well-developed body that follows at least two plot lines; (d) at least two distinct settings, relevant to the plot lines and the characters; (e) a clear and valid ending that shows resolution of both plot lines; (f) dialogue, correctly punctuated; (g) sentences of varying length and type, using correct grammar, syntax, spelling, and punctuation; and (h) language that is mature, interesting, and includes at least two figurative devices.

♦ An original science experiment may use a rubric that requires the following: (a) a clearly defined problem to solve; (b) at least three hypotheses about viable solutions; (c) evidence that the three hypotheses were considered in the light of if-then thinking; (d) the assembly of pertinent information to clarify and further explain the hypotheses; (e) a carefully designed experiment that controls for all the variables; (f) notes and documentation that show how the experiment was carried out; (g) valid conclusions drawn about the results; and (h) pertinent questions developed to suggest further inquiry.

The 80% can still work, providing the scoring rubric can be leveraged to yield a valid proportion. But there are other *Performance Indicators* for which that may be a struggle, including oral reading for fluency, writing an original poem, conducting error analysis of mathematical problems, building a model (i.e., a volcano), doing an interpretive dance, delivering a political speech, or giving a dramatic reading of literature—not impossible, but requiring careful, thoughtful discussion and several tryouts to see that every possible scenario has been covered.

❓ Is Mastery Permanent?

What if a student has shown mastery in October, but by March has completely lost it? For consistence, the level of mastery reported must reflect the level demonstrated at that point in time. It may be that the earlier mastery reading was a false positive, or this later reading a false negative. But there are typically enough *Performance Indicators* measured in a grading period that one misfire will not jeopardize a student's overall rating. And in most cases, the missed *Indicator* will reappear later in another unit anyway.

❓ How Does *Performance Indicator* Mastery Affect Letter Grades?

This is an extremely important issue and one that, while it cannot be rushed, must not be postponed too long. The answers lie in the district grading policies themselves and what the Board has approved as allowable for the determination of an A, a C, an F, or any other rating system, including narrative comments that indicate success or failure. Among the most common "allowables" are scores on tests and quizzes, checklisted skills observed by the teacher, and grades on various projects and laboratory reports. In essence, if the current system of awarding letter grades is well conceived and proven effective, inserting the *Performance Indicators* will not be a major hassle. But if the current system is haphazard and subjective, attempting to insert *Performance Indicators* into the mix will be like attempting to herd more cats. The thing teachers soon realize is that if students are mastering all of their *Performance Indicators*, they should not be getting C's or D's. On the flip side, if students are failing to master the majority of the *Performance Indicators*, they should not get A's on their report cards. In both situations, something is wrong. But like the previous mastery issues, the letter-grade–*Performance Indicator* connection will be easier to discuss after the Pilot.

Appendix C is a table that displays the various techniques to assess mastery, including teacher observation, paper-pencil tests, student logs or journals, and performance assessments with scoring rubrics. More information about determining mastery will be included in Chapter 8.

WHAT TO DO DURING THE PILOT ■ OF THE *PERFORMANCE INDICATORS*

The above questions are completely legitimate questions and concerns that must be addressed. But at this stage in the **Instructional Design** process, it's too early to make any firm decisions. Participants simply don't know enough. Until teachers and administrators have actually experienced the Pilot and begun the monitoring process, their discussions are merely hypothetical conjectures. By the end of the Pilot, participants will discover that several of their worst fears never materialized, some of their concerns were easily resolved, and other difficulties emerged that no one even anticipated.

The point is that a bridge cannot be crossed until you get there, and it is only during an actual Pilot that the specific issues and conditions surrounding mastery in each building (which may differ across the district) fully emerge. And by then, teachers and administrators will make decisions that are informed by experience and practicality. School staffs are urged not to attempt to finalize anything before the Pilot. But the key is to have a well-organized and data-based Pilot.

Monitor Each Student's Mastery of Every *Performance Indicator*

Teachers should keep track of each student's progress in mastering the *Performance Indicators*, even if using a simple Excel spreadsheet or a sheet of graph paper. This may require some additional release time for teachers to manage, but it is well worth the investment to discover as many issues as possible during the Pilot. These Pilot mastery data will be extremely helpful in making needed adjustments.

Keep Track of Difficulties and Questions About the Mastery Process

While teachers are "green inking" their Pilot documents, they can add notes about individual student mastery: "If Rachel's *PI* mastery were to be translated to a letter grade, she'd have had a D during most of the grading period but an A by the end." "Darren's high-stakes test scores are decent, but he's mastered only half the *PI*s." "Several of my best *PI*-mastery students aren't doing their homework." "I have some students whose mastery is nearly 100%; how do they, and I, distinguish this stronger showing from routine mastery of, for example, 8 of 10?"

Share These Notes and Trends With Others During Team Meetings

As shown in the "wedding cake" diagram in Chapter 1, the detail on each layer includes specific roles for teachers and administrators. One of the roles for teachers is to regularly share information with team members about the mastery portion of the Pilot. But be careful not to allow the conversation to slip into panic mode or a rush to decide. Trust us, by the next month, another group of issues will have surfaced that would nullify or compromise some of those decisions anyway. A perfect role for the building principal and designated central office staff is to attend these meetings and to ask pertinent questions about the *Performance Indicators* being piloted. Beginning at this early stage, these conversations will forge significant pedagogical bonds among the participants that will become stronger as the project proceeds, sufficient to withstand the inevitable setbacks as well as to celebrate the assured successes.

Begin to Decide on How to Decide

As the Pilot proceeds, communal definitions will gain traction, and several issues that had been ambiguous or even obscure will emerge with greater clarity. Hypothetical scenarios will begin to sound more definite, and those who began the Pilot fearful that the sky is falling will become knowledgeable problem-solvers. Ideas for mastery ranges and levels will be commonplace, and the early certainty that "We just can't do all this" will give way to "This will work if ___, ___, and ___ are in place."

Think How Best to Communicate With Parents/Guardians

If at all possible, at least some parents/guardians should be kept informed about the Pilot. In many districts, parents/guardians have been involved in the reform process from Day 1 and have helped to develop the overall Reform Plan. Many buildings have very active parent/guardian-involvement programs and have a tradition of relying on parents/guardians for guidance and support. In these schools, parents/guardians have already been advised about state content standards and *Performance Indicators* and that the instructional program is under renovation. To involve already supportive and knowledgeable parents/guardians in the Pilot process, particularly in discussions about mastery, is indeed a wise move. Parents/guardians should be included in discussions about the *Performance Indicators* and consulted about how mastery will be determined. They need to have a voice in how mastery, or lack thereof, will affect their children's permanent records. To decide without them may send the signal that their input is neither appreciated nor valued, and it may be the kill-shot for an otherwise effective system.

Procure or Design a Cost-Effective and User-Friendly Monitoring System

Even though the mastery issue is in some ways separate from the system to keep track of it, school staffs cannot think clearly about the pedagogical aspects of mastery if they are preoccupied about the logistics of doing so. Even the most productive and exhilarating work by teachers in developing their *Performance Indicators* will grind to a screeching halt if record keeping is a burden. From the beginning of the **Instructional Design** reform process, a committee consisting of central office administrators, building principals, and teachers should be appointed to explore the various options for such a system. This was suggested in the "wedding cake" whole-staff involvement diagram in Chapter 1 (see Figure 1.2). The mission of this committee will be to determine which of the commercial systems would be appropriate for the district, or whether it would be better to develop its own. Naturally, the financial and logistical support needed for start-up and for continuation and maintenance are primary considerations. But the deliberations must also include candid discussions about time commitments and workloads, and throughout the Pilot, the issues surrounding mastery in each school should be considered by this exploratory committee.

"ARE WE THERE YET?"   ■

During the Pilot year, district leaders, teachers, and parents/guardians are frequently disappointed that they don't see an immediate and noticeable increase in test scores. These districts must be reminded that their present state of need did not materialize in only one year, and it cannot be reversed in one year. As corroborated in the school reform research, it may take two to three years to fully implement comprehensive reform, and the curricular and instructional portion of the effort will require at least a year or so before teachers substantively change what they are doing in classrooms.

But there are those who still don't get it. A few years ago, a principal from a school in a fairly large southern city called us in the spring to ask about providing them assistance in curricular and instructional reform. Once we determined what it was that she had in mind, we asked about the time lines, expecting to hear the customary 18- to 24-month window. To our surprise, she responded, "Well, I want to start right away so our November test scores will show an improvement."

As much as we know about the power and potential of *Instructional Design*, we know that at the end of the Pilot year, there may be only trace indications of improved student performance. It typically requires at least two years of concerted effort to begin to see any significant improvement in group test scores. But with disaggregations and the examination of more finely-parsed levels of performance (including individual scores), small but promising gains for specific students can be documented almost immediately. But the changes in staff performance will be enormous. And for everyone in the school community—staff, parents/guardians, and students—it will be totally apparent that things are no longer "business as usual." Most profound will be the increased academic expectations of students and parents/guardians and the expanded level of student accountability to perform or construct.

On the infrastructure level, the staff working to develop *Performance Indicators* will have experienced unprecedented growth, not only as individuals but as part of a team having enjoyed a collaborative effort on a professional project that will actually make a difference in the lives of children. The **Building Leadership Teams** will have helped circulate the draft *Performance Indicators* among the Critical Friends, participated in and encouraged fellow staff during the Pilot, and helped assemble the "green ink" to prepare for revisions. By design, this strategic involvement with the faculty will have enlarged the Leadership Team's capacity and their level of trust from the staff to provide the leadership necessary to proceed through the rest of the *Instructional Design* process. As the base of staff involvement is broadened, terms such as *PI* and *Performance Indicator*, *"green ink," mastery, standards-based*, and so on will become second nature and part of the building vernacular, an essential foundation on which to build the remaining components of the process.

■ SUMMARY

As described above, the process of developing and piloting *Performance Indicators* is fairly complex. But it is the most important step in the *Instructional Design* process, since the indicators for each subject drive the entire instructional program. Table 2.4 is the sample time line provided at the end of Chapter 1. It shows how the development and Pilot of *Performance Indicators* fits into the big picture of the entire process.

Table 2.4   Sample Three-Year Time Frame

		Year 1			Year 2			Year 3		
		Summer	*Fall*	*Winter/ Spring*	*Summer*	*Fall*	*Winter/ Spring*	*Summer*	*Fall*	*Winter/ Spring*
Two Subjects, PreK–12; for example, Reading and Math	*Performance Indicators (PIs)*	Develop, Pilot Critical Friends →			Revise, Implement →			Continue (annual review) →		
	Curriculum Maps	Develop, Pilot Critical Friends →			Revise, Implement →			Continue (annual review) →		
	Unit Plans				Develop, Pilot Critical Friends →			Revise, Implement →		
	Continuous Monitoring	Unofficially keep track of student mastery			Develop, Pilot Critical Friends →			Revise, Implement →		
	Benchmark Assessments	Collect classroom tests measuring PIs			Develop, Pilot Critical Friends →			Revise, Implement →		

PART II
Planning

3

Curriculum Mapping

NOT A NEW CONCEPT ■

Once adopted, the *Performance Indicators* are ready for classroom implementation. This requires that teachers attach them to content units, which typically address a particular theme or topic. While the unit idea is certainly nothing new, inserting a set of *Performance Indicators* into each and structuring the entire unit around them may be. Traditional curriculum models feature the content and activities of a unit as the INPUT to be provided to students. In a standards-based curriculum, the focus shifts to an OUTPUT model, and the *Performance Indicators* are what students are expected to do, having experienced the unit activities. Several of the *Performance Indicators* may be inserted into more than one unit to provide students with multiple opportunities for mastery.

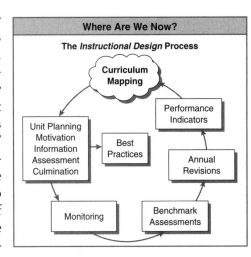

In the **Instructional Design** process, this linkage of the *Performance Indicators* to the *Unit* topics is the first step toward the *Curriculum Map*. Once developers identify the other components they feel would make an effective *Map* and select a physical layout, the *Map* becomes the yearlong planning guide by which teachers organize their course content across the school year. Together, the *Performance Indicators* and *Curriculum Maps* comprise a contract between the district and its community, an assurance that the Board is serious about standards-based curriculum and that it will indeed be evident in every classroom.

A convenient metaphor for the *Curriculum Map* is its namesake, the road map, or AAA's TripTik as shown in Table 3.1.

Table 3.1   Comparison of a Traditional Road Map with a *Curriculum Map*

The Road Map/TripTik		The Curriculum Map
destinations	⇔	*Performance Indicators*
each "leg" of the trip	⇔	units, chapters, themes—they go by several names
important features in each leg (e.g., terrain, historic sites, cultural events, etc.)	⇔	key concepts, processes, skills, terminology, etc.
routes taken	⇔	methods and materials used
special attractions	⇔	integration with other subjects, technology, guest speakers, field trips, mentorships, etc.
detours	⇔	▪ intervention (both remediation and enrichment) ▪ building events (parent conferences, open house, testing, picture day, etc.)
distances and schedules	⇔	time frames

The *Curriculum Map* has been a staple of classroom instruction for decades. The basic components of most *Curriculum Maps* are time frames; clusters of related content; references to content standards (or *Performance Indicators*); and major assessment events, such as state testing or benchmark tests. An annotated review of literature—available, by chapter, on request from the authors—acknowledges the various scholars who have contributed to the mapping discourse. Several *Mapping* formats are available online, and it is important that each school select the layout and components that are most helpful for its staff. *Mapping* is a versatile and effective course tool that codifies the yearlong implementation of the *Performance Indicators*. When implemented schoolwide, *Curriculum Map* benefits every stakeholder: (a) the classroom teacher maintains a continual sense of the big picture, or "where we've been and where we're headed;" (b) the principal can quickly see how the *Performance Indicators* are unfolding in each classroom; (c) parents/guardians can anticipate the plan of action for their children's school year; and (d) it is helpful to older students as a syllabus for the course. It is ideal if the *Curriculum Maps* are developed by a Team of teachers, at least a core of whom were also involved in devising the *Performance Indicators*. Although each teacher may wish to personalize his or her *Map* by adding further detail, for consistency, we recommend that each grade level and subject operate from a common *Map*.

As with all of the course tools in the **Instructional Design** process, the first draft of each *Map* should be circulated among Critical Friends for input and feedback. *Curriculum Maps* are, however, never etched in stone; they breathe and are adjusted as the months pass. The most effective *Maps* are rife with "green ink," indicating that they are being used to drive instruction and yet are accommodating unforeseen circumstances.

Although they are flexible, *Curriculum Maps* aren't shapeless and indefinite. They give a sturdy but resilient framework to the school year and document the use of state content standards in every classroom. Like the well-used road map to a traveler, the *Curriculum Map* is a handy reference for teachers and serves as an overall guide to the terrain of the school year; it allows for necessary and interesting side trips without losing one's way.

FEATURES AND PHYSICAL ■
LAYOUT OF THE *CURRICULUM MAP*

Most Teams appreciate seeing various models of *Curriculum Maps* to get a sense of the features or components that could be included and the options for physical format or layout. Portrait or landscape work equally well; some users prefer 8 ½ by 11 inch to fit into a three-ring binder, and others select 11 by 17 inch to provide more detail (which, when folded in half also fits nicely into a three-ring binder). Perusing these samples helps Teams decide which will be the most effective for their school. The two components suggested by **Instructional Design** are the *Performance Indicators* linked to specific content units and a sense of time or duration. Beyond these, a Team should include those components that they know will be the most helpful. Typically, a common *Map* format and components are selected for a school, but the choices at elementary school may differ from middle and high school. The key is to select what will be the most functional and convenient for the teachers and administrators who will use it. Among the most popular components are the following: (a) essential questions, (b) key concepts and vocabulary, (c) cites for textbook and supplemental, (d) differentiation strategies, (e) nonprint media, (f) Special Needs adaptations, (g) major building events that will affect instruction, (h) technology, (i) cross-curricular references, (j) products or assessments, and (k) lead-up or enabling skills.

More detail about these features is included in the Frequently Asked Questions section toward the end of this chapter. These initial format decisions may be adjusted as Teams proceed through the work, but making a tentative decision early on helps a Team maintain a visual focus to guide their work. Two popular layouts are shown here, but we encourage districts to customize their *Maps* for maximum efficiency. With the magic of word processing, *Maps* are easily input and subsequently edited, and districts that are serious about ensuring the success of their reform efforts should provide for clerical assistance. In some cases, it is simpler to subcontract this production and distribution function; in others, it is best handled in-house. In addition, we strongly urge districts to post the *Maps* on the building (and/or district) Web site to expedite teacher access, not only of their own grade level but at adjacent grade levels, too.

Since the *Curriculum Map* is the vehicle for piloting the *Performance Indicators*, teachers will be using "green ink" to make edits and adjustments in the context of actual classroom use. The two sample formats below include "green ink" illustrations. One principal said it best: "How do I know we're using the maps? We're in our second box of green pens."

THE *INSTRUCTIONAL DESIGN* APPROACH TO *CURRICULUM MAPPING*

The development of a *Curriculum Map* is not merely an exercise in scheduling that parodies the scope and sequence of a textbook or linear curriculum guide. It is a professional development experience during which teachers, working in grade-level or course-alike Teams, make important decisions about how to organize, sequence, and pace their work for the year.

Teams developing the maps make several key decisions based on the overall intent of the course and the way the content standards are translated into the *Performance Indicators*. For each grade level, the discussions should include the following:

- Examine the current content for developmental appropriateness and adequacy.
- Divide the content into teachable chunks or units (some grades prefer chapters or themes).
- Now that the *Performance Indicators* are part of the equation, how do they factor into each unit?
- Which *Indicators* need to appear in more than one unit, since they may take longer to master?
- Given the distribution of the *Indicators,* there may be content that needs to be moved to another grade level.
- Place the units into the most appropriate developmental sequence across the year.
- Identify interdisciplinary connections (e.g., a History Day project that will cross into several subjects).
- Given the various options as to *Map* layout and the features it may display (see Tables 3.2 and 3.3), select the most doable for the staff represented by the Developing Team. (More detail about the optional features is included in the Frequently Asked Questions section toward the end of this chapter.)

What Mapping Is Not

With the advent of the standards-based curriculum has come the pacing guide, or **calendar** of standards. A calendar of standards is not a *Curriculum Map.* For the reasons listed in Chapter 2: *Performance Indicators,* the content standards are not classroom ready, and typing keywords from the standards out of context into a window-pane calendar does not make them any more ready. Indeed, it only widens the isolation of the skills and concepts in each standard.

A second pseudo *Curriculum Map* is the **scope and sequence chart of the textbook**. Although publishers claim to fully and faithfully reflect the standards in every state, a close examination reveals that this "reflection" is often the mere mention of a concept or perhaps a few words. In some texts we have reviewed, several standards are referenced repeatedly, but a few standards are actually missing. Second, the majority of textbooks include a surplus of content and activities to provide for reteaching, differentiation, year-round schooling, block schedules, and structured interventions. With

(Text continues on page 62)

Table 3.2 Sample of a Horizontal Map

Content Topics may prefer to list bullets (e.g., supply and demand)

Performance Indicators (abbreviated for illustration) representing multiple strands

Identifying Information typically the name of the school, the subject, grade level, year, and names of the developing team

Concepts/Key Vocabulary typically, the key ideas, major concepts, principles, and terms that will be focus

Cross-Curricular References links to other subject areas (as appropriate) to broaden context

Products a list of expected unit outcomes to document mastery

Text Materials may prefer to include page numbers, chapter titles, Web sites, etc.

Unit Title, Length ⇦

⇨ **Components Building Event**

Sample "Green Ink" (would be written right on the *Map*) e.g.,
✓ don't need that much time for PreTest
✓ terrible editing skills; better add that to several units

Sample "Green Ink" (would be written right on the *Map*) e.g.,
✓ next time, read simpler selections
✓ their understanding of poetry is basically song lyrics; build on this

Curriculum Map for Tippecanoe Middle School

Grade: 7   Developing Team: *Althea, Bernie, Enrique, Jamal, Ruth*

Subject: *Language Arts*

Topics/Materials	PIs	Concepts/Vocabulary	Integration	Products
Unit # 1 August—Mid-September (2 weeks) "Who's Here ?!" (Open House; Meet-the-Parents)				
Fiction "The Lottery" **Nonfiction** (current editorial on beliefs) **Poetry** "Dreams" **Video** CNN and FOX talking heads on common topic	I D 22 . . . the elements of fiction, nonfiction, and poetry I E 16 . . . comparison among different genres/same topic II B 9 . . . written summary of literature selections II C 31–42 . . . spelling, grammar, punctuation III B 7 . . . extemporaneous speech on assigned topic	Elements of fiction (plot events, character, setting; how they interrelate) Elements of nonfiction (main idea/supporting details; organizational pattern; Pgh structure Conventions of poetry (thyme, rhythm, imagery, voice, etc.); types Caliber of evidence (re: date, clarity, accuracy, adequacy, etc.)	**Science:** use of science text passage to assess knowledge of Greek/Latin word origins **Social Studies:** use of Internet "treasure hunt" to assess ability to access Internet	Results of **PreTests** on ▪ Basic reading skills ▪ Basic writing and editing skills ▪ Basic listening and speaking skills ▪ Internet access
Unit # 2 Mid September–Mid-October (4 weeks) "Mythology"				
Myths (text) p. 304 p. 389, etc. continued	I B 24 . . . Greek and Latin word parts, origins I C 40 . . . summarization continued	affixes roots derivatives summary vs. recall continued	**Social Studies:** maps of ancient Greece and Rome (Troy, etc.) continued	Journal entries: ▪ reaction to myths ▪ key words ▪ summaries continued

Note: these are just the first few details of the next unit

✓ need to explain "Journal" ASAP; they were clueless
✓ need to give them sample Journal pages

Table 3.3   Sample of a Vertical Map

Synopsis
a brief snapshot or big-picture overview of the unit; typically one or two sentences indicating the key events and what students will be doing.

Identifying Information
typically the name of the school, the subject, grade level, year, and names of the developing team

Curriculum Map

Developers: Luca, Nancy, Marge, Theo   **Grade:** 2   **Subject:** Math   **Time:** 3 wks
[actually took 4 wks]

Synopsis

August- September Unit #1 "All About Me" Students gather data about themselves (e.g., date of birth; birth length/weight; current height; hair color; etc.); these data will be used to make computations, comparisons, graphs. Each student will create a time line of his and her major life events; these dates will be used for addition and subtraction, and students will compare time lines and data collected. Instruction will include fact families but not drill on facts. [Will need to have generic data available; some Ss couldn't get birth info]

Performance Indicators

I A 37 . . . whole numbers . . . place value concepts . . . write numbers in expanded forms

I C 6 . . . solve addition/subtraction problems . . . various strategies . . . properties

II B 8 . . . appropriate units of measure within same system . . . common reference for each (e.g., portion of finger = 1 inch) to measure objects) ⇦ [maybe not the best PI]

IV C 1 . . . illustrate real-life qualitative changes (growing taller, etc.) . . . quantitative changes (2 inches taller) . . . addition and subtraction

V A 6 . . . read, construct time lines to sequence events . . .

V B 2 . . . read, make comparisons, interpret data represented on charts, graphs, etc.; . . . distinguish true from untrue statements made about the data

Performance Indicators ⇨ (abbreviated for illustration)

representing multiple strands

[ ] = "Green Ink" notes

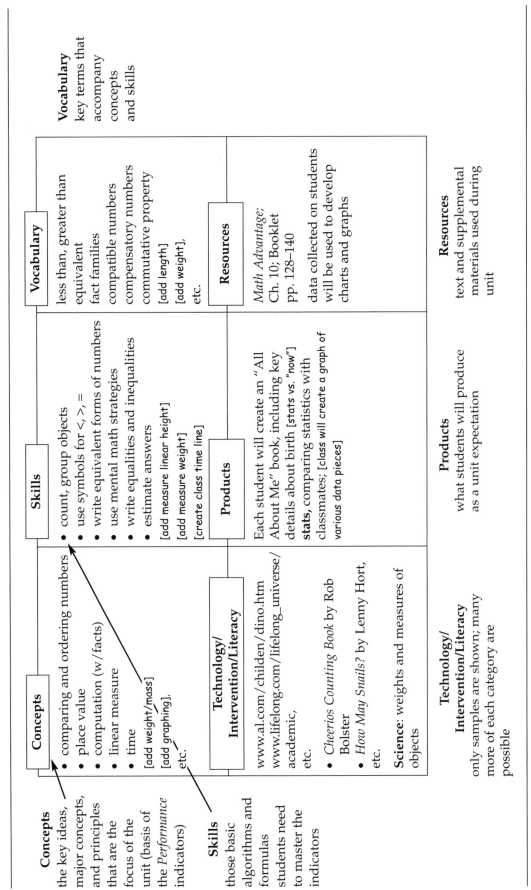

Concepts

- comparing and ordering numbers
- place value
- computation (w/facts)
- linear measure
- time

[add weight/mass]
[add graphing].
etc.

Skills

- count, group objects
- use symbols for <, >, =
- write equivalent forms of numbers
- use mental math strategies
- write equalities and inequalities
- estimate answers

[add measure linear height]
[add measure weight]
[create class time line]

Vocabulary

less than, greater than
equivalent
fact families
compatible numbers
compensatory numbers
commutative property
[add length]
[add weight].
etc.

Technology/Intervention/Literacy

www.al.com/childen/dino.htm
www.lifelong.com/lifelong_universe/academic,
etc.

- *Cheerios Counting Book* by Rob Bolster
- *How May Snails?* by Lenny Hort,
etc.

Science: weights and measures of objects

Products

Each student will create an "All About Me" book, including key details about birth [stats vs. "now"] **stats**, comparing statistics with classmates; [class will create a graph of various data pieces]

Resources

Math Advantage;
Ch. 10; Booklet
pp. 128–140

data collected on students will be used to develop charts and graphs

---

Concepts
the key ideas, major concepts, and principles that are the focus of the unit (basis of the *Performance* indicators)

Skills
those basic algorithms and formulas students need to master the indicators

Technology/Intervention/Literacy
only samples are shown; many more of each category are possible

Products
what students will produce as a unit expectation

Vocabulary
key terms that accompany concepts and skills

Resources
text and supplemental materials used during unit

[ ] = "Green Ink" notes

61

so much extra material, teachers must prioritize and select which portions they will use for initial instruction, which for differentiation, and which for remediation. In addition, they need to decide the sequence in which the units will be taught. Progressive and enlightened districts use the textbook as only one source of information. In these districts, students are exposed to primary sources such as diaries, manuscripts, technical manuals, sets of instructions, treaties, letters, eyewitness accounts, op-ed pieces, and transcripts—the kinds of information students will encounter in life. In addition, they hear various audiotapes and view visual media (paintings, wall art, film) that draw on different intelligences and add a richness beyond print. And to help students manage the continual barrage of electronic stimuli, these districts include selected Internet sites, CD-ROMs, blogs, and other technological media in their sources for information.

The *Instructional Design* approach to *Curriculum Mapping* brings together the efficiency of the pacing guide and the richness of quality textbook materials, adding to them the list of *Performance Indicators* to reflect state content standards. But what energizes the process is the Team of teachers working collaboratively to make thoughtful decisions about how best to organize the list of indicators into a meaningful work plan for the instructional year. This organization allows for differentiation and remediation as well. Absent this critical feature of teacher discourse and decision making, year-long planning typically becomes an empty ritual of blindly following the textbook.

Step-by-Step Successful Mapping

As summarized earlier, the *Instructional Design* approach to *Mapping* brings together grade-level or course-alike Teams of teachers to develop grade-level or course *Maps.* In middle schools that follow a community model, the grade-level Teams may be interdisciplinary and develop multi-subject *Maps.* The *Curriculum Mapping* Teams should begin their work by making several important decisions:

1. Link the Performance Indicators to the Appropriate Unit(s)

Imagine each *Performance Indicator* for a subject and grade level being printed on a 3 by 5 inch note card. The Team assigned to develop the *Curriculum Maps* for that grade level and subject would then assign each *Indicator* to the appropriate unit(s) across the school year, several appearing in multiple units. Often, secondary teachers prefer chapters rather than thematic units, since that's how their texts are organized. The key to this discussion is deciding if the organization and/or themes set forth in the textbook (and other adopted materials) is appropriate in the light of the *Performance Indicators*. In most cases, there is far more in the text than can be used within a typical 9-month time frame, particularly when there will be interruptions (e.g., for testing), and there may be additional building or district priorities to include (e.g., pullout reading or math labs). With "elementary" Teams, the key is to assemble the usual array of multiple texts and supplemental materials and then coordinate them to provide what is appropriate to the *Performance Indicators*. Thematic units are not usually a problem in the elementary grades. If anything, the difficulty lies in giving up cherished content when the corresponding standards have reassigned to a different grade level.

2. Determine Which Indicators Need to Appear in Multiple Units

During the assignment of *Indicators* to units, the *Mapping* Team also decides which need to be addressed multiple times across the year in different units. Some *Indicators* are written with the intent that they will not be fully mastered until the end of a school year but with interval mastery as the year goes along (e.g., Math "computation through 100,000" or "letter-sound relationships through three-letter blends"). Other *Indicators* are fairly complex and require multiple contexts and opportunities for students to demonstrate full mastery (e.g., "observation versus inference" in Science or "factors of production" in Social Studies).

3. Sequence or Order the Units

Once the *Performance Indicators* have been clustered into units, the next decision becomes the most appropriate sequence or order in which the units are presented. In addition to the structure of each discipline (i.e., the most appropriate sequence developmentally), this decision is affected by what must be included within a grading period or a semester and what must be covered before the state test is given. The standard patterns or structures for "ordering" content are the following: (a) **chronological** or time order (typical of History, some Science, some Literature); (b) **spiral** or developmental (typical of Math, Reading, some Foreign Language); and (c) **topical** or thematic, the order of which is interchangeable (typical of Science, Geography, Writing).

4. Select Indicators From Multiple Strands

The key is to make the text and supplemental materials work *for* the *Indicators* and not the reverse. You may remember an earlier discussion about the standards books themselves admonishing users not to teach each standard in isolation but to link them and to work across strands to broaden the context for students and help them see the standards in more authentic applications. Table 3.4 contrasts the traditional, single-strand method of planning with the integrated approach made possible by the *Performance Indicators* and the added dimension they bring to the same topics.

5. Decide Whether to Develop Multisubject Maps

In most cases, single-subject maps are the easiest to manage. But some Teams prefer to develop parallel maps to ensure that certain content pieces are taught at the same time. For example, if The Research Project is to be a cooperative venture between the Language Arts and Science (or Social Studies) classes, the two subject area Teams can develop their respective maps to coordinate their time accordingly. But in some cases, the district is committed to interdisciplinary teaching; the multiage elementary, the community-model middle school, or a high school Humanities block are three such examples. In these situations, and in Pre–K and Kindergarten classes, the most functional *Mapping* format may indeed be interdisciplinary.

Table 3.4   Traditional Unit Content Compared to Standards-Based Content

In Math, What Was . . .	Now Becomes . . .
The "Fractions" Unit With objectives from the *Number Theory* strand (fractions and mixed numbers in "naked" computation, with word problems that *may* have involved measurement but no product or construction of meaning is required)	**The "Blueprints" Unit** With *Performance Indicators* from the following strands: *Measurement* ♦ convert among units of measure ♦ select the correct measurement tool ♦ prepare "blueprints" of rooms to remodel *Algebra* ♦ develop algebraic equations to show how to scale up and scale down a blueprint ♦ use formulas to solve for an unknown, including inverse operations *Number Theory* ♦ compute with fractions and mixed numbers, decimals, ratios, and percents

In Social Studies, What Was . . .	Now Becomes . . .
The "U.S. Constitution" Unit With objectives from the *History* strand (text presents incidents from post-Revolutionary times as evidence of difficulty in handling "freedom"; focus on key events, dates, people; does not require investigation *behind* events, the examination of other world governments at the time, or the impact on ordinary people)	**The "Struggle for the Constitution" Unit** With *Performance Indicators* from the following strands: *Government* ♦ compare forms of government (monarchy, democracy, dictatorship, etc.) ♦ compare states' rights versus the powers of the federal government ♦ identify missing elements in the U. S. Constitution *People in Societies* ♦ distinguish individual rights versus the common good ♦ document the denial of rights to subpopulations ♦ describe diverse populations in the new nation *History* ♦ identify difficulties facing the nation after the Revolution ♦ explain the need for structure and organization ♦ analyze the role of key events and individuals ♦ evaluate the document itself

In developing their grade-level *Curriculum Maps*, the developing Teams will have wrestled with all of the questions and issues listed above, in addition to plenty others that surfaced during the discourse. But once those first *Maps* are printed out and readied for distribution among the Critical Friends, the excitement among the Team members is palpable. They are justly proud of their accomplishment: the culmination of weeks or even months of hard work. Developing the *Performance Indicators* and getting them adopted is a major accomplishment, but at that point, they are still fairly abstract. But once committed to a *Curriculum Map*, the *Indicators* are elevated to a whole new level of significance. Henceforth, they will prescribe the teaching-learning practices in every classroom.

TEACHER-ADMINISTRATOR ACCOUNTABILITY   ■

With the adoption of the *Performance Indicators* as the official achievement targets of the district, the *Curriculum Maps* verify to the district's parents/guardians and community members that the new curriculum is indeed standards-based. Additionally, every classroom will be driven by higher expectations and the commitment to help every student make AYP. But these are just the initial steps in the newly-enacted curriculum. The *Maps* must be installed in each classroom as the core planning document to guide the delivery and assessment of instruction. As with any reform initiative, the entire staff must assume their respective accountability for the implementation and continual monitoring of the new curriculum.

Administrator Role

The responsibility for the development, implementation, and annual update of the *Curriculum Maps* should be assigned to at least one central office administrator (typically, the Director of Curriculum) and the principal in each school. Albeit the central office may be invested with one level of position power, teachers quickly realize that the actual power resides with the person who evaluates them. Ideally, the facilitation of the *Curriculum Maps* should be a joint effort by the central office and the principal in each school.

Central Office

Acting as the official agents of the Board of Education, the Central Office Team is responsible for translating the Board's mission for the district's educational program into the PreK–12 curriculum and instructional plan. They must assure the Board and the community that the adopted curriculum (and its various course tools, materials, and processes) is being implemented as intended in classrooms throughout the district. That assurance can only be given when there are collaborative and cooperative links between the central office and each school. It is a wise superintendent indeed who builds school reform into the job descriptions and annual performance review criteria of both the key curriculum person on the central office staff and each building principal. Specifically, the central office is responsible for obtaining the equipment, materials, and other resources needed by teachers and other school staff members to implement the *Performance Indicators*. They must also communicate the importance of the classroom reforms to parents/guardians and community members. While this latter role seems more about public relations than pedagogy, the community must be assured that its schools are responding to the emerging needs of society and doing everything possible to prepare students to be successful world-class citizens. But that same community must also be fully involved in and informed about the changes in the district's curricular and instructional program and be totally clear that things are not "business as usual."

Building Principals

Although the responsibility for establishing the official curriculum and instructional program lies with the Board and the Central Office, the effective principal knows he or she is accountable for its implementation. Metaphorically, it's like depending on the superintendent and his or her staff to chart the course, but as instructional leaders, effective principals know they need to steer the boat. The savvy principal realizes that his or her own success will be largely determined by the performance of the teaching staff. With the use of *Curriculum Maps*, each teacher's implementation of the *Performance Indicators* is not left to chance. The principal's involvement with *Curriculum Mapping* includes (a) maintaining an aerial view of each class (and grade level) for the year; (b) asking teachers to use the *Map* as the basis for daily lesson plans (if they are required); (c) using the *Maps* as a tentative schedule for pacing the year's curriculum, and to determine better or worse times for assemblies, fieldtrips, and special events; (d) distributing the *Maps* to parents/guardians or community members at orientation or open house; (e) determining equipment and material needs for the building; (f) providing professional development for specific areas of staff weakness; (g) referencing the *Maps* during preobservation and postobservation conferences as part of teacher appraisal; (h) obtaining teacher feedback about components of the *Map* that may need revision as indicated with the ongoing application of "green ink"; the most frequent adjustments are in pacing, the clustering of *Performance Indicators*, and how well a set of materials worked, or didn't; and (i) using the *Maps* as the focus of Team meetings (grade-level, department, multidiscipline, community, etc.) to discuss student performance.

Teachers

As an employee of the district, each teacher signed a contract to abide by the policies and procedures of the Board of Education, and that includes implementing the adopted curriculum. Teachers are not self-employed. But it is the intelligent and enlightened principal who gets the most from his or her teachers by providing them an environment of support and encouragement of their creativity while requiring them to meet a distinct set of professional expectations in the performance of their duties. But the truth is that many teachers find themselves working with principals who have nothing to do with curriculum and instruction, whether by their own design or through no fault of their own. Nonetheless, teachers are obligated to follow the adopted curriculum of the district, and the *Curriculum Map* provides a practical, reasonable structure to follow. And even though the *Map* is developed by a Team, the Critical Friends network provides every teacher a voice in its precise detail. In our experience, teachers derive the maximum benefit from the *Curriculum Maps* in the following ways:

♦ They use the *Maps* ("green ink" and all) in meeting with parents/ guardians to remind them of the complexity and detail of thoughtful instructional planning and to counter the popular belief that "Anyone can teach; they just follow a book and use a bunch of worksheets." This *is* a profession, and if teachers intend to reclaim respect, they need to do so one parent/guardian at a time.

♦ They can easily access their own *Maps* as well as those of their colleagues at adjacent grade levels and courses via their building Web sites.

Once the *Maps* are completed and revised (usually, the second iteration of most *Curriculum Maps* is far superior to the first), they should be posted, and a directory should be disseminated throughout the district.

♦ They rely on the members of their Building Leadership Team to address particular difficulties or barriers they encounter in using their respective *Map.*

In effect, a district's (or building's) *Curriculum Maps* are the physical documentation that its teachers are adhering to the state content standards and to the Board's adopted curriculum, or the *Performance Indicators.* Their use by teachers, as verified and confirmed by the principal and the Building Leadership Teams, attests to the fact that the entire staff is holding itself accountable for implementing the adopted curriculum and for seeing to it that every student is provided adequate opportunity to master the world-class standards it represents.

FREQUENTLY ASKED QUESTIONS ABOUT THE *CURRICULUM MAPPING* PROCESS

Over the years, we have learned many valuable lessons about what works and does not work in the development and rollout of *Curriculum Maps.* Below are several issues that seem to raise the most interest and concern.

? Who Should Serve on the Development Teams?

Ideally, the developing Team for the *Curriculum Maps* should include those same teachers who served on the *Indicator* Teams. But for some members, the additional time commitment to devise Maps may just not be possible. Borrowing from Will Rogers, there's more to celebrate at harvest if we haven't worked the plow horses to death. And to increase the level and quality of staff inclusion, the circles need to be expanded to include additional members wherever possible. The best-case scenario is to include a core group from each *Performance Indicator* Team to anchor the *Curriculum Map* Teams to ensure continuity and a consistent focus. Since a *Map* is developed for each grade level and course, the number of teachers involved should be expanded proportionately to build capacity and broaden the base of ownership and accountability.

? What Are the Preferred Logistics for Developing the Maps?

Ideally, the districts should plan for two stages to complete the *Maps:* (a) the initial training in *how-to*, including the selection of the format, typically, a three-hour session, and (b) the actual development of the *Maps.* Depending on how the work is divided, the actual development of a *Map* typically requires between 8 and 12 clock hours and can be done outside a workshop setting. Naturally, this time may be shortened or lengthened, depending on the cohesiveness of the work Team and the complexity of the detail they decide to include.

In our experience, teachers in medium-sized and larger districts have been amazingly creative in dividing the workload and circling back with each other to continue the discourse. In very small districts, however, there may be only one or two teachers at a grade level and only one secondary teacher assigned to a course. In these cases, the *Map* is developed exclusively by the one teacher who will use it. A great option for smaller districts is to collaborate with similar-size districts to develop their *Maps*. Working together, single teachers can see past the limits of their own experience. Otherwise, they have a tendency to preserve their own status quo. Regardless of the size of the developing team, working as a group brings diverse perspectives to organizing and sequencing the content and strengthens the overall quality and versatility of the map.

? What Are the Most Popular Features or Components of a Map?

As mentioned earlier, the absolute minimum features should be the *Performance Indicators*—nested in each content unit—and an indication of how much time is allocated for each unit. In addition, the following components have become popular; many of these appear in the two sample maps in Tables 3.2 and 3.3:

♦ the **content topics** to be addressed, in addition to the title and length of each unit: This provides a consistent focus for multiple users and need only be a bulleted list.

♦ the key **vocabulary** and/or **concepts** to be addressed.

♦ **text pages** and other **resources**: Many teachers appreciate chapter headings, page numbers, or titles of key selections and activities from the text. But developers are encouraged to supplement the text with primary source documents as well as materials students must use in real life.

♦ **multiple media and nontext resources**: Developers are urged to include print and nonprint materials, primary and secondary source documents, and multiple genres as well. For example, (a) Language Arts needs to move away from the Drama unit or the Poetry unit and include a variety of genres from fiction and nonfiction in every unit, inserting poetry and drama in various units throughout the year; (b) Math teachers are encouraged to include actual life materials that show math in real-world context, including catalogues, instructions, consumer guides, travel schedules, blueprints, data tables, recipes, and so on; (c) Science teachers should include scientific journals and technical manuals, newspaper and magazine articles of current events, and TV and radio transcripts of science specials in addition to the regular text and lab manuals; and (d) social Studies is strongly urged to supplement the regular text with political tracts; primary sources such as treaties, diaries, letters, and interviews; court transcripts; speeches; recordings from C-SPAN, and so on.

? What About When Students Are Missing So Many Skills Coming In?

Some districts who do not have a structured course of study or a clean developmental flow between grades like to include *enabling or lead-up skills and concepts*. By placing them in the *Maps*, they remain a focal point in every classroom. This feature provides direction to prior as well as current grade levels and offers the present grade-level teachers with an indication of where to remediate. If key Vocabulary has not been listed elsewhere, this is also a popular spot for it.

❓ We Have Always Used "Essential Questions;" Can They Appear on the *Map*?

This feature is popular in the current reform literature and provides a more specific sense of direction than topics alone. Many developers identify these questions as a way to structure their thinking about the other components.

❓ What About Cross-Content Integration? Does It Always Have to Be Formal, or Can It Also Be Casual?

Even in single-subject *Curriculum Maps*, the designation of links to other subjects is often extremely helpful and at times downright essential to helping students master the *Performance Indicators* for a specific subject. This feature prevents single-subject instruction from lapsing into isolated sets of abstractions and theories that are disconnected from real-world contexts. Moreover, it is a popular notion among students not only because it feels to them like they are killing two birds with one stone, but it provides a legitimate glimpse at how seamless learning really is. A few examples are suggested: (a) the collection of data via surveys or observations (Math, Science, and Social Studies); (b) reading nonfiction and fictional accounts of the Dust Bowl (Social Studies and Language Arts); (c) the relationship between geography and climate (Science and Social Studies); (d) charts of economic trends or population growth (Math and Social Studies); (e) problems dealing with navigation; time, space, and distance (Math, Science, and Social Studies); (f) a real-time action research project (Language Arts and Science; e.g., which school drinking fountain has the greatest concentration of bacteria?); (g) city maps or grids (Social Studies and Math); and (h) letters to the editor (any subject and Language Arts).

In addition to two or more subjects actually planning activities, another useful technique is for the supplemental performing areas to augment academic instruction. For example, when Math is dealing with fractions, Music teachers can help students experience fractions in musical beats and rhythms. Art teachers are extremely adept at helping students understand geometry, using shapes and patterns in one- and two-dimensional artwork. When English teachers are beginning poetry, Music teachers can help with song lyrics and the various figurative images they convey.

❓ Where Is Technology? Our District Is Big in This.

For districts that have prioritized the use of technology as a learning tool, many developers use the *Map* to designate Word Processing, Excel or Access, HyperStudio, PowerPoint, approved Web sites, and Internet applications. Some developers also include software applications here as well (i.e., designated Web sites, CD-ROMs, etc.), rather than print materials.

? What About Students With Special Needs?

Handling this component requires an extra measure of finesse and patience. We confess, it is one of the most difficult features to nail down, mainly because decision makers in Washington and at the state capitals can't seem to arrive at a definite decision about whether Special Needs students are to master on-level standards (or *Performance Indicators*) or below level as a form of accommodation or modification. With the mounting pressures of NCLB and AYP, many districts are trying to be proactive in seeing to it that these students are provided every possible access to the general education curriculum and its performance expectations. But without clear and definite interpretations, this, too, becomes a cosmetic addition that may help a district comply with the letter of the law but totally avoid the spirit. State departments of education seem to have the immediate authority on how students with Special Needs fit into the reforms of curriculum and instruction, and we have found considerable variance state-to-state.

■ ENSURING A SUCCESSFUL ROLLOUT OF THE *CURRICULUM MAPS*

Appoint Someone to Oversee the Rollout

The road to school reform is littered with discarded course tools that were never properly rolled out for use in classrooms. We strongly suggested that one person (usually the Director of Curriculum) be designated to oversee this important task. Without a carefully planned and fully monitored rollout plan, and the accompanying year-end collection of "green ink" revisions, the entire process will collapse. It may take a time or two to iron out the bugs, but once it has been successfully established, it will flow each year with comparative ease.

Don't Overlook the Clerical

Some developing Teams put their *Maps* together with cuttings and pastings from various teacher manuals, printouts from the Internet, and their own notes, particularly if several people are working on it at once. Other Teams use chart paper, and some like the flexibility of note cards. Increasingly, development Teams are requesting a template and word process the map as they go along. It would be smart to allow Teams to proceed in whatever way is most effective for them, but assign a submission date at least a month before the distribution. Once the *Maps* have been collected, the designated central office staff member and building principal should review them for legibility, content, and adherence to the adopted format. Then they should be word processed by a qualified typist, using a consistent template that is attractive and easily read but that gives the maps a polished and professional look. This is especially critical since the *Maps* will be shared with parents/guardians and community members, and they should be placed on the district Web site for access by staff and other stakeholders along with other public documents. Although the final pilot versions (and the revised versions thereafter) should have a uniform, official look to them, they should not be commercially printed. That is not only a needless extravagance, it suggests a permanence that contradicts the notion that the documents are dynamic and responsive to the needs of students and to new materials and curriculum developments. Word-processed documents with attractive, functional graphics and shading, boldface print, symbols, the use of space and highlights, consistent labels, and a clear interpretive key will do just fine. It will telegraph a message that the Board regards the *Curriculum Maps* as important professional documents and is paying attention to the requisite detail it expects of teachers.

Circulate the Draft Through the Critical Friends Network

As quickly as possible, the first drafts of the *Curriculum Maps* should be input and circulated through the Critical Friends network for input and feedback. Based on their response, some editing may be needed. This done, the maps and the *Performance Indicators* are ready to be piloted.

Conduct the Pilot

The Board's adoption of the *Performance Indicators* as the district's official achievement targets typically includes language that specifies something like this: "The processes and documents to be used for implementation of the *Performance Indicators* in each content area will include a *Curriculum Map* for each course and grade level." This wording not only allows the *Performance Indicators* to be piloted but provides for the *Curriculum Maps* as the vehicle for doing so. In addition to a new level of accountability for student performance, many teachers have used only a textbook to guide their year-long planning. This will be their first experience with a *Curriculum Map*, one they are expected to use. To discuss reform and the need to improve curriculum and so on in the abstract is quite different from actually dealing with it.

During the Pilot, the "green ink" pen becomes a most important tool. Typically, the reality of working with actual students reveals all sorts of *uh-ohs* that the developing Teams could never have anticipated. Throughout the Pilot year, the developing Teams should discuss the implementation of the *Maps*, using the "green ink" to plan for revisions and adjustments. Typically, the first map is the worst map. Until teachers have actually used a *Map*, they can't really know how it will play out with students and which features are more or less effective. Once the use of *Curriculum Maps* becomes a consistent routine throughout each school, it will become part of the deep culture and one of the primary features of the way we do business here.

Teachers report that the very process of piloting, "green inking," and discussing needed revisions has expanded and enriched their capacity to develop and evaluate their curriculum beyond anything else they've attempted. Someone said, "If you want to be sure that a boat is safe, sound, and seaworthy, be sure the builder is the first passenger."

Monitor

Throughout the school year, the *Curriculum Maps* should be among the key documents referenced during conversations among teachers, and between teachers and principal about how classroom instruction is proceeding. As information is assembled about student mastery of the *Performance Indicators*, the order and organization of the content and the other related components as set forth in the *Curriculum Maps* will be part of the discussion, particularly if students are not mastering the *Performance Indicators* at the rate and level expected. Among the most common revisions are (a) the pacing; either too much or insufficient time has been allotted; (b) how the *Indicators* are clustered; they may need to be reshuffled a bit, or some need to be repeated; and (c) the designated materials; they may prove inappropriate or inadequate for the students, particularly for differentiation. If adjustments such as these are made with thoughtful and informed judgment, the *Map* is an invaluable tool for keeping the curriculum appropriate, current, and responsive to the students being served. Whenever the infrastructure is mentioned in the school reform process, the use of *Curriculum Maps* should be in the same sentence.

Some issues that typically surface during the pilot are the following:

? *Why do we all have to use the same materials? If I find a different short story (or an alternate lab manual, set of treaties, airline schedule, etc.), may I use it?*

Our response to this is, "yes," providing it falls within the scope of the unit topics and matches the intent of the *Performance Indicators* involved. But this is an excellent question to be fielded by the principal. It will give him or her a golden opportunity to examine the alternate material in the context of the developing Team's original idea and build the principal's capacity to demonstrate knowledgeable leadership in the **Instructional Design** process.

? *Math follows a developmental sequence, but in some of the other subjects, the units are more topical or thematic and can be taught in any order. Why do we all have to follow the same order?*

This one is a toughie. If there is a limited number of classroom sets of materials (e.g., in Science or for Literature Circles), alternating the order of units may be essential. But in other cases, the district or building has a special reason to require that each grade level follow a consistent order. That's the district's call, but the decision should be valid and well-thought-out. Nothing more quickly destroys a staff's confidence in any reform process than to get directives from an administrator who is uninformed and disconnected. The answer to this question bears careful consideration.

? *Do we have to use the same pace in all classes? Some kids can go faster, and some need more time.*

In the spirit of differentiation and to provide both enrichment and remediation, our answer to this one is, "within a window." Ideally, teachers who work with several classes of children will keep the classes within a few days of each other, differentiating the materials and the activities rather than creating huge and awkward differences in time. But whether a teacher works with four sections of 25 each or one group of 25 all day, the same rules apply. In our experience, teachers who wait until every student has mastered every *Performance Indicator* before moving to the next unit get woefully bogged down and never really recover. But to race ahead too quickly, leaving the majority of the class behind, is unwise. Differentiation research advocates finding a middle ground, or moving at a reasonable pace for the critical mass of students, allowing for the fact that some may not have kept pace and others may be eager to move on. With effective planning, the advanced students will have been provided more self-directed activities or more challenging reading materials in lieu of (not in addition to) those being used with the mainstream group. The less successful students will have been provided more guided tasks with more frequent checks by the teacher and using materials at their reading levels. They will move ahead with the group. Those things they did not master will be addressed in a later unit; will be the target of remediation; or will remain unmastered until next year. Here again, the questions of pacing and different rates of mastery are excellent ones for the principal to build his or her capacity for instructional leadership.

Review the Maps Annually

Each year, the developing Team should evaluate the *Curriculum Maps* for completeness, accuracy, validity to guide instruction, and user-friendliness. Just as every other professional reviews and updates his or her materials each year, so must classroom teachers. The antiquated five-year review of curriculum should be relegated to the same museum as the one-room schoolhouse and desks bolted to the floor. Each spring, the "green ink" for every *Map* should be coordinated into appropriate revisions to be certain that the most current edition is ready for the next school year. For this annual review, the building principal and designated central office administrator play crucial but respective roles. They should meet with the developing Teams to discuss the needed revisions, to verify that the changes are consistent with the state content standards and the mission of the district Board of Education, and to be sure that the materials and equipment needed will be available for the upcoming school year. Unless teachers see that their decision makers are knowledgeable about the *Maps*, obsess about their relationship to the state content standards, and are dead serious about their use, the entire reform process is compromised. If teachers haven't learned anything else in three decades of school reform, they have learned that the only reforms they really need to worry about are the ones with which their administrators are directly involved and for which the Board is holding them and the administrators accountable. Everything else won't matter much.

THE THREE-YEAR TIME FRAME ■

As described in this chapter, the process of developing and piloting the *Curriculum Maps* is fairly complex. But it is indeed a critical step in the **Instructional Design** process, since the *Maps* document the implementation of the *Performance Indicators*. Table 3.5 is a reprint of the sample time line provided at the end of Chapters 1 and 2 and highlights how the *Curriculum Maps* fit into the big picture of the entire process.

Table 3.5   Sample Three-Year Time Frame

		Year 1			Year 2			Year 3		
		Summer	*Fall*	*Winter/ Spring*	*Summer*	*Fall*	*Winter/ Spring*	*Summer*	*Fall*	*Winter/ Spring*
Two Subjects, PreK–12, for example, Reading and Math	*Performance Indicators (PIs)*	Develop, Pilot Critical Friends →			Revise, Implement →			Continue (annual review) →		
	Curriculum Maps	Develop, Pilot Critical Friends →			Revise, Implement →			Continue (annual review) →		
	Unit Plans				Develop, Pilot Critical Friends →			Revise, Implement →		
	Continuous Monitoring	Unofficially keep track of student mastery			Develop, Pilot Critical Friends →			Revise, Implement →		
	Benchmark Assessments	Collect classroom tests measure *PIs*			Develop, Pilot Critical Friends →			Revise, Implement →		

4

Unit Planning

Rationale and Format

INTRODUCTION ▪

Where Do Unit Plans Fit Into the Process?

Once the *Performance Indicators* have been adopted by the Board as the district's official achievement targets, and the *Curriculum Maps* have assigned the *Indicators* to content units for implementation across the school year, the next point of focus is the unit itself. After all, the *Performance Indicators Maps* detail *what* will be taught and *when*, but the *how* is the domain of the unit itself. The **Instructional Design** approach to the *Unit Plan* begins with the *Performance Indicators* on which each unit is based and identifies specific strategies to provide instruction and to assess student learning. The simple, one-page format has been developed from the principles of learning theory, authentic and constructivist teaching, and the more recent Best Practices

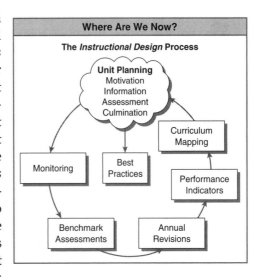

research. Complete annotations of the entire research base, available from the authors on request, detail the scholars whose work informed our approach to *Unit Planning*. Districts who worry that developing *Unit Plans* is too much work should remember the fitness analogy. No matter how many fancy workout togs and what state-of-the-art equipment we buy, until and unless we change how we eat and exercise, we will still look and weigh the same. Every school reformer on the speaking circuit opens his or her address with some variation of, "Unless we change what teachers do in the classroom, we will get what we've always gotten from students."

"It's Not Your Father's Unit Plan"

Just the mention of the term "unit plan" typically casts a pall over an entire room, and reflexive yawns burst forth unbidden. The very prospect conjures up all sorts of negative associations, typical of which are the detailed documents in three-ring binders submitted during Methods 306 or Student Teaching. Our experience has shown that most conventional unit plans are not only cumbersome, they are pedagogically flawed, particularly with what the research has revealed about Best Practices and student achievement. One of the most popular comments about best practices is, "Does this list of Best Practices presume a list of worst ones?" There certainly are worst practices in classroom instruction, in even the best schools. We have been keeping track of the ones we've encountered over the years, listed below with a ☹. For each, we offer how the *Instructional Design* format has taken pains to avoid them (listed below with a ☺).

☹ Units that are planned around provocative themes or topics and with interesting activities but not connected to academic standards. The Worst Practice here is the deception that the standards will be covered without planning for them.

  ☺ The *Instructional Design Unit Plans* are built around the standards in the form of *Performance Indicators* assigned to *Units* in the *Curriculum Map*.

☹ Units that are disconnected from those that precede and come after, adhering to the Worst Practice that each series of learning experiences should be a thing of beauty on its own, untrammeled by links to other units.

  ☺ Because the *Instructional Design Unit Plans* for each grade level or course are developed from the *Curriculum Map*, they are developmentally linked to each other. Each *Unit* builds on the skills and understandings from prior *Units*. For example in intermediate Science, if one *Unit* deals with the atomic and molecular systems, the next dealing with the solar system will build in the concept of "systems." It can actually use the understanding of how electrons revolve around the nucleus as an advanced organizer for how the planets revolve around the sun.

☹ Units that pay little or no attention to the various mental processes (called *cognitive demand* in the academic standards books) required of students to demonstrate independent mastery. These units illustrate the worst practices of (a) limiting expectations to memorization and low-level skill applications, or (b) skipping directly to the upper levels without an adequate foundation.

  ☺ The *Instructional Design Unit Plans* provide for the various levels of Bloom's Taxonomy, both to strengthen a student's mental versatility and to provide for Differentiation.

☹ Units that make no provision for determining what students already know about the topics involved or what skills they already have. These units make the worst practice assumption that students know nothing and should be dragged through the entire unit, regardless of their entry level skills or special needs.

☺ The *Instructional Design Unit Plans* provide for determining what students bring to the *Unit* and make adjustments accordingly. In fact, one of the Best Practices is for teachers to use this entry-level information to help students set at least one personal and one academic goal for each *Unit Plan.*

☹ Units that assume all students learn at the same rate and can be successful using identical activities, using the Worst Practice of "one size fits all."

☺ The *Instructional Design Unit Plans* include several different activities to help students master the *Performance Indicators,* including various modalities and learning channels and various options for students to demonstrate what they have learned. Each *Unit Plan* provides for Differentiation, including strategies for intervention or remediation as well as enrichment. For students with Special Needs, specific modifications and accommodations are included.

☹ Units that are largely workbook-driven and/or teacher-centered, relying on (a) a majority of teacher-talk, with students playing passive roles; (b) limiting the bulk of student activity to drill-and-practice worksheets or study guides, with very little opportunity or requirement to construct new meaning; and (c) group activities in which accomplishments are attributed to all students as "mastery," overlooking the reality that some students may be missing vital skills.

☺ By contrast, the *Instructional Design Unit Plans* identify for each activity a Best Practice teaching strategy and an active, engaged response from each student. The priority is for every student to construct meaning, and the teacher role is to monitor individual student mastery, even in group activities.

☹ Units in which there is no concern for triangulation (i.e., congruence) among the teaching-learning activities, the intended outcomes, and the means of assessment, resulting in such Worst Practices as the following:

Expected Outcome	Teaching-Learning Activity	Test
Analyze a passage containing figurative language to predict why an author might have used such imagery.	Students practice identifying various types of figurative language in sample passages.	Students are asked to write their own examples of figurative language.
Make three observations to draw three inferences from a scientific experiment (that student conducts).	The teacher conducts the experiment and leads the class in making observations and inferences.	A multiple-choice test that asks students to select the correct observations and inferences.
Create a scale drawing of a geometric atrium or garden that could be constructed in the school courtyard, including access walkways from multiple doors.	Students do sample geometric measurements from workbooks.	Students are asked to solve word problems about scale drawings of gardens, patios, etc.

☺ The *Instructional Design Unit Plans* focus on triangulation from the very outset and monitor it throughout the development process. Class activities and assessments are congruent with Unit objectives.

☹ Units that end with a paper-pencil test and provide no real performance or authentic assessments, compounding that error with an even worse Worst Practice of labeling frivolous activities as performance assessments. Among the actual examples we have encountered are collages, coats of arms, food fairs, imaginary animals, and rap.

☺ In comparison, the *Instructional Design Unit Plans* require that several authentic or performance assessments be completed by each student to demonstrate independent mastery of the *Performance Indicators*. Even though some of these may be group activities, they are constructed to determine each student's mastery.

■ THE UNIT PLAN FORMAT
FOR *INSTRUCTIONAL DESIGN*

Having plenty of experience with poor unit plans and equipped with two decades of research on what is effective in classroom instruction, putting a format in place was not difficult. In devising the *Instructional Design* approach to *Unit Planning*, we pulled together several theories about learning and how students successfully process information, including experiential learning, the process-product research, constructivism and performance assessment, differentiation, and the more recent Best Practices methods.

A Synthesis of the Research About Effective Teaching and Learning

The research on the effective delivery and valid assessment of classroom instruction can be synthesized into several basic assumptions that inform the development of valid *Unit Plans*.

♦ *Units* should be directly based on the content standards (or *Performance Indicators*) selected by the district as their official achievement targets, and all teaching and testing strategies should be congruent with these standards.

♦ Students learn the most and retain the longest in classrooms where the instruction is student centered rather than teacher directed. This requires students to be actively engaged from the outset, and teacher-talk should be limited.

♦ Delivery strategies must be appropriate to the content and cognitive demand of the standards (or *Performance Indicators*) of the Unit. Samples include explanation, demonstration, guided discussion, inquiry, the Socratic Seminar, Learning Circles, and the Advance Organizer. For each activity, students must be assigned a specific task or role in which they are actively involved and engaged.

◆ Students must construct meaning for themselves rather than respond only to prompts from the teacher or the text. This minimizes such passive staples as seatwork, worksheets, and the questions at the end of the chapter. Instead, students should negotiate new materials on their own and produce original products, such as compositions, models, performances, math problems, science experiments, treaties, laws, resolutions, and so on. To prepare students for this new approach to learning, the research cites several specific Learning Constructs or scaffolds: (a) showing students how to identify the organizational patterns in text (e.g., compare-contrast, cause-effect, chronological sequence) to unlock meaning; (b) helping students summarize information using these same organizational patterns; (c) showing students how to use structure and context clues to better cope with unfamiliar vocabulary rather than memorize lists of words in isolation; (d) using various levels of questions to help students comprehend material and showing students how to construct these different level questions for their classmates; (e) helping students recognize similarities and differences within and among pieces of information or passages of text; and (f) using graphic or visual organizers to represent key concepts, displaying the relationships among the terms and ideas provided.

◆ Throughout the unit, teachers should continually monitor student performance, using formative assessments that indicate progress and prescribe subsequent instruction. These assessments should be (a) criterion-referenced to the content standards (or *Performance Indicators*); (b) diagnostic in that the error analysis will indicate any mislearning and the need for reteaching; (c) used by students for meta-analysis, to discover their own mistakes and error patterns; and (d) be parallel to the high-stakes tests students will be taking for NCLB, including multiple-choice and constructed response items.

◆ Authentic or performance assessments must be included to give students the opportunity to demonstrate a more concrete and independent ownership of the standards. These performance assessments draw together what has been presented in class into holistic, authentic tasks that extend beyond the classroom; encourage divergent, creative thinking; and ask students to solve the types of problems they face in life. A few samples are: (a) writing an original piece of literature or a composition; (b) devising a treaty or a contract between two parties; (c) collecting, analyzing, and displaying data; (d) designing and conducting an original experiment; (e) analyzing the error patterns in solved problems; (f) developing original problems to solve; (g) preparing a script for a TV talk show or newscast; and (h) creating a business plan for a cottage industry.

The Physical Layout

Every unit planning system has its own format. We sought a layout that would be simple and easily converted into a template but, more important, be symbolic of the teaching-learning process it represents. See Table 4.3 (*Note:* Although several systems use a four-quadrant diagram, ours was first influenced by Bernice McCarthy's 4-MAT system and then expanded by the work of other researchers.) We began with what seemed to us to be the two key learning axes.

Concrete to Abstract Axis

The things that we learn well began as Concrete examples or illustrations. We handled and manipulated objects or ideas related to the "thing," to see how it worked, or heard a performance or verbal description and reacted with laughter or anger or sadness. Conversations were held about the "thing" being learned, and its physical or emotional attributes got into our heads as visual, auditory, or feeling sensations and established sensory memories there. Eventually, we became facile with the underlying concepts of the "thing," enough to understand them in the Abstract. We just intuitively knew how they work and no longer required a Concrete experience to use the concepts or generalize them to a related situation. Most important, we could apply the "thing" to solve problems, to make predictions about ___, and to interpret other ideas or situations we may not have experienced directly. This same Concrete-to-Abstract sequence can become the template for the teaching-learning activities we provide students. (See Table 4.1.)

Reception-to-Production Axis

If the Concrete-to-Abstract axis describes the developmental progression by which a student processes information, the second axis, Reception-to-Production, describes the student's developmental progression from taking in information to producing something that demonstrates mastery. To step back a minute, when we learned our new "thing," we were provided information through our various senses. We saw, heard, tasted, smelled, and/or touched it, either literally or vicariously. In this Reception stage, the activities are structured, and we would have been guided through the learning experiences; we depended on external prompts to internalize the "thing" and its underlying concepts. Eventually, however, we could demonstrate what we knew on tests. But we could also perform authentic, holistic tasks such as an original performance or composition, a construction, a project, or a comprehensive analysis. In this Production stage, we were expected to perform independently and with little guidance to construct meaning. Table 4.2 provides an illustration.

The Conceptual Flow Within the Format

Symbolically, we think of the four quadrants as forming a clock face. The Concrete-to-Abstract axis is a line that connects 12:00 to 6:00, and the Reception-to-Production axis connects 3:00 to 9:00. This means the horizontal axis loses its left-to-right orientation. But keeping the clock face in mind, the *Unit Plan* begins at 12:00 and proceeds clockwise around the dial. With such a familiar image, we trust the user can live with the Reception-to-Production axis as moving from right to left. As the source or inspiration of every *Unit Plan*, the *Performance Indicators* are placed directly above the clock face as a continual reminder that the *Unit Plan* begins and ends with them.

Table 4.1   The Concrete-to-Abstract Axis

Example A	Example B
Concrete	**Concrete**
Students use various measuring tools to determine the length of objects. ⇩ ⇩ ⇩ ⇩ ⇩ ⇩ ⇩ ⇩ ⇩ ⇩	Students "feel" distinct emotional messages when hearing "The Battle Hymn of the Republic" and can identify words or draw pictures that describe or represent their feelings. ⇩ ⇩ ⇩ ⇩ ⇩
Abstract	**Abstract**
Students can estimate the length of an object, using a common referent; compare it with an object of similar length, and identify the most appropriate tool and unit to express length; they can do the same for an object they only hear about.	Students can analyze a song or verse they hear or a passage they read for its tonal qualities, recurrent "images," or underlying "message"; they can verbalize (orally or in writing) how the author uses language, sound, and rhythm to communicate his or her message; and they can identify other pieces that remind them of the one in reference.

Table 4.2   The Reception-to-Production Axis

Example A	
Reception ⇨ ⇨ ⇨ ⇨ ⇨	⇨ ⇨ ⇨ ⇨ ⇨ **Production**
Students are provided activities to see and use various tools to measure the length of objects and to realize the importance of the appropriate unit of measure (i.e., centimeters; inches; meters; yards; etc.).	Students estimate, select the appropriate tool and unit to measure objects, and verify or adjust their estimate; they can decide how best to measure unfamiliar objects (tool and unit) and evaluate a given measurement, both in terms of accuracy and the appropriateness of the unit.

Example B	
Reception ⇨ ⇨ ⇨ ⇨ ⇨	⇨ ⇨ ⇨ ⇨ ⇨ **Production**
Students are guided through activities during which they "feel" various emotions when hearing "The Battle Hymn of the Republic," thinking about a beloved pet who has been "put-to-sleep," or viewing a comic-tragic film such as *Brian's Song* or *Saving Private Ryan*.	Students compose a letter of condolence to a friend that conveys genuine sympathy and offers emotional support; they also send a letter to the editor objecting strongly to the removal of an important cultural landmark to build a parking lot; they can also locate evidence to support their viewpoint.

Figure 4.1   Combining the Axes

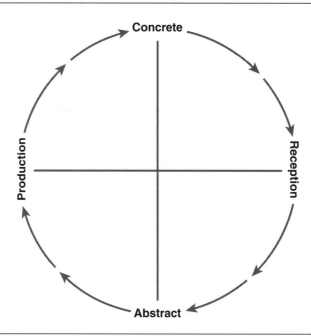

The Clock Face as Four Quadrants

The *Unit Plan* clock face (as shown in Figure 4.1 above) is divided into four quadrants, and the two quadrants on the right contain activities that provide students with what they will need to demonstrate mastery; beginning at the 12:00 position:.

♦ Quadrant 1, called *Motivation*, draws students into the *Unit*, determining what they already know (and don't know), setting expectations by previewing the Culminating activities, and helping students set academic and personal goals for the *Unit*.

♦ Quadrant 2, called *Information*, is a variety of teaching-learning activities through which students are provided the knowledge and skills they need to master the *Performance Indicators*. Each activity has a teacher behavior (a delivery strategy and learning construct appropriate to the concepts and ideas embedded in the indicators) and a student response.

Looking to the left side of the clock face, Quadrants 3 and 4 house strategies for determining student mastery, beginning at the 6:00 position.

♦ Quadrant 3, called *Assessment*, designates tests and observations that measure student mastery of the *Indicators* in a traditional way. Still in the "abstract" section of the vertical axis, the paper-pencil tests ask students to respond to multiple-choice prompts and short-answer items that imply or infer mastery. They cover a sampling of the *Unit* concepts, and there is a narrow range of correct answers. They are teacher-directed and deliberately constructed to yield diagnostic data that will indicate the need for reteaching or other intervention. Although students are now producing information, they are still in an "abstract" or theoretical mode, and their work is relatively convergent. In addition to traditional paper-pencil test, other assessments include teacher observations, write-ups for lab experiments, journal entries, and quizzes.

♦ Quadrant 4 is the *Culmination* quadrant. These activities are holistic tasks or performances through which students demonstrate independent mastery of one or more *Performance Indicators*. Students create or develop a product or process, solve real-world problems, or evaluate the merits of ABC as per XYZ criteria. Like the Assessments, students are being asked to produce what they know to show mastery; but in this Concrete or practical mode, the work is more divergent, and students control and shape the outcome, albeit within guidelines. Rather than a scoring key, this work is evaluated using a rubric based on the *Performance Indicators*.

Another way to think of the clock face is that the right side—the Motivation and Information quadrants—represent the INPUT of the unit, and the left side—the Assessment and Culmination quadrants—represent the OUTPUT.

The Visual Display

Table 4.3 provides a horizontal synthesis of the *Unit Plan* format. For each quadrant, the criteria described above are summarized, the position of the quadrant in the format is highlighted, and sample strategies and activities are listed. Following Table 4.3 is a sample *Unit Plan* called "Discovering Africa" (see Table 4.4) illustrating the *Performance Indicators* and how the four Quadrants might appear.

CONSIDERATIONS IN DEVELOPING *UNIT PLANS* ■

Developing Teams

As with the *Performance Indicators* and *Curriculum Maps*, the ideal arrangement for developing *Unit Plans* is to use representative Teams of grade-level teachers. For continuity and consistency, at least some members of the grade-level *Unit Planning* Teams should be teachers and the designated administrator(s) who served on the Teams to develop the *Performance Indicators* and/or the *Curriculum Maps*. Since there are typically 8 to 10 *Unit Plans* devised for each year-long course, there is proportionately more labor involved, and so the *Unit* Teams may be larger to broaden the base of involvement and divide the workload among several teachers. As with the *Curriculum Maps*, some districts devise separate *Unit Plans* for each subject at a grade level; others may decide to develop integrated *Units,* featuring two or more subjects. Either works.

Embedded Training

In our experience, the development of *Unit Plans* works best when it is actually embedded into the school year. If the training and development are spread across the school year, participants can actually try out the *Unit Plans* as they are developed. If also tried out by the Critical Friends,

(Text continues on page 87)

Table 4.3 The Horizontal View of the Four Quadrants

Component and Definition	Placement in the Format		Examples
Title: The title and length of the Unit Plan are taken directly from the Curriculum Map			

Performance Indicators (called "PIs")
■ taken from *Curriculum Map*
■ include multiple strands
■ may include other subjects (integration)
■ represent a common theme or topic
■ imply or state teaching and testing strategies
■ typically involve a product
	Performance Indicators
	——————
	——————
	——————
	
	Culmination / Motivation
	
	Assessment / Information
			Integrated
			    popular in self-contained classrooms
			
			Single Subject
			    more prevalent
			
			"Cross-Overs"
			    activities are shared (e.g., the English teacher allows the science essay to satisfy an English requirement, or vice versa)

Motivation (Concrete-Reception) ■ actively involve students in a direct experience ■ determine what students know and don't know ■ establish connections to prior and subsequent learning ■ pique students' interest ■ set expectations for completing the unit ■ help students set personal learning goals	*Performance Indicators* —————— —————— —————— Culmination / **Motivation** Assessment / Information		■ pretest ■ brainstorm ■ KWL chart ■ video ■ manipulation of objects or ideas ■ intriguing question or puzzlement ■ concept web ■ song ■ artifacts ■ oral reading ■ conduct a poll ■ what-if scenario ■ demonstration ■ role-play or simulation ■ expert ■ speaker ■ error analysis ■ extended analogies or extended metaphors
Information (Abstract-Reception) ■ delivery strategies and student responses <u>match</u> the *Performance Indicators* ■ students have an active, constructive role ■ include variety in grouping patterns and learning modalities ■ indicate how all *Performance Indicators* will be taught (including options for differentiation: remediation, enrichment) ■ require multiple levels of thinking ■ involve continuous assessment, feedback	*Performance Indicators* —————— —————— —————— Culmination / Motivation Assessment / **Information**		**Learning Constructs** ■ organizational patterns ■ summarizing ■ note taking ■ graphic or visual organizers ■ context and structural clues for vocabulary ■ various levels of questioning ■ similarities and differences **Delivery Strategies** ■ lecture ■ demonstration ■ guided discussion ■ inquiry ■ Socratic Seminar ■ literature circles ■ action research ■ advance organizer

Assessment (Abstract-Production)
■ traditional tests to determine mastery (paper-pencil or teacher observation)
■ multiple-choice items (validly constructed; match the *Performance Indicators*; congruent with teaching-learning activities)
■ short-answer, extended response items
■ are diagnostic to identify needed intervention
■ are selective to infer mastery
	Performance Indicators
	——————
	——————
	——————
	
	Culmination / Motivation
	
	Assessment / Information
			tests/quizzes that parallel high-stakes tests:
			■ multiple-choice items (with choices that are diagnostic upon analysis)
			■ answer items that involve—
			    ✓ problem-finding, solving
			    ✓ making inferences
			    ✓ evaluating, making judgments
			    ✓ explaining
			■ observation checklists, journal entries, maps, data compilation

Culmination (Concrete-Production) ■ are holistic, life-related tasks extending beyond the classroom ■ draw together the unit learning experiences ■ allow students options for completing these tasks ■ help students measure their own goals ■ scored with a rubric based on the *Performance Indicators*	*Performance Indicators* —————— —————— —————— **Culmination** / Motivation Assessment / Information		■ writing an original piece of literature or a composition ■ devising a treaty or a contract between two parties ■ collecting, displaying, and analyzing data ■ designing and conducting an original experiment ■ analyzing error patterns in a series of "solved" problems; developing original problems to solve ■ preparing a script for a TV talk show or newscast ■ formulating arguments

Table 4.4   Best Practices Unit Plan

Unit Title: "Discovering Africa"	Course/Grade: Grade 6 Social Studies Time frame: 4 weeks

Performance Indicators or Learning Targets (shortened to make the sample easier to read)

I A 9   Construct a multitiered time line to represent the development of a region politically, economically, culturally (class has begun a time line, beginning with *Unit* 1, and they add to it as each unit progresses).

I F 2   Compare ancient civilizations (the Nile, Africa) re: government, religion, culture, language, etc.; construct a matrix.

II C 5   Analyze how world regions interact . . . diplomacy, treaties, alliances, military conflicts, trade . . . class structure, gender roles, beliefs/religion, traditions, language, agriculture, government, economic interests, etc. . . . present as a TV broadcast.

III A 12   Locate countries, cities, landforms and bodies of water, use coordinates (latitude and longitude) to identify specific points.

III B 10   Interpret maps, charts, graphs to explain the distribution patterns of economic activity (e.g., mining, agriculture); use T-chart.

III C 7   List the positive and negative consequences of modifying the environment (e.g., dam-building, urbanization, education).

III D 2   Explain push-pull factors that cause people to migrate from one place to another, create a visual display, write an editorial.

IV A 8   Compare different regions in terms of geography, available resources, goods/services produced . . . interdependence, brochure.

V A 16   Create a graphic to show composition of a (country>state>city>town), explain sovereignty over country not geographically connected (i.e., mother country), border changes as a result of global events (e.g., war), interactions with neighbors.

VI A 6   Identify the characteristics . . . democracy, monarchy, dictatorship . . . re: citizens' rights (e.g., owning land); prepare a lesson.

(concrete)

(production)

Culmination (individual students)

1. Create an annotated map of Africa that displays various migration patterns from (a) *outside-in* (e.g., Europeans); (b) *inside-out* (e.g., the slave trade); and (c) from country to country *within* (e.g., famine, cultural ties, etc.); include physical changes (e.g., deforestation, border changes, desertification); specify the *who, what, when, where, why,* and *how* of key events

2. Write letters home (as if from the train) that describe major civic issues at each stop (e.g., voting rights, apartheid, etc.); explain how they impact life, and compare each stop to a similar region in the United States

3. Write a persuasive essay re: four environmental changes to modernize Africa (e.g., dam building, urbanization, etc.); follow established guidelines

4. Reflect on progress toward personal and content goals

Motivation

Have on wall (a) a giant outline map of Africa and (b) an empty matrix; these will be filled-in with pertinent details as the unit progresses.

1. Students draw an outline map of Africa (kept in their notebooks); as a pretest, students fill in as much as they know (borders of countries, cities, landforms, bodies of water); will add to

2. Brainstorm what students know about Africa re: geography, art, history, climate, politics, etc.; students pose 3 questions they have

3. Review the daily journal and note-taking formats; provide samples

4. Preview the Africa railroad trip; explain Culminating activities

5. Help students set personal and content goals; direct where to record the goals and how to self-monitor

Assessment

1. Journal entries, as per directions during Information

2. Map location test: countries, cities, major landforms, bodies of water, longitude and latitude, etc.

3. Paper-pencil test (multiple-choice, extended response, and essay; taken from students' own Levels I, II, and III questions)

4. Completed map of Africa (cities, landforms, water, etc.)

5. Compiled data charts (distances, precipitation, population, temperature, economic factors, etc.) ⇦ apply math skills

(T = Teacher; Ss = Students) Information

1. T tells Ss that Africa has two major regions: (a) Saharan and (b) Sub-Saharan; Ss predict likely attributes of each; in dyads, they verify or adjust their hunches with information from *directed* areas of the text; add information to the wall map

2. T explains that the class will take a trip aboard the Cairo-to-Capetown railroad, stopping at Cairo, Nairobi, Livingstone, and Capetown; Ss will keep a travel journal, recording information they will need for the wall map, wall matrix, and their own maps and assignments. At each stop, the following will be addressed:
   a.   notable landmarks
   b.   significant historic and current events

(reception)

(abstract)

(Continued)

Table 4.4 (Continued)

(production)

   c. geographic and climactic information
   d. economic, political, cultural, social, features

3. Students will chart distances between stops; record latitude and longitude; highest/lowest points re: sea level; average temperature and precipitation; highs and lows of both; income and demographic rates; and apply math to notable features (e.g., the pyramids)

Students will work in different dyads at each stop. When small group is used, this will be two dyads joined.

4. *Stop 1: Cairo, Egypt* [Column 1 on Wall Chart]
   a. notable landmarks: the Nile, Pyramids, Sphinx, Cleopatra
   b. historic significance: the Nile Valley as birthplace of first humans (i.e., "Lucy," Dr. Leake)
   c. geographic and climactic features
   d. economic, political, cultural social features

Ss take notes; work in small groups to develop Levels I, II, and III questions about the stop; each student adds detail to own map

T draws Ss together to decide what detail to add to the Wall Chart and the class map

5. *Stop 2: Nairobi, Kenya* [Column 2 on Wall Chart]
   a. notable landmarks: the Serengeti, the Great Rift Valley
   b. historic significance: location of grand safaris (President Roosevelt, etc.); historic game preserve; US Embassy bombed in 1988 by Osama bin Laden
   c. geographic and climactic features
   d. economic, political, cultural social features

Ss take notes; work in small groups to develop Levels I, II, and III questions about the stop; each student adds detail to own map

T draws Ss together to decide what detail to add to the wall chart and the class map

6. *Stop 3: Livingstone, Zambia* [Column 3 on Wall Chart]
   a. notable landmarks: Victoria Falls, museums, national park
   b. historic significance: site of first European explorer (David Livingstone)
   c. geographic and climactic features
   d. economic, political, cultural, social, features

Ss take notes; work in small groups to develop Levels I, II, and III questions about the stop; each student adds detail to own map

T draws Ss together to decide what detail to add to the wall chart and the class map

7. *Stop 4: Capetown, South Africa* [Column 4 on wall chart]
   a. notable landmarks: diamond exports, Vasco DeGama; Cape of Good Hope; fine wines, exotic plant life
   b. historic significance
   c. geographic and climactic features
   d. economic, political, cultural, social, features

Ss take notes; work in small groups to develop Levels I, II, and III questions about the stop; each student adds detail to own map

T draws Ss together to decide what detail to add to the wall chart and the class map

(reception)

Side trips: T assigns small groups of students (different combinations than previously) each to take a "side trip."

Side trips to Morocco, the Congo, Liberia, Namibia, Madagascar, Mali, and Timbuktu. Groups locate the same information as was located for the group stops; each group enters info on wall map and wall chart [Columns 5–11]

8. T discusses push-pull factors that cause Africans to migrate; e.g., Europeans in, slaves out, migration across countries; Ss have guided discussion on how these impacted the continent; each small group prepares a summary of notes taken and discussion ideas
   a. In and Out of Africa:
      ♦ slaves taken out
      ♦ Europeans coming in
      ♦ citizens leaving due to famine, wars, lack of jobs
   b. Within Africa:
      ♦ famines, poverty, starvation
      ♦ political unrest
      ♦ natural disasters
      ♦ economic shifts

9. Ss consider modernization efforts (e.g., mining for diamonds and gold; dam building; energy production and use; urban growth in major cities); in triads, Ss locate two articles describing the modernization efforts from different perspectives (e.g., positive, negative) re: impact on the country; triads share findings with class

10. T reviews with students how to develop a persuasive essay or speech (i.e., take a position, support it with evidence from viable sources, acknowledge alternate points of view, etc.); Ss practice reading sample persuasive essays to identify attributes, suggest improvements

11. Ss practice taking notes from sources and paraphrasing to prepare for Culminating activities, letters home; Ss cite sources accurately

12. T monitors student notebooks, journal entries (for letters home); questions developed; etc.; T meets with each student to discuss progress on unit goals—the S's individual goals as well as the unit goals

13. T lectures/explains the major *economic factors* of Africa:
   a. the *how* and *why* of trade and commerce *within* the 57 African countries (food, minerals, manufactured goods)
   b. the *how* and *why* of trade and commerce with other countries (i.e., *exports:* gold, diamonds, ivory, copper, etc.; *imports:* food, medicine, clothing, machinery, technology)
   c. interdependence
   d. lowest opportunity cost
   e. economic decisions involving trade-offs

14. T and Ss continually add to course Time line, wall map of Africa, and wall chart comparing regions and countries.

Web sites:
http://www.EnchantedLearning.com/school/Africa/Africamaps.html

http://www.ahsd.25.k12.il.us/curriculum%20info/africa/abutaf.html

this will expedite the editing process for a full-blown pilot the following year. Whether it is held in the summer or during the school year, the training is best split into two phases:

♦ Phase I is a two-day session to learn the basic *Unit Plan* format and to master the criteria for each Quadrant. And since the Unit topics have already been set forth in the *Curriculum Maps*, the major decisions about *Performance Indicators*, the materials to be used, and perhaps some of the major outcomes may have already been determined for each *Unit Plan*. This will considerably expedite the development process, allowing participants to focus their energies on the identification of effective teaching and testing methods.

♦ Phase II consists of 36 clock hours of training in the Best Practices, typically held at intervals across the school year. Most districts accomplish this with one or two release days each quarter, or four 3-hour sessions after school. This quarterly approach provides time for developing Teams to devise the *Unit Plans* for the next grading period. As the Teams learn specific Best Practices strategies and then bring the results of their tryouts back to each subsequent session, they become increasingly facile at enriching their prior work and in developing more mature units. Because they are piloting these units with their own students, users discover the need for Differentiation, and remediation, and/or enrichment, and the "green ink" given to the developing Teams reflects not only how this year's students responded but anticipates the needs of next year's students as well.

The Best Practices Components

This chapter has been devoted to the rationale and basic format of the *Unit Plan* process as it is approached in the **Instructional Design** process. It corresponds to Phase I of the training explained above and offers guidance on how to get the development of the *Unit Plans* underway. Phase II will be addressed in the next four chapters, each of which addresses specific detail about each quadrant and how the Best Practices can be leveraged to enrich and extend the *Unit Plans* devised during Phase I.

Chapter 5:	**Motivation and Information**	Quadrants 1 and 2: the INPUT side of the clock face
Chapter 6:	**Learning Constructs**	scaffolding activities to help students construct meaning
Chapter 7:	**Delivery Strategies**	teaching methods that match the *Performance Indicators*
Chapter 8:	**Assessment and Culmination**	Quadrants 3 and 4: the OUTPUT side of the clock face

The Consortium Approach

Throughout the book, we have mentioned the advantages of a consortium approach to school reform, and for districts with limited funding and little or no support staff, it is often a necessity. But sharing the expenses of training and/or data management does not force member districts into identical planning or decision-making. Each district still conducts its own needs assessments (or self-study), devises its own Action Plan, and honors its own vision and mission about the needs of its students and the demands of its community. The collaboration among teachers and administrators is an excellent venue to consider what really matters: What is good for students and how can we provide each the highest-quality curricular and instructional program possible?

In our experience, the course tools developed and the professional growth resulting from multidistrict collaboratives are far superior to those that occur when a district works in isolation. When districts work alone, even wealthy districts, their perspective is limited to their own experiences, and their expectations are confined to what they observe in their own students. Through the exchange of ideas, the discussion of mutual concerns, and hearing about alternative methods of problem solving, the capabilities and confidence of every staff member are expanded geometrically. The quality of both teaching and administrative practice is greatly enhanced in every district when participants learn about more creative and diverse approaches that actually work. This is particularly true in considering ways to Differentiate and to provide alternative activities for remediation and enrichment. Of equal importance are the support networks formed from such collaboration, extending beyond a set of workshops. By posting their course tools and ideas on their district Web sites, consortium members have immediate access to alternate resources they can use tomorrow morning.

Clerical Services

As was recommended with the *Performance Indicators* and the *Curriculum Maps*, we strongly suggest that the district set aside enough dollars for clerical services to input the *Unit Plans* as they are developed. Understandably, some development Teams prefer to be given a template and to word process the *Units* as they go along, and this is useful in the early drafting stages. However, once teachers begin to backfill their initial *Unit Plans* with Best Practices and "green ink" edits, it is much easier if these editing functions are provided by a clerical person who is facile with the templates and knows how to edit them. Naturally, continuity in format and correctness in spelling and punctuation are essential to creating a polished and professional-looking document, and a clerical person can attend to this polish work quickly and efficiently. And since the final versions of each *Unit Plan* will be disseminated throughout the district and be posted on various Web sites, they must have a consistent, official look to them. They should not, however, be commercially printed. Not only is that a wasteful extravagance, it suggests a permanence that totally contradicts the notion that the *Unit Plans* are dynamic and responsive to the needs of students and to new materials and curriculum developments. Word-processed documents with attractive, functional graphics and shading, boldface print, symbols, the use of space and highlights, consistent labels, and a clear interpretive key will do quite nicely. It will telegraph a message that the Board regards the *Unit Plans* as important academic documents and is willing to equip teachers with professional-looking course tools.

An Effective, Strategic Rollout

The careful preparation of the *Unit Plans* is all for naught without an effective rollout plan. It is strongly suggested that one person (usually the Director of Curriculum) be designated to oversee this task. Our experience has shown that without a carefully planned rollout process, and the year-end collection of "green ink," the entire *Unit Planning* initiative will collapse. Once the process is debugged, it will flow with relative ease. For most teachers, this will be their first formal experience with a *Unit Plan* that anyone actually expects them to use. But once the *Unit Plans* are part of a consistent routine throughout the school, they will be part of the building deep culture and flash an unmistakable signal of "the way we do business here."

Replacing Daily Lesson Plans With the Unit Plans

In buildings or districts requiring teachers to submit daily lesson plans, we strongly urge decision-makers to consider the *Unit Plan* as a better approach. Although most *Unit Plans* include a few pages of attachments (i.e., handouts, activity guides, tests, performance assessment prompts, and one or more scoring rubrics), the essence of each unit is captured on its *face pages*, or those pages that reflect the four quadrants. With that in mind, the teacher submits a clean copy of these face pages each Monday, highlighting the activities planned for that week. Alternatives we've seen include placing days and/or dates beside the highlighting; using different colors for different days of the week; or even recycling the same highlighted pages from one week into the next, updated as needed. Whatever works.

Since the original intent of lesson plans was to help teachers organize their instructional delivery, that purpose is served even more comprehensively by the *Unit Plan*. And since a secondary reason for lesson plans was to keep the building principal informed, the combination of *Curriculum Map* and *Unit Plans* is far more functional than a collection of piecemeal two-inch squares. In knowing how to interpret the *Curriculum Maps*, the principal has an immediate wide-angle view of the year's curriculum: how the *Performance Indicators* have been assigned to *Units* and how these *Units* have been sequenced and paced from September through June. Familiarity with the *Unit Plan* acquaints the principal with specific delivery and assessment strategies being used in each classroom and how each day's lesson is derived.

The Role of the Principal

Throughout the book, we have suggested several flash points in the reform process that will require the diligent stewardship of the principal if the effort is to succeed. Chapter 9 will wrap these responsibilities together into a discussion of how to fully integrate the enacted reforms into the deep culture of each school. But since the *Unit Plans* are typically developed during the school year, seeing to their implementation and monitoring how well they are working requires an extraordinary measure of the principal's attention. With this in mind, it may be helpful to consider some specific steps a principal can take to facilitate the *Unit Plan* process:

♦ Make timely and appropriate arrangements for the release (with substitutes) of the developing Team members.

♦ Support and encourage the efforts of the developing Team to informally pilot the initial *Unit Plans*; take a direct and sincere interest by discussing the pilot with team members and facilitating discussions between them and the other teachers who are piloting.

♦ Help parents/guardians understand any and all reform processes and their effect on classroom instruction.

♦ Assume a direct role in the more formal pilot of the *Unit Plans* by explaining the importance of the "green ink" to all staff; meet with confused or reluctant teachers to more fully clarify expectations; schedule meetings among staff members to discuss the pilot effort; and help to collect and synthesize the "green ink" at year's end.

♦ Meet with lead teachers (or members of the Building Leadership Team) and members of the developing Team to plan the most efficient and appropriate way to implement the *Unit Plans* as a regular part of the building's curriculum and instructional program, including how best to encourage and support reluctant and/or uncooperative teachers.

♦ Take proactive and responsive steps to help make *Unit Plans* (and their continual renewal) part of the school's daily routine and one of the primary indicators of "the way we do business here."

Annual Review and Revision

Each year, the developing Team should review the *Unit Plans* for completeness, accuracy, and user-friendliness, synthesizing the "green ink" for each into needed revisions. This will ensure that the most current edition is ready for the next school year. For this annual review, the building principal and designated central office administrator play crucial but respective roles. They should meet with the developing Teams to discuss the needed revisions, to verify that the changes are consistent with the state content standards and the mission of the district Board of Education, and to be sure that the materials and equipment needed will be available for the upcoming school year. Unless teachers see that district decision-makers, and the building principal in particular, are knowledgeable about the *Unit Plans* and serious about their use, there will be understandable skepticism. To paraphrase the eulogy of many school un-reforms, "This too shall pass; it's just another 'flavor-of-the-month,' and next year it'll be something else." As was suggested in Chapter 3, if teachers haven't learned anything else in three decades of school reform, they have learned that the only reforms they really need to worry about are those for which their administrators are being held accountable.

FREQUENTLY ASKED ◼ QUESTIONS ABOUT *UNIT PLANS*

The *Unit Plans* in the **Instructional Design** process are not scripts. The intent is to list activities that will guide teachers in using effective delivery and assessment strategies. And although most teachers realize the logic of using the same core *Unit Plans* at a grade level, they need to be reassured that the intent is not that they be clones of each other. Each teacher is expected to enhance the *Unit Plans* with his and her personal style and creativity. But some of the questions that arise need to be anticipated. A few are listed below.

❓ Must We Use the Same Strategies? What if We Know a Different Strategy That Works Just as Well?

Our response to using a different strategy is "yes," providing it falls within the scope of the *Unit* and matches the *Performance Indicators* involved. But this is an excellent question to be fielded by the principal. It provides a golden opportunity to examine the alternate material in the context of the developing Team's original idea and build the principal's capacity to demonstrate knowledgeable leadership in the **Instructional Design** process.

❓ Can We Use Alternate Materials as Long as They Are Parallel to Those Suggested in the *Unit Plan?*

The answer depends on whether there are "adopted" materials at each grade level and in each course. One dangerous trend to be avoided is what we call the "johnny-one-note rut:" that is, Language Arts teachers who fall back into the Short Story *Unit* or the Essay *Unit* rather than include a cross-section of genres in every *Unit*. Or Math teachers who fall back to the Fractions *Unit,* and students solve only the problems at the end of the chapter. But beware, this rut is at times more subtle. For example, a thematic *Unit* in Language Arts such as "Looking Out for Others" may seem fine until one looks at the materials and sees only the short story. Or in Science, a unit called "Using Simple Machines to Move Mountains" is a catchy title, but it is stifled by the exclusive use of workbook pages. And the Social Studies *Unit Plan* called "Life on the Underground Railroad" uses no primary sources. Much of this will be caught in the early development stages, but occasionally, there are teachers who use the invitation to be flexible and to apply their creativity as license to take their teaching back to traditional practices.

❓ Do We All Have to Go at the Same Pace? Some of My Kids Might Need More Time.

Since the pacing of the *Unit Plans* for a course has been established in the *Curriculum Map,* the pacing is predetermined. While the time frames are not absolute, teachers must be careful not to slip too far behind, especially if some of the *Performance Indicators* will reappear in other *Unit Plans* later in the year. Naturally, some students may need more time to master than others, but teachers are advised not to wait until all students have mastered every *Indicator.* The intervention and reteaching may need to occur during subsequent *Units.*

❓ Do We Have to Use the *Unit Plans* in the Same Order?

In some districts, equipment and/or materials may need to be shared among classes. In such cases, the order of the *Unit Plans* will need to vary accordingly. But this must be carefully and thoughtfully planned during the development of the *Curriculum Maps.* Remember, the *Unit Plans* are designed to build on each other, and if the order is shifted, the connections will need to be adjusted as well.

❓ What About the Students With Special Needs Who Are Included in My Class?

As was admitted in Chapter 3, this issue is extremely sensitive and difficult to pin down until the law is more precisely interpreted. When it is fully developed, after both Phases I and II of the training have been completed, each *Unit Plan* provides for Differentiation and for remediation or enrichment. In addition, each *Unit Plan* can also be enhanced to include accommodation or modification. With the mounting pressures of NCLB and AYP, many districts are trying to be proactive in seeing to it that students having Special Needs are provided every possible access to the general education curriculum and its performance expectations. But without clear and definite interpretations, this can become a cosmetic policy that may help a district comply with the letter of the law but totally avoid the spirit. State departments of education seem to have the immediate authority on how students with Special Needs fit into curricular and instructional reforms, and there is considerable variance state to state.

■ THE THREE-YEAR TIME FRAME

As described above, the process of developing and piloting the *Unit Plans* is fairly complex. But it is nonetheless a critical step in the **Instructional Design** process, since the *Unit Plans* guide the delivery and assessment of classroom instruction. And they are indeed the course tool for making it possible for students to demonstrate mastery of the *Performance Indicators.* The sample time line in Table 4.5 shows how *Unit Planning* fits into the big picture of the entire process.

Table 4.5   Sample Three-Year Time Frame

		Year 1			Year 2			Year 3		
		Summer	*Fall*	*Winter/ Spring*	*Summer*	*Fall*	*Winter/ Spring*	*Summer*	*Fall*	*Winter/ Spring*
Two Subjects, PreK–12; e.g., Reading and Math	*Performance Indicators (PIs)*	Develop, Pilot Critical Friends ⟶			Revise, Implement ⟶			Continue (annual review) ⟶		
	Curriculum Maps	Develop, Pilot Critical Friends ⟶			Revise, Implement ⟶			Continue (annual review) ⟶		
	Unit Plans				Develop, Pilot Critical Friends ⟶			Revise, Implement ⟶		
	Continuous Monitoring	Unofficially keep track of student mastery			Develop, Pilot Critical Friends ⟶			Revise, Implement ⟶		
	Benchmark Assessments	Collect classroom tests measuring *PIs*			Develop, Pilot Critical Friends ⟶			Revise, Implement ⟶		

PART III

Best Practices in *Unit Planning* and Delivery

5
Unit Planning

Motivation and Information

INTRODUCTION ■

Fixing the Plane in Flight

After Phase I of the *Unit Plan* training, the developing Teams are familiar with the format and have enough information in the *Curriculum Map* to devise a basic *Unit Plan* or two to start the school year. Perhaps in a perfect world, school would be stopped to conduct Phase II, or the entire canon of Best Practices, but that's not reality. And since the research clearly supports embedding professional development into the context of actual classroom instruction, learning how to build the Best Practices methods into each *Unit Plan* as the year progresses has its advantages. But during Phase I training, developers must be helped to fully understand the format and the conceptual links among the four quadrants, since this is the framework to which developers will apply the Best

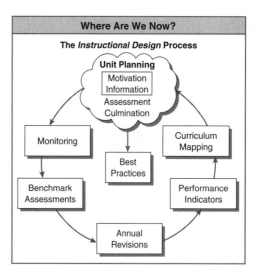

Practices. As Phase II training occurs during the school year, developers will be provided successive portions of the Best Practices methods to both backfill earlier basic *Unit Plans* and continue to develop richer subsequent units as the training progresses. To that end, we will provide detailed information about each quadrant in the next four chapters. This chapter will closely examine *Motivation* and *Information*, or the INPUT section of the *Unit Plan*. Chapters 6 and 7 will provide an in-depth look at the Best Practices methods, since they are initially applied to these two quadrants. Chapter 8 will address the *Assessment* and *Culmination* quadrants, or the OUTPUT side of the *Unit Plan*. Depending on the *Performance Indicators* involved, and the methods used in the INPUT quadrants, many of the Best Practices are equally at home in the OUTPUT portion of a *Unit Plan*. Each component is fully validated in the research, and annotated descriptions of each cite are available from the authors on request.

The Significance of INPUT

It is during the *Motivation* and *Information* activities in the *Unit Plan* that students take in and organize the information they will need to master the *Performance Indicators*. The significance of these INPUT teaching/learning activities is multifold:

♦ They are guided activities, carefully structured to help teachers lead students to construct meaning for themselves through learning experiences that are rich, interesting, and suitably complex.

♦ Each activity specifies (or implies) a teacher behavior or strategy and an active role for students.

♦ The activities serve the dual purposes of providing students with new information while helping them make connections with what they already know.

♦ Collectively, the INPUT activities address all of the *Performance Indicators* designated for the *Unit*; each activity typically addresses multiple indicators.

♦ Beginning with a diagnostic activity and continuing throughout both quadrants, teachers continually monitor student performance to check for understanding.

♦ To Differentiate, information can be provided in smaller and large doses, in multiple modalities, and in various grouping patterns, all choices informed by student needs.

■ MOTIVATION

The *Motivation* activities are the essential first steps in the teaching/learning process. Here, teachers help students not only to become familiar with the unit content but also to anticipate what will be expected by the end of the relationship. But it's about a mind-set, too. In these initial activities, good teachers illustrate and reinforce a classroom culture that values high-level performance and pride in workmanship, not necessarily perfection. They acknowledge that much of what students will encounter during the upcoming unit will challenge and may frustrate them, but failure will not be an option. Best Practice teachers know that with suitable *Motivation*, students will see problems and mistakes as golden opportunities to try again. It is said that Thomas Edison insisted he didn't fail in 6,000 attempts to find the right filament for his light bulb; he discovered 6,000 things that didn't work. Psychologists call this *joyful persistence*. Negative stress and destructive anxiety are the result of students' fearing failure and punishment. **Instructional Design** teachers should generate positive anticipation and minimize students' stress by encouraging them not to accept failure but to keep trying and to work hard at attaining some measure of success, and to do so with every unit.

Reflective of the Concrete-Reception quadrant, the *Motivation* activities provide students with concrete experiences using or observing the concepts that undergird the *Performance Indicators*. It is not necessary to have a Motivation activity for each *Indicator* but rather to design two or three activities that capture the big picture of the *Unit*. The students are closely guided through these activities, not only to ensure their readiness for the remainder of the *Unit* but also to give the teacher an overall idea of their level of interest in and knowledge of the topics to be addressed. The Motivation quadrant (see Table 5.1) has been excerpted from Figure 4.3 to remind readers of the criteria for effective *Motivation* activities as well as a few sample strategies.

The Criteria for Effective Motivation

As practical and intuitive as these criteria seem, we often have difficulty getting teachers to see the value of actually specifying them as an important and necessary feature of the *Unit Plan*. To clarify, a brief explanation of each criterion will be provided, illustrated by the Africa unit that appeared in Chapter 4 (Figure 4.4).

Actively Involve Students in a Direct Experience

The research is conclusive that when students have a direct or hands-on experience with the concepts, skills, and ideas to be considered in the *Unit*, they develop a sensory image or memory to call upon throughout the *Unit*. In many cases, these concrete experiences also provide students with a real-world context for the concepts, skills, and ideas and help them see their significance—or the *so what*—as they begin. In the Africa *Unit* from Chapter 4,

Table 5.1   The Motivation Quadrant: Horizontal View

(criteria for the quadrant)   (sample strategies)

| **Motivation (Concrete-Reception)**
■ actively involve students in a direct experience
■ determine what students know and don't know
■ make connections to prior and subsequent learning
■ pique students' interest
■ set expectations for completing the unit
■ help students set personal learning goals | *Performance Indicators*
———————
———————
———————

Culmination / Motivation

Assessment / Information | ■ pretest
■ brainstorm
■ KWL chart
■ video
■ manipulation of objects or ideas
■ intriguing question or puzzlement
■ concept web
■ song
■ artifacts
■ oral reading
■ conduct a poll
■ what-if scenario
■ demonstration
■ role-play or simulation
■ expert speaker
■ error analysis
■ extended analogies or extended metaphors |

using the wall-sized outline map of Africa, having students fill in their own outline map of Africa as the *Unit* proceeds, brainstorming what students know about Africa, and previewing the train trip are all direct or concrete experiences that are images to be revisited throughout the *Unit.*

Determine What Students Know and Don't Know

There are very few topics about which twenty-first-century children know absolutely nothing. Bringing forth what they already know about the *Unit* topics accomplishes two things: (a) it supplies a home base to which students can always return when they become disoriented, and (b) it gives the teacher a foundation on which to build the remainder of the *Unit,* especially if there is misinformation to be corrected. Most *Unit Plans* use a formal or informal Pretest to obtain such diagnostic information. It is not an exaggeration to say that omitting this step is as foolish as leaving a number out of an equation or a key character out of a movie. In the Africa *Unit,* imagine how unfortunate not to know that a couple students had traveled to Africa, another was born there to parents in the armed forces, and one had a pen pal from Kenya. And what if the teacher missed discovering that many students thought Africa was a country, while several had been with a fifth-grade teacher who took them through an elaborate study of the African rain forest?

Make Connections to Prior and Subsequent Learning

Structuring at least one *Motivation* activity to form bridges or links backward while reaching forward will pay off multifold once students get to the OUTPUT portion of the *Unit.* These links are sensory images and mental signposts that can be recalled by students as needed; they are part of that home base to which students can always return to begin again. In the Africa *Unit,* the display of the multitiered Time line for the course, with the ongoing addition of relevant information, helps students directly witness the chronological relationship among historic events. It is also particularly useful in helping students see how cultural, scientific, and economic developments affect the events on the Time line and how the removal of any one would affect the others. Students' prior map-reading and map-making skills and their understanding of geography will be challenged, but also greatly enhanced, as they are applied to the enormously varied landscape of Africa. How well students understand data—their collection, organization, and interpretation—will be evident as they assemble data on regional precipitation, population, and economic factors and attempt to use the information to make generalizations. Obviously, students' experience writing letters, summaries, and persuasive essays will be taken to another level as they attempt to capture their impressions of Africa's beauty, mystery, and fascination.

Pique Students' Interest

Although many teachers are skeptical that students beyond age 8 have any interest to pique, giving up on it is not an option. They may be in the minority, but there are still students who are eager to learn and are willing to put forth the effort it takes to do so. Hopefully, the majority of students who work hard at behaving with hostility or indifference toward learning will either grow out of it or are actually hiding a deep-level fear of failure that can be assuaged with academic success. Both experience and research tell us that even if students don't show any outward expressions of enthusiasm, classroom activities that allow them choices or options in how they may participate, actively involve them in constructing meaning for themselves, and/or allow them to involve a hobby or special interest will pull them into the *Unit,* even if reluctantly. In the Africa *Unit,* finding out what students already know, and don't, about Africa will yield a lively discussion, particularly if several students have had direct or even vicarious experiences there and/or other students have all sorts of misconceptions about Africa. The anticipation of taking a train trip, keeping a travel journal, and sending letters back home will be fascinating to many students. On a subliminal level, the physical stimuli of huge outline wall maps and empty wall charts holds the appeal of seeing what goes in them, especially if the students themselves do the filling in.

Set Expectations for Completing the Unit

Teaching graduate classes confirmed for us the necessity of clarifying at the outset of each course not only the syllabus of topics and expectations during the semester but precisely what is required of students as their final course projects. In the **Instructional Design** format for *Unit Planning,* teachers are asked to include in the *Motivation* quadrant an explanation or preview for students of what is expected of them by the end of the *Unit.* This typically includes showing students samples of work done by previous students as concrete models of what they will produce, not mimic or copy. Not only is such a preview an advantage for the student, it benefits the teacher as well. It is through these final projects or what will be Culminating tasks that students demonstrate their independent or concrete mastery of the *Performance Indicators.* Hence, the tasks must be strategically planned in advance as the endgame of the *Unit,* and the teaching/learning activities that occur throughout the *Unit* should contribute to them in some way. Such deliberate planning cannot help but make every *Unit* stronger and more viable. In the Africa *Unit,* the students need to realize that they will develop their own working map of Africa, complete with all of the features that are on the wall-sized map. They will also see what annotations are and how they enhance graphics of all kinds. Since students will be writing letters home as if from a real train trip, they need to see models or sample letters, as much to pique their interest in these exotic places as to reassure them that letter writing is actually a very familiar activity. On the other hand, the persuasive essay may appear to be a daunting prospect. Most Grade 6 students have written essays, but *persuasive* may not have been among them. So seeing an example of a persuasive essay, addressing a relevant topic such as school dress codes or policing the Internet, gives students at least a target toward which to aim.

Help Students Set Personal Learning Goals

This particular criterion for an effective *Motivation* quadrant doubles as a Best Practice. The research identifying the Best Practices has consistently shown that students who set their own content and personal goals form a more direct attachment to the content, take a proprietary interest in it, pay closer attention to their work, and accept responsibility for their successes and shortcomings. A more complete discussion of student goal setting is provided later in this chapter. In the Africa *Unit,* students might set the following content goals: (a) to know more about Africa by learning basic information about its regions and (b) to learn how other countries in the world took advantage of Africa. Sample personal goals might include (a) to use the Internet to locate information, (b) to work with a partner to complete tasks, and (c) to "keep up with my journals."

Boilerplate Examples of Motivation Strategies

The following sections are sample *Motivation* activities (see also Table 5.2), shown in the context of specific content units. Note how strongly they suggest possible *Performance Indicators*. These examples are easily adapted by switching out the content.

Table 5.2   Sample Motivation Activities

Brainstorm what students already know about the unit topic(s) or concepts; list on board or wall-chart and/or record as the "K" in a KWL chart. Variation: can later go back and label or cluster into common categories.
Math: "Financial Analysis" (Grade 6) Brainstorm current knowledge about finances and how to calculate them; list ways that people can work and invest to increase their financial holdings. **Language Arts:** "The Musical—a Mirror of America" (Grade 10) Record which shows the students have seen; what they know; how they felt about "musical"; etc. Later classify as titles, types, message, theme, technical elements, etc.

Role-play or imagine "what-if" or hypothetical situations; jot down attributes displayed, and reflect on how they are significant (i.e., if they had not been present).
Language Arts: "I Say, Holmes!—Murder Mysteries and Other Nail-Biters" (Grade 5) Provide a brief synopsis of a murder (or other mysterious event); students play detective and pose questions to lead the investigation (full-class or small groups). **Science:** "Animals" (Grade 1) Play the "Who Am I?" game about animals children already know (e.g., "I live in a hive. I take pollen from flowers and make honey. Who Am I?"

Display artifacts, products, or samples as (a) a mystery object for prediction; (b) a model of what students will make; or (c) a point of interest.
Social Studies: "Who WERE These People?" (Grades 9, 10) Provide a trash-bag full of artifacts; students work in 3s to select an artifact, and hypothesize that the family who used it may have been like—where they lived, their possible occupation, their daily routines, etc. If verification data are available (e.g., Amish, Native American, etc.), students check their hypotheses against the actual fact. **Arts and Other: (Music)** "Asymmetrical Music" (Grades 9–12) Provide examples of asymmetrical music as the students come into the classroom (e.g., "Come Home From the Sea" by the Manhattan Stem Roller) **(Art)** "Masks and Such" (Grade 6–8) Display masks from various cultures (some made by students—made prior years); students use authentic materials to make masks depicting a specific tradition in their own or an adopted culture OR "Drawing Still-Life" (Grades K–3) Guide students to set up still life displays (e.g., sports items, favorite toys, musical instruments, fruits, flowers, dried weeds, garden vegetables, etc). Students draw or sketch.

Read aloud an editorial (story, etc.) as an example of what students will produce (concepts they will address).

Math/Language Arts: "Sorting" (K) Teacher reads *Frog and Toad Are Friends* by Arnold Lobel and discuss the attributes of each; line up 3 students, and have a student describe one of them using several attributes; others try to guess who is being described, narrowing it to 2 students, then to 1.

Science: "Pesticides and Other Hazards" (Grades 9–12) Read aloud a passage from Rachel Carson's *A Silent Spring* (1962), which exposed the hazards of the pesticide DDT, questioned humanity's faith in technological progress, and helped set the stage for the environmental movement.

View a __partial__ video, listen to portions of a speech or story; predict subsequent events or details; later confirm or revise. __Variation:__ substitute details and consider impact on the piece.

Arts and Other: "Stories in Stone" (Grade 4) Show part of the video *K'uu T'ahn—Rockmarkings*; explain to students that these are petroglyphs from the Southwest in North America; help students predict how the rock markings describe life in that culture.

Language Arts: "H.G. Wells—A Man Before His Time" (Grade 9) Show students partial video of *The Time Machine* (e.g., Wells leaves the 1890s to the scene after WW II when he stops to visit); students predict what will happen (later, they will see what happened, and confirm or revise their predictions).

Teacher demonstrates a usual or surprising event, asks students to answer (and/or devise) a few questions or formulate one or more hypotheses about what happened. Later confirm or revise hypotheses, citing evidence to support or reject. Variation: substitute variables; "what-if ___ instead of ___?"

Math: "Fractions" (elementary) Ask students to predict the effects on baking a cake if the wrong fractions were used; e.g., ½ tsp of salt rather than ¼, 1½ cups of sugar rather than 2½ cups, etc. Verify the predictions with the actual activity, or interview a science or home ec teacher; discuss how a recipe can be tripled or halved; have students rewrite the recipe as it should be.

Science: "Fire! Fire!" (Grade 8) Douse a cotton handkerchief in alcohol; ignite it, but students see that it does not burn; have students hypothesize why this might happen (the alcohol burns at a temperature below the kindling temperature of the cotton; the heating and vaporization of the water removes the heat and prevents the cloth from burning).

Conduct a class poll to obtain data on 2 or 3 variables (1 for primary students); organize, represent, and summarize; identify ways the data can be used. Variation: identify what data are missing and how to collect them.

Social Studies: "Stereotyping" (Grade 8) Students conduct a survey of several classes to capture perceptions about stereotypes that are often associated with e.g., teenagers, people with body piercings, African Americans, the elderly, etc); compile the results, display as a graph or table, and note any patterns among respondents.

Science: ""Variations Among Us!" (Grade 3) Collect measurements of familiar living objects (e.g., femurs, kidney beans, adult grasshoppers, apples, etc.); organize and graph the data, and consider the variations within the same living thing. Predict how such variation occurs and how it can be an advantage or a disadvantage.

(Continued)

Table 5.2 (Continued)

Conduct a Pretest that is (a) formal, consisting of some items from the final test; or (b) informal, consisting of a few casual items (oral and/or written). Use the results for student goal-setting.

Math: "Percents" (Grade 7) Distribute newspapers with pages of merchandise offered at sale prices, plus an extra discount coupon; have students create percentage problems for each other to solve.

Language Arts: "Laugh 'Til You Cry" (Grade 8) Pretest that includes various techniques used by authors to create humor in fiction and nonfiction and sample passages for students to identify the "humor" features used by the authors.

Science: "Nature or Nurture—Genetics or Environment" (Grade 7) Ask students to respond to a list of facts and fallacies about old-wives tales versus scientific fact about inherited traits (e.g., if your mother is obese, you can't help but be obese also).

Social Studies: "The Cold War—Gone but Not Forgotten" (Grades 11, 12) Give Government students a pretest on the Cold War, and how it continues to impact American government today. Each student uses his or her results as a fact sheet to collect information throughout the unit.

Arts and Other: "Art and Music—The Mirrors of a Culture" (Grade 5) Give students a pretest of terms associated with art and music in Latin America, the Slovakian countries, Asia, Polynesia and the Caribbean, Africa, Scandinavia, Canada, and various sections of North America.

Conduct a class discussion, either (a) formal, as a guided discussion (students use given information to formulate a response); or (b) informal, consisting of a give-and-take exchange (teacher role may be observer or participant).

Math: "Problem-Solving" (Grades 3, 4) Read the book *The Math Curse*; discuss actual math "fears" among students in the class; assure them that this is normal.

Language Arts: (Grade 7) Given basic bio facts about Poe and Billy Joel (including a sample poem by Poe and song lyrics by Joel), groups discuss how a composer's work is a metaphor of his or her life and a mirror of the reader's/listener's life.

Provide maps, graphics, diagrams that create a context for the unit and get filled in as the unit progresses.

Social Studies: "Mapping the Ancient World" (Grade 6) Show students a succession of maps representing the "world" as it was known in the Biblical eras, Marco Polo's time, just before Columbus sailed, etc. Help them link each "generation" of map to the political and cultural events of the day.

Arts and Other: "A Riot of Color" (Grade 5) Give students a color wheel that displays primary and secondary colors. Discuss intermediate (tertiary) colors; help students mix tints and shades, and help them understand color planning and complementary colors.

Goal Setting

The Best Practices research confirms that students who make their own individual connections to content by setting their own content and personal goals attain higher levels of achievement than those who do not. This individual goal setting falls nicely within the "active student involvement" and "connecting prior and subsequent learning" criteria. And what could be more concrete than setting one's own goals? We insist that these goals be set for each *Unit* and documented in a journal for continual reference. To have students set year-long or even quarterly goals is a waste of time. Not only does it necessitate that the goals be generic, it removes them so far from immediacy that they are completely forgettable.

Although it is affirming to students and the teacher to see the student's individual goals accomplished, it is more important that students see themselves making progress toward the goals by the end of the unit. We refer to this as "seeing if the needle moved." Some goals may well be continued in the next *Unit*; others may be discontinued or modified. The key is that students rate themselves on these individual goals, giving themselves a letter grade or point value (as established at the outset). Bear in mind, this is the one aspect of the *Unit* over which students have control; they identify the goals, monitor them, and rate themselves on their success. It is thus important that the goals be revisited at the end of the *Unit*. Time should be allocated for students to reflect on the progress they have made toward their goals during the *Unit* and the status of those goals as it draws to a close. The following suggestions are offered for goal setting:

♦ Each student should formulate at least two goals for each unit: one content and one personal. Two each is the ideal, but begin with at least one each.

♦ For a *Unit* or two, model the goal-setting process with one's own goals for the *Unit* and a few sample goals from which students may choose. One prime source for student goals is the diagnostic assessment or pretest (one of the Motivation activities). By the third *Unit*, students will be able to select their own.

♦ Ask students to write each goal in their journals (or notebooks); ask that the goals be submitted for review. Offer a written comment to each student to endorse his or her goals and/or to make suggestions.

♦ Remind students that they will be expected to monitor their progress toward reaching each goal, even if the goals aren't completely achieved. Assure students that the important point is "progress toward." Actually attaining each goal is wonderful, but not essential. Help students think through how they will monitor their progress and how they will know when progress is being made.

♦ As the *Unit* proceeds, give students time to revisit their goals and to make adjustments as needed; most important, have students record any progress they have made toward each goal.

♦ At the end of the *Unit*, ask students to review the progress they made toward accomplishing their goals and to give themselves a rating. Provide encouraging feedback to students about their progress and this summative self-appraisal.

Samples

"All About Me" (Grade 2, Math)

- Content goals: (a) learn to collect information from my friends, (b) graph my friends' birth weight, length at birth, time of day born, (c) change numbers in my head to add and subtract.

- Personal goals: (a) get facts about my birth, (b) measure things at home to see how long they are.

"The Settlement of Ohio: Native Americans" (Grade 4, Social Studies)

- Content goals: (a) find out how the Indian tribes living in Ohio were affected by the settlers in their territories, (b) explain why settlers came to Ohio, (c) read and interpret different kinds of maps.
- Personal goals: (a) learn to read a time line, (b) trace my family history to see if any were Native Americans or European settlers.

"Mythology" (Grade 7, Language Arts)

- Content goals: (a) improve my writing vocabulary using a thesaurus; (b) write more believable, interesting narratives; (c) get better at recognizing errors in mechanics.
- Personal goals: (a) apply themes and symbols from what we read to my own life; (b) be more confident in my public speaking (less fearful, fewer "ums"); (c) improve my listening skills: get the info correct.

"The Universe" (Grade 8, Science)

- Content goals: understand how time relates to distance in terms of light-years and how it is used to measure faraway objects in the universe; (b) explore the solar system, universe, and galaxies so I can compare the different bodies.
- Personal goals: (a) gain an appreciation for astronomy, which has always been abstract and difficult to understand; (b) read at least two space-type science fiction books.

■ INFORMATION

Quadrant 2 of the *Unit Plan* format is *Information*. This is the primary teaching portion of the *Unit,* or the meat-and-potatoes of the INPUT side. We jokingly acknowledge to teachers our wish that we could just stick a funnel in students' ears to pour the information directly into their brains, but since that only works in cartoons, other methods must be employed. The *Information* quadrant (see Table 5.3) reflects the full intent of the *Performance Indicators* in the *Unit* by detailing *what* needs to be taught and *how* it is best presented to help every student achieve mastery. In effect, the concepts, skills, and ideas that underlie the *Indicators* are addressed in the business end of the *Unit Plan.*

In many cases, multiple *Indicators* are accommodated in the same activity. For example, when students write an original short story, they may address *Indicators* dealing with story elements, the narrative genre, figurative language, writing fiction, point of view, and various language mechanics. Or when they collect data and display it in original tables, they may be working on *Indicators* in all four math operations, measures of central tendency, and data analysis.

With more densely constructed *Indicators,* however, it may be necessary to have *more* than one activity, particularly if Differentiation is likely.

Table 5.3   The Information Quadrant: Horizontal View

Information (Abstract-Reception)	*Performance Indicators*		Learning "Constructs"
<ul><li>delivery strategies and student responses <u>match</u> the *Performance Indicators*</li><li>students have an active, constructive role</li><li>include variety in grouping patterns and learning modalities</li><li>indicate how all *Performance Indicators* will be taught (including options for differentiation: remediation, enrichment)</li><li>require multiple levels of thinking</li><li>involve continuous assessment, feedback</li></ul>	_____ _____ _____		<ul><li>organizational patterns</li><li>summarizing</li><li>note-taking</li><li>graphic or visual organizers</li><li>context and structural clues for vocabulary</li><li>various levels of questioning</li><li>similarities and differences</li></ul> **Delivery Strategies** <ul><li>lecture</li><li>demonstration</li><li>guided discussion</li><li>inquiry</li><li>Socratic Seminar</li><li>literature circles</li><li>action research</li><li>advance organizer</li></ul>
	Culmination	Motivation	
	Assessment	Information	

One example is an *Indicator* from Grade 8 Social Studies dealing with the American Revolution. Students are expected to identify and explain the sources of conflict leading up to the Revolutionary War, including the Proclamation of 1763, the Stamp Act, the Townshend Acts, the Tea Tax, the Intolerable Acts, the Boston Tea Party, the boycotts, and the Sons of Liberty. Although all of these events are included in the same *Performance Indicator*, each source has its own set of circumstances and would be considered in separate activities.

In reflecting the Reception-Abstract axes, the *Information* activities are strategically designed to help students take in information but process it in ways that develop key concepts and ideas on an abstract level sufficient to use them without a concrete example. Developers are encouraged to include a wide array of activities in this quadrant, anticipating the need to provide for Differentiation in the initial teaching scenario as well as the likelihood that remediation or enrichment may be needed later. These activities should include various grouping configurations and multiple learning channels or modalities through which students obtain information and demonstrate what they have learned. As the teacher monitors student performance, opportunity should also be provided for students to assess themselves, becoming increasingly proficient at reflection and self-correction in these formative stages of the *Unit*.

In keeping with the intent of standards-based curriculum and the Best Practices approach to teaching and learning, students should solve real-world problems and apply critical and creative thinking skills in doing so. To this end, **Instructional Design** includes training in Bloom's Taxonomy to help teachers structure their teaching/learning activities at various levels of mental processing. The final section of this chapter is devoted to Bloom as our way of helping teachers think about how to construct teaching/learning activities at various levels, even in their initial *Unit Plans*. Bloom is the perfect readiness tool to prepare teachers for more granular Best Practices.

In this section, the Information section is explained, and an illustration is provided from the Africa unit. Looking ahead, Chapter 6 will focus on the Learning Constructs, or scaffold-type supports to help students process information and construct meaning for themselves. Chapter 7 will deal with Delivery Strategies, or the specific techniques selected by teachers to convey new information to students.

The Criteria for Effective Information Activities

Delivery Strategies and Student Responses Match the Performance Indicators

One intimidating aspect of the *Unit Planning* process is that some of the favorite and comfortable teaching/learning activities, for both teachers and students, no longer match the *Performance Indicators*. In the abstract, most teachers admit that the *Indicators* will make different demands on them and that they may even lose some of their favorite content. But when they come face-to-face with the reality, comments such as, "Oh, but you don't mean my tadpole unit. The kids just love it!" become commonplace. But once they finally come to grips with letting go of those topics not authorized by the standards, as well as taking on those that are new to a grade level or subject, teachers proceed much more efficiently through the rest of the unit development. In the Africa unit, every teaching/learning experience reflects one or more of the *Performance Indicators*. There simply isn't time for extraneous activities that don't lead to mastery of the *Indicators*.

A second difficulty in matching the teaching/learning activities with the *Performance Indicators* lies in the cognitive demand of the *Indicator*. If students are asked to "analyze" an amendment, having them "label" an amendment is not a match. Nor does it work to have students "solve math problems on a worksheet" if the indicator calls for "writing original math story problems." In the Africa unit, the *Performance Indicators* require students to construct, compare and contrast, analyze, locate, interpret, list, explain, and identify. The teaching/learning activities in the *Motivation* and *Information* quadrants strategically reflect these cognitive demands.

Students Have an Active, Constructive Role

With so much content to cover and so little time to do so, it is easy for teachers to lapse into a *telling* mode and for students to become passive recipients of what they are told by the teacher and/or the text. In such cases, students' active involvement is limited to seatwork, note taking, filling in worksheets, or answering questions at the end of the chapter. Even lively discussions can be dominated by a few verbal students, allowing the majority of the class to sit in silence. A further complication is that many teachers were taught using this approach and thus see nothing inappropriate about it.

Across the years, we've seen districts spend enormous amounts of money bringing in a famous guru to *tell* teachers about active student involvement (no irony there!). Months later, district leaders lament that nothing has changed in their classrooms and that students are still basically passive. The reality is, unless teachers are *shown* how to more actively involve students and provided the time and assistance to develop or adapt their own classroom materials, they will continue to do what they have always done. It's like healthy snacking: If veggies and cheese are already prepared, we'll grab it. If we have to stop and get it ready, we're more likely to go for the chocolate. Teachers will use what's prepared.

Looking at incorrect methods, developers can quickly see how to revise them, typically by replacing passive student roles with active participation and the construction of meaning. For example,

♦ "The teacher will explain XYZ" can be swapped out for "Students will work in groups to examine passages about XYZ, and develop three questions."

♦ "Students will look up the list of vocabulary words" can be replaced by "Student partners will scan a section of text to locate the words on the board and make predictions about meaning from context."

♦ "The students will solve the story problems at the end of the chapter" can become "In threes, students will examine two sample problems to identify (a) what the problem is asking to be done, (b) the best strategy to find the solution, (c) what order of operations is to be used, and (d) how will we check for accuracy? They will also devise one problem to exchange with another triad."

In the Africa *Unit,* students' active involvement includes the following: (a) draw (maps and features); (b) write predictions and look them up to verify; (c) take notes with regard to suggested format; (d) develop Level I, II, and III questions; (e) chart distances and record geographic details; (f) keep a travel journal, recording specific details and observations; (g) participate in guided discussion and summarize consensus; (h) locate information for their "side trips" to Morocco, and so on; (i) add details to the wall map and wall matrix; (j) locate articles about modernization efforts in Africa, and share the findings with classmates; (k) review sample essays as per criteria, and make edits to improve; (l) paraphrase notes taken from sources; prepare citations; and (m) develop graphic organizers.

Grouping

As with the "active student involvement," unless variety in grouping is planned for, the typical defaults are whole class, "get into groups," or each student working alone. Worse, if the tasks have not been well planned, the group activity may lapse into a "bull session" with students accomplishing very little. Our experience has shown, and the research supports, several tips for successful grouping:

♦ Decide which activities are best done in groups rather than whole class or individually. During classroom observations, the comments students make to each other can be amazingly insightful about the profession. One of the most humorous (but enlightening) is when they wink at each other and say, "He must have just gone to a grouping workshop." It's the old adage that once we learn to use a hammer, everything becomes a nail. In the current frenzy by schools to meet AYP, there has been an alarming tendency to use the need to Differentiate as an excuse to use "ability groups." Like the hammer, grouping can be misused. The key is to use it appropriately, and only if it's the right idea.

♦ Determine the intended outcome and appropriate time frame. For example: Is there a product to be developed (within a few minutes, long-term)? Is it a spot check or sponge activity (to check for understanding during whole-class presentation)? Is it a discussion or process activity (typically completed within the class period)? Will each group do the same activity or different activities? If the latter, how will the *different* activities be linked? Will the groups "share-out" or simply submit their work to the teacher?

♦ Decide if it is a high-stakes or low-stakes activity. If high stakes, the purpose is mastery, and there is a direct alignment to one or more *Performance Indicators*. There is a specified outcome and a convergent focus, and the task should include a rubric to guide the group's effort. If low stakes, the purpose is experiential, or an opportunity to try out ideas; the key purposes are diversity of thought, creativity, and viable speculation, and there is little risk of failure; the focus is divergent, since mastery is not intended.

♦ Be sure the payoff is worth the effort. This point is best made by some of the horror stories we hear from teachers about grouping. Examples follow:

◊ "I just can't afford to take time to group. The last time I did that, it took four weeks for all the groups to read *West Side Story* and then another four weeks for them to read *Romeo and Juliet*. They wouldn't stay on schedule, and my class discussions were useless because some of the groups had read the material and other groups claimed they couldn't follow the language or understand the worksheet. It was a disaster."

◊ "That grouping nearly killed off my Spanish II class. Each group was to create a model of a locker, one of the cupboards in the classroom, or the entrees in the school cafeteria line. They had to include all the objects in their model and label each with the correct Spanish name. You have no idea what a mess that was. They just ruined the entire thing. Some got all carried away and created these incredibly complex models, and others just threw something together. Most of the groups claimed that at least two of their team members didn't do enough. Yikes, that was the last time I'll try any group Spanish project."

◊ "Oh, the first time I did a group thing, it went well. It was election time, and each group had to assemble the results in one of the city precincts: how many people were registered, how many voted, who received the most votes, and what issues won and lost. The groups did a fairly good job, too. But then the next year, the project was a total bomb: no one, not even my good kids, did anything. When I asked why, they said it was because the project counted toward only 10% of their 9-weeks' grade, so they decided it wasn't worth it."

◊ "Well, I've had my fill of group activities in elementary math. I had each group take one of the problem-solving strategies and create a poster that explained how it was to be used. Then each group was to teach the rest of the class how to use that strategy. Now mind you, I had already taught all of the strategies and given them examples, so it should have been easy for them, right? Wrong! They got all caught up in the decorative aspect and used examples that were completely out of context, so we had to rework most of them. Once is enough of that."

These teachers fell into the "big effort/little benefit" trap with both feet, and their experience taught us the following lessons:

♦ Take care that the group activity is not too elaborate; limit the amount of class time used for students to prepare the product (e.g., two class periods, or 2 to 3 hours, maximum).

♦ Provide clear guidelines about how the final product should look, taking care that it does not eclipse the concept to be mastered; remember, the product may be a demonstration, a simple sheet of paper, or a wall chart; be sure that artistic products are fresh and original and not merely copying.

♦ Be sure the product reflects mastery of one or more *Performance Indicators* and is not merely fun or busywork; the amount of credit should be proportionate to the amount of effort, and the production should be a part of the learning toward mastery.

♦ Limit the amount of class time needed to present the product (e.g., two periods for a major product such as a research study and one period for lesser products); bear in mind, there may be little profit to students to hear 25 (or even 5) renditions of the same thing; consider having each student present to three other students. Whenever possible, have each group do a different but complementary aspect to increase the amount learned by the entire class. Watch out for PowerPoint; it may have already become technology's hammer.

♦ Be certain there is a productive, engaging role to be played by the students as the audience.

♦ Make the task suitable for the developmental needs of students: (a) Are students capable of self-direction, or do they need continual supervision? If the former, be sure to build in checkpoints; if the latter, be sure the supervision is provided. (b) Can students handle multistep tasks and follow the proper sequence, within the allocated time? Again, build in checkpoints. (c) Have students mastered the social skills needed to interact with a partner? Or is it more a matter of just working solo but sitting beside each other? Teamwork skills may need to be taught or reviewed.

♦ Vary the types and composition of the groups. Students need to work successfully alone, with a partner, and in small groups. They also need to work with different partners and in various group compositions.

- **skill-alike:** Students with like academic needs may be grouped for a specific activity; these pairings or groupings are never permanent and never posted. Some tasks appropriate to skill-alike groups are pronouncing words and practicing structural cues, making up word problems in math, or reading passages on the same topic written at various developmental levels. But bear in mind, skill-alike grouping should not be a ruse for tracking.

- **cross-ability:** Students with various levels of academic ability may be paired or placed in the same group; these groupings are not permanent since students' strengths vary in different areas. Appropriate to cross-ability groups are multistep tasks that can be divided among (or between two) group members and require each to be accountable (e.g., planning a road trip, conducting an investigation of a puzzlement). But bear in mind, cross-ability grouping should not become peer tutoring. More capable students should not be used as surrogate teachers, and we urge caution that a good technique not be abused.

- **random:** This is typically accomplished by numbering off (e.g., 1s, 2s, 3s) or drawing names from a hat. Some tasks appropriate to random grouping include brainstorming lists at the introduction of a concept, reading assigned material and comparing perspectives, applying a concept to practice problem solving, having a guided discussion, and so on. *Random* should not be construed as haphazard; the tasks of this group are as deliberately planned as the others, but the composition of the group is not as strategic.

- **interest:** Students are paired or grouped according to expressed interest. Some tasks appropriate to interest grouping include those where fact-finding is the priority and student selection of the topic is part of the motivation. It may be hobby based or involve selecting among several options; e.g., the five biomes.

Excluding skill-alike groups, teachers can preselect and post a few standing combinations, so that students can get into them quickly. Whether students work alone, in dyads, triads, or small groups or remain as a whole class should be carefully thought-out and written directly into the *Unit Plan.*

In the Africa *Unit,* students work in several combinations, including *whole class* (e.g., brainstorming what students know about Africa and the teacher's presentation of the persuasive essay); *individual* (e.g., students' individual maps of Africa, setting personal goals, and writing the travel letters home); dyads (e.g., recording information at each stop along the railway); triads (e.g., locating information on the modernization efforts); and various small groups (e.g., devising various levels of questions, taking each of the various "side trips" to Morocco).

Students' use of multiple modalities to receive information as well as to process it has become one of the staples in the *how-to* of successful classroom reform. But to accomplish this, teachers must deliberately plan for students to hear some of the information; read some of it, verbalize portions of it to each other; act out, role-play, or dramatize some of it; and manipulate objects or pieces of paper for part of it. In the Africa *Unit,* students see all sorts of visuals on the wall and in the text; note in particular that the time line, the wall map of Africa, and the wall matrix to compare the regions remain posted throughout the *Unit* to provide students with a continual referent. In addition, students (a) draw maps (outlines, features, landmarks, etc.); (b) call out during brainstorms (and see their ideas recorded); (c) devise various levels of questions; (d) record individual goals, data, notes, and journal information; (e) provide summaries both orally and in print; (f) hear explanations of the "train trip" and see samples of travel-journal entries; (g) write and verbalize hunches, then locate information online and in print to verify or revise; (h) discuss assigned tasks with other students (decide how to proceed, review progress); (i) hold conversations with the teacher to explain progress, identify concerns, and ask clarifying questions; (j) read and process text passages and sample essays; (k) compile data and display in graphs and charts; (l) calculate distances, and note similarities and differences in data from various regions; (m) identify patterns and trends indicated by data; (n) answer questions orally and in writing; (o) write letters; (p) write an essay; and (q) prepare annotations of diagrams, maps, and other visualizations.

Indicate How All Performance Indicators Will Be Taught

During the development of each *Unit,* Teams must make certain they address each of the *Performance Indicators* identified, including how the relevant content or skill will be taught and how students are expected to respond as they wend their way toward mastery. And the Teams need to constantly remind themselves that they will make adjustments as they learn more Best Practices and do so in the context of piloting their *Unit Plans.* Some of the nuances and variations that they may eventually add, including options for Differentiation and remediation or acceleration, will become more apparent during the Phase II training.

In the Africa *Unit,* all 10 *Performance Indicators* are addressed in the 15 teaching/learning activities listed as the *Information* quadrant. In summary, the *Indicators* require students to use a variety of map skills to locate features and compare regions; to compare the physical, social, and political features of regions, and to analyze the interrelationships among them; to list the positive and negative consequences of modernization; to explain push/pull factors that result in migrations in and out of the countries of Africa; to contrast the concepts of sovereignty and protectorate; and to distinguish among various types of government (monarchy, democracy, and dictatorship). Each of the teaching/learning activities in the Africa *Unit* are constructed to reflect the requirements of the *Performance Indicators.*

Although the Best Practices are not yet labeled in the Africa *Unit,* the foundation for them is there. And as participants learn more about Learning Constructs and Delivery Strategies, these Best Practices will be more fully displayed, labeled with a surrounding box—including various options for Differentiation.

Require Multiple Levels of Thinking

This advice has become so widespread in the list of must-dos for successful classroom reform, publications that don't include it are virtually nonexistent. And yet it is far easier to talk about than to put into practice. And while we don't claim to have completely overcome it, we have had considerable luck helping teachers manage it over the years by reconnecting with Bloom's Taxonomy. And since we include a section devoted to Bloom's Taxonomy, we will defer the discussion of it here.

Involve Continual Assessment and Substantive Feedback

Another of the trendy phrases batted around school reform cocktail tables is formative assessment. For many of us, formative assessment has never *not* been a major emphasis. But the twenty-first-century variation has added the "assessment for learning" as distinct from "assessment of learning," or summative assessment. The continual monitoring of student performance and subsequent adjustment of instruction is one of the core principles of **Instructional Design**, and it is provided for in every *Unit Plan*. Within the array of teaching/learning activities that comprise the Motivation and Information quadrants of each *Unit*, the following assessment and feedback strategies are to be ever-present:

♦ Formal or informal *Preassessments* at the outset of the *Unit* as well as at the introduction of a major concept to determine what each student is bringing to the work: These may take the form of paper-pencil tests, the performance of a task, or a teacher carefully listening to what students say. These results are not only instructive to the teacher, they inform student goal setting as well.

♦ Individual academic and *Personal Goals* for the unit set by each student based on his and her own needs and interests: As indicated in the previous section describing goal setting, these goals should be recorded in the student's Log or Journal, revisited throughout the *Unit*, and evaluated by the student at the conclusion of the *Unit*. Again, the importance is not so much attainment of each goal but progress, and the student recognizing the link between his and her effort and that progress (or lack thereof).

♦ Continual documentation via Journals or Logs in which students record not only their personal goals but also perceptions and reflections: In addition, the Journals may house specific written assignments (e.g., words in context, math problem-solving strategies, class notes, quick-writes); the teacher should review these Journals at least weekly, and provide substantive comments about strengths and needs for growth.

♦ Out-of-class Homework, excluding mere busy work without academic purpose: A sore spot with us, we have found all sorts of atrocities from homework assigned as punishment to homework never looked at by teachers. For legitimate homework (i.e., that which links directly to one or more *Performance Indicators* and involves students in authentic, valid practice, application, or extension of class work), teachers should provide substantive feedback. Most legitimate homework results in a written product of sorts, which makes it more convenient for teachers to provide feedback. Students need to be reinforced in areas where they succeeded, shown where and how they made errors, and told specifically how to improve.

♦ In-class Comprehension Activities, providing they legitimately and accurately reflect the student's level of proficiency in applying or extending the concepts taught: In fact, the criteria for "legitimacy" is similar to that for out-of-class homework: (a) a direct link to one or more of the *Performance Indicators*; (b) students required to construct meaning, not mimic or parrot that of the teacher or the text; and (c) options for students to redo in the event they are unsuccessful. Comprehension activities may result in a written product, displays, or verbal discourse. Whichever, teachers need to monitor each student's performance and provide substantive feedback as to specific areas of success, failure, and how to go about making improvements. In-class work to check for understanding or comprehension is most effective when it is checked during the class period and students know immediately if they are on the right track or need to relearn some or all of the skill or concept in reference.

In the Africa *Unit*, several activities provide opportunity for the teacher to monitor each student's performance and provide substantive feedback. These include the following: (a) the daily journal and class lecture notes; (b) the results of student predictions; (c) the charting of distances and data displays for populations, precipitation, temperatures, economic features, and so on; (d) the questions developed by students; (e) the details added to the wall charts by each group; (f) the data found in taking the various "side trips"; (g) the guided discussion about push/pull factors; (h) the articles located about modernization and the way they are summarized to share with the class; (i) the persuasive essays, improved by students' edits; (j) practice paraphrases in preparation for assessment and culminating activities; and (k) the personal maps constructed by each student.

[... 🖋] **More Testing Than Teaching?** Although we are strong supporters of assessment for learning and are assisting several districts in so doing, we have lately discovered a rather disturbing backlash. There may indeed be more testing than teaching going on in many of the nation's classrooms. This is discomforting on two levels. First, it occurs in districts where subgroups have failed to make AYP, the very students who need more instruction and guided practice, not less. For reformers who are desperate to narrow the gap in achievement between "advantaged" and "disadvantaged" students, this is the perfect crusade. Is NCLB all about making sure every child successfully masters the curriculum or obtains a certain test score? But on a deeper level, we are concerned about what this is doing to the profession. An actual anecdote from a recent research study is the best way to illustrate what we mean.

In a Value-Added study, principals were interviewed about what they could identify that may have made their test scores higher between one year and the next, as predicted from previous scores. Responses such as the following were painful to hear: "Oh, that's easy. We give a short-cycle assessment on Monday, reteach all week, and retest on Friday." and "Every Friday is test day, when we give practice tests to get ready for the [state's high-stakes test]. We practice all week and give the test on Friday. Our kids are getting better and better."

Has school reform, and the catalytic effect of NCLB, come down to scores on a test, irrespective of real learning and deep-level mastery that is transferable to leading a productive adult life and having a healthy, informed society? If so, why worry about highly qualified teachers or spending four or five years preparing them, much less paying them $50,000 in salary and fringes? Just train paraprofessionals to give tests, provide remedial tutoring, give more tests, tutor again, and so on. Think of the money it would save. The whole thing could be done online, just like higher education. And then we might not even have to operate traditional schools. The savings would be mind-boggling. *Scary, isn't it?*

■ BLOOM'S TAXONOMY

One of the best ways to make teachers comfortable with levels of cognitive demand is to ask them to apply Bloom's Taxonomy to the teaching/learning activities in their *Unit Plans*. Bloom is relatively familiar to most teachers, and it is an ideal advance organizer for the varied levels of mental processes required of students by the new standards. When teachers are asked to identify examples from their own teaching of the various levels of Bloom, the discussion is rich and energetic. At times, there is healthy disagreement about which level a certain activity represents. Participants quickly discover that the distinctions are more grey than black-and-white and that the key lies in how much information a student is given versus how much he or she must construct. This discourse is invaluable in getting teachers to examine what they do. As an aside, some scholars have taken it upon themselves to update Bloom by switching the top two levels: Evaluation and Synthesis. In their judgment, Synthesis is the more constructive of the two and should be the higher level. We prefer to use the original version.

Sometimes, it helps to think of the Taxonomy as a continuum of mental processes rather than the six distinct silos in which it is typically published. This developmental approach not only helps teachers level their own activities, but they quickly see how each can be tweaked to move it to a different level. Naturally, it isn't necessary that every concept be taught at all six levels. But *which* level(s) to use is an important decision, and the key to using the Taxonomy to its greatest advantage.

Inevitably, one or more of those colorful laminated lists of "Bloom verbs" surfaces during a workshop. But once they become facile with the Taxonomy, participants realize the business end of each level is not the verb but what students are expected to do with the information. As an example, these colorful lists always relegate the verb list to the Knowledge level. But when high school students "List three reasons why cloning may be morally wrong," they are thinking at the Evaluation level. Or the verb *combine* typically sits in the Synthesis column. But if students combine root words and affixes to form new words, they are operating at the Comprehension level.

Table 5.4 displays a quick snapshot of the Taxonomy, including definitions and a few examples. On the pages that follow, we provide the definitions and criteria for each level and several sets of concepts developed through the six levels.

Knowledge

Although it is the most basic level, Knowledge is the workhorse for the entire Taxonomy in that it powers and sustains the other levels. Students are functioning at this level when specific, literal, factual detail is required, either from memory or by looking it up. No interpretation, reflection, evaluation, or higher-order association is involved. Each Knowledge activity is situation specific, and transfer is not a priority. Some general Knowledge-level tasks include the following:

Table 5.4 Bloom's Taxonomy: Basic Definitions and Distinguishing Criteria

Knowledge	Comprehension	Application	Analysis	Synthesis	Evaluation
recall information from memory; file and retrieve literal detail as stated	put information into own words (i.e., explain, translate, paraphrase, summarize); use given prompts, formulas, or cues to solve problems; make verifiable predictions	solve problems, form hypotheses, or locate information without prompts, formulas, or cues	separate a concept, idea, or object into component parts to determine how each part works together to comprise the whole	rearrange or combine information to create a process or product new to the student	make a judgment about the value or worth of an object, idea, concept, etc. using a set of valid criteria

Examples

Knowledge	Comprehension	Application	Analysis	Synthesis	Evaluation
list the steps to how a bill becomes a law	explain to a younger child how a bill becomes a law, giving relevant examples	formulate a series of action steps to repeal or amend a specific rule in the school or law in the community	examine a current bill being proposed as a law; which portions are likely to be objectionable to the democrats, republicans, and special interest groups; what are viable compromises?	write a bill that could become a law to address an important social or economic issue (e.g., voting, abuse of the Internet, school funding, etc.)	decide the merits of a law or a bill (dealing with an important social or economic issue) in terms of equity, cost-benefit, and impact
⇧	⇧	⇧	⇧	⇧	⇧

Note: Students working at these two levels are working "inside" the material given by an author or the teacher; activities are situation-specific and have low rates of transfer.

Note: Students working at these four levels are working "outside" the material given by an author or the teacher; they are applying or extending what they have learned to *new situations*. Even if the activities are situation-specific, the rate of transfer to other situations gets progressively higher.

♦ recount a series of facts or details (e.g., number, letter, historic, scientific);

♦ read information presented in a table, chart, or graph;

♦ describe or characterize an object, person, and so on, using literal terms, details;

♦ complete the template of a written document that requires literal information (e.g., application, resume); and

♦ recite a rhetorical piece (e.g., a poem, treaty, formula, law, theorem, scientific principle).

Comprehension

Although it is one link above Knowledge on the food chain, Comprehension is really short-term learning; it is situation specific, requires prompting to use again, and the rate of application or transferability is quite low. Students are using the Comprehension level when they put information into their own words; i.e., translate, paraphrase, explicate, or rephrase what has been said, viewed, heard, or read. There is some need to interpret, associate, and make low-level inferences but *within* the confines of the material. Students are given formulas or algorithms to solve problems, and they follow a prescribed set of steps to complete the work. However, in contrast to Knowledge, which requires students to work from memory in an automatic way, students working at the Comprehension level have run the information through their own filters and can select from among options to process information and to arrive at solutions. Some general Comprehension-level tasks include the following:

♦ solve math or science problems using a formula provided by the text or teacher;

♦ explain a scientific process or historic event;

♦ paraphrase or summarize a passage, speech, rule, or dialogue;

♦ make a verifiable prediction about a text, an event, or a person based on partial information; and

♦ compose a written piece from a formula prewrite.

Application

Probably the most difficult and frequently misunderstood level, Application is the first rung of the higher-order thinking ladder. Where Knowledge and Comprehension occur inside the material provided by the teacher or text and include low levels of transfer, when students work at the Application level, they are operating outside or beyond the material and are knee-deep in transfer. In fact, they are using what they have learned to solve new or unfamiliar problems. Students are functioning at the Application level when they solve problems, generate viable hypotheses, or address dilemmas for which there is not an automatic, formulistic solution. Typically, there are multiple approaches to solving the problem, developing the hypotheses, or approaching the quandary, and students select from among the options. In essence, they are constructing meaning for themselves as opposed to restating (Knowledge) or paraphrasing (Comprehension) someone else's meaning. In Mathematics and Science, they are solving problems without being given the formula(s) or the prompt(s) as to what they must do. Students must sort out the problem with all that they know to decide what is appropriate to use and how to use it. Remember that in Comprehension, the formula(s) or leads are provided. Some general Application-level tasks include the following:

♦ Decide how best to determine the dimensions and area of an irregular-shaped object or area (e.g., to determine how much water is needed for a swimming pool, what size air conditioner to buy for an L-shaped basement, how much equipment can be fit into a 12-by-20-foot storage shed that is one third full).

♦ Reorganize or reclassify objects (events, ideas, etc.) in ways other than are typically found (e.g., Civil War battles by military strategy rather than whether won by the North or South; toys that enable children to learn versus those that are mainly for entertainment).

♦ Prepare an alternative interpretation of a passage, rule, speech, or other piece of writing, provided in a different context (e.g., how the story would have ended had the main character made another decision; how the northern border of the U.S. might be different had the English *lost* the French and Indian War).

♦ Compare and contrast facts and inferences resulting from observations (e.g., which age groups tend to remain in the fast food restaurants to eat versus take their meals out; how can our knowledge of bats be helpful in aerial warfare; what might be some ways to benefit from floating asteroids).

♦ Generate hypotheses as to the possible reason for phenomena or events, including action-steps to test them.

♦ Prepare a written piece using an organizational pattern appropriate to the prompt, including a prewrite.

Analysis

We joke that if we gave teachers $10.00 every time they use the verb *analyze* but collected it back each time they used it incorrectly, we'd come out ahead. In the same way everyone calls all tissues "Kleenex," teachers oftentimes incorrectly think every activity above memorization is analysis—or at least call it that. We've discovered it's because they were never shown Bloom's definition of *Analysis*. Most people think *analyze* means to tear apart or divide into component parts. But that's only half right, according to what Bloom himself wrote in his original treatise [As noted earlier, each component is fully validated in the research, and annotated descriptions of each cite are available from the authors on request]. The complete definition is to examine a concept (event, idea, etc.) for the purpose not only to identify its components but to discover how each component relates to the other and how they work together to comprise the whole. When thinking at the Analysis level, students demonstrate their deep-level understanding of complex people, places, objects, actions, events, and states of being by examining and explaining the relationships between and among them. In contrast to inferences made in Comprehension (which are drawn from the detail of the material and can be more like opinions), the inferences made in Analysis go beyond the material and are supported by objective evidence, both from the material and from outside sources. Some general Analysis-level tasks include the following:

♦ Conduct an "error analysis" of a word problem to determine whether errors exist and (if so) what they are (e.g., the overall approach, computation, the order of operations), how the error(s) would have been avoided, how the error affected the final answer, and whether there are alternate ways to solve the problem.

♦ Analyze a complete work of fiction to determine how each of the literary elements (i.e., character, setting, plot events) and the author's style (i.e., language, mechanics, rhetorical devices) work together to achieve the overall effect of the piece.

♦ Analyze a complete work of nonfiction to determine how each of the conventions (i.e., the thesis or controlling ideas, the supporting details, key transitions, rhetorical devices, language, organizational pattern, etc.) work together to achieve the overall effect of the piece.

♦ Analyze a scientific article (e.g., on using DNA in criminal investigations) to distinguish facts from hypotheses, that is, viable hunches about the "why and how" of a puzzlement of inquiry (contrasted with opinions, which can be more subjective and represent lower-order thinking).

♦ Distinguish logical (consistent, supported) from illogical (inconsistent, unsupported) arguments, inferences, and conclusions; discern propaganda techniques in a political campaign speech.

♦ Compare and contrast the specific and implied provisions of two or more documents not previously compared (using the internal elements of each item as the basis for these original comparisons; e.g., Lincoln's "First Inaugural Address" on March 4, 1861—assuring the southern states he would not interfere with slavery—and his "Emancipation Proclamation" on January 1, 1863—abolishing slavery).

Synthesis

Bloom defines *Synthesis* as combining ideas and details in an original or new way—new to the student, not necessarily the universe—to accomplish a specific purpose. Students create an original set of relationships for a unique pattern or structure. Compared with Comprehension, where students rearrange traditional concepts and ideas within the material being considered, students working at the Synthesis level are constructing new and original meanings that extend beyond the material. Some general Synthesis–level tasks include the following:

♦ Bring together mathematical, scientific, political, historic, economic, cultural, linguistic, and/or literary concepts or ideas in doable ways that have not (in the student's experience) been linked. Examples include (a) discover an original way to solve a mathematics problem; (b) propose an alternate school funding plan; (c) conduct an original scientific experiment, for example, to identify which drinking fountain has the most bacteria; (d) create an original sculpture; and (e) compose and present a stage play.

♦ Rearrange given information into a new application (e.g., increasing the use of the military for prevention of conflict and peacetime enterprises, harnessing the energy of asteroids to provide fuel and other energy for the earth).

♦ Create a new category or pattern (e.g., type of television talk show).

♦ Create a new formula or algorithm (e.g., foolproof ways to locate and use primary and secondary research for a report; a humane, legal, and preventive way to deal with juvenile crime).

Evaluation

Shortly behind Analysis, *Evaluation* is the most misunderstood and misused of the levels. Many users mistakenly assume that if a student expresses an opinion, he or she is indeed performing at the Evaluation level. A closer look at what Bloom himself intended for Evaluation reveals that its significance, and the reason he considered it the highest level stage of cognitive processing, lies in its requirement that students apply viable and rigorous criteria to render an opinion as to the quality or worth of something.

At times, students will use internal evidence—that is, the logic, consistency, and accuracy within the material—to support their opinions. At other times, they will use external evidence, or comparing the material with other recognized work or the opinions of acknowledged experts in the relevant field. In some case, they will use both.

Unlike the other five levels, Evaluation commits a student morally to another person (the author or originator of the thing being evaluated) or society as a whole. In essence, the student is taking a public position that may affect how others hereafter perceive an idea, product, or person (including the one giving the evaluation). Granted, in the safety of the classroom, a student's judgment will not result in life or death, the loss of prestige, or the denial of a property or civil right. But students should learn to use the same thorough, introspective, and fact-based type of reasoning as that used by any trial judge, movie critic, or consumer advocate: anyone who interprets the law, enforces human rights, helps consumers make choices, or shapes public opinion.

In addition, this level of thinking takes students into that sensitive realm of making value judgments and can involve them in considering something or someone based on their integrity, honesty, worth, and merit. In the past, nearly every social, political, and scientific issue was fair game for students to consider, but in the present climate of caution about delving into family and religious values, many of these are off-limits. This is an unfortunate irony, because students should become knowledgeable about such life-changing issues as a military draft, gay rights, Medicare, abortion, and evolution versus intelligent design, but schools must include them with extreme caution.

This is certainly not to say that schools should abandon activities at the Evaluation level. We find that in the *Unit Plans* devised by teachers in our training, there are plenty of not-so-risky areas in which students can think at the Evaluation level. Students should learn to take an informed (by criteria) judgmental stand on important issues or ideas that forces them to define their own ethical and moral beliefs and values. They should articulate a clear-cut position and develop it with viable evidence and support (both internal and external), including an acknowledgment of the opposing point(s) of view. Some general Evaluation-level tasks include the following:

♦ Critique a written, oral, or artistic presentation (e.g., news casts, movies, TV shows, paintings or sculptures, music, dance, drama, print and online materials) using established criteria but also including one's own supported opinion.

♦ Distinguish between products that do and do not adhere to prescribed criteria for merit, value, or worth, citing evidence for the distinction.

♦ Articulate an opinion about a substantive issue based on given or original criteria (e.g., school uniforms, stem-cell research); include opposing points of view, giving the relative merits of each.

♦ Judge the merit, worth, and/or quality of an item (object, event, action, decision, etc.) based on established guidelines (e.g., judging science fair projects, peer review of compositions).

♦ Set standards for ethical or moral decision making (e.g., the required behavior of elected public officials, a code of conduct for scientists conducting research with live animals).

■ SUMMARY

This chapter has addressed the INPUT section of the *Unit Plan* format—specifically, the *Motivation* and *Information* quadrants. We provided explanations of each criterion and offered several examples, one of which was a sample unit on Africa that we used to illustrate all of the criteria for the two quadrants, at least as far as the initial *Unit Plans* are to be developed. In addition, samples of Motivation activities and personal student goals were also included. The final section of the chapter provided a discussion of Bloom and the use of the Taxonomy to help teachers distinguish among levels of thinking and to establish a readiness for Differentiation. We felt this would make an excellent backdrop against which to begin the presentation of the Best Practices. Several examples are provided for teachers to adapt.

Chapter 6 will address the Learning Constructs (or various cognitive scaffolds) found in the Best Practices research to help students construct their own meaning. Chapter 7 will present several Delivery Strategies from which teachers can select those that best match the *Performance Indicators* for the unit. Together, these two chapters will capture how the **Instructional Design** process integrates the Best Practices research into the reform of classroom instruction.

6

Unit Planning

Learning Constructs

INTRODUCTION ■

At last count, the number of academic content standards promulgated by the nation's professional associations topped 3,000. It's been said that if the district curriculum included them all, a student's school career would approach a quarter-century. And with knowledge increasing exponentially every five years, the reality is that schools must prioritize what can be addressed within the time frame provided. This is not to diminish the importance of what's left; rather, it's an acknowledgment that part of the school's mission is to equip students with tools they'll need to learn on their own and for the rest of their lives. While many of these tools are habits of mind and self-discipline, several are academic processing techniques that can be taught.

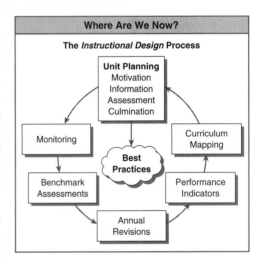

This chapter will discuss a series of Best Practices called **Learning Constructs**; they are an array of techniques used by students to process information and construct meaning for themselves. They are often referred to as *scaffolding*, or structures students use to reach the material. Once students become facile at using these Constructs, they can apply them independently to new situations both in and outside the classroom.

It relates to the adage about giving someone a single fish versus teaching him or her to use a pole. In past generations of school reform, this was called *learning to learn*, and there are still many school researchers who argue that competence in using these Constructs or independent learning tools is equal in importance to the mastery of content knowledge and skills. In recognition of this, many state content standards have included various Process skills as either a separate strand or to be integrated into the other academic strands.

In the **Instructional Design** process, these Learning Constructs can be easily inserted into the *Unit Plans* as the deep core of the INPUT side of the Plan, or the Motivation and Information quadrants. For each of the following Constructs, we will provide a definition or explanation and suggestions for how to build it into the *Unit* for use with students: Organizational Patterns, Summary, Note Taking, Math Problem–Analysis and Problem-Solving, Vocabulary and Context Clues, Graphic or Visual Organizers, Levels of Questioning, and Similarities and Differences.

■ ORGANIZATIONAL PATTERNS

What They Are

The successful reading and comprehension of text passages is challenging for good readers and virtually hopeless for poor readers. Worse, many of today's students assiduously avoid reading passages of any length, accustomed to an era of sound bites, graphics, and visual effects to convey meaning. We've had teachers tell us that their students complain if even bulleted information is too long. Whether working with students who lack the necessary comprehension skills and can't successfully derive meaning, or those who lack the necessary ambition and won't, teachers face a daunting task. How can they help students negotiate lengthy passages successfully without word-for-word reading? One coping skill is to scan the material to ferret out its *Organizational Pattern*, or the rhetorical structure used by the author to put his or her thoughts together. As can be seen in the explanations that follow, each Pattern represents a thinking construct, a way that information is organized verbally as well as in print. Although there is some overlap, each has a relatively discrete set of attributes or conventions that differentiates it from the others, and these distinguishing attributes must be clearly understood by students if they are to recognize the logic behind each Pattern when an author has used it. This will also provide students with an advantage in developing their skill narrative, expository, descriptive, and persuasive writing skills.

The discussion of these Patterns should begin as early as possible, well before students read on their own. Thus, in the next section, **How to Use With Students**, we include special notes to primary teachers. We understand that most primary students aren't required to read complex text independently, but several Pre–K through Grade 2 teachers with whom we have worked report considerable success (a) reading to their students and then debriefing on these patterns, (b) using basic versions of the *Patterns* to present verbal explanations and information, and (c) asking students to restate the information, including the *Pattern*, albeit in developmentally appropriate language.

Patterns A through D below are the most common.

A. **The Fictional Narrative.** Although the majority of the text in reference is nonfiction, many authors use the narrative structure, borrowed from fiction. Using the **Fictional Narrative** format is an advance organizer to help students understand the concept of an Organizational Pattern. In prose and drama, the narrative pattern includes characterization, setting details, plot events, and sometimes flashback, foreshadowing, dialect, and so on. As the earliest type of reading material to which students are exposed, it is typically the easiest to recognize and interpret. However, mature stylistic techniques such as parallel plot lines; multifaceted characterization; multiple, shifting settings; and use of symbolism and figurative language may make even the common narrative challenging for poor and/or disinterested readers. Most Language Arts teachers address the conventions of fiction (as well as its various stylistic variations) during their analysis and interpretation sessions. But the **Fictional Narrative** as a *Pattern* is still the best hook to begin understanding nonfiction.

B. **The Nonfiction Narrative** has similar elements to the **Fictional Narrative**, but it is based on an actual account or series of experiences that actually happened, presented in chronological sequence. In contrast to its fictional counterpart, the **Nonfiction Narrative** is not distinguished by intricacies in style and deep-level introspection. After all, the intent is not so much to be entertained or emotionally engaged as to be informed. But the narrative elements of character, a sequence of plot events, conflicts, and settings serve to engage the reader and provide cognitive "pegs" on which to hang the expository information. Some of the best media examples of this technique are found on the History Channel. Viewers learn about historic events via the **Nonfiction Narrative**, augmented by appropriate music and sound effects, authentic costume, and the use of flashback and foreshadowing to heighten the dramatic effect.

C. **Main Idea** followed by **Supporting Details** is the nonfiction *Pattern* most frequently encountered by students. It consists of a controlling idea, stated at the outset, followed by a series of clarifying, defining, and explanatory details; it usually includes examples and illustrations. Most authors use this format for its simplicity, directness, and clarity. After all, most nonfiction authors hope their readers will be impressed by the information they provide, not the particular style of writing.

D. **Supporting Details** leading to a **Main Idea** is the reverse of the above (C). Authors of nonfiction who use this *Pattern* feel their message will be best delivered if they provide a series of examples that illustrate or provide evidence that build a case for and then culminate in the main idea.

Within these major *Patterns* are several *Subpatterns* or *Specialty Patterns* that give each piece its distinct character, the cognitive structure or internal logic used by the author to make his or her point. Unfortunately, it is often this very logic that seems so illogical to struggling readers. These **Subpatterns** are described below.

1. **Chronological Sequence.** One of the most common nonfiction *Patterns* is to present items or events in the time order they occurred. It is called *Chronological Sequence*, and it is the preferred format of most History texts, upper-level Literature anthologies, and biography/autobiography. Authors are careful to place the events in the context of the point in time represented to help students understand the links and interrelationships among political, artistic, economic, scientific, and/or social events of the time. For example, the Renaissance cannot be fully understood apart from the entire constellation of scientific, political, and social events within which it occurred.

2. **Description.** Much of the descriptive text students will read is in English class and is typically found in fiction as careful, intricate detail about characters or settings. But many nonfiction authors also choose descriptive writing, and its appeal to the senses, to add perceptual clarity to their thesis and to establish a vivid mental and sensory image of what they are presenting. For example, the most memorable accounts of the Great Depression include vivid sensory details of sight, sound, smell, texture, and location to help readers vicariously experience what the people going through it must have suffered. Such detail provides the reader with a permanent mental and psychological image of the starvation, homelessness, and desperation that is almost unimaginable in a country that now boasts so much prosperity.

3. **Compare-Contrast.** Sometimes, two or more ideas or objects are made clearer when each is considered in comparison and contrast to the other. In this *Pattern*, the author provides parallel details about each idea to show likenesses and to reveal differences. For example, in comparing percentages, decimals, and fractions, the similarities include the following: (a) all three are part of the whole, (b) all three show proportion as well as portion, and (c) all three can be converted among each other. Among the differences are that fractions are based on 1s, decimals on 10s, and percentages on 100s.

4. **Cause-Effect.** In this format, the author either implies or directly states that one event or condition is the result of one or more other events or conditions. Evidence is presented to support at least one cause-effect relationship and sometimes secondary causal relationships as well. The text may also present a chain of events that are part of a domino effect, and students are expected to understand that one consequence may indeed be a cause for the next event, and so on. For example, to explain why the leaves change color in the fall, an author might point out that leaves are green in the summer due to the chlorophyll they contain, which is a byproduct of the tree's food-making process. In the fall, when trees rest and no

longer make food, the chlorophyll disappears from the leaves, leaving the gold and brown color. These colors were there all along but were covered by the green chlorophyll. Some maple leaves turn a bright red from trapped glucose that is changed into red by the sunlight and cool night temperatures. The terms *cause* and *effect* were never used, but the relationships are nonetheless apparent.

5. **Persuasion.** In conventional persuasive text, the author presents a controversial issue, takes a position, and supports it with compelling evidence, emotional appeals, and/or logic. Some authors include the opposing argument and then refute it. In other cases, the author remains neutral, presenting enough information about each position for the reader to make up his or her own mind, or at least decide to look further into the issue. For example, an author might attempt to persuade the reader that the current two-party system is ruining American democracy because important governmental decisions are made on the basis of party affiliation and not what is best for the country. An author might take a position and so attempt to persuade the reader, or he or she may present both sides of the issue with the intent to prompt the reader into careful consideration. With persuasive text, the reader must be on the alert for author bias, even when the author claims to be neutral.

How to Use With Students

Once the use of *Organizational Patterns* becomes part of the learning culture in a building, it will not be necessary to reteach it each year to every student, particularly if students begin to use it at the primary level. But until it becomes second nature to the students, it should be retaught in the fall and revisited throughout the year to keep it one of students' most active and potent Learning Constructs. Bear in mind, the *Organizational Patterns* are not only the methods for assembling text; each is also a cognitive structure or boilerplate format to think about and process information. In recognition of their seminal importance to the delivery of verbal as well as printed information, these *Patterns* reappear in several other Learning Constructs, namely the *Summary, Note Taking,* and *Graphic Organizers.* Throughout the chapter, we will emphasize these links to make the case that time spent on helping students identify specific *Patterns,* first as a way to think about information and then as the way an author chooses to organize the text, pays off in multiple dividends. It is recommended that the following strategies be used by teachers to address *Organizational Patterns:*

Strategy 1: Draw attention to the concept of Organizational Patterns as a way to think about information.

Most teachers do this anyway, but they may not use the label *Organizational Pattern.* We've seen it referred to as *cognitive structure, cognitive demand,* or *patterns of thought.* Whatever it's called, the important thing is to draw students' attention to the fact that information isn't typically just thrown together at random. It is usually organized in a way that makes it comprehensible to the listener or reader in the first place and then makes it easier to recall afterwards. The most prevalent *Patterns* listed below are the ones addressed in the book.

- Fictional Narrative
- Nonfiction Narrative
- Main Idea Supported by Detail
- Simple Listing
- Supporting Detail Leading to Main Idea
- How-To
- Chronological Sequence
- Description
- Compare-Contrast
- Cause-Effect
- Problem-Solution
- Persuasion

The best strategy for teachers to help students become aware of these thinking and composition *Patterns* is to use them to present information and to point them out in common text read by the entire class. Students should hear and see the appropriate label, and they should also see the graphic representation for each *Pattern*. For example, the Venn diagram represents *compare-contrast*, the flowchart represents *chronological sequence*, and so on. Table 6.3 illustrates a visual or graphic organizer for each *Pattern*. In addition, the final section of this chapter is devoted to the *Graphic Organizer* as a Learning Construct. What follows next are a few suggestions about how to help students distinguish among the *Patterns*.

Fictional Narrative. The conventional elements of fiction work well. The use of character, setting, and plot details (including at least one conflict) are relatively familiar. Childhood stories, movies, and TV sitcoms are helpful illustrations. But be sure to advise students that the narrative, as presented by an author, is not always sequential. Authors who use the flashback and/or foreshadowing techniques deliberately take the reader back and forth within the actual sequence of events. *Note to Primary Teachers:* Story telling and retelling—observing the basic conventions of who, what, where, and when—is an effective readiness for nonfiction. But be careful that students do not see *fantasy* as synonymous with *fiction* and *facts* as the critical attribute of *nonfiction*. We've seen situations where these have been mistakenly used as the distinguishing features of fiction and nonfiction. Most fiction includes some basis in fact, and not every work of fiction contains fantasy.

Nonfiction Narrative. Most of the conventions of the Fictional Narrative are included, but the material is strictly nonfiction in that it is actual or real. Notice we avoid the term *factual* because fiction also contains facts. Good teaching examples are the TV documentaries that attempt to dramatize the events in reference. Other good examples are biographical and autobiographical sketches, which, by the way, are special favorites of high-stakes test publishers. *Note to Primary Teachers:* With a strong sense of story and grasp of the elements of fiction, students can begin to understand nonfiction stories about science, social studies, and math concepts, made memorable by their association with characters, setting details, plot events, and an occasional problem (conflict) to resolve. By the end of Grade 1 in some districts, students read on-level nonfiction accounts, simple though they are. These early *Patterns* can then become templates for more complex passages that will appear in actual content texts.

Main Idea Supported by Detail. Students should be shown how the big idea or thesis appears early in the text and is followed by an array of details that explain, develop, or support it. What's tricky here is that the author may use other *Patterns* such as *cause-effect, compare-contrast,* or *description* to provide this support. Be sure this doesn't trip them up. The conventional outline is a good physical prompt, and a metaphor about legs on a table or pillars holding up a roof are helpful. *Note to Primary Teachers:* Where possible, students should at least hear (and ideally read) actual text that uses the Main Idea-Supporting Detail format. Present information to students using the language of this *Pattern* (i.e., big idea, supporting detail) and call it by name while writing nonfiction stories on chart paper or as Big Books. This early activity will instill the mind-set that much of life's information is presented in this way.

Simple Listing. Very few authors make life this simple, but occasionally students will encounter it. For example, "The United Nations consist of _____, _____, etc." While some lists are truly simple in that they are random, many are not. Students should be alerted to look for an order within the list. The most common is alphabetical, but some authors might use size (or other numerical value), others might use date of membership, and so on. The term *simple* is often a mislabel.

Supporting Detail Leading to Main Idea. The reverse of Main Idea-Supporting Detail, this *Pattern* is being used with greater frequency, perhaps to keep readers' attention by holding them in suspense while drawing them closer and closer to the thesis or big idea. The supporting detail typically consists of examples or incidents. Good teaching examples include sightings of UFOs, a list of government acts leading to a culminating revolution, or crime scenarios that argue for better security in schools. *Note to Primary Teachers:* Since many of the television shows early learners watch and the fairy tales they hear use this event > event > event > big idea scenario, typically in 3s, they will benefit from hearing and retelling nonfiction stories that use this *Pattern*. In addition, they should create such stories of their own, again seeing them in print as they do. But it is important that little ones can accurately distinguish make-believe (only some of which is fantasy) from that which is actual, real, or truly did occur.

How-To. This *Pattern* is extremely common, and its most recognizable feature is that it clarifies the task at the outset and then proceeds to give step-by-step instructions as to how it can be accomplished. From the first day of preschool, most students are exposed to this format, both verbally and in writing.

Chronological Sequence. The distinguishing attribute of this *Pattern* is "events placed in time order." An excellent teaching method is the *time line,* particularly the multitiered time line to help students see multiple factors that affect the original sequence of events. Most students recognize the Pattern with little difficulty, but when they cannot, immediate and in-depth intervention is needed. A sense of time-order is one of the most fundamental requisite skills for other learning. As students mature, they should also be able to distinguish chronology that just happens to be in that order versus chronology whose sequence of events are causally related. A quick teaching example is the following two lists:

Noncausal—Sequence Random	Causal—Sequence Important
Saturday chores—	Preparing for a party—
Clean my room	Plan the party
Wash the car	Send invitations; get RSVPs
Tidy the garage	Prepare the house
Mow the yard	Decorate

Note to Primary Teachers: Young students are typically inundated by this *Pattern*, but seeing it in print, reading it aloud, and seeing the events on a time line are excellent ways to prepare prereaders to recognize and interpret it in their textbooks.

Description. The major distinguishing feature of descriptive text is the focus on sensory details: visual, auditory, olfactory, taste, and touch or texture. In some cases, atmospheric details are also featured. Typically, the adjective and adverb certainly show off, but in the hands of a skillful descriptive writer, the nouns and verbs are equally remarkable. The best teaching technique is to give students practice identifying the descriptive and sensory details that occur in their own daily experiences. *Note to Primary Teachers:* Most pre- and beginning readers love the opportunity to think of imaginative words. They become experts in supplying all sorts of adjectives and suggesting creative action verbs. If these words are captured in their Big Book stories or wall chart text, and it becomes clear to them how such words create pictures in the mind of the reader, primary students will be better prepared to react similarly when they read such descriptive detail on their own.

Compare-Contrast. This *Pattern* is fairly distinct; the author is describing how two or more things (concepts, ideas, etc.) are alike and/or different in terms of parallel attributes. Students first need to identify the attributes being compared (e.g., size, number, color, function) and then be sure they can assign the detail of each attribute to its respective "comparee." Some authors list all of the attributes for one thing first and then the same for the other(s). Or the author may describe each attribute, alternating between (or among) the things being compared. Students need practice with both types. *Note to Primary Teachers:* Pre- and early reading students should have multiple experiences hearing about and discussing likenesses and differences between two things: how two things are compared and contrasted. Students should learn to "tell" nonfiction stories that focus on two objects and stress the parallel likenesses and differences between them.

Cause-Effect. One of the more subtle *Patterns,* cause and effect, is often difficult to spot. In many cases, the text includes some cause and effect, but it may not be the dominant or only *Pattern* in the passage. But even if the entire passage is not devoted to it, the use of cause and effect is an important feature in the author's presentation and not to be missed. The best teaching technique is to practice with students using fairly obvious cause and effect relationships, helping them to identify which is the cause, which the effect, and any multiple causations. Some authors call the presence of multiple causation *chaining*, and others refer to it as *cascading*. One caution for teachers is to help students distinguish causation from correlation and coincidence, for example, the fact that 10 of the 14 cars towed to Ben's garage in the past 6 months were red is coincidental, the fact that 13 of the 14 were from the same city block is correlational, and the fact that they were all illegally parked is causation. *Note to Primary Teachers:* Cause-effect is an obscure concept for all students, and younger children in particular often have difficulty grasping the actual causes for specific events as well as the actual result of others. Teachers should help young students by modeling these relationships using very clear and simple illustrations (e.g., "if we cut in line, we lose our turn" or "snow happens when cold temperatures makes the rain freeze," or "if we break this object in half, we have two"). It will take patience and considerable practice for young readers to master the cause-effect *Pattern* in when they see it in print.

Problem-Solution. Most science and social studies texts use the familiar format of "Here's a problem, and here's how it was solved." Most students easily recognize this *Pattern*, and it is not extremely difficult. The use of several examples typically suffices. What may be tricky is the inclusion of several alternate solutions, particularly if more than one is viable. Helping students distinguish among multiple solutions, recognizing why each may work or why it won't, can be challenging for students.

Persuasion. Persuasive text is another fairly obvious *Pattern*. At its core is a controversial issue (or problem) and at least one argument as to how it should be resolved. Some authors take a definite position, while others remain neutral. Either way, the object is to convince the reader of the merits of one position and the demerits of the opposite one. But the reader's "crap detector" must be intact to be certain that the supportive evidence offered is valid, complete, and relevant. Persuasive text often suffers from bias (even if subtle) and any number of fallacies in reasoning. This is known as propaganda, and students must learn to recognize it if they are to be intelligent consumers of information. Teachers should alert students to the 10 or 12 most prevalent forms of propaganda, post them on the classroom wall, and refer to them often. *Note to Primary Teachers:* As with cause-effect, mastering the persuasion Pattern may be developmentally too difficult for beginning readers. But little ones do have a profound sense of fairness and equity, and they can be shown how to state and support their opinion about an issue. Furthermore, they can select one viewpoint over the other, including a *why* statement (e.g., "I think Shawna should not be allowed to play since she did not eat her snack." or "I think the Indians should have been allowed to keep their land since they were there first.") Again, using the persuasive *Pattern* in class talks and putting opinions in print, compared with facts, helps primary students develop such habits of logic that later are recognizable in text.

Strategy 2: Use sample passages to train students.

Teachers should use sample passages from their textbooks, the Internet, news stories, or supplemental materials—all of the print sources to be used by their students. It is prudent to tackle only two or three *Patterns* at once, spreading them out a bit to avoid overloading the circuits. There will be opportunities in every *Unit* to revisit previously studied *Patterns* as well as to encounter new ones. They are everywhere. The sample texts should be made into overheads (with students having their own copy) and analyzed as a whole class. As the teacher marks the overhead, the students mark their copies. It may take several examples and repeated practice, but eventually, students will come to recognize the key words and syntactical cues that distinguish each *Pattern* from the others. If every student does not master every *Pattern*, all is not lost. Knowing a few of them is better than none at all, and a majority of students will master nearly all of them. Using generic and simple samples is fine at first (or for remediation), but teachers need to be continually on the lookout for print and electronic passages students will actually encounter.

For primary grades, the samples should be only a few lines, similar to the length of passages teachers read to them and that they see in print. At the intermediate through high school stages, the teaching samples should be at least 300 to 400 words, the approximate length students are required to read on their high-stakes tests. For students who are overwhelmed by the prospect, shorter, single-paragraph samples excerpted from longer passages work well as a start.

Gradually, these excerpts can be extended, and before they know it, the students who had struggled earlier can get through the entire passage successfully. Some passages may reflect multiple *Patterns*, and that's okay. But we suggest not using these in the initial training; save them for later. Or they may be a perfect Differentiation strategy for students who need a challenge.

Strategy 3: Have students be on the lookout for passages.

Before long, the students themselves will be able to bring in examples. Once they learn to recognize some of the *Patterns*, students suddenly notice them everywhere. Try offering a few points of extra credit for correctly labeled and course-relevant samples; this will be particularly good for struggling readers. They'll see the points as a great freebie, and only the teacher need know that in looking for *Patterns*, the strugglers are actually strengthening their reading muscles and exposing themselves to print material.

Strategy 4: Combine the use of Organizational Patterns with other Learning Constructs.

In the sections that follow, we will present the *Summary* and *Note Taking*, both Learning Constructs linked to the *Organizational Pattern*. Later in this chapter, Table 6.3 displays how to coordinate all three of these Learning Constructs, and how to connect them with the appropriate Visual or Graphic representation.

◾ WRITING SUMMARY

What It Is

The *Summary* has long been the yardstick of choice to measure student comprehension of a text passage or excerpt from Literature. And the Best

Practices research has determined that *Summary* is one of the essentials for students to construct their own meaning. Most high-stakes and norm-referenced tests include the *Summary* as an extended or constructed response item. But the *Summary* has had difficulty on at least two levels. One, students are frequently misled to think that the format for all summarization is *who, what, when, where, what,* and *how*. Although this may work for **fiction**, unless the piece being summarized includes the *why* and *how*, they cannot be included. The format for the *Summary* of **nonfiction** is actually the *Organizational Pattern* of the piece. Second, students often confuse *Summary* with its sister, the Retell. Although they are closely related, the Retell is an event-by-event account of the passage, as a video might portray. By contrast, the *Summary* is a synopsis or snapshot of key details. Table 6.3 illustrates the link between the *Organizational Pattern* and the *Summary*.

How to Use With Students

To appreciate the contrast between the *Summary* of **fiction** and **nonfiction**, students need to practice both. One template for summarizing fiction is illustrated in Table 6.1. This format not only guides students in writing summaries of fiction but, when compared to the *Summary* formats for **nonfiction**, helps them see the distinction between the two.

Table 6.1   Organizing Rubric for Summary of Fiction

		(Summary as written by a middle schooler)
Lead:	The first sentence should identify the selection by title, genre, subject (if not obvious), author(s), and date of publication, if available.	"The Ransom of Red Chief" is a short story written by O'Henry in 1910. The story occurs near a western town, and it is told by Sam, one of the main characters. He and his partner, Bill, kidnap a young boy for ransom, and the three hide in a cave to wait for the payoff. But things do not go as planned. The boy calls himself Red Chief, and he spends his kidnapping doing all sorts of ornery and painful things to Sam and Bill. After two days of being tortured by Red Chief, the kidnappers not only do not collect the ransom they asked for, they actually pay the boy's father to take him back.
Who:	One sentence should identify the main character(s) and/or narrator, indicating point of view.	
Where:	Another sentence should identify the setting(s) in which the piece occurs and indicate if there are shifts.	
When:	Along with the *where* should be the date in which the piece is set, the duration or time frame of the piece, and if flashbacks or foreshadowing have been included.	
What:	The key plot events should be *briefly* described; this is typically the most difficult part of the summary; students are inclined to *retell* the piece instead of *summarize* it.	
Author's Message:	**Only if it is so stated**; most authors of fiction *do not* tell the reader, preferring that the reader glean it from the text	

Summary of Nonfiction

Since the majority of the print and electronic material students read in school is nonfiction, the nonfiction *Summary* should be given priority as a Learning Construct. The most effective way to summarize nonfiction is to use its *Organizational Pattern* as the template. After all, *that* is the internal logic of the piece and the key to unlocking the author's message. Teachers need to give students practice summarizing **nonfiction**, written in several different *Patterns*. The length of the practice passages should be 300 to 500 words (adjusted to the developmental needs of the students). As with every Best Practice, we recommend that teachers provide corrective and affirmative feedback on each *Summary* so that students know if they are writing them correctly. At intervals, students should exchange *Summaries*, without revealing the *Organizational Pattern*. If properly written, the *Summary* should lead the partner to identify its *Pattern*. Three sample passages and *Summaries* are provided below. The ability to write a successful *Summary* is an important and empowering Learning Construct for every student.

Descriptive Passage: "The Discovery of King Tut's Tomb"

> The first sensation was the rushing sound of hot, escaping air and then the flicker of torches in a swirling mist of sand and dust. Carter was standing in the first and largest of four rooms, a 12 by 26 foot rectangle called the Antechamber. His position was just left of center along the long near-wall. The chamber was heaped with chairs, footstools, and chests of alabaster, ebony, and ivory. There were also strange couches of gilded wood in the form of animals, one of which was a cow and one a lion. Beneath the cow bed were egg-shaped food containers made of clay. . . . The second room was guarded by two gold-encrusted statues of Tutankhamen. Through this door lay the Burial chamber, the one holding the King's sarcophagus. It too was rectangular, measuring 18 by 22 feet, and was positioned perpendicular to the Antechamber. Tutankhamen's elaborately carved stone coffin rested inside a series of four nested wooden cases, each covered with gold leaf. Nested inside the rectangular stone coffin were three richly gleaming mummy-shaped coffins, one inside the other. The innermost of these coffins was solid gold, and it was in this last coffin that the actual mummy of the dead King was found. [His] head and shoulders . . . were covered in a solid gold mask inlaid with blue lapis lazuli, other semiprecious stones, and colored glass. The mask shows the king in a youthful, serene, and noble pose . . . wearing the ceremonial false beard and the striped head cloth of royalty. At the center of his brow is the royal cobra and vulture. The mummy itself was wrapped in 13 layers of linen bandages containing 143 precious gold and bejeweled objects, including necklaces, pendants, bracelets, rings, belts, gold-sheathed daggers, gold sandals, and slender golden tubes encasing the mummy's fingernails and toenails.

Sample Summary for Descriptive Passage

> "The Discovery of King Tut's Tomb" reveals a four-room treasure trove of unimaginable splendor. The sights, sounds, and smells of the tomb are brought to life as the author sets forth the precise location, size, features, texture, composition, and exact color of furniture, jewels, statues, weapons, and other artifacts. He provides rich and

vivid details about each object, particularly the king's mummy. Most of the ornamentation, clothing, protective devices, and precious gems with which Tut was buried were really well preserved.

Cause-Effect Passage: "The Rainbow"

The rainbow is one simple, lovely example of nature's atmospheric mysteries. You can usually see a rainbow after a rain shower or in the fine spray of a fountain or waterfall. Although our sunlight appears to be white, it is actually a blend or aggregate of colors, all the colors of the rainbow. We see the rainbow of multiple colors because millions of tiny raindrops act as mirrors and prisms on the sunlight. (Prisms are glass or plastic objects that bend light, splitting it into bands of color.) The bands of color form a perfect semicircle, and from the top edge to the bottom, the colors are always in the same order: red, orange, yellow, green, blue, indigo, and violet. The brightness and width of each band may vary from one minute to the next. The sky within the rainbow is lighter than the sky above the arc, as the light that forms the innermost or violet band is more spread out than the light that forms the top red band. In the morning, rainbows are always seen in the west, since the sunlight is in the east; likewise, the evening rainbows appear in the east, since the sun is in the west. For a rainbow to appear, the sun can be no higher than 420, or nearly halfway up the sky. If the sunlight is strong and the water droplets very small, a double rainbow may appear. This happens because the light is reflected twice in the water droplets. But in the second rainbow, the color bands are fainter and in the reverse order, as if to emulate or provide a mirror image of the first.

Sample Summary for Cause-Effect Passage

"The Rainbow" describes how and why the rainbow is formed. As sunlight strikes drops of water from rain or a fountain, the water acts like a prism and breaks the light into colors. The sky within the arc is brighter than the sky above the arc because the innermost violet band spreads the light out more than the outermost red band. Morning rainbows are seen in the west, since the sun is in the east; evening rainbows are seen in the east, since the sun sets in the west. If the sun is strong enough, the light may be reflected twice, resulting in two rainbows.

Compare-Contrast Passage: "Clothing in the Colonies"

The clothing of the American colonies varied from the north to the south. It reflected not only the differences in climate but in the religion and the ancestries of the settlers. The clothes most often seen in the New England colonies where the Puritans settled were very plain and simple. The materials were wool and linen, both very warm and sturdy. Rich or poor, they had strict rules about clothing; no bright colors, ruffles, or lace were allowed, and jewelry was strictly prohibited. The Puritan woman wore a long gray dress with a big white collar, cuffs, apron, and cap. A Puritan man wore baggy leather breeches (or knee-length trousers) and long woolen stockings. The adults and children dressed in the same type of clothing. In the middle colonies, the clothing ranged from the simple clothing of the Quakers

(Continued)

(Continued)

to the more colorful, loose-fitting outfits of the Dutch colonists. Similar to the Puritans, the Quaker religion required one's dress to be low-key and conservative. The Quakers wore clothing similar to the Puritans, except the men's coats and women's capes and hats were slightly more decorative with brass buttons and some lacing. But the Dutch women wore brightly colored dresses with fur trim and petticoats that made their skirts stand out. The men wore silver buckles on their shoes, their coattails were longer, and their hats were decked with curling feathers. The poorer people dressed plainly, similar to the Puritans. In the southern colonies, there were no religious rules about dress. The wealthy men wore brightly colored silk breeches and fancy silk stockings. Their coats were similarly colorful and made of silk or velvet. The women's gowns were made of the same fancy silks or velvet, and they were festooned with all sorts of ribbons, ruffles, and lace. The larger the diameter of their petticoats, the better. Both men and women wore powered periwigs tied in the back. As in the middle colonies, the poor people dressed much like the Puritans.

Sample Summary for Compare-Contrast Passage

"Clothing in the Colonies" compares what people wore in the three main sections of the colonial America. In New England, the rich and poor Puritans wore plain but sturdy clothing and allowed no lace or decoration. In the Middle colonies, the Quakers required the same low-key dress as the Puritans, except they allowed a bit of lace and some brass buttons. But the wealthy Dutch in the Middle colonies wore bold colors with fur trim and silver buckles. The poor people dressed plainly, much like the Puritans. In the Southern colonies, the wealthy French and Spanish wore clothing of brightly colored silks and velvet, and their garments were decorated with lace, ribbons, ruffles, and feathers. Like New England and the Middle colonies, the poor Southern colonials dressed in plain, drab garments similar to the Puritans.

■ NOTE TAKING

What It Is

In our experience, *Note Taking* is largely overlooked as one of those things that "everyone just does." Asking teachers if their students are good note takers brings a predictable "Are you kidding?" groan throughout the room. The follow-up questions, "So at what grade level do the students learn to take notes? and "Where does it appear in the curriculum?" bring a profound thud of silence, followed by much throat-clearing and noticing the patterns in the rug for the first time. The truth is, no one actually teaches students how to take notes. It falls on each teacher to do it him- or herself. And as convenient as it would be to leave it on the doorstep of language arts, its importance in every content area makes it a universal Learning Construct. Many teachers make an excellent case for the fact that students need to learn several note-taking strategies and to recalibrate their note taking to fit the various demands of each subject. And we agree. In fact, Table 6.2 illustrates three of the most common formats that teachers have shared with us over the years.

Table 6.2   Formats for Note Taking

Traditional Outline	in writing	Informal Outline

I. Big idea
   a. Subtopic (detail)
     1) example or subdetail
     2) example or subdetail
   b. Subtopic (detail)
     1) example or subdetail
     2) example or subdetail
   c. Subtopic (detail) etc.
II. Big Idea
   a. Subtopic (detail)
   b. Subtopic (detail)
   c. Subtopic (detail)
	⇦ typically used for traditional research papers, classical-format essays, or other expository writing
	
	typically used for nontraditional research papers, informal writing of all types; is a favorite prewrite ⇨
	
	in oral communication
	
	⇦ used for traditional or high-church sermon outlines, formal diplomatic speeches, where detail is the priority
	
	typically used for informal talks and presentations where clarity and brevity are priorities ⇨
	
	variation
	
	filling in portions of the outline in advance, and asking students to complete it from what they hear, read, or see
		Big Idea
		  ■ bullet (detail)
		  ■ bullet (detail)
		  ■ bullet (detail)
		
		Big Idea
		  ■ bullet (detail)
		  ■ bullet (detail)
		  ■ bullet (detail)
		
		Big Idea
		  ■ bullet (detail)
		  ■ bullet (detail)
		  ■ bullet (detail)

The Cornell Method	Regular Notes	Graphics, Reflections, Peer or Teacher Notes
This is the process of splitting the notebook paper in half or 2/3 and 1/3. Students use only the left portion for regular notes. The right side is used for reflections, graphics, summaries, etc. Or, it can be used for the teacher or peers to write notes to the student.	Class _____ Date ____ Topic _____	

But *Note Taking* is more than a decision about format; it is actually a matter of "sussing out" the *Organizational Pattern* as the internal logic or rhetorical structure of the materials. In fact, we encourage teachers to structure their lectures, explanations, and handouts using the appropriate *Organizational Pattern*. As shown in Table 6.2, there are direct and mutually strengthening links among the *Patterns*, the *Summary*, and *Note Taking*.

How to Use With Students

We encourage teachers to consciously work *Note Taking* into their *Unit Plans* as a means for students to process print and electronic text and to use as they listen to auditory or verbal information. For some students, *Note Taking* may well be a personal and/or an academic goal established at the outset in one or more *Units*. In our experience, the few teachers who don't complain about students' *Note Taking* are the ones who consistently review the notes, reinforcing students when they are on track and making specific suggestions when improvements are needed.

For young students, specific *Note Taking* lessons should be provided to allow teachers to model the various formats. For intermediate students, the teacher will need to be specific about the format to use, perhaps to the point of reviewing various formats throughout the year. Most important, students should be required to take notes in their journals or notebooks, and teachers should provide corrective and supportive feedback. For many students, the teacher actually helping them structure and organize their *Note Taking* and then giving them feedback as to how well they did it is a new idea altogether.

Granted, showing students how to take notes in several formats and to make adjustments on call will take time, and it will no doubt require additional practice and more checking than has been the case, but the extra effort will pay off in triplicate. Perhaps a building staff can agree to share the responsibility and disperse the practice across several classrooms.

■ MATH-PROBLEM ANALYSIS AND PROBLEM-SOLVING

What It Is

Problem-Solving in math is not only about arriving at an answer to a word problem but about what the problem is asking, what information is needed and not needed, and determining a method to solve it. It relies not as much on computational skill as experience with analyzing problem situations. By learning to analyze math problems as the precursor to *Problem-Solving*, students acquire ways of thinking, habits of persistence and curiosity, and confidence in unfamiliar situations that will serve them well outside the mathematics classroom. *Problem-Solving* is an integral part of all mathematics learning, and so it should not be an isolated *Unit* or strand of the mathematics curriculum. Rather, it should become how students work within each *Unit* of instruction.

Most mathematical concepts can be conceptualized number scenarios from the students' world. Good problem-solvers tend naturally to analyze numerical situations in mathematical terms and to propose solutions based on previous or similar situations they encountered. They first consider simple problems as a hook or enabler for solving more complicated problems. The following describes the developmental sequence for understanding the way mathematics works.

Addition/Subtraction

Students first encounter addition and then subtraction. To successfully work with contextualized mathematics, students must consider different ways to illustrate the same problems, in effect, how addition and subtraction are inverse operations. Traditionally, they are shown the following and asked to find the ***result***:

- Bob has 3 cookies. He is given 2 more cookies. How many cookies does he have now?

(Text continues on page 143)

Table 6.3 Links Among Organizational Patterns, Summary, Note Taking, and Relevant Graphic Organizers

Structure of Organizational Pattern	Format for Summary = Sentence	Note Taking	Visual/Graphic Organizer
Specific Detail → General Topic: detail or example detail or example } thesis idea (key concept) detail or example detail or example For example, show students a series of congruent figures in isolation and in context, including a description for and use of each; lead up to the concept of congruence	▪ synthesis of details or examples that support thesis ▪ thesis idea	} thesis idea or key concept	
General Topic → Specific Detail: thesis idea (key concept) } detail, example detail, example detail, example detail, example For example, start with the Salem Witch Trials followed by several details of what, how, where, and why; include results	thesis idea synthesis of details or examples to support	thesis idea (key concept) } detail detail detail	
Chronological Sequence (secondary) For example, the events of the Renaissance in Europe in the context of the political, economic, artistic, scientific, etc. events happening at the same time	event or cluster of events synthesis of lead-up events other contextual events happening simultaneously	Historic Economic Political Social	event > event > event > event event > event > event > event event > event > event > event event > event > event > event **Time line** **Flowchart**

(Continued)

139

Table 6.3 (Continued)

Structure of Organizational Pattern	Format for Summary = Sentence	Note Taking	Visual/Graphic Organizer

Problem/Solution

problem (puzzlement) (quandary) — various facets: how, when, where (etc.) — criteria for solution (each facet) — solution of "best fit"

For example, present a quandary (e.g., the class' pet gerbil bites); ask students to identify the facts of the problem, identify the criteria for a solution, pose several solutions, and then apply the criteria to select the best one

Format for Summary: synthesis of problem, including various facets, criteria for solution, and solution of "best fit"

Note Taking:
Problem
• ___
• ___
• ___

solution criteria
• ___
• ___
• ___
etc.

best solution

Visual/Graphic Organizer: Problem Criteria Solution (with various for viable of facets) solution "Best Fit"

Persuasion/Argument

• takes a position
• remains neutral; helps reader make a choice

Controversial issue → Position → support #1, Position → support #2 { May or may not take a position

For example, present the issue: Should the U.S. bring democracy to 3rd-world countries? Offer both perspective: yes, they'll be better off because...and no, not every culture benefits from democracy because . . .

Format for Summary:
▪ synthesis of issue
▪ alternate positions
▪ indication of support or neutrality

Note Taking:
issue
• ___
• ___
• ___

position #1
___
___
position #2
___
___

Visual/Graphic Organizer:
(with rationale)
or
(with rationale)

Nonfiction Narrative Sequence

• setting (time, place)
• character(s)
• conflict

presented as a { story — 1st or 3rd person point of view

For example, present the discovery of sulfur matches as a narrative; include settings, key people, mishaps and failures, and the final success

Format for Summary:
▪ plot scenario, setting, character(s)
▪ resolution and "message"

Note Taking:
setting ___
character ___
plot ___
point of view 1st, 3rd?

Visual/Graphic Organizer:
etc. | plot events
Resolution
conflicts | setting

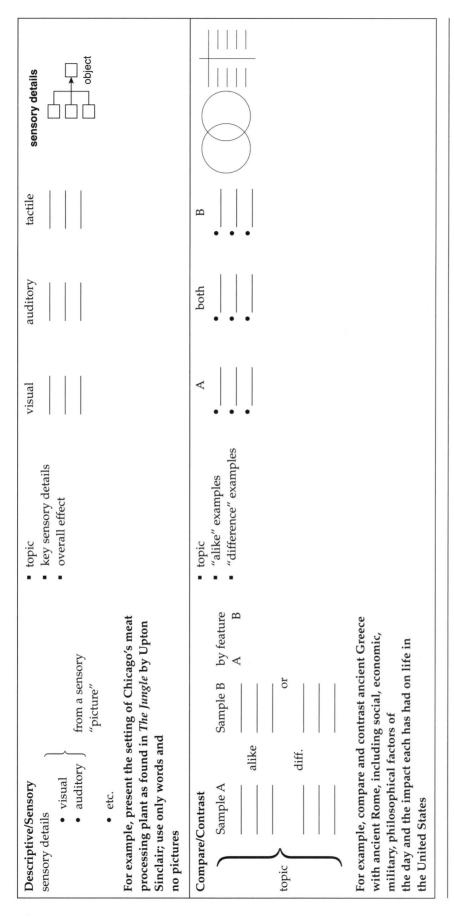

Descriptive/Sensory

sensory details

- visual
- auditory } from a sensory "picture"
- etc.

- topic
- key sensory details
- overall effect

sensory details

visual   auditory   tactile

object

For example, present the setting of Chicago's meat processing plant as found in *The Jungle* by Upton Sinclair; use only words and no pictures

Compare/Contrast

Sample A   Sample B   by feature
                              A   B

alike

or

diff.

topic

- topic
- "alike" examples
- "difference" examples

A   both   B

For example, compare and contrast ancient Greece with ancient Rome, including social, economic, military, philosophical factors of the day and the impact each has had on life in the United States

(Continued)

Table 6.3 (Continued)

Structure of Organizational Pattern	Format for Summary= Sentence	Note Taking	Visual/Graphic Organizer

Cause—Effect

Topic — causal Factors — effects — may be 1:1 (single) or multi

For example, show students the drawing of a box that holds a cup of sand; then make two sides bigger to show how the change in measurement impacts the volume

Format for Summary=Sentence:
- topic
- synthesis of causes-effects
- multiple or chaining (if applicable)

Note Taking:
- causes _____
- effects _____

Visual/Graphic Organizer:
- single (1:1)
- multiple

"How-To"

Steps in sequence

Topic (secondary) (may vary) — or —

For example, explain how to devise a Research Plan to guide an Action Research project; use an example (e.g., which drinking fountain in the school has the greatest amount of bacteria?), including drafts and final copy

Format for Summary=Sentence:
- topic (what, why)
- synthesis of steps, procedures
- variations, options (if applicable)

Note Taking:
- Steps
  1. _____
  2. _____
  3. _____
  4. _____
- checkpoints ✓ _____ ✓ _____
- product

Visual/Graphic Organizer:
- Time line
- Flowchart

But teachers should also show students the following and ask them to identify the *start*:

- Bob was given 2 cookies. Now he has 5 cookies. How many cookies did he have in the beginning?

To solve this problem, young children might count on from 2, keeping track with their fingers, to get to 5 (addition). But they should also learn that the problem uses the inverse operation of addition to solve for an unknown. They actually use the fact that $5 - 2 = 3$ to write the number sentence that reflects the problem: either as $\triangle + 2 = 5$ or $5 - \triangle = 3$.

A third scenario would be for students to find the *change*:

- Bob began with 3 cookies. Now he has 5. How many cookies did he get to have 5?

Multiplication/Division

Beyond addition and subtraction, students must also recognize situations involving multiplication and division. Traditionally, they are shown

- Each class member has 5 tickets, and there are 20 students in the class. How many tickets does the class have?

But teachers should also show them

- The class has 100 tickets to see the movie. If each student has 5 tickets, how many students are in the class?

Working with these types of problems helps students comprehend the relationships among the operations, and they are able to see the similarity of addition to multiplication and subtraction to division. They are also able to recognize that addition and subtraction are inverse operations, as are multiplication and division. Students must (a) recognize that the same operation can be applied in problem situations that on the surface seem quite different from one another, (b) know how operations relate to one another, and (c) have an idea about what kind of result to expect.

Fractions/Decimals/Ratios/Percentages

Students' intuitions about operations should evolve as they work with an expanded system of numbers in Grades 6 through 8. For example, multiplying a whole number by a fraction between 0 and 1 (e.g., $8 \times \frac{1}{2}$) produces a result less than the whole number. This is counter to students' prior experience with whole numbers where multiplication always resulted in a greater number. Students must become proficient in creating ratios to make comparisons in situations that involve pairs of numbers. Students should know the ratio/proportion in problems such as the following: If three packages of cocoa make 15 cups of hot chocolate, how many packages are needed to make 60 cups?

In our 35 years of experience, we have rarely seen these fundamentals of contextualized math instruction in the majority of classrooms. Instead, we have encountered more of the following:

♦ Math computation is taught in isolation, without regard for lifelike scenarios. Contextualized math should begin with problem-solving scenarios and pull computation from them. In fact, the high-stakes tests expect students to wrap skills together and apply them to solving real-life problems. Students enduring their first exposure to fractions are rarely shown how fractions work in their daily lives in advance of how to compute with them.

♦ Math textbooks and teacher-made tests ask students to find the final *result* in a problem. By contrast, the high-stakes tests present the questions so that students must determine the *change* or the *start* in a problem. But because students are accustomed only to finding results, they are stymied by the problems on high-stakes tests. They quickly give up attempting to solve the extended response or short answer items, thinking that these are things they do not know.

♦ Many math programs use the "silo" approach. Each *Unit* has its own set of skills and concepts focused on an individual strand (i.e., Measurement or Geometry or Data Analysis). There is no deliberate attempt to link strands, such as placing Measurement in the context of Geometry. Furthermore, there are weak or nonexistent connections between the present *Unit* and the one that precedes or follows it. The inference is that the teacher will do this intuitively, but in many cases, teachers feel they lack the time and the expertise to do this on their own.

♦ In the lower grades, it has becomes commonplace to teach students what are called *trigger words* or *signal words* that are intended to cue them as to what operation is needed to solve a word problem (e.g., how many in all, how many are left). We find that students memorize the trigger words, and without actually reading what a problem is asking, they jump to the computation too quickly. While trigger words may be a useful first step, we strongly suggest that teachers wean students away from this crutch. The key to finding the solution is being able to think through what a problem asks, not just do the computation.

It bears repeating that many high-stakes tests don't actually ask for the correct answer; rather, they ask students to identify "what is needed to solve a problem," "how a problem was solved," or "what errors were made?" The onus on students is to show their ability to analyze the problem and identify the thinking required to arrive at the solution. These questions are more concerned about the students' ability to think than to calculate the right answer. With students long accustomed to going for the "right answer," these questions make both teachers and students extremely uncomfortable.

How to Use With Students

It is suggested that elementary Math teachers rethink their approach to Math *Problem-Solving*, understanding that it is more than a series of steps posted on the bulletin board. They need to help students analyze or dissect common problems, such as those listed at the outset with Addition/Subtraction and Multiplication/Division, to identify what each problem asks. With practice, they can come to recognize that some ask for the *result*, some want to know the amount and direction of *change*, and some ask for the number or quantity at the *start*. It is suggested to begin with simple numbers and one-step operations and then more complex numbers to show how the same principles work with multiple operations involving larger whole numbers, decimals, fractions, integers, and so on. The big idea is this: Math *Problem-Solving* is really about multiple ways to look at the same problem. We found a chart that summarized these problem types in mathematics, including variations on each type. With the authors' permission, we have reproduced it as Table 6.4.

Various Types of Problems Illustrated

Borrowing from the first column of Table 6.4, the four major *Types* of problems encountered by students require them to (a) **join** (add/multiply), (b) **separate** (subtract/divide), (c) examine **part-to-part or part-to-whole**

Table 6.4   Problem-Solving: Different Ways to Consider the Unknown

Problem Type	*"Unknown" That Students Are to Find*		
JOIN (add/multiply)	(Result Unknown) *Connie has 5 marbles. Jon gave her 8 more marbles. How many marbles does Connie have?*	(Change Unknown) *Connie has 5 marbles. How many more marbles does she need to have 13 marbles?*	(Start Unknown) *Connie has some marbles. Jon gave her 5 more marbles. Now she has 13 marbles. How many marbles did Connie have to start with?*
SEPARATE (subtract/divide)	(Result Unknown) *Connie had 13 marbles. She gave 5 to Jon. How many marbles does Connie have?*	(Change Unknown) *Connie had 13 marbles. She gave some to Jon. Now she has 5 marbles. How many marbles did Connie give to Jon?*	(Start Unknown) *Connie has some marbles. She gave 5 to Jon. Now she has 8 marbles. How many marbles did Connie have to start with?*
PART-PART-WHOLE (fractions/decimals/ ratios/percentages)	(Result Unknown) *Connie has 5 red marbles and 8 blue marbles. How many marbles does she have?*	(Part Unknown) *Connie has 13 marbles. Five are red, and the rest are blue. How many blue marbles does Connie have?*	
COMPARE	(Difference Unknown) *Connie has 13 marbles. Jon has 5 marbles. How many more marbles does Connie have than Jon?*	(Compare Quantity Unknown) *Jon has 5 marbles. Connie has 8 more than Jon. How many marbles does Connie have?*	(Reference Unknown) *Connie has 13 marbles. She has 5 more marbles than Jon. How many marbles does Jon have?*

Source: The chart was adapted from *Children's Mathematics: Cognitively Guided Instruction;* 1999; by Carpenter, T.; Fennema, E; Franke, M. L.; Levi, L.; Empson, S. B. Reprinted with permission of the authors.

(fractions/decimals/ratios/percentages), and (d) **make comparisons** (how many more, etc.).

Working across the chart by row, students are to find the *Unknown*, which varies for each problem Type:

- for the **join** and **separate** problems, the unknown may be the *result*, the *change* that occurred, or the *start*
- for **part-whole** problems, the unknown may be the *whole* or the *part*
- for the **compare** problems, the unknown may be the *difference*, the *compare quantity*, or the *reference*.

Teachers and textbooks both are very proficient at asking *result* questions. An example of a **join** problem:

- Jane has 3 cards; Roy gave her 5 more; how many cards does Jane now have? (**result**)

However, if we were to take the same problem, we could also ask it so that students would need to focus on the *change* or the *starting point*:

- Jane has 3 cards; how many more cards does she need to have 8? (**change**)
- Jane has some cards; Roy gave her 5 more, and now she has 8; how many cards did Jane have to start? (**starting point**)

All three questions above deal with the same concepts, but students have to think differently to address the last two: although *result* problems are most prevalent in texts, the *change* and *start* problems are more life-like. Students must learn to represent each situation mathematically:

Result: $3 + 5 = \triangle$

Change: $3 + \triangle = 8$

Start: $\triangle + 5 = 8$

This one rather simplistic problem shows how students can use *counting on* as a strategy, or to understand inverse operations, and to balance an equation. The different structure of the problem focuses on the logic of math as a thinking process, not a rote skill. Children should begin by using concrete (direct modeling) strategies involving the use of counters or other objects to represent the problem; over time, more abstract counting strategies evolve. Eventually, counting strategies such as counting on, doubles, doubles plus 1, and so one are replaced by number facts, but the number facts become internalized when students understand them in context and in relation to the other math operations, not from hours of drill or memorization.

The following section presents questions adapted from several high-stakes test to illustrate the four Types of math problems displayed in Table 6.4. Our intent is that teachers adapt these examples to design *Unit Plan* activities that allow their students to work regularly with the different Types. This will ensure that students are exposed to situations requiring them to solve for various types of unknowns in problem situations.

1. Join (Add/Multiply)

Result Unknown

> **Grade 3:** David grew 12 pea plants; Karen grew 17 pea plants. Write a number sentence to show how to find the total number of plants they grew.

> **Grade 6:** Evelyn rode her bike 3½ miles on Monday, 2¼ miles on Wednesday. On Saturday, she rode 5⅛ miles. How many miles did Evelyn ride in the 3 days?

Change Unknown

> **Grade 3:** What is the rule for this INPUT-OUTPUT table?

Input	Output
3	12
5	20
8	32

(multiply by 4)

> **Grade 7:** The table below shows the total balance in four people's savings accounts at the end of each month:

Name	Jan	Feb	Mar	Apr	May	Jun
Julie	50	65	80	105	120	135
Stuart	70	80	90	100	110	120
Sarah	100	120	140	160	180	220
Mike	90	100	110	130	150	180

> In which person's account did the balance show a constant rate of increase over the six-month period?

Start Unknown

> **Grade 3:** In the Bean Bag Toss game a player can score points by tossing a bean bag in a hole of 5 points, 6 points, 7 points, 8 points, and 10 points; Max tossed three bean bags in the same hole and two bean bags in a second hole. What is the highest score that Max could receive for these five tosses? Alissa also tossed five bean bags into the holes. She scored 45 points; show how Alissa could have gotten this score.

> **Grade 6:** A coach paid a total of $175.00 for 14 baseball uniforms. What was the price of each uniform?

> **Grade 7:** Jackson bought groceries that totaled $16.07; he received $4.00 in change. What amount did Jackson pay the cashier for the groceries in order to receive the $4.00 change?

To illustrate how to make one problem work for the three unknowns, let's examine the first problem presented above for Grade 3. For teachers to make the best use of this information, the key is to show students how one question could be turned around and asked in different ways. The **result** question was the one posed on one test, but the **change** or **start** question below could just as easily have been posed to the third graders.

Result:

> David grew 12 pea plants; Karen grew 17 pea plants. Write a number sentence to show how to find the total number of plants they grew.

Change:

> David grew 12 pea plants; how many more plants will he need to grow so that he has 29?

Start:

> David has pea plants. Karen grew 17, bringing their total to 29. How many plants did David have to start with?

2. Separate (Subtract/Divide)

Result Unknown

> **Grade 8**: Rob wants to buy a $20.00 CD that is on sale for 15% off. He estimates that he will save at least $4.00. Tell whether Rob's estimate is reasonable, and show how you determined your answer.

Change Unknown

> **Grade 9:** The pilot of a small aircraft was given permission to land, and she lowered the wheels at an altitude of 1,500 feet. Two and a half minutes after lowering the wheels, the aircraft landed. What was the plane's rate of descent, in feet per second, from the time the wheels were lowered to the time the plane landed?

Start Unknown

> **Grade 7**: The Acme Carpet Company received an order for 240 square feet of carpeting. The order form showed that the length of the rectangular room was 20 feet. What width should the company cut the carpeting to fit the room?

> **Grade 8**: Mrs. Stanley has 32 pieces of ribbon, each ¾ yard long. How much ribbon did Mrs. Stanley have to cut her pieces of ribbon?

3. Part-to-Part or Part-to-Whole (Fractions/Decimals/Ratio/Percentage)

Whole Unknown

> **Grade 7:** The Amazon basin has received 23 inches of rain so far this year. This amount is 25% of the average yearly rainfall. What is the average yearly rainfall in the Amazon basin?

Part Unknown

> **Grade 6**: Ms. Andrews allowed her students to print, write in cursive, or type their essays. Sixty percent of the students printed; 10% of the students used cursive; and 30% of the students typed their essays. Ms. Andrews teaches 150 students; how many students typed their essays?

> **Grade 7**: A book that sells for $13.50 is on sale for $10.80. What fraction represents the discount being offered on the book?

4. Compare

Difference Unknown

> **Grade 9**: Two years ago, Monique paid $5.50 for the rookie baseball card of her favorite New York Yankees player. The card is now worth $17.00. Sean, her brother, paid $12.00 for his favorite card, and it has a current value of $27.00. Sean says that his card has increased more in value than Monique's card. Monique says that her card has increased more in value than Sean's card. Show how both Monique and Sean can be correct. Support your answer by showing work or providing an explanation.

Compare Quantity Unknown

> **Grade 7**: Patty found the table below on the back of a pasta box. She needs 10 cups of cooked pasta. How many ounces of uncooked pasta does she need?

Amount of Uncooked Pasta in ounces	Amount of Cooked Pasta in cups
4	2
8	4
16	8

> **Grade 9**: The population density of a state, in people per square mile, is found by dividing the population of the state by its area in square miles. Florida has an area of 53,936 square miles. In 1998, Florida had a population of 14,915,980 and a population density of 276.5 people per square mile. Describe the conditions under which a different state could have a smaller population than Florida but have a greater population density.

Reference Unknown

> **Grade 7:** A water tower casts a shadow 70 meters long; at the same time, a fence post 1 meter tall casts a shadow 1.4 meters long. How tall is the water tower?

Problem-Solving Strategies

Once students have determined what the problem asks them to do and how it should be solved, they then need to go about the business of getting the correct answer. In our experience, successful math teachers help their students build a toolkit of strategies from which they can draw. Some students will nearly always want to make a chart, table, or visual of some type; other students will tend to use the work-backward strategy, while others like the make-it-simpler technique. "Whatever works" is the key, but if the toolkit is to be effective, students must know how to use each tool or *Problem-Solving* strategy in the kit and when to use it. It is strongly recommended that teachers show students multiple *Problem-Solving* strategies to solve the same problem so that they make informed choices when confronted with various types of problems on the high-stakes tests. Rarely does the test dictate what strategy a student should use; test makers are relying on the fact that students know them all and will apply what is most appropriate for the problem at hand.

■ VOCABULARY AND CONTEXT CLUES

What It Is

According to the Best Practices research, a student's level of *Vocabulary* is one of the most powerful predictors of success, both in school and as an adult. Studies have found extremely high correlations between a student's vocabulary and his or her (a) level of intelligence, (b) ability to comprehend new information, and (c) level of income (as an adult). Regardless of the occupation, there is little argument that the ability to understand *Vocabulary* and to use it effectively in writing and speaking is the passkey to success. And those without it are relegated to jobs requiring very little intelligence.

One of the most predictive variables to a strong *Vocabulary* is environment. Even children of average and below-average levels of intelligence who come from vocabulary-rich environments have considerably less difficulty with language and self-expression than children with above-average intelligence from vocabulary-poor backgrounds. These findings have prompted major efforts in preschool compensatory programs such as Head Start to augment children's lack of experience and language development. And they show that a strong command of language and *Vocabulary can* be taught.

General Versus Content-Specific Words

1. The *Vocabulary* in reference here is not so much the technical words affiliated with each content area or subject. Authors are typically careful to define those words as they go along. For example, *photosynthesis, irrational number, imperialism,* and *verisimilitude* are likely to be explained, a number of times. The *Vocabulary* that we're addressing in **Instructional Design** is that huge canon of general words that authors use but rarely stop to define. The fact is, even the most skillful and practiced adult reader will not comprehend the meaning of every general word encountered. Even if he or she can readily pronounce any of the following—*acetify, cadaster, ecdysiast, hadal, imbricate, kermis, paronymous, valorise*—8 of every 10 readers have never seen them before, may never see them again, and couldn't care less what they mean. And the only reason

the adult reader would take notice of them at all is if the overall meaning of the passage were somehow tied in with them. Before skipping such words altogether or giving in and going to the dictionary, most adult readers will try (a) context clues to see if the surrounding words will be any help; (b) structure clues to see if the word can be divided into familiar roots, affixes, or word-parts; or (c) part of speech to see if the way the word is used in the sentence might help. Let's start at the end and work backwards.

(1) Part of Speech. Does the part of speech help us out? Let's check to see.

1. *acetify*:
   ♦ *-ify* usually signifies a verb (e.g., rectify) ⇨ yes, acetify is a verb

2. *cadaster*:
   ♦ *-er* usually signifies a noun (e.g., toaster) ⇨ yes, cadaster is a noun
   ♦ *-er* often signifies "a person" (e.g., master) ⇨ not this time; cadaster is an object

3. *ecdysiast*:
   ♦ *-ast* usually signifies "a person who" (e.g., gymnast) ⇨ yes, ecdysiast is a person

4. *hadal*:
   ♦ *-al* usually signifies an adjective (e.g., tidal) ⇨ yes, hadal is an adjective

5. *imbricate*:
   ♦ *-cate* usually signifies a verb (e.g., replicate) ⇨ yes, imbricate is a verb

6. *kermis*:
   ♦ *-is* usually signifies a noun (e.g., epidermis) ⇨ yes, kermis is a noun

7. *paronymous*:
   ♦ *-ous* usually signifies an adjective (e.g., poisonous) ⇨ yes, paronymous is an adjective

8. *valorise*:
   ♦ *-ise* may signify a noun (e.g., treatise), a verb (e.g., advise, revise), or both a noun and a verb (e.g., promise, exercise, surprise) ⇨ in this case, valorise is a verb

(2) Structure Clues. How about any familiar roots or affixes? Perhaps. Let's look.

1. *acetify*: maybe, if the reader associates *acid*, but other readers may be misled by *acedia* or boredom.

2. *paronymous*: sometimes, *par* is associated with nearly or almost, but the *-onymous* may get confused with anonymous.

3. *valorise*: valor has to do with courage and honor, but valorise has nothing to do with either.

4. *hadal*: maybe, if the reader thinks of Hades, or hell.

5-8. *cadaster, ecdysiast, imbricate, kermis*: not really any such clues for the average reader.

(3) No luck so far. So, let's consider context clues. Below are two groups of sentences; first look at Group A.

Group A

1. The pathologist was baffled as to why the fluid in one organ after the other had begun to acetify.

2. It was clear from the cadaster that as many as 40 homes would be affected.

3. With so little job security, the ecdysiasts have been forced to unionize.

4. Astronomers wonder if, like the Earth, the seas on Jupiter and Mars have hadal sections.

5. Military historians marvel that even when facing an enemy of twice their number, the Roman generals would imbricate their troops.

6. Because of the rash of car thefts and assaults last year, the sheriff assigned twice the number of deputies for this year's kermis.

7. During World War II, Japan was unable to break the Rutland code because it used strings of paronymous terms.

8. One strategy for economic recovery is to valorise the amount paid in income tax.

Well, there certainly isn't much help there, either. These sentences illustrate the fact that not every author takes pains to use context clues to help the reader determine what an unusual word might mean. If our nettlesome words appeared in sentences such as those above, they would be what we call *a-contextual*, meaning that the context is little or no help. In cases such as this, the reader simply has to skip the word or give in and go to the dictionary. But before you do either, look at the sentences in Group B below.

Group B

1. My grandpa made his own vinegar by setting aside a portion of homemade cider and allowing it to acetify or ferment.

2. The judge could not rule on the new mall project until it could be determined who really owned the land and its tax value, and somehow the county cadaster or public record of that information had disappeared.

3. Until the 1950s, the League of Decency prohibited modern-day ecdysiasts such as Gypsy Rose Lee or the exotic dancers we see on TV today to appear in movies.

4. Despite the advances in oceanographic technology, the hadal regions below 6,000 meters have remained unexplored.

5. A favorite technique of Spanish builders is to imbricate the roof tiles like scales on a fish or feathers on a bird's wing.

6. To raise money and provide an enjoyable outing for families, churches rely on the parish kermis, or carnival.

7. The words *hydrosphere*, *hydrologic*, and *hydrofoil* are paronymous, or linked by their derivation from the same root.

8. Experts feel the uncontrolled surges in gasoline prices could be stopped if the oil countries would valorise the per barrel price rather than raise and lower it in response to demand.

Now that's more like it. The reader may still not know the precise definition of each word, but he or she can at least make an intelligent guess. And that's enough to get the overall meaning. So let's take a look.

1. *acetify* (it has something to do with souring or making vinegar)

2. *cadaster* (it has something to do with records about land ownership and taxation)

3. *ecdysiasts* (are apparently strippers or belly dancers)

4. *hadal* (that must be where the ocean is really, really deep!)

5. *imbricate* (so the roof tiles are put on in staggered rows like fish scales)

6. *kermis* (it has something to do with a street-fair or carnival)

7. *paronymous* (are several words from the same root or base)

8. *valorise* (it suggests fixing the price and leaving it there)

How to Use With Students

There are no guarantees that these three techniques—the part of speech or syntax within the sentence; the word structure, including roots or affixes; or the context clues in the surrounding words—will be useful in every situation. But teaching students to use all three, and then to provide them with plenty of practice, is to give them the gift of a Learning Construct that just gets stronger and stronger with each year of experience.

Part of Speech or Syntax

One way to help students get accustomed to using syntax or part of speech is the replacement technique. First, have students identify a familiar word for a noun (e.g., car), verb (e.g., walk), adjective (e.g., blue), and adverb (e.g., slowly). Then, ask them to replace the tough word with their familiar one, based on the part of speech and/or syntax. It doesn't reveal the definition, but it provides a placeholder. In most cases, students will comprehend the overall passage without defining each of these words, but if they do need to come back to look up a few of them, where to look will be clearly marked with *car, walk, blue,* and *slowly.*

1. Several flags were thrown after the play, and it took several minutes to sort out who committed the blatant penalties. (Since the tough word is an adjective, replace it with a familiar one, or blue.)

2. The Hindenburg debacle prevented the airship from becoming a major weapon in aerial warfare. (Since the tough word is a noun, and the subject, replace it with the familiar one, or car.)

3. Although spiritual beliefs are based on faith, an important part of worship centers around religious icons. (Since the tough word is a noun, but an object of a preposition, replace it with the familiar one, or car[s].)

4. The treasure was divided proportionately among the families who found it. (Since the tough word is an adverb, replace it with the familiar one, or slowly.)

5. Judges often sequester the jury for high-profile cases that have created strong public feelings. (Since the tough word is a verb, replace it with the familiar one, or walk.)

Structure of the Word

A second technique is to analyze the structure of the word to identify roots or affixes. As with parts of speech or syntax, the "word-parts" strategy may not always work. But students need to be ready for those occasions when roots or affixes do give clues as to the possible meaning of the word. The following words illustrate how this might work.

bulbous	*root*: bulb =like a bulb	*affix*: -ous = having	
equidistance	*root*: distance = length	*affix*: equi- = the same	
indeterminate	*root*: determine = length	*affix*: in- = not	-ate = the same
multinational	*root*: national	*affix*: multi- = many	-al = characteristic of
premeditation	*root*: meditate	*affix*: pre- = before, prior	-tion = state of
circumnavigate	*root*: navigate	*affix*: circum- = to circle	

Context Clues

Before addressing how the context clue technique can be taught to students, we need to establish the following ground rule for teachers. Never, never should *Vocabulary* be taught as the old list on the board for students to define and use in a sentence. Growing *Vocabulary* is just like cultivating a seed, and students who encounter new words in isolation will internalize them about as well as seeds scattered on the driveway will become flourishing plants. The words may stick at a memory level long enough to pass a test, but they will be quickly forgotten. (And the awful sentences most of us wrote are far better forgotten.)

Multiple Meanings. Many words have multiple meanings and depend on context to be understood. Basic examples—*back, cast, drum, flood, hold, key, left, part, rise, trace, water,* and *yield*—should be pointed out and practiced in the early grades. Students will become familiar with these words and the basic concept of multiple meanings by the time they leave the intermediate grades. But other more formidable examples await them from Grade 5 through adulthood. These include *account, direct, founder, honor, index, justify, manipulate, perch, relative, saturate, temper,* and *value,* all words that can be accurately interpreted only in context.

Types of Context Clue. The most frequently encountered context clues are as follows:

1. *definition or explanation,* for example,

    a. The roots of the old cedar tree were **sinewy**, or twisted and knotted like thick rope.
    b. Once it was discovered that the boys had eaten infected meat, they had no choice but to take an **emetic**, or a substance that would cause them to vomit.
    c. Because the strings are so rough, many classical guitarists use a **plectrum**, or thin, flat piece of plastic or horn as a pick.

    And from our earlier list,

    d. The judge could not rule on the new mall project until it could be determined who really owned the land and its tax value, and somehow the county **cadaster** or public record of that information had disappeared.
    e. The words hydrosphere, hydrologic, and hydrofoil are **paronymous,** or linked by their derivation from the same root.

2. *synonym,* for example,

    a. Many of the farmers or their sons became soldiers, and most of the fields lay **fallow** or unplanted for the entire Civil War.
    b. During the war, the underground communicated by leaving messages in the **stoups** or basins for holy water in occupied churches.
    c. Newspaper apprentices were never hard to spot; their cuffs were always **imbrued** or soaked with printer's ink.

    And from our earlier list,

    d. My grandpa made his own vinegar by setting aside a portion homemade cider and allowing it to **acetify** or ferment.
    e. To raise money and provide an enjoyable outing for families, churches rely on the parish **kermis,** or carnival.

3. *antonym*, for example,

   a. Rather than being glad to have avoided all the hassle, Jonathan now **rued** his decision to skip the concert.
   b. The Senator thought her amendment was fully developed, but the committee thought it too **inchoate** to seriously consider.
   c. In the jury's mind, the additional testimony only managed to **obfuscate** as opposed to clarify the issue in question.

   And from our earlier list,

   d. Experts feel the uncontrolled surges in gasoline prices could be stopped if the oil countries would **valorise** the per barrel price rather than raise and lower it in response to demand.

4. *example*, for example,

   a. Rachel's **metamorphosis** from lab partner to prom date was like the caterpillar that became a beautiful butterfly; Sean could not believe his eyes!
   b. The surface of the cave wall was **glaucous** with tiny mushrooms, as if they were clusters of grapes.
   c. In rugby, the **scrum** reminds me of pigeons scrambling for a cracker.

   And from our earlier list,

   d. Until the 1950s, the League of Decency prohibited modern-day **ecdysiasts** such as Gypsy Rose Lee or the exotic dancers we see on TV today to appear in movies.
   e. A favorite technique of Spanish builders is to **imbricate** the roof tiles like scales on a fish or feathers on a bird's wing.

5. some authors use *allusions* to create a particular image; these are mythological, biblical, or famous familiar figures or expressions.

   a. Once a man or woman contracts AIDS, fighting even the common cold becomes a **herculean** task for his or her weakened defenses.
   b. Professor Carter, the man who discovered King Tut's tomb, was indeed the **Indiana Jones** of his day.
   c. Students who want to avoid school fights often find themselves having to **turn the other cheek**.

   And from our earlier list,

   d. Despite the advances in oceanography, the **hadal** regions below 6,000 meters have remained unexplored.

Of course, students need to verify in the dictionary the hunches they form about the meaning of words using context. But the more practice they get at using context, the more successful they will be. Naturally, they cannot check themselves during a test, but their past success will give them well-founded confidence sufficient not to panic when they cannot use any external aids. As students become more and more successful in using context clues, they will no longer be stymied by dense passages with "tough words." And that's just one less intimidation for the struggling reader.

Teaching Strategies

Preteaching

Researchers claim (research citations are available from the authors upon request) that students are 33% more likely to understand the words they encounter if the words are pretaught. The sequence of teaching events identified by most specialists is as follows:

1. Determine if any students already know the term or one like it, but it will be doubtful.

2. Present a brief, clear definition or explanation of the word but also include the context in which the word is found, even if the context is noninstructive.

   > A *pogrom* is an organized sanctioned massacre of an entire group, for example, from a news bulletin. "A spokesman for Hezbollah denied that the killings were a pogrom of the Asian immigrants, authorized by their leaders."

3. Present a visual representation of the term, that is, a picture, diagram, drawing, and so on; concepts such as *metamorphosis* can be represented as a larva to a butterfly; a *pogrom* can be illustrated with a cartoon of three officials sitting like the three monkeys (i.e., hear no evil, see no evil, speak no evil), with one monkey handing orders to a death squad.

Imaging

Another respected technique is imaging, or thinking of a visual or graphic that defines or explains the term. Researchers claim that students who used the imaging technique scored 34 percentile points higher on standardized tests than those who did not. For example, students could think of the larva-butterfly thing to remember *metamorphosis* or the nerdy-looking lab partner blossoming into a beautiful dance partner.

Revisit

Probably the greatest barrier to expanding both student and adult *Vocabulary* is the limit to which the newly learned words are integrated into daily writing and speaking. Naturally, the unlimited number of words encountered by students makes this a formidable challenge. But the next best thing is for classroom teachers to identify 25 to 30 of the most critical nontechnical words their students must know on sight, words not associated with any one subject area but those that are part of everyday living and communicating. In addition to the words identified by the teacher, students could be asked to make a list of the words they hear on the news or read in the newspaper at least five times in the course of a week. This list of 25 to 30 words should be strategically revisited in conversation, writing, class discussion, and the teacher's presentation several times during the year. This requires a conscious effort to place the words into the *Unit Plans.* As an added incentive for students to use the designated words, it may be smart to offer points for identifying someone's use, double points if it's a classmate, and triple points if they appear in the student's own writing.

Denotation and Connotation

Another means to strengthen student *Vocabulary* is the use of value associated with many of the words they will encounter in reading and listening. Even though words are merely ink strokes on paper, they often convey a feeling or tone. Some are negative or critical (such as *skinny* or *miser*) and others are positive or complimentary (such as *slender* or *thrifty*). Still others are neutral; they can be either positive or negative, or neither (such as *thin* or *cost-conscious*).

The neutral sense of a word is its *denotation*, or dictionary definition. The feeling or attitude in a word is known as its *connotation*, either positive or negative. What's difficult is that without context, it is often impossible to tell which is which. Students should see several examples of all three types of words and in various contexts, noting that the attitude is not always absolute but rather conditioned by the context. For example, words such as *criminal*, *distasteful*, *horrific*, and *vermin* are negatively charged, irrespective of their context, and words such as *angel*, *commend*, *flawless*, *luxury*, and *personable* typically carry a positive connotation.

But there are other words that could be positive, neutral, or negative all in the same passage, depending entirely on the context in which they are used. For example,

1. *alliance* is *neutral* in the sense of simply joining forces for a common purpose, *positive* in reference to joining forces against evil, but *negative* if talking about a network of drug dealers.

2. *resistance* is *neutral* if the context of physical fitness, *positive* if avoiding a destructive habit, but *negative* when combatants refuse to compromise.

3. *eclipse* is neutral (as in the context of solar and lunar), except when discovering that red ink has *eclipsed* our profits (negative) or referring to an injured athlete's courage and determination eclipsing adversity (positive).

Some of the samples should reflect the three-part connection shown in the table below.

Positive	Neutral	Negative
assertive	forthright	aggressive
discrete	cautious	secretive
considering	undecided	equivocal
loyal	faithful	sycophant
individualist	nonconformist	renegade

The CLOZE Procedure

Although it is typically associated with reading tests and the identification of that grade-level material where a student comprehends what he or she reads, a handy adaptation of the CLOZE method is a great way to strengthen *Vocabulary*, particularly in passages that must be very well understood. For example, since students must understand the Declaration of Independence very well, and the language is somewhat intimidating, placing blanks in key spots for students to supply the correct word (or synonym) is an excellent way to ensure deep-level comprehension. The same is true for complex mathematical or scientific explanations as well as a densely worded passage from Literature. Students themselves can prepare these as study guides; they love to try to stump each other, and the bonus is that the developers are as familiar with the pieces as those attempting to fill in the blanks.

GRAPHIC ORGANIZERS   ■

What They Are

One of the most popular of all Learning Constructs is the visual or *Graphic Organizer,* also known as nonlinguistic representations, semantic maps, and concept maps. Just for simplicity, we will use the term *Graphic Organizers.* By definition, they are pictorial representations of information, the layout and content of which depict the direct and implied relationships among ideas and details. They are a translation of abstract information into concrete symbols and images to provide students with a visual or graphic memory of material that may otherwise be obscured in text. And for most learners, these pictures truly are worth a thousand words. Just ask the advertising industry. Icons such as McDonald's golden arches, Disney's mouse ears, Prudential's outline of Gibraltar, Target's white bull's eye on the red field, or Master Card's intersecting orange and red circles all are immediately recognizable to the global culture.

Why Use Them

The use of nonlinguistic representations is nothing new; textbooks have included illustrations, charts, diagrams, maps, cartoons, and graphic displays for decades. But using graphic organizers to represent or even displace text is relatively recent and exploits the technology of computer art and digital graphics. Nearly every modern textbook uses colorful, two- and three-dimensional illustrations to represent ideas and concepts, particularly when they are too abstract and difficult to describe linguistically. Moreover, *Graphic Organizers* have been included among the academic content standards. In several states, the standards in all four core subjects require students to interpret and to construct—yes, construct—*Graphic Organizers.*

By placing bits of key (not superfluous) information into physical spaces and lines in a particular order and proximity to other bits of information, a teacher or an author can display the conceptual thinking and relationships among the detail that is the core of a particular text or set of data. The most successful of such visual diagrams illustrate how process skills connect important items of content. Ironically, it is the process of tearing something apart that enables the learner to better understand it intact. When students can interpret *Graphic Organizers,* they demonstrate an understanding not only of what is contained in the discourse or text, but how it is structured and how the various ideas, facts, concepts, and terminology interrelate to make the whole. Once they can interpret the *Organizers* presented to them, students are required to construct their own *Organizers* to represent their deep-level understanding.

Watch Out!

When appropriately constructed, *Graphic Organizers* are one of the most effective of all Learning Constructs. Hundreds of articles, monographs, and Web sites provide teachers with thousands of *Organizers* from which to choose. The secret is in knowing which *Organizer* best illustrates the relationships in reference. If sequence is the basis of the relationship, it would be foolish to use a Web; if there are only differences and no likenesses in two parallel terms, a T-chart is preferable to a Venn diagram. We have encountered several instances where *Organizers* have been used incorrectly. A few examples follow:

a. **The KWL chart** was intended for use with topics or concepts about which students know a little and want to know more, implying that what follows will be interesting, somewhat divergent, and will result in a fairly clear but nonabsolute set of outcomes (the What I Learned part). We've seen it used for overly broad topics such as pollution or totally boring ones such as adverbs, neither of which will result in a memorable list of What I Learned. (We feel the KWL chart is better as a goal-setting strategy than as a graphic representation of material learned.)

b. Another misuse is the **Web organizer**. Like its namesake, the individual pieces of the Web are connected in some way. There is a relationship among them that helps define the term in the center, and the outlier pieces are to be consistent. Done correctly, a Web of the Great Lakes would show the Great Lakes in the center (hub) and have each of the five Lakes at the end of the spokes. Radiating from each lake name should be the same four or five attributes (e.g., size, bordering states, best known for, and economic significance). Less effective is using the Web as a brainstorming technique, with dozens of spokes going every which way. At the ends are disparate terms such as *Erie, cold, the Edmund Fitzgerald, sailing, ore boats,* and so on, a brain dump of word associations. This is a great mind dump, but not a Web in the sense of reflecting an internal logic.

c. A third culprit is the **Venn diagram**. The intent of the Venn is to compare and contrast comparable and meaningful concepts (terms, ideas, etc.). We find it being used to compare everything and anything, irrespective of comparability or value. Class time is too precious to squander it dragging students through a comparison of *Romeo and Juliet* with *King Lear,* horses with cows, greatest common factors with least common multiples, plants with animals, or movies with hubcaps. A second difficulty with Venn is to keep the points of comparison parallel. To compare the Republican with the Democratic party is perfectly worthwhile, but not when what's listed for the Democrats is *party origin, number of presidents, number of "blue" states in the last election, and their key platforms,* while on the Republican side is listed *animal symbol, number of presidents, influential women, and synthesis of the mission statement.*

The points to be compared and contrasted must be parallel. Otherwise, the exercise is merely a brainstorm.

Don't Throw the Baby Out With the Bath Water

We ourselves fell into some of these traps, so we realize how easily it happens. And teachers don't deliberately misuse the *Organizers*. But we feel strongly that to use any Learning Construct incorrectly is worse than not using it at all. Since the *Graphic Organizer* is so important to the state content standards as well as the Best Practices research, we feel is it too valuable to forego.

The Most Frequently Represented Relationships

Although there are dozens of organizational structures and conceptual relationships that can be displayed in printed text or verbal presentations, the most frequently used are closely aligned to the *Organizational Patterns* that led off this chapter. We have included eight of the most popular. For each type, we provide a brief explanation—particularly distinguishing it from the other types—and offer several sample *Graphic Organizers* that are easily adapted, or may be used intact.

☐ Sequence	☐ Cause-Effect
☐ Classification or Categorization	☐ Problem-Solution
☐ Comparison-Contrast	☐ Text Mapping
☐ Concept Webbing	☐ Data Display

Sequence

Many speeches, movies, TV broadcasts, and expository texts are presented in a chronological or developmental sequence. Although it may at first appear obvious, there are frequently subtle nuances and variations in the order of presentation that may confuse the student. Material that uses sequence as its dominant *Organizational Pattern* expects students to see the major events or steps that, when taken together and in the order they occurred, lead to an endpoint. The endpoint may be an idea, a concept, a plot resolution, or a document, but it is the culmination of the prior events or steps and is usually affected by what has preceded it.

Which Organizers?

The most frequently used **sequence** is linear; that is, events proceed developmentally as if along a horizontal line.

Sequence may overlap somewhat with cause and effect, and teachers must be cautious that students do not equate all events in sequence with cause and effect. Three samples are provided on the following page.

Cause-Effect Sequence. Juan heard the doorbell, and he ran up from the basement to answer. The delivery truck was pulling away. Juan ran waving and shouting to the end of the sidewalk. The driver stopped and pulled back up to the house. The driver unloaded a large package. [The final event *was caused by* or was the *effect of* those preceding it.]

Non-Cause-Effect Sequence. Juan dressed in running clothes; he pulled on a windbreaker and headed out into the backyard. After two laps around the house, Juan jogged out to the doghouse to check on Queenie's new litter.

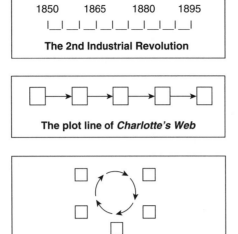

The **Time Line** reflects a chronological relationship among events, and multitiered time lines display other events—scientific, artistic, economic, etc.—occurring simultaneously.

The **Flowchart** reflects a series of steps or events that occur in sequence; parallel lines may flow off one or more steps as appropriate.

The **Cycle** reflects a sequence in which the steps or events occur in a specific order but which are repeated, mostly in self-perpetuation. Typically, the cycle is displayed in a clockwise direction and implies that one "starts" at 12:00. In other cases, the "start" can be at any point.

He scratched Queenie's head and hugged each puppy. [The final event was not necessarily caused by those preceding it.]

Alternate Steps. To fully understand sequence, students must be able to determine the order of the events or steps in reference and the precise relationship between each event or step. But the deep-level understanding of sequence occurs when students can identify key points in the sequence where **decisions** are (or could have been) made. It is at these decision points that **alternate steps** could be taken that would trigger a different chain of events or steps. If students can make viable predictions as to "what would have happened if . . ." and can verify these hunches in the text, they have reached the deepest level of understanding sequence.

Content Examples for Sequence

Language Arts	Math	Science	Social Studies
1. a plot diagram 2. the writing process 3. character development 4. the research paper	1. steps in division 2. solving story problems 3. multiples (numerical sequences) 1 2 3 ... 11 12 13 ... 21 22 23 ... 31 32 33 ...	1. cell division 2. the rock cycle 3. the scientific method 4. stages of butterfly development	1. the economic cycle 2. a time line of events 3. how a bill becomes a law 4. biographical information about historic figures

Classification or Categorization

When students can sort items (i.e., objects, people, ideas, events, actions, ideas, concepts, states of being) into categories, they have identified the common attributes or traits that make those items alike and, simultaneously, the distinctions that make them different from each other.

The physical and visual act of moving items around, dividing them as well as grouping them, calls forth prior associations and combines the tactile with the visual sensory channels, strengthening the overall impression on the brain. The simplest way to classify or **Categorize** is to physically or graphically place actual objects or strips of paper into labeled circles or boxes. But students must also be able to place objects, events, ideas, and so on into categories without the benefit of physical objects.

Which Organizers?

There are several types of Visual or *Graphic Organizer* for **Categorization.**

The federal and state government

The **Natural Tree** Diagram is an excellent means for younger students to understand the classification concept—the trunk splitting into large branches and then splitting into smaller ones, but all leading back to the "trunk." For older students, the "roots" may be included to suggest causation.

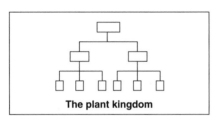

The plant kingdom

The **Line Tree** Diagram displays the hierarchical arrangement of "categories," displaying various sublevels. The key for students is to see that there may be several ways to categorize objects or ideas, but that once the "division" begins, the subsequent levels must consistently fall out accordingly.

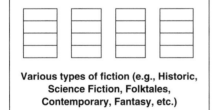

Various types of fiction (e.g., Historic, Science Fiction, Folktales, Contemporary, Fantasy, etc.)

The **Classifying Chart** or table comes as close as possible to the physical act of sorting. But what goes into each "stack" must be homogeneous, distinct from the other stacks by way of identifying attributes, traits, or characteristics.

Content Examples for Categorization or Classification

Language Arts	Math	Science	Social Studies
1. parts of speech 2. types of writing (e.g., narrative, descriptive, persuasive) 3. literary genres 4. figurative language devices	1. prime, composite numbers 2. odd and even numbers 3. types of graphs 4. the English system of measurement	1. the five kingdoms 2. rocks and minerals 3. bodies in the solar system 4. types of chemical reaction (e.g., single displacement, decomposition)	1. Native American tribes 2. types of government 3. explorers of the Western hemisphere 4. regions of the world

Compare-Contrast

The identification of similarities and contrasts among objects, events, people, ideas, and so on sits atop most of the Best Practice lists currently in use. It is thought that when students can see how two or more items are alike but also how they are different, they demonstrate a deeper-level understanding of each item than when considering them one at a time. When **comparing and contrasting,** the essential elements are as follows:

a. **Comparable**, meaning that the items are homogeneous enough to provide likenesses and differences. For example, comparing *carnivores*, *herbivores*, and *omnivores* would yield important understandings about all three as well as how they coexist. But to attempt a comparison of mollusks with mammals would yield too many dissimilarities to be helpful.

b. **Meaningful**, meaning that it matters. Frankly, we've seen many compare-contrast activities that were really not worth the effort. The comparison and contrast of two short stories about a child discovering that he or she has been adopted would be worthy in terms of the content and structure of each story and the common features and messages they provide. But to compare two pieces of literature on completely different topics would not be very instructive.

c. Keeping the features **Parallel**, using the same criteria for both items. An example of what not to do is shown below. A huge Venn diagram is on the bulletin board, neatly lettered and decorated, just beckoning a closer look. The two items being compared were Ottawa, Canada, and Washington, D.C.

Ottawa, Canada	*(same)*	*Washington, DC*
• noted for landscaping • lots of bed and breakfasts • nineteenth-century trolleys in use • government buildings here • wealthiest city in Canada • high tech center of Canada	• capital of the country • tourist attractions • tight security • served by three airports	• food and lodging expensive • tour buses easier than cars • cannot be seen in one day • all buildings open to public • most popular tourist site in U.S. • oldest original train station in U.S.

This is an interesting brainstorm of facts about the two cities, but the features being compared are not parallel, so the contrasts are actually lost.

d. **Fully Developing** both the **Likenesses** and the **Differences** is essential if there is to be an actual comparison and contrast. The example below shows a comparison of snacks eaten by adults with those consumed by adolescents.

adolescents	*(both)*	*adults*
type of food snacks (amount, frequency) type of liquids consumed (amount, frequency) exercise regimen (frequency) metabolic rates	common types of food common types of liquid common exercise regimen common metabolic rates	type of food snacks (amount, frequency) type of liquids consumed (amount, frequency) exercise regimen (frequency) metabolic rates

As teachers plan a **Compare-Contrast** activity, if they are unable to identify a reasonable number of attributes that the items have in common as well as how they differ (in parallel ways), perhaps the comparison is not really strong enough to be instructive.

Which Organizers?

There are several Visual or *Graphic Organizers* for **Compare-Contrast.**

The **T-chart** is usually considered the most preliminary graphic, since it displays only compare *or* contrast—not both. But this is actually an advantage, since *both* likenesses and differences need not be developed in the same activity. We recommend that to get started on the right foot, the comparisons or contrasts be parallel rather than random.

The North vs. the South in the Civil War (i.e., the major purpose of entering the war, budget/resources, number of troops, military advantage; turning point, . . . etc.)

The **Venn diagram** is the most popular graphic to display comparison and contrast. But with the requirement that the similarities (overlap) be *fully developed* and that the comparisons be parallel with each other, using it appropriately is a challenge.

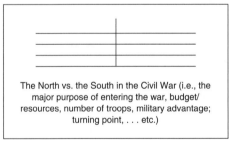

Physical and Chemical change

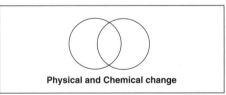

Cinderella Around the World

	Europe	*Africa*	*Japan*	*The US*
Subject				
Setting				
Theme				
Impact on Culture				

Compare various versions of *Cinderella* (e.g., US, Europe, Africa, Japan, Scandinavia, etc.)

The **Comparison Chart** or matrix compares *multiple* parallel items (across the top) using *several* parallel features (along the left side). Each cell contains unique details, some of which seem comparable to others and some dissimilar. The key to the matrix is to use multiple parallel items that have common formats or structures. In examining the completed matrix, several comparisons and contrasts jump out, cell by cell.

Content Examples for Compare-Contrast

Language Arts	Math	Science	Social Studies
1. poetry and song lyrics 2. the protagonist and antagonist of a piece 3. the Romantic and Victorian eras in British Literature 4. three different versions of the same story	1. fractions, decimals, and percents 2. addition/ subtraction and multiplication/ division 3. determine the "best" buy 4. mean, median, and mode	1. diffusion and osmosis 2. ionic and covalent bonds 3. renewable vs. nonrenewable resources 4. metamorphic, igneous, and sedimentary rocks	1. the Greek and Roman forms of government 2. Robert E. Lee vs. Ulysses S. Grant 3. state, federal, and shared powers 4. the Vietnam and Iraq Wars

Concept Webbing

Concept Webbing is the systematic dissection or analysis of an idea, event, action, principle, and so on to identify the defining characteristics, functions, or examples. The term *systematic* is significant to distinguish **Concept Webbing** from a word association or brainstorm of random, unparallel thoughts about the item. In one sense, it is the inverse operation to clustering, or putting items into distinct categories. It is analyzing or taking the item apart to look at its structure or internal logic.

The term being analyzed is placed in the center, and key terms resulting from the analysis are placed in circles that orbit the term. The essential requirement for a correct **Web** is that the items in each orbit are homogeneous. This means that there can't be a type of body system at the end of one or two "spokes," an ailment at the end of another, organs at the end of three, and a function at the end of two more. *That* is a brainstorm, not an analysis of the Body Systems concept.

The following diagram is the most familiar way to structure a Concept Web, and we've used a simple concept, the Body Systems, for illustration. Notice that the surrounding circles are parallel, homogeneous categories.

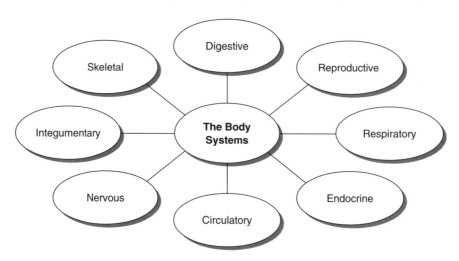

Multiple Orbits

The use of orbits is strategic. A second-order **Web** might well be the components of each body system, and spokes shooting out of each system would lead to such components. For example, spokes radiating from the digestive system might lead to Eustachian tube, stomach, small intestine, large intestine, and so on. A third-order **Web** (another orbit) might focus in functions and another on diseases. Again, the key is homogeneity. At some point, it will be important to show connections between and among systems; this can be accomplished with, say, dotted lines.

One variation in the homogeneity theme is to use a consistent set of heterogeneous attributes. In our training materials, we have an excellent Concept Web dealing with Proportion. The first-order **Web** (or orbit) displays the four terms *percent*, *fraction*, *ratio*, and *decimal*. Around each of these (the second orbit) are the terms *labeled with*, *based on*, and *used with*.

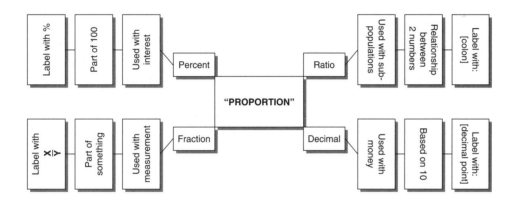

Content Examples for Concept Webbing

Language Arts	*Math*	*Science*	*Social Studies*
1. literary devices 2. persuasive writing 3. the fantasy genre 4. coming of age in nonfiction	1. balancing linear equations 2. measurement tools 3. percentages 4. 3-dimensional shapes	1. the structure of the atom 2. ecosystems 3. inert gases 4. the five senses	1. types of government 2. private (free) enterprise 3. federalism 4. the NAFTA Treaty

Cause-Effect

Many events, ideas, and concepts are best understood in terms of their association with causes and effects. At times, it is difficult to distinguish causes from effects, and it often seems as if they are interchangeable. In many cases, there are multiple causes for an effect; in other cases, a single cause leads to multiple effects. Some **cause-effect** specialists feel that **cause-effect** is not a singular relationship but rather a chain of causes that lead to effects, which become causes which lead to effects which become causes, and so on. A full understanding of **cause-effect** requires students to disaggregate events or outcomes in terms of the factors or conditions that led to or at least contributed to their occurrence. Students must also be able to distinguish causation from its cousins: correlation and coincidence.

Fire inspectors do this for a living; they sift through the *effects* (e.g., a burned building) to identify what may have *caused* the blaze (e.g., a faulty furnace, bad wiring, a fireplace left unattended, arson). The fact that the fire occurred on Wednesday is a *coincidence*. But wait! If there are 20 fires each in June, August, and September, that too may be coincidence. But if 50 of the 60 fires occurred on a Wednesday, there is a strong likelihood that we have an arsonist with a thing about Wednesdays. Now what had been coincidence (day of the week) takes a different turn. It still does not mean that Wednesday was the direct cause of the fire, but there is now a *correlation* between day of the week and at least 50 of the fires.

> **Correlation** is an intriguing concept in and of itself. By definition, it means that two events or conditions often occur in conjunction with each other, but one does not cause the other to occur. For example, there is considerable evidence that high and low school attendance is correlated with high and low student achievement, respectively. This is not to say that simply being in school every day will directly result in high achievement, nor that not being in school is the direct cause of low achievement. And although logic and experience tell us it is difficult to do well in school without being there, we all know of situations where students with low attendance do quite well academically.

> **Coincidence.** At times, students confuse correlation with coincidence. We have a colleague who swears that whenever she books a golf trip to Myrtle Beach, it rains the entire week. Or there are sports fans who are sure they are to blame for their team's loss because they didn't watch the game from their customary chair. Back to the fires, if all 60 were on a Wednesday but all caused by something different—and let's say only one by an arsonist—the *Wednesday* thing is purely a coincidence.

In our experience, **cause-effect** is one of the most difficult concepts for adults to understand, never mind students. We urge participants to begin in the early grades, use clear examples at first, and help students develop hooks to distinguish among **cause**, **correlation**, and **coincidence** for the best results.

Which Organizers?

There are several *Graphic Organizers* for **cause-effect**. Notice that some Organizers have also appeared in prior relationships. In our experience, the same half dozen or so *Organizers* are versatile enough to be used in multiple situations.

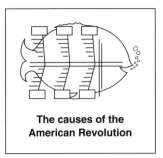

The causes of the American Revolution

The **Fishbone** displays a physical connection of ribs (causes) leading into a backbone (effect); once words are inserted, this pictorial association helps young children develop a cause-effect hook. For older students, the fishbone can do double duty in that upper ribs might represent one set of causes (events in Great Britain) and the lower ribs another (events in the Colonies) to understand the "effect" (the Revolutionary War).

The plot line of *The Canterbury Tales*

For cause-effect, the **Tree** diagram is especially useful in that it shows roots as in original causes, the trunk as a major effect, which then leads into several branches, which in turn spawn subbranches. This multiple cause-effect sequence is an easy graphic to picture for students of all ages.

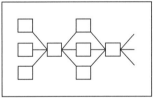

The **Joined Spiders** typically show multiple **cause-effect** relationships (moisture, instability, and wind-shear result in a tornado; which results in destruction of property, flooding, loss of life; which results in shortages, unemployment, displacement, etc.).

Content Examples for Cause-Effect

Language Arts	Math	Science	Social Studies
1. the development of characters in fiction 2. support for thesis in persuasive essay 3. multiple conflicts in plot development 4. the development of language	1. projecting growth in a trend line 2. calculating time, distance, rate 3. analyzing error patterns 4. the effect on volume of changing dimensions on probability	1. simple machines 2. analysis of a disease 3. weathering and erosion 4. the impact of moisture and light on fungi	1. economic developments and population shifts 2. the emergence of third-world countries 3. the impact of religion on political behavior 4. the causes and effects of the Great Depression

Problem-Solution

Students are continually faced with their own problems to solve, and they hear about problem-solving throughout the world in every nightly newscast. Most problems require multiple steps to arrive at a solution (e.g., getting into shape), many have multiple viable solutions (which diet and exercise plan to choose?), and a few cannot really be solved (e.g., a limited budget or having diabetes). These latter problems just have to be managed or lived with. The tricky part about problem-solving is to select from many options the one that is likely to be the most satisfactory. At times, there is no one perfect solution, and it's a matter of selecting the lesser of the evils. The choice of solution often depends on the ripple effects into other dimensions, since nearly every decision affects someone or something else further along the line. The whole getting-into-shape illustration above is a perfect example of this domino effect.

For some students, the study of **Problem-Solution** in their own lives or at least within their family is the ideal concrete reference and the place to begin. For others, problem-solving at school provides a slightly more remote and thus safer backdrop. In either case, we've noted that the **Problem-Solution** process needs to be experienced on three levels: real-time, hypothetical, and retrospective.

Real-Time. The most authentic **Problem-Solution** activities are real-time; that is, they are actual dilemmas, and students participate directly in the process of finding solutions. Students can track their steps and reflect on their work. Some real-time scenarios are immediate. For example, (a) How can we distribute and collect class materials with less disruption? (b) How can we regulate the moisture in the class terrarium to keep the animals comfortable? (c) What can we do to be better peer edit each other's compositions? and (d) How many containers (and what size) will we need to store our crayons and markers?

The solutions to some real-time problems are *not immediate* but can be seen sooner than the weight-loss problem above. For example, (a) How can we increase voter registration over the last election (Social Studies)? (b) How can we set up our class store to raise money for a field trip (Math)? and (c) How can we use simple machines to create a scale that can actually weigh objects (Science)?

Hypothetical. A second type of **Problem-Solution** activity is the hypothetical, or *what-if*, type. These problems cannot be solved by students but rather present quandaries or dilemmas that they can consider vicariously. And since there is no actual outcome, the *reflection* process is limited to how students defined the problem, identified possible solutions, examined each for viability, and arrived at their preferred answer. For example, students might consider the dilemma of declining interest in joining the military: How can the strength of the military be restored? At what level should drug testing for athletes be required? or What regulations should be imposed on stem-cell research to keep it safe yet productive? Contemporary issues make ideal subjects for hypothetical problem-solving.

Retrospective. The third type of **Problem-Solution** scenario is to consider an actual historic or literary problem situation that has already occurred to offer a deep-level analysis and/or an alternate solution. Some scholars call this *off-camera* analysis. For example, students might consider what alternatives there might have been to end World War II, rather than the atom bomb. Or suppose Abraham Lincoln had not been assassinated? In Literature, students might discuss what might have happened had Romeo and Juliet's families been good friends, or what if Ahab had not actually found Moby Dick? Granted, these may be after-the-fact analyses of problems already solved by someone else, but they are nonetheless instructive as to how the process works.

Which Organizers?

Graphically, the **Problem-Solution** process typically includes the steps taken, points of decision, if-then scenarios, and outcomes. Some diagrams also include preliminary or fact-finding steps as well. There are several Visual or *Graphic Organizers* for **Problem-Solution** activities.

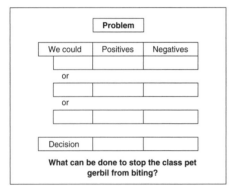

What can be done to stop the class pet gerbil from biting?

The **Positive-Negative Solution template** is helpful for students to track the discussion of two or three options. By identifying several choices, including the up-side and down-side of each, students can "land on" the most viable (if not the perfect) solution. It is actually in using the process of considering and weighing options with classmates that students develop their own ability to use the format.

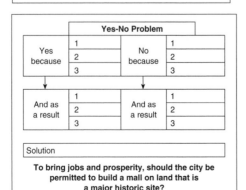

Which is *really* the best buy on tennis shoes?

The **Locks and Keys** template illustrates the multistep nature of problem-solving: what are the keys (and in what order) to unlock the quandary or dilemma? Looking at multistep math and other content area problems prevents students from leaping to single-step conclusions.

Yes-No Problem				
Yes because	1	No because	1	
	2		2	
	3		3	
And as a result	1	And as a result	1	
	2		2	
	3		3	
Solution				

To bring jobs and prosperity, should the city be permitted to build a mall on land that is a major historic site?

The **Yes-No** template is more complicated than the Positive-Negative, but illustrates a similar concept. For any problem (including "yes-no"), there are consequences to either choice, and the final decision may need to be a compromise between "yes and no." The key is that students give serious and frank consideration to *both* alternatives to be certain they have given full consideration to the immediate and long-term ramifications of each.

Content Examples for Problem Solution

Language Arts	Math	Science	Social Studies
1. making predictions about fiction 2. completing an action research problem 3. taking sides in a persuasive argument 4. analyzing a character's problem-solution dilemma	1. which is the best method to calculate the amount saved at a sale? 2. how can this parking lot hold 20% more cars? 3. which containers hold the most for shipping 4. how using the wrong display of data leads to erroneous conclusions	1. using the scientific method to grow mold 2. a device for dogs with no front legs 3. correcting a dietary deficiency (e.g., lack of calcium) 4. how can space travel become a vacation option?	1. imposing democracy on third-world countries 2. tax law revision to achieve greater equity 3. balancing security with the right to privacy (i.e., the Patriot Act) 4. irrigation techniques to control annual forest fires

Text Mapping

Text Mapping is the analysis of highly complex passages to identify the underlying structure and internal logic and then using a *Graphic Organizer* to display it. It is most frequently used with nonfiction, although there are times when fictional material is sufficiently complex. **Text Mapping** is a deep-level version of the *Organizational Patterns*, a learning construct considered earlier in the chapter. We provided a few utility graphics to accompany each of the *Organizational Patterns* previously examined (Table 6.3), but when students perform **Text Mapping,** they not only determine the overall pattern used by the author to organize the piece but also drill down into the text to unlock the concepts or ideas presented.

Which Organizers?

There are several *Graphic Organizers* for **Text Mapping.** One is called the "Character Map." It is a technique to help students profile themselves, historic characters, or the characters from stories or books. Key attributes and qualities are featured for younger students, and older students will include more subtle and indirect descriptors.

1. Another variation of the "Character Map" is below.

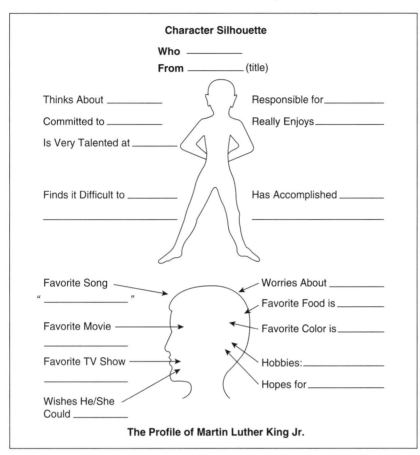

Character Silhouette

Who _____
From _____ (title)

Thinks About _____

Committed to _____

Is Very Talented at _____

Finds it Difficult to _____
_____

Responsible for _____

Really Enjoys _____

Has Accomplished _____
_____

Favorite Song _____
" _____ "

Favorite Movie _____
_____

Favorite TV Show _____
_____

Wishes He/She
Could _____

Worries About _____

Favorite Food is _____

Favorite Color is _____

Hobbies: _____

Hopes for _____

The Profile of Martin Luther King Jr.

2. A second strategy is the "Text Map."

who   when   where

what   why
?

Huckleberry Finn

For fiction, one popular text map is the identification of *who, what, where,* etc. using visual icons that can remind students of key literary elements. Developmentally, younger students use a simpler schema (shown in the diagram), while older students benefit from additional icons about types of conflict, parallel plot lines, and multiple settings.

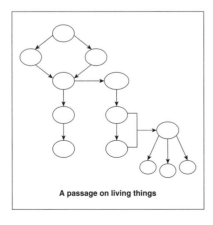

A passage on living things

In text mapping, the **Flowchart** is used to map a passage that is particularly dense. The diagram will feature key terms and connections between and among them show how the passage is structured.

Content Examples for Text Mapping

Language Arts	Math	Science	Social Studies
1. technical documents or manuals 2. expository material for research materials 3. the plot structure of a play (e.g., *Macbeth*)	1. technical documents containing mathematical detail 2. nonmath passages containing mathematical detail	1. technical manuals or pamphlets (e.g., the process of refining petroleum) 2. scientific text material (e.g., DNA) 3. expository material for the research	1. political pamphlets and speeches 2. expository material for research paper 3. manuscripts (e.g., the interrelated causes of the Korean War) 4. social studies text material (e.g., the factors of production)

Data Display

In many content area classes, including but certainly not limited to math, students are confronted with data tables and charts of various types. Many authors oblige the reader with colorful graphs to provide concrete references that help clarify the data and create a lasting memory hook. The editors of *USA Today*, for example, provide at least one such graph daily and even use symbolic icons to make the data even more noteworthy. For example, to display world trends in pipe smoking, they might use pipe stems as the bars in the graph, complete with the little bowl at the end. For England, the little bowl would be the calabash used by Sherlock Holmes; for the United States, the bowl might be a corncob pipe; for Germany, a meerschaum would do the trick; for a Middle Eastern country, a hookah would appear; and so on. Whether or not the reader smokes a pipe, the graph is eye-catching and memorable.

Other materials encountered by students will not show such concern about clarity and aesthetics. These authors see colorful graphs as an unnecessary distraction and simply list the data or perhaps even embed it in the rhetoric. In such cases, students may need to put the data into an explanatory chart or graph for themselves. The entire point is to capture the numbers in a way that reflects their significance and their relationship to each other. Such graphic displays allow students to analyze the data and to make inferences and generalizations from it, and to pose questions for further study.

Which Organizers?

There are several Visual or *Graphic Organizers* for data display. Notice that some of these same visuals have also appeared in prior relationships.

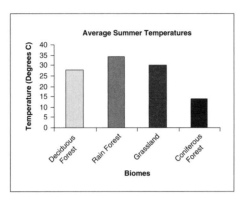

The **Bar Graph** compares quantities on the vertical axis with those along the horizontal and shows the data as bars or columns. It is meant to show a one-to-one relationship between the two axes and does not attempt to show progress across time. What's clear is that if these temperatures and biomes were described as text, it would be difficult to fully understand.

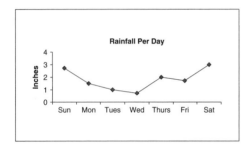

The **Line Graph** also compares the vertical with the horizontal axis but shows the data as points of intersection rather than columns. In addition, the "points" are connected with a line—which shows progress across time. Without this graphic display and the connecting lines, it is not clear how drastically the temperature declined during the week.

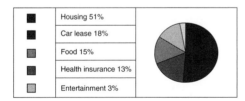

The **Circle Graph** displays data as proportion—or what portion of 100% (the entire circle) is each data set. It is important to see not only how quantities are divided but how each quantity relates to each other as well as the whole. Students can see that amount of income is less important than how it must be spent.

The Stem-and-Leaf Plot, Histogram, and Box-and-Whisker Plot are illustrated on the next page.

	Game		Game		Game
1: 50		7: 66		13: 44	
2: 65	Game	8: 65	Game	14: 56	Game
3: 70	Game	9: 70	Game	15: 66	Game
4: 35	Game	10: 35	Game	16: 60	Game
5: 40	Game	11: 29	Game	17: 44	Game
6: 57	Game	12: 33	Game	18: 50	Game

The stem-and-leaf plot for these scores would look like:

Stem	Leaves				
2	9				
3	3	5	5		
4	0	4	4		
5	0	0	6	7	
6	0	5	5	6	6
7	0	0			

Coach Smith's last 18 basketball game scores for the 7th grade Wildcats

The **Stem-and-Leaf Plot** is a frequency diagram that displays the actual data together with its frequency. It does so by taking each piece of data (e.g., 46) and using part of its value (i.e., the 4) as a class or group (i.e., the stem) and actually lists the other part (i.e., the 6) as leaves. Even if the scores were listed in a column, their exact distribution is not as clear as if diagrammed, such as is shown to the left.

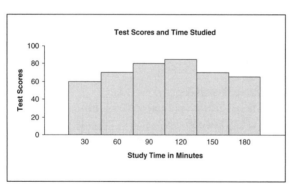

The **Histogram** is a graph that uses bars to show the frequency of data within continuous intervals. This helps students see how large quantities of data (e.g., minutes studied and test scores) can be sorted to show a trend or make comparisons.

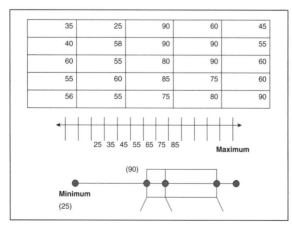

The **Box-and-Whisker Plot** is a diagram that shows the median of data and measures of spread to upper and lower quartile ranges. This then shows the entire range of data in the set and provides a sense of how high or low it is overall. If attempting to make sense of the data by only looking at the scores, the reader will miss the distribution of the results and how many more scores were above than below the median.

Content Examples for Data Display

Language Arts	*Math*	*Science*	*Social Studies*
1. frequency of sentence types used in writing 2. proportion of each genre read 3. comparing numeric data from primary and secondary sources 4. number of speech rehearsals and final grade	1. cost of items at several different stores 2. test scores and measures of central tendency 3. hours spent watching TV (etc.)	1. daily temperatures 2. temperature relative to precipitation 3. the phases and tides of the moon 4. mass compared to weight at and above sea level	1. proportion of populations on a continent 2. gas prices relative to supply and demand 3. voting patterns by zip code 4. the casualties in major global wars

How to Use Graphic Organizers With Students

Like all of the Learning Constructs, *Graphic Organizers* can be used at appropriate times throughout a *Unit Plan*. The key with any of the Constructs is to use the one that matches the activity, which, of course, must match one or more of the *Performance Indicators*. For reference, the eight *Graphic Organizers* just addressed are reprinted below.

☐ Sequence   ☐ Cause-Effect
☐ Classification or Categorization   ☐ Problem-Solution
☐ Comparison-Contrast   ☐ Text Mapping
☐ Concept Webbing   ☐ Data Display

It is no mere coincidence that these names capture precisely the patterns of thinking that students will use consistently throughout their school years. And the fact that *these* patterns are the deep-level companions to the *Organizational Patterns* discussed earlier confirms for students that the way information is presented to them, the way they process it, and the way they construct meaning are each part of the same seamless whole.

For teachers to augment their initial *Unit Plans* with Visual or *Graphic Organizers*, the keys to success are as follows:

Advanced Preparation

In our experience, teachers are always happier with *Graphic Organizers* when they have planned for them in advance and used them strategically. This advanced and strategic preparation consists of two steps:

1. **Select viable passages (or chunks of information).** Find actual passages from texts, media, lectures, or demonstrations, and other authentic print materials that students will be expected to digest. Make sure the passages are significant and pithy, not watered-down material that is unimportant, doesn't really contain much information, and for which students are not accountable.

2. **Plan accurate organizers.** Identify the type of *Graphic Organizer* that will accurately reflect the patterns and conceptual structures in each passage. Construct a makeshift diagram to use as a demo with students. While the computer-generated *Organizers* are slick and trendy, the teacher's hand-drawn versions are normally the most accurate. If teachers decide to use computer-generated graphics, they must take special care to be certain that the *Organizer* fits the passage and that they aren't attempting to retrofit a passage into an attractive graphic.

Show Students How-To

Once teachers throughout the building are using *Graphic Organizers*, this step may be unnecessary, or might be used as a pretest. But a quick annual review of the *Organizational Patterns* and the accompanying *Graphic Organizers* using simple passages will never hurt. With a mental image of, say, "The Three Little Pigs" as a three-part Venn diagram or "Pinocchio" as a **Cause-Effect** fishbone, students have memory hooks to use for application in their content material. Students must also be shown how to devise their own *Graphic Organizers* to represent simple, familiar ideas or text passages.

Provide Viable Practice

But please no phony drill-and-kill practice with workbook pages and no-brainer worksheets. *Viable* practice means asking students to **interpret** given *Organizers*, as well as to **devise** the appropriate *Organizers*, for legitimate print and auditory materials.

■ LEVELS OF QUESTIONING

What It Is

The research on *Questioning* is as diverse as it is plentiful. Beginning with Socrates, asking questions as a teaching-learning strategy has been a Best Practice throughout recorded history. The research on *Questioning* tells us that as much as 80% of classroom time is spent this way, but the number of questions teachers reported asking was significantly lower than the number they actually asked. Not only are teachers unaware of the number of questions asked and answered, they lack a sense of what proportion of the questions are academic versus those that are logistical or directional. We often script lessons, and teachers are always amazed to see that what they thought would be a question-answer session on, say, "The Preamble" turns out to be 3 questions about the topic (e.g., 2 by the teacher and 1 by a student) and 8 to 10 other questions that pertain to the directions or logistics such as "Is this for a grade?" or "Scott's absent; what about his part?" or "Can we finish after lunch?" or "Did you say it had to be in ink?" or "What do we do if the printer won't work?" It's not that students should never ask logistical questions; that's part of every classroom, and it's inherent to following directions. But when a disproportionate amount of the teaching-learning time is consumed with nonacademic questions compared with academic ones, *Questioning* can become counterproductive.

Even in classrooms where academic *Questioning* does take precedence, we find that the majority are limited to the recall of facts. Only a small proportion of questions ask students to think at inferential levels, and in only rare instances are they asked to construct meaning beyond the material. But to be fair, most of us were never really taught how to develop higher-order questions, nor to help students devise constructive-level responses.

In our experience, effective *Questioning* must be planned for, and students must be shown how to process information at different levels and answer corresponding questions. Thereafter, they must also become proficient at developing questions at these various levels. Many of the academic standards in several states include the requirement that students answer various levels of questions, and some stipulate that students must also construct questions at various levels of difficulty. To that end, we have developed three levels of questions for teachers to integrate into their *Unit Plans*.

Level I

Level I questions ask students to use stored or immediate knowledge. They ask for literal or fact-level information that students have read or been given. Level I questions typically deal with the *who, what, when,* and *where* of things because that's what the author or speaker has provided. If the information given also includes a *why* or *how*, these too can become Level I questions. If such information is not given, it must be inferred, and that at a higher level of thought. Another way to describe Level I questions is that they address what the author (or speaker) actually writes or says. For example,

- Where do Spanish names appear in American geography?
- What were the three little pigs trying to accomplish?
- Who is the mayor of _____?
- When during the month is a female most likely to become pregnant?
- Which is more pie, 2/3 or 3/4?
- How many legs does a grasshopper have?

Remember, a *why* question may also be a Level I if the information is provided or is common knowledge.

For example, "Why did Abraham Lincoln go to Gettysburg?" is a Level I question, since it is common knowledge that he went to dedicate the battlefield.

Level II

Level II questions ask students to make inferences, draw conclusions, or see implications in the given information. In contrast to Level I questions, they cannot be answered only from the literal detail provided in the material. Students must read between the lines or think about what the author or speaker may have meant by what he or she said. Sample Level II questions are as follows:

- How is it determined whether to use Santa or San?
- Why did it take the third little pig longer than the first two to build his house?
- What does the city government have to do with the way the schools are run?

- How does the unborn fetus react to alcohol or drugs?
- What do we need to do to know how much total pie we have? (2/3 of one pie and 3/4 of another)
- How is a spider different from a grasshopper?

In contrast to Level I questions that deal with one concept or skill, Level II questions include two or more concepts and involve relationships between and among them. Both Level I and II questions are *convergent*; that is, they tend to have a limited range of correct answers, and sometimes only one.

Level III

Level III questions ask students to construct meaning beyond the given information and to think at the *what-if* or the hypothetical level; in addition, Level III questions may also ask students to evaluate the material in reference. Students cannot adequately answer, nor create, Level III questions without a firm foundation of background information (Level I) and a sense of the relationships among the concepts involved (Level II). In contrast to the convergent nature of Level I and II questions, Level III questions are more *divergent* in that they involve thinking beyond the material and require students to delve into creative but viable possibilities. In reference to the *Performance Indicators*, many of them are constructed to require Level III–type student mastery.

As with Bloom's Taxonomy, it is not necessary to ask students questions at all three on the same topic, but the samples we've included show the developmental relationships among the levels. Sample Level III questions are as follows:

- Suppose everyone in school spoke Spanish except you? How would you communicate?
- What if all three little pigs built one house; how could they all have had the things they wanted and still be safe?
- Why don't we just have the city run the schools?
- How does having a baby while you are a teenager make your life different from your friends' lives?
- If we needed to serve pie to 3 football teams of 11 players each, and each player wanted 1/4 of a pie, how would we decide how many pies are needed?
- Is it possible for grasshoppers and other insects to get as big as the monsters in the horror films? Why or why not?

Teachers must take care that students are not fooled into looking for cue words. Just as *who* and *when* questions can be Level I or Level II, depending on the amount of information given, *what-if* questions are not always a Level III. For example, "What if we substituted Splenda for sugar in this recipe? How much would we need?" is a Level I question, since the answer is literal. And for that matter, a *who* question could very well be a Level III; for example, "who would be the most likely candidates to test the new stem-cell technology?"

How to Use With Students

In our experience, *Levels of Questioning* is one of the most popular of all the Learning Constructs. Teachers like the way it gently forces them to be better prepared for class discussions and reminds them to include the various levels of questions on their tests. From the earliest grades, students should be shown how to answer questions at all three levels and to distinguish among the three levels in terms of internalizing the information. Being able to <u>answer</u> questions at all three levels about the information reflects a student's ability to comprehend the material at an independent level. The ability to <u>develop</u> questions at all three levels indicates his or her capacity to construct meaning at an even more intuitive level.

SIMILARITIES AND DIFFERENCES ■

The Best Practice known as *Similarities and Differences* is based on a student's ability to compare and contrast, or to show how two or more things are alike and different. As a Learning Construct, researchers feel that it has the highest effect size or correlation with students' academic success. (Annotated research citations are available from the authors upon request.) Students who can use *Similarities and Differences* successfully can sort things into categories or classes based on features or attributes that distinguish them from others. Researchers understandably feel that *Similarities and Differences* offer teachers an important lever to help students construct meaning for themselves. We have assembled the various Constructs associated with *Similarities and Differences* into the following five methods: **Categorization**, **Comparison**, **Critical Attributes**, the **Metaphor**, and **Analogies**. These methods can be applied separately or together as appropriate to the *Performance Indicators* featured in each *Unit Plan*.

Categorization

What It Is

Categories are the mental "bins" we use to sort things by common attribute. Daily, we are inundated with a wide array of people, words, objects, and ideas that we continually sort, categorize, and associate with what we already know to make sense of them. At its simplest level, **Categorization** is like the way "big-box" home-improvement stores are organized.

There are separate sections for lamps, candles, rugs, clocks, and electronics. As new products come along, they are placed into the proper category with similar items. The operant motive is *quick access and convenience*, in and out. Unfortunately, many classroom workbooks stop here. Students are provided sets of fairly homogeneous items tossed into a jumble, which they are asked to sort into preselected categories.

But most of life isn't that conveniently presorted. To extend the retail analogy, life often presents us with the "furniture store" instead. The various products—lamps, candles, rugs, furniture, and so on—are placed into authentic groupings to simulate an actual room. Here the operant motive is *browse and linger*. In fact, the shopper really must browse through every furniture grouping to find just the right lamp, for example. Both types of store offer many of the same goods, but the display is totally opposite, and the context provided by the furniture store settings helps distinguish the Colonial theme from the Tuscan or the Contemporary. As learners, we are often faced with a similar composite of learning stimuli—embedded in a particular context—and must do the sorting on our own. We soon discover that some items do not fall into only one category; lamps can be sorted by theme (Colonial, Tuscan, etc.), but also style (candlestick, mock-Tiffany ginger jar, etc.), or type (incandescent, fluorescent, sunlight, etc.), and those categories tend not to be mutually exclusive.

While we're in the store analogy, life often provides a third type: the antique shop. Here the wares are randomly strewn about to look as much like an unkempt attic or abandoned garage as possible. Connoisseurs claim that there is a strategic order in the apparent disorder, but for the sake of discussion, let's call it totally random. In contrast to the furniture store, the context is irrelevant; one might see a piece of scrimshaw leaning against a statue of Howdy Doody wearing a Nixon-Agnew pin, lit by an Aladdin's lamp, the whole thing resting on a Coca-Cola tray from a USO canteen. Here the motive is *search*. Only the trained eye can discern worthless junk from a real find, and dealers prosper from the sales of both. Items in an antique shop are often even more difficult to sort than the furniture store, since they fit into several categories such as by object, by period, by composition, by value, by manufacturer, by taste, and so on.

These three types of retail displays are analogous to the kinds of **Categorization** students must do to master the skill. In our experience, most teachers have had access only to the "home-improvement store" model. Items clearly represent distinct categories but are then thrown together for students to resort into predetermined categories. While this is an important basic skill, it is certainly not sufficient. Students also need the "furniture store" as well as the "antique shop" experiences to become fully proficient in categorization on two levels: (a) of information provided to them, and (b) to construct their own categories from noncategorical information.

How to Use With Students

In our experience, even the most effective teachers are lulled into a false satisfaction about their students' **Categorization** prowess. This is because the level of sorting asked of their students is limited to the "home-improvement store" model. Then when high-stakes tests require the "furniture store" or "antique shop" models, many of their students have no idea how to respond. Worse, when asked to construct their own categories from noncategorical material, most students won't even make an attempt. Teachers need to teach their students the skill of deep-level **Categorization.** This involves using analogies like our retail stores to be sure students understand the different levels of **Categorization.**

According to learning theorists who've made a study of it, everything that we learn can be sorted into one of several "bins" that progress in difficulty. The most frequently used bins are the following: **people, objects, places, events, actions, conditions,** and **concepts.** These bins offer a nice variety of topics or concepts for teaching students how to practice categorizing information. As a sorting taxonomy, it will help students master categorization as a learning construct to cut their way through the various thickets of complex material and information they face every day. The items listed in each bin can be easily replaced by those closer to a teacher's content area as needed. Note also that the examples beneath each bin proceed from the literal and concrete to the more hypothetical or abstract. These too are only samples and can be swapped out for other examples aligned with a teacher's subject matter.

People: accountant, air marshal, Congressperson, nurse, orchestra conductor, pathologist (e.g., duties, training requirements, hazards or unusual circumstances, place in our society)

Objects: biography, hunting license, extension ladder, personal budget, snapshot, thermometer, and so on (e.g., definitions, attributes, various uses or functions)

Places: baseball diamond, city park, hospital, national monument, restaurant, shopping mall, university (e.g., function or purpose, physical attributes, who works there, who goes there, relevance)

Events: the discovery of DNA, the Lindberg kidnapping, the surrender at Appomattox, Super Bowl XXV (e.g., dates, persons involved, decisive moments, lead-up or prior conditions, historic implications)

Actions: exercising, forecasting weather, getting married, justifiable homicide, impeaching a president, quitting a job (e.g., definitions, rationale, steps involved, implications, the aftermath, evaluating the consequences)

Conditions: errors in math problems, a hostage standoff, a life-threatening injury, a controversial school rule (e.g., description of situation, what is known, current effect, what if left as is, viable solutions)

Concepts: euthanasia, fuel rationing, hypnotism to elicit confessions, NSA surveillance, narcissism, stem-cell research (e.g., definition/rationale, terms and conditions, civil liberty implications, overall effect on society)

Here is a very simple **people** sort using famous men:

Clyde Barrow
William McKinley
George Washington
  Carver
Henry Wadsworth
  Longfellow
Theodore Roosevelt
Dwight D. Eisenhower
Martin Luther King Jr.
	Ulysses S. Grant
	William Colin Powell
	George Armstrong
	  Custer
	Oliver Wendell Holmes
	John F. Kennedy
	Charles A. Lindberg
	William Bonney
		Thurgood Marshall
		Gerald Ford
		Alexander Graham Bell
		Horace Greeley
		Richard Nixon
		George Herbert Walker
		  Bush
		Robert Byrd

The first-level sort can be by noteworthy occupation; one category that will surface is U. S. Presidents. Playing off Presidents, a second sort can be living and nonliving, political party, and/or served in wartime. By the third sort, the students can be asked to create their own categories, either going back to the original list or remaining with Presidents. Such categories as birthplace, economic background, and family history typically surface. One test of students' **Categorization** prowess is if they can supply an additional name to the category. For example, if the Presidents get sorted into "served in the military," can students supply another President who served (e.g., Andrew Jackson)?

When students have truly mastered **Categorization,** they can, within all seven classes of knowledge and without prompts, do the following with lists of categorical information: (a) sort terms into categories and sub-categories, (b) supply additional items for each overall category, (c) supply additional items for each subcategory, (d) create sub-subcategories (e.g., Presidents > nineteenth century > reelected), (e) create new categories that would also work (e.g., made a career-ending mistake while in office), and (f) distinguish between examples and nonexamples.

Categorization is the foundation for the other four methods in the *Similarities and Differences* Construct. And teachers need to help their students see **Categorization** as a mental bookmark to which they can return if they become confused by any of the other three methods that comprise the *Similarities and Differences* construct.

Comparison

What It Is

The second of the *Similarities and Differences* methods is **Comparison**. Once students understand the concept of Categorization and can sort or classify items according to their common attributes, they are ready to make more extensive **Comparisons** of two or more items in the same category, noting how they are alike and different. This could be two or more people (e.g., colonial first ladies Abigail Adams, Dolly Madison, Elizabeth Monroe), objects (e.g., a paper cutter, a pair of scissors, a straight razor), or highly abstract concepts (e.g., collaboration versus competition).

As discussed with *Organizational Patterns* and *Graphic Organizers*, two of the most common techniques for displaying comparisons and contrasts are (a) the T-chart and (b) the Venn diagram. But to compare several homogeneous items on multiple dimensions, (c) the Comparison Matrix is a useful tool. All three are illustrated below.

The **T-chart** allows for either the comparison or contrast of parallel attributes, but not both.

Narcissus	*Orpheus*
• known for being extremely handsome • did not return the love of Echo (she died for love of him) • used his good looks to charm himself • was cursed to look at himself in the pool and wasted away looking at his reflection	• known for being a musical genius • willing to risk his own life to save Eurydice (they were in love, and she died) • used his musical talent to charm the underworld • was cursed because he looked back and lost Eurydice to the underworld forever

The advantage of the T-chart is that students do not see both likeness and differences at the same time but one or the other. For difficult or entirely new concepts, the T-chart is preferable to the Venn diagram for developing students' early acquaintance.

The **Venn diagram** both compares and contrasts, the latter using parallel attributes.

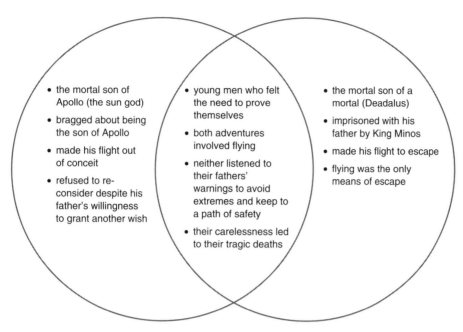

The **Comparison Matrix** displays a set of homogeneous items on one axis (e.g., familiar tragic Myths) and a set of criteria or attributes along the other axis (e.g., chief claim to fame, major weakness, and reason for demise). When completed, the cells in the matrix reveal multiple points of comparison. Unlike the Venn diagram, the intent is not necessarily to show totally parallel and direct comparisons but to use the information in the cells to make the direct and indirect comparisons.

Popular Tragic Characters From Mythology

	Chief claim to fame	*Major weakness*	*Reason for demise*	*etc.*
Daedalus (and Icarus)	Daedalus was the most skilled artisan and craftsman in Greece; discovered how to create wings that would enable him and his son, Icarus, to fly.	. . . while he and Icarus were flying, Icarus flew too close to the sun; his wings melted, and he fell to the sea and perished; Daedalus was too far ahead and did not hear Icarus' calls for help.	. . . when he discovered that his son had fallen into the sea, Daedalus blamed himself for the tragedy and never flew again.	
Narcissus	Narcissus was one of the most handsome, desirable youths who ever lived, but—because he was also very selfish—he could not return anyone's affection for him.	. . . rejected the affections and attentions of Echo, who wasted away with love for him; as punishment, he was cursed to love only himself.	. . . while gazing in a reflecting pool, he fell in love with his own reflection—so much so that he became obsessed with it and couldn't stop looking at it; he eventually wasted away gazing into the pool.	

(Continued)

(Continued)

	Chief claim to fame	*Major weakness*	*Reason for demise*	*etc.*
Orpheus (and Eurydice)	Orpheus had a talent for music; played the lyre for hours, charming even the animals and especially his girlfriend, Eurydice.	. . . went down to the Underworld to rescue Eurydice, using his music to charm those in charge; he was told not to look back at Eurydice as they left, but he forgot and looked, and she was snatched back to the Underworld forever.	. . . without Eurydice, he went into isolation and no longer played his lyre; he eventually starved himself to death as the only way he could return to the Underworld to be united with Eurydice.	
Phaëton	Phaëton was the mortal son of Apollo; he bragged about it so much to his friends that they challenged him for proof; he went off to find his father to obtain the proof.	. . . when Apollo asked what he wished for as proof, Phaëton asked to ride his father's chariot across the heavens. Apollo knew this was too dangerous and would probably prove fatal but couldn't talk his son out of it.	. . . as his father feared, Phaëton lost control. The chariot ran amok across the heavens, creating havoc on the earth and nearly burning it up. Jupiter had to intervene, sending a lightning bolt to kill Phaëton, removing him from the chariot, thus saving the earth.	
etc.				

To construct one's own meaning, facility with the Comparison Matrix also includes the ability to add rows and columns, inserting the pertinent information in each cell. While adding another selection may be relatively simple—in this case, another tragic Myth such as *Cupid and Psyche* or *Pygmalion*—the addition of a criteria or attribute is more of a challenge. It means that the student is familiar enough with the original Myths and the original criteria to know that they will work with additional Myths. Examples of additional criteria (or attribute) for Myths might be the following:

- alternate choice (or what could he have done differently?)
- lasting effect (or what legacy has he left that we still use today?)

In the sample Comparison Matrix carrying through the Mythology theme, students can see that

- some characters were "good" people, and some were self-absorbed and vain
- all of the characters were distinguished in some way (looks, talent, lineage)
- love was at the base of all the stories; some romantic, some familial
- only Orpheus deliberately took his own life
- only Daedalus survived his tragedy but would live with the painful memory thereafter

How to Use With Students

The T-chart and Venn diagram are extremely popular and have become a favorite in every classroom. But as we pointed out in the introduction to the *Graphic Organizers*, they are not always used correctly. Many are filled with a mind-dump or brainstorm of varied and random associations that may relate to the topic but do not indicate anything about its internal logic. Students can easily master all three types of comparison and contrast as shown above, but they must be provided practice in using them correctly. We suggest the following sequence of strategies and encourage the use of the seven bins used in the **Categorization** section. As quickly as possible, however, students should use material from their course content and deal with items that relate to their *Performance Indicators*. We suggest that teachers

1. for the **T-Chart:** make comparisons or contrasts, not both at once
    a. Show students several correct models of familiar topics (e.g., the sun and the moon, fiction and nonfiction, the Metric and U. S. Customary systems of measurement, the Union and Confederate armies).
    b. Next, use familiar topics done incorrectly to show students how it should not be done; ask them to make corrections.
    c. Finally, ask students to create a T-chart of their own, using text materials or other information for which they are accountable; many of the *Performance Indicators* either state or imply making comparisons or contrasts.

2. for the **Venn Diagram:** make comparisons and parallel contrasts simultaneously

    a. Show students several correct models using familiar topics (e.g., the assassinations of Lincoln and Kennedy; a comparison of Christianity, Islam, and Judaism; the circulatory and the respiratory systems; warfare tactics used by Napoleon and those used in Iraq; two major characters in a literary piece; two or more basic shapes).
    b. Next, show several examples done incorrectly; ask students to make the appropriate corrections.
    c. Finally, ask students to create a Venn diagram of their own, using text materials or other information for which they are accountable; many of the *Performance Indicators* either state or imply making comparisons and contrasts.

3. for the **Comparison Matrix:** compare multiple items using several criteria
    a. Show students several correct samples; take time to have students examine the cells for similarities (which they highlight in green) and differences (which they highlight in pink); samples may include the following:

2- and 3-dimensional shapes and figures

	Square	Rectangle	Rectangular prism	Circle	Cylinder
birthday party					
the circus					
the supermarket					
the airport					
etc.					

Vertebrate Animals

	Shark, skate, ray	Perch, bass, trout	Frog, toad, salamander	Turtle, lizard, snake, alligator	Robin, eagle, pelican	Human, bear, whale
outside covering						
temperature control						
limb structure						
reproduction						
etc.						

New World Explorers

	Spain	Portugal	France	Great Britain
earliest date of exploration				
general location				
type of government sponsoring				
reasons for coming				
etc.				

Types of Writing

	Expository			Narrative	
	Descriptive	Informational	Persuasive	Nonfiction	Fiction
purpose					
conventions					
how message conveyed					
typical genre					
sample					
etc.					

b. *Note:* There is really no purpose to be served by showing students examples of **Comparison Matrices** that are not done correctly. In contrast to the T-chart and Venn diagram, this device is relatively new, and students won't have seen it done incorrectly; in this case, showing them the wrong way may just confuse them.

c. Finally, ask students to create a Comparison Matrix of their own, using text materials or other information for which they are accountable; many of the *Performance Indicators* either state or imply making multiple comparisons (e.g., compare several articles about the same topic written by different authors from different perspectives).

The Popularity of the Comparison Matrix. The Comparison Matrix is an epiphany for many teachers. They may have used charts and tables ad nauseam, but the idea of using the matrix as a Learning Construct to compare and contrast multiple types of something and of actually building the matrix in class with students as the information is presented may be relatively new. The key to constructivism is that students produce their own comparison matrix from materials presented (easier) and/or materials they must locate (harder).

One of the most successful uses of the Comparison Matrix is as an assessment. On one level, the teacher provides information in 20% of the cells, and students are asked to fill in the remaining cells. At an even more constructive level, students may be asked to create an entire Comparison Matrix of their own.

Critical Attributes

What It Is

The third Construct in *Similarities and Differences* is to learn a concept by identifying its distinguishing attributes. Some learning theorists call this *concept attainment*, and some refer to it as *critical attribution* (research citations are available from the authors upon request). We call it the **Critical Attribute** method. It helps students discover a concept by looking at exemplars and nonexemplars of it and identify those or critical attributes that seem to make it what it is. That done, they can then identify other examples of that concept and distinguish it from other concepts.

A very simple example is that students are shown piles of what appears to be garbage or junk. One pile contains a used paper plate, a cardboard box lid, a piece of cotton, part of a wooden spoon, and crusts from toast; it is labeled *biodegradable*. The other pile includes a used Styrofoam cup, a wad of aluminum foil, a broken glass bottle, an empty pop can, a piece of vinyl wallet, and a broken plastic brush; its label reads *nonbiodegradable*. Students are asked to identify the attributes of the items in Pile 1 and the attributes of those in Pile 2. Then when they compare the two, they see some common or similar characteristics; perhaps color, function, or the fact that they are broken or used. But it should also dawn on most students that one distinguishing or **Critical Attribute** is that the biodegradable items are natural and have no chemical preservatives or synthetic resins. Hence, they will decay when left to the elements, and their ingredients will blend harmlessly back into the soil. In contrast, the nonbiodegradable items contain synthetic chemicals and resins that will not decay and return to the soil; instead, they will simply remain as unsightly garbage, or pollution. Older students will observe that some of these resins may be toxic and harmful to the environment.

When students truly understand the concept, they can supply examples and nonexamples themselves. In the sample, once they truly understand the concept of biodegradable, they can add a piece of leather belt to the biodegradable pile and a piece of plastic pen to the nonbiodegradable pile.

The important role for the teacher is not to tell students the concept but to ask them questions that prompt them to discover answers. Compared to the conventional method of simply explaining to students the underlying facts or definitions of a concept, the teacher requires students to do more than listen and take notes. They must construct meaning for themselves. Likewise, the teacher's role involves a different type of planning than the telling or presenting role.

Prior to the Lesson

    A. Determine the concept and prepare examples.

    B. Select clear-cut examples and sequence them from easiest to more complex, developmentally, allowing students to get to the desired concept.

During the Lesson

    C. Guide the process by helping students verbalize their thinking.

    D. Help students determine which attributes hold for the various examples.

    E. Have students explain why attributes are kept or discarded.

    F. Help students summarize their thoughts.

    G. Have students give new examples and nonexamples of the concept, verifying against the criteria.

Following the Lesson

    H. Debrief with students on the process.

    I. Ask students to reflect on their thinking and how they used the information in the dialogue to come to their conclusions.

We use three approaches to applying the Critical Attribute method as a Learning Construct with students.

The concept is not announced; examples and nonexamples are given separately. The teacher does not announce the concept but provides clear examples and asks students to describe the attributes of each. This initial list is followed by additional examples, and the teacher asks students to be sure their attributes still hold. Any criteria that do not hold for the examples are dropped. The teacher then poses nonexamples to compare against the examples, describing how they are different. The following is an example from a Grade 5 class studying fruits and vegetables.

The teacher shows the examples of an apple cut in half and a sliced tomato.

Students give the description as *things we eat; things that are alive; and things that grow on plants.*

The teacher shows nonexamples of a rock and a carrot sliced in half.

Students reexamine the three ideas/criteria they previously said. Since a carrot meets the criteria of *things we eat, things that are alive, and things that grow on plants,* but a carrot is not an example, students need to think more deeply. Their first three criteria no longer hold, and they must attempt to refine their thinking to develop new criteria.

Students may come up with: *parts of a plant that we eat that grow above the ground.*

The teacher gives examples of *avocado, peach, squash,* and *orange.*

Students now come up with *things we eat with seeds in them.*

The teacher gives more nonexamples: *celery, head of lettuce, artichoke,* and *potato.*

Students will finally get the attributes of the examples and discover the concept is, *fruits are foods we eat with seeds in the edible part; some foods commonly thought of as vegetables are really fruits.*

A variation of this approach is to provide students examples through pictures or illustrations, both as line drawings and as they appear in the environment, one at a time. If teaching four types of angles (acute, obtuse, right, and straight), the teacher might show students one or more samples of an acute angle, and ask them to identify the attributes. These are recorded on a piece of wall chart paper. Before going to the next drawing(s), the teacher would affix the first picture(s) to its attributes. This continues through the four types of angles. Once finished, students note the lists and attempt to identify similarities and differences, moving to the distinguishing attributes of each angle. Finally, students should be able to cite examples of how each type of angle appears in the environment.

A variation on the use of drawings or physical models is to use a map. By circling the Yucatan, Florida, Cape Cod, and so on, students discover that they are all land connected to a larger piece of land, jutting into an ocean or bay, surrounded on three sides by water. Putting the technical label on the concept is not as important as students showing they can identify still others on the map and that they can distinguish them from other landforms. The name *peninsula* is not as important as the concept.

A more challenging approach is to allow students to predict the concept from the examples. If students are given the following list of words—*bookcase, carport, earplugs, fireplace, sunshine*—most will get to the notion of compound words. When asked to identify the attributes of compound words, they typically arrive at "two words joined to make one word." But when students are shown this next group—*angel, carpet, format, father, carrot*—they are nonplussed. Their definition worked for the first group but certainly not this group. Eventually, students get around to the core attribute of compound words: two words joined together to form a word which retains part or all of the meaning of the original words.

The concept is not announced; examples and nonexamples are mixed. A second approach is to provide a list that contains both examples and nonexamples and, without revealing the concept, ask students to separate the items. In so doing, they reflect on what distinguishes the two groups. An example of this approach to teach the concept of complete sentences is shown below.

Consider the following list:

1. Hazel runs each morning
2. At 5:00 a.m. in the peace and quiet
3. Hazel finds morning a preferred time to run
4. As compared with running in the evening
5. The danger of evening traffic
6. Carlos enjoys running with Hazel
7. One morning, the mist rolling, Hazel and Carlos
8. Carlos was nowhere in sight
9. What began as a feeling of puzzlement but became a pang of fear as she saw what lay ahead

Most students can see that the list contains complete and incomplete sentences. The next step is to ask students to distinguish between them; most eventually see that there must be an "actor" and an "action" for the sentence to be complete. They can deconstruct each of the items to discover that 1, 3, 6, and 8 are complete sentences, and the others are not. As a test of mastery, students should be asked to revise the incomplete sentences to make them complete and to provide complete sentences of their own.

A variation of this approach is to present the items already labeled as Yes or No, asking the students to identify how the "Yeses" differ from the "Nos." This removes the need for students to do the initial sort, making it a bit easier to focus on the distinctions.

The concept is announced; examples and nonexamples are mixed. A third approach is to announce the concept at the outset (e.g., the relationship between fact and inference) and provide students a combined list of examples and nonexamples for facts and inferences that address a common topic (e.g., the repeal of the "blue laws" that ban retail business on Sundays). The students must separate the facts from the inferences, identifying the critical attributes that distinguish one from the other while identifying the linkage between them.

Fact or Inference?

F 1. The print-shop owner found a baby boy, carefully bundled in a small wicker basket, on his door stoop.

I 2. The boy appeared to be about six months old.

I 3. It must have been placed there by some neglectful mother who foolishly counted on the printer to find the child before it died.

___ 4. Aleesha and Latricia Mills, the famous sailing twins who recently won the Challengers' Cup, arrived at San Diego two hours ahead of their projected schedule.

___ 5. Their 36-foot cruiser, name *Gemini*, is appropriate, given the space exploration program of the same name.

___ 6. "It's about time women are recognized for their sailing prowess," Commodore Steward said. "The Mills victory proves they are as capable as men on the high seas."

___ 7. The United Nations' initiative to provide food and clothing for the southeast Asian countries devastated by the tsunami has been jeopardized by another storm that makes it impossible for the planes to land.

___ 8. Without these supplies, the survivors are at further risk of disease and starvation.

___ 9. The nations located nearby have agreed to come forward with aid, provided they are compensated by the United Nations.

Students typically realize even though facts and inferences are separate ideas, they are related. A valid inference is built on a verifiable fact. However, and this may be the tricky part for some students, facts do not necessarily announce their own inferences.

A variation in the approach where the concept is announced is to show students separate lists to illustrate the concept. For example, the commutative property of addition and multiplication might be shown as follows:

Examples:	
$4 + 3 = 3 + 4$	$45 \cdot 23 = 23 \cdot 45$
$1 \cdot 2 = 2 \cdot 1$	$91 + 18 = 18 + 91$
$18 + 22 = 22 + 18$	$71 + 16 = 16 + 71$
$12 \cdot 4 \cdot 3 = 3 \cdot 12 \cdot 4$	$3 + 2 + 6 = 2 + 6 + 3$

Students can see that the problems deal with addition and multiplication and that the answers are identical on both sides of the equal sign. No matter what the **order**, the answer is the same.

Nonexamples:	
$4 - 3 \neq 3 - 4$	$45 - 23 \neq 23 - 45$
$2 \div 1 \neq 1 \div 2$	$91 \div 18 \neq 18 \div 91$
$22 - 18 \neq 18 - 22$	$71 - 16 \neq 16 - 71$

Students can see that these problems deal with subtraction and division. By contrast, the answers are *not* identical on both sides of the equal sign when the **order** is reversed.

When students have truly internalized this concept, they realize that the "order" property holds for addition and multiplication, but it does not hold for subtraction and division. Students can identify their own examples and nonexamples, even to the point of creating word problems to illustrate their mastery. As students get older, they use the property to simplify computation with more complex numbers.

The entire point of the **Critical Attribute** method is to give students prompts that exemplify a concept and with the help of some nonexamples, assist them to deduce the concept for themselves. It's almost as if the concept is clarified by what it is not.

How to Use With Students

The **Critical Attribute** technique is not appropriate to teach every concept. It is most helpful with concepts that students will need to use repeatedly and on their own, without being retaught. The concepts should be fairly narrow and concise; more divergent and inclusive concepts such as *loyalty* or *humanitarianism* are difficult to capture in clear-cut examples and nonexamples. Moreover, they tend to be value laden, and students often confuse emotion and opinion with the those attributes that distinguish, say, "invasion of privacy" from "terrorism prevention." Far greater success will be achieved if teachers use more definitive concepts as, say, the climate variations in the seven major biomes.

Table 6.5   Content Topics That Might Be Taught With the Critical Attribute Strategy

Language Arts	*Math*	*Science*	*Social Studies*
Figurative Language	Symmetry	Gravity	Imperialism
Critical Analysis	Quadrilaterals	Interdependence	Scarcity
Subject-Verb Agreement	Density and Volume	Conservation of Matter	Socialism
Supported Argument	Congruency	Adaptation	Checks and Balances
Theme	Basic Shapes	Mammals	Landforms

We suggest that teachers use the same types of examples with their students as we have used in this text, adapted developmentally, of course. Teachers tell us that the toughest part for them is to decide which of the various approaches are best to use with which concepts. Furthermore, they puzzle over whether to announce the concept, whether to keep the examples and nonexamples separate, and whether to use visuals. The **Critical Attribute** technique is most successful when students have adequate experiential and knowledge hooks on which to build; it may be that these experiential hooks may need to be supplied by the teacher using other Learning Constructs as readiness for the **Critical Attribute** method.

The Metaphor

What It Is

The sign of genius, or so says Aristotle in *Poetics*, "The greatest thing by far is to be the master of the metaphor. It is the sign of genius, since a good metaphor implies an intuitive perception of the similarity in dissimilars." In the glossary of most Literature books, the **Metaphor** is defined as a figure of speech that directly compares two unlike things that have something in common (e.g., "Life is a voyage on the sea of opportunity," or "It's a jungle out there"). In contrast, the Simile is an indirect comparison in that it uses *like* or *as* to make the connection (e.g., "Life is like a voyage on a sea of opportunity," or "It's like a jungle out there").

Purists consider the Simile as a branch of the **Metaphor** family (there's a metaphor) and some claim that all figures of speech are **Metaphors**. That would include onomatopoeia (or words that sound like what they mean, e.g., buzzing bees, whirring tops); personification (or using a living attribute to describe a nonliving object, e.g., the breeze whistled softly); allusion (reference to another, better known image, e.g., Hercules, Moses, Gandhi, Osama Bin Laden, Helen Keller); and metonymy (or the use of a large, general term to represent a smaller one, e.g., "the White House says . . ." to represent the president).

Typically Associated With Literature. The literary **Metaphor** is a figurative device used by authors to help readers experience sensory images far richer than that conveyed in literal wording. The intent is to bring the reader as close as possible to the actual sensation of feeling, hearing, tasting, or visualizing what the author has written by associating his or her words with vivid images from the reader's own experience. The **Metaphor** transports us inside or beneath the words. For example, in the following lines from *Dreams* by Langston Hughes,

> For if dreams die
>
> Life is a broken-winged bird
>
> That cannot fly

The broken-winged bird is an especially poignant and tragic image because the bird's inability to fly means it will be forced to make a home on the ground (or finish its days in the same tree where it was injured); it cannot venture far from its nest to get food for itself or its young; and it will have difficulty escaping predators. An even deeper level of sorrow lies in the fact that the bird has a memory of what it was like to fly and faces the rest of its life in the misery of "what might have been" and "if-only." Students can relate to a person losing his or her sight at age 10 (for example) as compared to being born blind.

By contrast, the literal wording provides the identical information but without the same intensity.

> For if dreams disappear
>
> Life is bleak and may as well be over

Although the **Metaphor** is very much at home in Literature, it is also found in other aspects of life.

Popular Song Lyrics. Anything "literary" has always been a hard sell with adolescents and teenagers. But teachers have gained some traction with the lyrics of popular songs, albeit the relevant examples have a very short shelf life. A few years ago, Pink Floyd recorded a controversial CD called *The Wall*, the most celebrated song from which castigates education and disparages teachers. It refers to each pupil as "just another brick in the wall." Students can easily see how inconsequential the literal lyrics would be, referring to students as "of no real importance, lost among hundreds of others." Despite the obscenity and violence in many of the songs on this CD, they do include several other metaphoric lines, including a few similes:

> " [A girl is] . . . skating on the thin ice of modern life."

> " [The bored singer is] . . . cold as a razor blade; tight as a tourniquet; dry as a funeral drum [similes]"

> " [Urging the girl to stay?] . . . I need you, babe, to put through the shredder in front of my friends"

> " [On death] . . . don't help them to bury the light"

> " [A lover is] . . . receding—a distant ship smoke on the horizon"

> " Just make up your face with your favorite disguise—button-down lips and roller-blind eyes"

As Seen on TV. The use of the **Metaphor** in the classrooms of other content areas has not received much attention. Until recently, metaphoric thinking has been largely taken for granted as the way we speak and the way things are made clear, almost as an element of style. The generic **Metaphor** has become the stock-in-trade of sports announcers, newscasters, and political commentators. Who has not heard at least once a week about

> "lots of mustard on that one." [to describe a hard-thrown pass in football]

> "has captured the hearts and opened the pocketbooks of the entire world." [a humanitarian reaction to a natural disaster]

> "has broken a few bones on both sides of the Congressional aisle." [to indicate that both parties lost ground in a controversial political issue]

> "will release an entirely new arsenal of products to combat the Saber virus." [to describe a new product developed by a major software provider]

> "[the network] . . . has announced its fall lineup, although you can bet the farm it's not yet carved in stone." [saying that the lineup has been designed to change and probably will]

> " If words are the coin of students' thinking, most of them are working with little more than pocket change." [an op-ed columnist for the *Washington Post* upset that today's students read so little]

Other. For other industries that rely on public consumption, the **Metaphor** is second-nature. The examples below are from greeting cards, the movies, magazine advertisements, billboards, and sales pamphlets.

1. As the rain began to fall, the stadium suddenly mushroomed with umbrellas.

2. The miles of endless bare wire were broken only by the occasional knot of black crows.

3. The well-upholstered matron struggled to get into her theater seat.

4. This CEO may well be called the world's only living heart donor.

5. The tide spread her fan on the beach and then gently pulled it away.

6. The little boy's cheeks were a milky way of freckles.

7. Being so far from home, the soldier barely noticed as summer rusted into autumn.

8. Where are the police when these road hogs take over the highway?

9. While she was grounded, Monica became quite a couch potato.

10. Every morning is a clean sheet of paper.

The Life Metaphor. Sometimes it helps students to personalize the **Metaphor** by identifying a life metaphor to describe their own life or particular episodes in their lives. An example is to ask students to think of a training program as a baseball game; the student sees qualifying for the program as getting selected, getting into the program as coming to bat, and then passing each benchmark as getting to a base. Nearing graduation is "rounding third," and crossing home plate is graduation. This activity allows students to use a concrete example from another realm entirely to capture the sensations and ideas that characterize an episode in one's life. Earlier in the chapter, we used the three-part **Metaphor** of a home-improvement store, a furniture store, and an antique shop to illustrate various systems for displaying lamps, pillows, rugs, end tables, and so on. Most adults have used the following **Metaphors** at one time or another to describe a life experience, and they may also prove helpful for students: a carousel, a puzzle, a minefield, a game of tennis, a zoo, a roller coaster, a game of cards, a battle (land or sea), a building under construction, a forest fire, a journey, a marathon, a shopping mall, a horserace, a dance.

How to Use With Students

The difficulty for most teachers is how to teach students to interpret **Metaphors** when encountered in print material other than Literature. But the more basic question should be how to teach them about the **Metaphor,** what it is outside the printed word. Earlier, we discussed **categorization** using the store metaphor: the "big box" method, compared with the "furniture store" motif, compared with the "antique store" approach. The life **Metaphors** above help students think about their own lives (or someone's they know) on a metaphoric level.

Academic Subjects. With the advent of the Best Practices research, several school reform gurus have landed on the **Metaphor** as a means for teaching and learning otherwise difficult concepts. They are convinced that if students can interpret the metaphoric significance of an association, they can understand the deep-level concept upon which it is based. Most textbooks and many teachers have made these connections for students, hoping they will help to clarify. A few examples are shown below:

Social Studies

1. The Civil War was a knife in the heart of the Union.

2. Racists of all cultures can hear nothing when their ears are filled with the cotton of prejudice and ignorance.

3. Just as weather forecasters predict changes in the wind, temperature, and precipitation (influencing what we wear), economists predict changes in the production, distribution, and consumption of goods (influencing what we buy).

4. The industrial revolution was a train that transported an agricultural society to an industrial destination on the rails of invention and mass communication.

Science

1. A lunar eclipse is the moon being swallowed by the earth's shadow.

2. Gravity is the glue that holds us at home on the earth.

3. The water cycle is a Ferris wheel, up and down around the same point.

4. Mitosis is each cell making a Xerox copy of itself.

5. Erosion is nature's bulldozer.

6. The molecules in the three states of matter are so many bumper cars—in solids, they are all clumped together and simply vibrate; in liquids, they glide past each other; in gases, they ricochet off each other.

Math

1. Writing equations is balancing a set of scales with the equal sign as the fulcrum; both sides must be equal in value, even if they do not look alike.

2. Plotting points on a coordinate plane creates a partial picture, but it also allows us to predict the rest of the detail to complete it.

3. Finding the square root of a number is discovering a set of identical twins; finding cubed root is discovering triplets.

These examples demonstrate the logic that if students can interpret the image (e.g., that an equation is a set of balanced scales, or that molecules move differently in different states of matter), they will retain the concept and recall it through visualization or imaging. But these examples are provided to the students for interpretation. For students to have truly mastered the **Metaphor** as a learning construct, they must not only be able to translate those given to them but be able to develop **Metaphors** on their own. And herein lies the difficulty for most teachers. How do we teach students to construct **Metaphors**? And even more to the point, how do WE learn to construct them to model for our students?

Begin With Axioms or Sage Advice. Depending on the developmental levels of the students, it may be useful to begin with a few axioms and ask students to interpret them. Several examples follow:

1. Before you criticize others, you should walk a mile in their shoes.

2. Some folks are so obsessed by the door that closed, they miss the open window. (Helen Keller)

3. Some days you're the bug, and some days, you're the windshield.

4. Talk is cheap because supply exceeds demand.

5. Even if you're on the right track, you'll get run over if you just sit there.

6. If you're not a liberal at 20, you have no heart; if you're not a conservative by 40, you have no brain. (Winston Churchill)

7. Does it occur to you that Disney World is the only people trap operated by a Mouse?

8. Give a man a fish, and he will eat for a day; teach him to fish, and he will eat for a lifetime.

9. If it ain't broke, fix it until it is.

10. Effective leadership is the ability to step on a subordinate's shoes without ruining his or her shine.

Or Try Idioms. Most students will have heard these since their primary grades when they discovered Amelia Bedelia. But they do present concrete and easily referenced **Metaphors** that can serve as hooks for later reference to content area concepts: make a mountain out of a molehill; hit the nail on the head; paint everyone with the same brush; from the frying pan into the fire; born with a silver spoon in one's mouth; left in the dark; bark worse than her bite; butterflies in my stomach; having a green thumb; all in the same boat; throw in the towel; bought a lemon; pulling your leg; crying wolf; the blind leading the blind.

School reformers and specialists in learning theory are convinced that students who can interpret **Metaphors** to understand concepts will more permanently remember those concepts. At the highest level, they can then create their own **Metaphors** to represent concepts and can communicate them to others, just as do published authors and poets.

Not an Easy Task. With the exception of Language Arts teachers, most teachers would rather get root canals than attempt to deal with **Metaphors.** The majority of content teachers have difficulty imagining how they will plan lessons that use the **Metaphor** as a Learning Construct. They are comfortable with the **Metaphors** they already know and use, but they struggle with creating **Metaphors** to use with students.

Despite the challenge, since the **Metaphor** has been identified as a Best Practice, and thus is predictive of academic success, it deserves a place at the *Unit Planning* table. As tough a sell as it is, the percentage of teachers who try it and are pleasantly surprised at its success is gradually increasing.

Analogies

What They Are

The **Analogy** has become another important star in the constellation of Best Practices (say, there's a **Metaphor**) because of the established link between students' ability to interpret and construct analogies and their academic performance. In many states, the **Analogy** has been included in the academic content standards for Language Arts, Math, Science, and Social Studies. Closely related to the **Metaphor** and other comparisons, the **Analogy** is a natural fit within the *Similarities and Differences* Learning Construct. The **Analogy** is defined as a set of relationships between two things that identify a parallel relationship between two other and usually unrelated things. It is the relationship between the first pair, leading to that between the second, that is the key to mastering the **Analogy.** A few examples are as follows:

green is to *go* as *red* is to *stop*
- [green is associated with *go*, and red is associated with *stop*]
- [↦ relationship: color to activity]

curtains are to windows as sunglasses are to eyes
- [curtains protect furnishings from the sun; sunglasses protect eyes from the sun]
- [↦ relationship: function]

fish is to swim as duck is to waddle
- [fish motate by swimming; ducks get around by waddling]
- [↦ relationship: movement or motation]

$\frac{4}{5}$ is to 80% as $\frac{1}{3}$ is to $33\frac{1}{3}$ %
- [$\frac{4}{5}$ and 80% are two ways to show the same proportion; and $33\frac{1}{3}\%$ . . . likewise]
- [↦ relationship: equivalent fractions and percentages]

These are very basic and simple examples. Anyone who's been subjected to the *Miller Analogies Test* or its equivalent knows how arcane and esoteric some of the relationships can be. For the purposes of helping students understand the **Analogy** and feel comfortable using it, we will stick with the fairly standard types.

Considered by many to be the most advanced of the *Similarities and Differences* techniques, the **Analogy** requires students to identify multiple relationships simultaneously and to use reasoning to identify the one that is being requested. For example, in the following **Analogy,**

grapes : wine :: apples : _____ (a) red (b) sauce (c) sweet (d) cider

there are several relationships between grapes and apples, as indicated in the choices. On the surface, the answer may appear to be (b) *sauce*, since grapes make wine and apples make *sauce*. But on closer examination, a more precise answer is (d) *cider*, since wine is produced by fermenting grapes, and cider is produced by fermenting apples.

Like the other techniques in this cluster—Categorization, Comparison, Critical Attribute, and Metaphor—the **Analogy** helps students to identify relationships between items and then to use those relationships to identify other relationships. But the **Analogy** is somewhat more difficult in that it requires students to identify one of several possible relationships between two sets of two items. One teacher quipped, "It's like identifying a double relationship." Learning theorists are convinced that a student's proficiency with **Analogies** will equip him or her to

1. use one situation to resolve another (e.g., if that widget worked to solve that problem, then this widget can be used to solve this one)

2. analyze "how things work " to devise a new or alternative application to accomplish the same thing with more efficiency

When **Analogies** appear on a high-stakes test, students are typically given choices from which to select the correct answer. In life, the idea is for students to use the **Analogy** as a tool to analyze problem situations or to describe difficult concepts. However, life doesn't give students answers from which to choose, and they are essentially on their own. To that end, we encourage teachers to supplement their use of multiple-choice **Analogies** with activities asking students to interpret and construct **Analogies.**

Common Types of Analogies Most Likely Encountered by Students

Whether trying to isolate the correct answer from several choices, or using Analogic thinking to interpret a situation or solve a problem, students MUST discover the underlying relationships between each word pair as well as the one that links the two pairs. Remember the grapes/apples thing. What follows are 15 common types of **Analogy,** including a very simple example for each.

1. **Synonyms** (e.g., purchase : buy :: throw : pitch)

2. **Antonyms** (e.g., purchase : sell :: throw : catch)

3. **Grammar** (i.e., parts of speech; language; sentence parts, rhyming words, etc.) (e.g., it : it's :: you : you'll)

4. **Causes and Effects** (e.g., cut : bleed :: ignite : burn)

5. **Part-Whole** (e.g., tail : dog :: mane : horse)

6. **Actions** (e.g., chickens : roost :: moles : tunnel)

7. **Examples or Types of** (e.g., isosceles : triangle :: epic : poetry)

8. **Homonyms (homophones, homographs)** (e.g., knight : night :: great : grate) (e.g., read : read :: wind : wind)

9. **Tool-Function (also called *object/function* or *object/purpose*)** (e.g., hammer : nails :: wrench : bolts)

10. **Location** (e.g., Mount Rushmore : South Dakota :: Grand Canyon : Arizona

11. **People (i.e., scientists, entertainers, artists, military heroes, statesmen, etc.)** (e.g., Fulton : steam :: Edison : electricity)

12. **Mathematics** (e.g., 1/4 : $.25 :: 4/5 : 80%)

13. **Associations (e.g., mascots, state flowers, symbols)** (e.g., buckeye : Ohio :: swastika : Nazism)

14. **Characteristics or Attributes** (e.g., athlete : endurance :: artist : creativity)

15. **Members of a Group** (e.g., gulls : flock :: cattle : herd)

Independent Mastery. To be fully proficient in the use of **Analogies** as a Learning Construct, students must know how to work with them on at least three developmental levels: (a) interpret and define the relationship in complete **Analogies,** (b) complete partial **Analogies** and define the relationship, and (c) create **Analogies** that illustrate various relationships. All three steps are illustrated below:

1. interpret completed **Analogies,** defining their defining relationship

   coffee : beverage :: canoe : boat (an example or a type of: coffee is a type of beverage, and canoe is a type of boat)

   triangle : 180° :: pentagon : 540° (the number of degrees in a shape: there are 180° in a triangle and 540° in a pentagon)

   Ontario : Canada :: Trees : Forest (part to whole: Ontario is part of Canada, and trees are part of a forest)

   education : ignorance :: employment : poverty (means to deal with or overcome: education is a means to overcome ignorance; employment is a way to overcome poverty)

2. complete **Analogies** that contain blanks, and define the relationship

   tomato : red :: lemon : _____   [↦ color]

   bird : chirp :: cat : _____ [↦ characteristic sound]

   _____ : back :: entrance : exit [↦ opposites]

   Mount Vernon : _____ :: Monticello : Jefferson   [↦ location]

   .80 : _____ :: .25 : $\frac{1}{4}$ [↦ decimal-fraction equivalent]

3. create **Analogies** that appropriately illustrate various relationships

_____ : _____ :: _____ : _____   [↤ **synonyms**]

_____ : _____ :: _____ : _____   [↤ **cause-effect**]

_____ : _____ :: _____ : _____   [↤ **part of speech**]

_____ : _____ :: _____ : _____   [↤ **color**]

_____ : _____ :: _____ : _____   [↤ **homonyms**]

It may help students to get started if the teacher supplies topics and one or more terms at first.

Connection to the Metaphor. As discussed earlier in the Metaphor section, the **Analogy** and the **Metaphor** are frequently used interchangeably, and experts argue over which came first or which is the subset of the other. We have found that most Literature anthologies and glossaries list the **Metaphor** (along with the Simile, the Pun, the Idiom, the Onomatopoeia, etc.) as creating a *figurative* relationship between two otherwise dissimilar things. In contrast, the **Analogy** defines a more *literal* relationship between two things and then identifies a *parallel* relationship with two others. The whole idea in both is to gain a deeper understanding of an intended literal link or emotional response through figurative or analogic thinking.

In their actual use, the **Metaphor** and **Analogy** often seem to refer to much the same thing. But structurally, they differ slightly. For example, to use the **Analogy** "The British House of Lords is analogous to the U.S. Senate" admits to being a comparison. But to use a **Metaphor** to describe the U.S. Senate such as "This House of Lords has gotten too far away from the people," the implication is that the Senate is behaving as if it were the House of Lords. The comparison is embedded rather than announced.

The distinctions get really blurry when examining the Extended Metaphor and the Extended Analogy. For example, to represent one's life as an ocean voyage might use

- the *launch* to refer to birth
- the *ship's wheel* to steering ones' course
- *smooth sailing* to suggest moving along as planned
- *rough seas* to denote troubled times
- *pulling into port* as major milestone events
- *anchor* to indicate special people or events that hold one fast to his or her beliefs
- *mayday* to represent impending disaster
- the *lighthouse* to serve as a guiding beacon
- *fog* to suggest an inability to see clearly what lies ahead
- *shipwreck* or *founder* to describe mishaps and disasters
- *crew members* as persons of significance, both helpful and not
- *mothballing* as retirement

Metaphor. The single **Metaphor** here is the *voyage* to represent *one's life*. The Extended **Metaphor** would apply if the student were to write an entire story or poem that repeated the image of the voyage, threaded throughout the text.

Analogy. The separate **Analogies** included within the above comparison are

launch : birth :: mothballing : retirement

the ship's wheel : steering :: the anchor : stopping

fog : danger :: the light house : safety

An Extended **Analogy** would be the point-by-point, acknowledged and literal comparison between the human life and a ship's voyage, as shown above.

Obviously, the entire image of life as a voyage is wrapped into the parallels between the events of a person's life and the elements involved in sailing a ship, and the exact label **(Metaphor or Analogy)** seems to depend on how literal **(Analogy)** versus implied or artistic **(Metaphor)** one chooses to be. Either way, the label is not as important as the student's understanding of the underlying comparisons.

How to Use With Students

For many students, classroom exposure to **Analogy** is limited to the "daily **Analogy**" or similar worksheet-type activities. While this is helpful to some extent, it typically occurs outside the authentic learning context of an actual subject area. We urge participants to provide students with a more directed instruction about Analogic thinking. Many of the examples and illustrations we have used above to discuss the **Analogy** are appropriate, and during the **Analogy** portion of the *Unit Planning* workshops, we provide several more examples and ideas.

Most learning experts suggest specific steps to help students understand the Analogy:

1. Examine the first pair to identify the relationship between the words. For example,
   - banana is to [:] peel
   - coffee : beans
   - hexagon : six
   - 360° : circle
   - epic : poetry

2. Add the second pair, helping students see the parallel relationship. While students are learning, it is best to use the same parts of speech in both pairs (e.g., noun : adjective :: noun : adjective.
   - banana is to [:] peel as [::] corn is to [:] _____
   - coffee : beans :: _____ : leaves
   - hexagon : six :: _____ : eight
   - 360° : circle :: 180° : _____
   - epic : poetry :: _____ : "Trees"

3. At a more advanced level, the Analogic relationship is between Terms 1 and 3 or 2 and 4. For example,
   - banana is to [:] corn :: peel : husk
   - coffee : tea :: beans : leaves

- hexagon : octagon :: six : eight
- 360° : 180° :: circle : triangle
- epic : poetry :: *The Odyssey* : "Trees"

Equally Challenging. As with the **Metaphor,** the **Analogy** is not an easy strategy to incorporate into the *Unit Plans*. But most participants realize the importance of showing students how to master the art of Analogic thinking and make a respectable effort to do so.

SUMMARY ■

This chapter has attempted to provide a brief but useful look at the eight most prevalent Learning Constructs that we believe are one of the two pillars that support the Best Practice methods essential to every classroom. As a synopsis, students who master the entire array of all eight will be able to

- analyze the *Organizational Patterns* of written and spoken text on their own
- create original *Summaries* using the Organizational Patterns
- take *Notes* using the Organizational Patterns
- analyze math problems to determine what is needed and apply the correct Math *Problem-Analysis* and *Solving* strategy without teacher prompting
- predict the meaning of difficult Vocabulary words from *Syntactical*, *Structural*, or *Context Clues* as well as identify the type of clue they used and whether the word has a positive, negative, or neutral connotation
- (1) interpret a *Graphic Organizer* supplied by the teacher, but also
  (2) devise their own appropriate Graphic Organizer to demonstrate comprehension
- (1) answer questions at varying levels of difficulty, but also
  (2) develop their own Level I, II, and III *Questions*
- (1) categorize information and
  (2) create their own *Categories* from noncategorical as well as categorical material
- (1) interpret and
  (2) generate T-charts, Venn Diagrams, and Comparison Matrices to demonstrate proficiency in *Comparing and Contrasting*
- identify the distinguishing or *Critical Attributes* of a concept and distinguish it from others
- (1) interpret *Metaphors* and
  (2) develop their own
- (1) interpret *Analogies* and
  (2) devise their own

This means that students have taken all the samples provided by their teachers and textbooks and internalized them to the point that they can construct the Construct. And it doesn't get any better than that.

7

Unit Planning

Delivery Strategies

■ INTRODUCTION

Where Are We Now?

The *Instructional Design* Process

Unit Planning
Motivation
Information
Assessment
Culmination

Monitoring

Curriculum
Mapping

Best
Practices

Benchmark
Assessments

Performance
Indicators

Annual
Revisions

This chapter is devoted to the set of Best Practices we call Delivery Strategies. Used in conjunction with the Learning Constructs from Chapter 6, through which students create meaning, the Delivery Strategies are the methods by which teachers deliver to students the information they use to create that meaning. Together, the Learning Constructs and Delivery Strategies are the two pillars that bear the weight of classroom reform in the *Instructional Design* process. Although nearly all of these Delivery Strategies appeared in the education literature 20 years before the term Best Practices was even conceived, they are still highly respected by twenty-first-century school reformers and are considered integral to the Best Practices approach to reform classroom instruction.

Since there are dozens of strategies, the teacher's toughest decision is to select those that are congruent with the *Performance Indicators* in the *Unit*. But there are some hints. In most cases, the teams who developed the *Performance Indicators* will have discussed how best to teach each indicator, and the team who put together each *Curriculum Map* will have discussed what teaching-learning activities would go best with each *Unit*.

Some Classic Mismatches

We have found that the best way to drive home the importance of this congruence between desired learning outcomes and teaching methods is to show some samples of incongruence. In the samples below, the *Performance Indicator* is in bold print, and the strategies are in nonbold print; the *"Note:"* suggests how to rectify the incongruence. For each Delivery Strategy, the teacher's behavior and the students' response should be stated or implied.

[Grade 1 Science] **Describe the sequence of a larva becoming a butterfly, and display as a time line with pictures and words to explain.**

- Teacher reads stories about butterflies; tells students about each stage
- Teacher shows students pictures of the various stages of the butterfly
- Students find and display pictures of various butterflies on the bulletin board, printing the name of each

Note: What's missing is an opportunity for students to construct meaning for themselves. They need to hear technical information, in developmentally appropriate language, about what happens to the larva at each stage, approximately how long each stage lasts, and practice describing and drawing each stage, including key terms and labels. A teaching example might be a baby, growing to a toddler, then into a child, displayed on the time line. Ideally, a few tadpoles in an aquarium could change into frogs during the course of the butterfly discussion. If not, pictures of the tadpole-frog metamorphosis should be used as an example.

[Grade 3 Math] **Count money and make change for single and multiple purchases at a class store using coins and bills to ten dollars; draw pictures to represent the transactions, including the bills and coins involved.**

- Teacher uses PowerPoint to show how bills and coins are related
- Students complete worksheets
- In small groups, students practice making change from overhead prompts
- Students solve story problems involving money from text

Note: What's missing is an opportunity for students to connect their knowledge of bills and coins to actual problems in life. For example, dyads could look at newspaper fliers to see how to spend, say, $10.00. They could create word problems based on the fliers, showing they can spend up to $10.00. Then the students could create a simulated class store (using price tags and pictures from the fliers) from what they find in the ads. Small groups could prepare separate sections of the store, for example, school supplies, first aid supplies, healthy snacks, and so on. From these prices and pictures, students could show their mastery of making purchases and getting change from $10.00.

[Grade 6 Language Arts] **Interpret a piece of fictional literature as to how the author's choice of words appeals to the reader's senses and**

creates a distinct mood; prepare at least five multilevel questions to exchange with classmates that help them analyze the mood of the piece as important to the author's message [submit answers and page numbers on which answers can be found].

- Teacher asks students about mood (brainstorm)
- Teacher points out mood words in the fictional piece to be read by all students
- Students read selection, and answer text questions at the end
- Students write an original piece using mood words as found in the selection

Note: What's missing is student practice actually interpreting the language that conveys mood. Following the brainstorm, students need to see and read aloud sample passages that contain mood words that create a distinct feeling, which they need to identify. They then need to read the selection without the teacher pointing out the examples of mood, and record the places where they feel the author used mood to convey his or her message. In small groups, students should read additional selections (perhaps poetry or a short story or even nonfiction, or view video segments) that use mood to convey the author's message. Ultimately, students should be able to describe the language that conveys mood. Answering comprehension questions may be important, but it doesn't get at this *Performance Indicator*. Writing various level questions is what's needed. And composing an original piece to reflect mood is a great idea, but it's not required to master the indicator.

[Grade 11 Civics] **Compare the structure and function of the federal, state, and local governments, including the concepts of federalism, states' rights, check-and-balance, and local control; use a matrix to display the comparisons, and include concrete examples at each level of government.**

- Teacher assigns textbook chapter
- Teacher assigns students to find newspaper items that feature federal, state, and local government at work
- As teacher discusses chapter, students take notes
- One student brings in an op-ed piece criticizing the federal government's manipulation of the United Nations

Note: While it's good that the teacher used the student's article as a discussion point, the students weren't well-enough prepared to look for articles yet, and so this article isn't what the teacher had in mind. The op-ed piece about the United Nations will draw the focus away from the role of each level of government and into an opinion by one writer about international relations. Before students are sent to look for articles, they need to be given criteria of what to look for. For example, an article about the federal government's use of NCLB to interfere with local school operations would be what the teacher had in mind. Second, the assignment to read the chapter without an advance organizer of what to look for (i.e., key terms and distinctions among the levels) will make the reading unfocused. The teacher's lecture should target the key terms and government levels as set forth in the *Performance Indicator* (perhaps completing a wall-sized matrix as it unfolds) and use authentic examples from the students' own local and state governments to distinguish them from the federal government. These respective roles and relationships must be clearly understood before students know enough to look for news articles.

In addition to their lack of congruence with the *Performance Indicator*, the above examples of incongruence have another major flaw: they are heavily teacher and textbook driven; students are not as actively involved as they could be and are not constructing meaning for themselves. We will address both of these issues throughout the chapter.

Beware of the Text

To be fair, a good deal of the responsibility for such disconnects as the ones illustrated lies with publishers who assure districts that their texts have fully integrated the state content standards and that all of their activities and strategies are congruent with the spirit as well as the letter of the standards. On close examination, we have found that many publishers credit themselves with full integration of a standard when they merely list the term or concept on a page or two. Textbook drills and exercises are convenient, but they are not always congruent with what the standards require of students.

List of Strategies

Several Delivery Strategies are featured in this chapter; they will be numbered for the reader's convenience.

1. Lecture (or Explanation)

2. Demonstration

3. Guided Discussion

4. Inquiry (or Hypothesis-Testing)

5. Learning Circles

6. The Socratic Seminar

7. Action Research

8. The Advance Organizer

For each Delivery Strategy, the following format is used:

A. The **Definition**: including its key attributes and how the Strategy delivers information

B. **When to Use It**: what concepts and skills lend themselves to this Strategy

C. **How-To** use it, specifying the role of both the teacher and the student

D. Some **Cautionary Notes** about the Strategy: those things we learned the hard way

As with the Learning Constructs, we have <u>underlined</u> each Delivery Strategy, and for the reader's convenience, we have boxed in the Learning Constructs whenever they are used as examples. This will reinforce the importance of integrating the two for the most effective use of Best Practices in the Information quadrant. Moreover, each Delivery Strategy should indicate what the teacher plans to do and how he or she has planned for students to respond.

■ LECTURE OR EXPLANATION

Definition

Lecture (or explanation) is the primarily spoken presentation of information on a particular subject or topic, typically including technical and abstract information unfamiliar to the listeners. It follows a logical sequence, beginning with an introduction to set forth its purpose and ending with a summary or a set of lead-ins to another segment. In our experience, the keys to effective *Lecture* are as follows:

- The **general** structure typically follows one of two paths:
  A. Main Idea developed by Supporting Details, or
  B. Supporting Details leading to the Main Idea
- The **specific** detail follows an Organizational Pattern that is appropriate to the material (e.g., chronological sequence, compare-contrast, persuasion, narrative)
  A. It is **developmentally appropriate** to the students in language, examples, and length
- It is accompanied by one or more clear, pertinent visuals or **graphics**
- It is **listener-friendly**, using familiar examples, entertaining anecdotes, and humor; and
- It directly **involves the audience** to help them process the information and to help the speaker check for understanding.

When to Use

As with every Delivery Strategy, deciding whether to use the *Lecture* depends on the *Performance Indicators* in the *Unit*. Among the indicators for which the *Lecture* is usually appropriate are those requiring students to take in and use **new information** that is complex and contains unfamiliar language and relatively technical terms. This information is not easily processed by students and relies on teacher clarification or reexplanation. It may also be appropriate when **time is limited**, and a great deal of information needs to be conveyed. In addition, it is the ideal way to present information synthesized from a variety of sources—such as college notes, several Internet sites, a primary source document such as a diary or private letters, and so on—and **not otherwise available** to the student. In effect, the *Lecture* is the method of choice to convey information that the listener could not internalize as effectively another way. If the *Lecture* is delivered in real time, the speaker has the advantage of immediately seeing confusion or uncertainty and can adjust his or her delivery accordingly.

This live response to the audience—as well as other direct engagement activities such as question-answer, wait-time, or audience participation— make the real-time lecture or explanation more interactive than its prerecorded cousin. Recently, though, we've seen teachers record their *Lectures* (on video or audiotape, or even as blog entries) as a differentiation or intervention strategy to permit students to rewind as needed and save the teacher from repeating the whole thing. Or, teachers may record special TV *Lectures* such as the President's State of the Union address or a Congressional Hearing.

Although the recorded version is convenient and can be stopped and started and replayed as often as needed, the speaker cannot interact directly with the audience, and in particular, cannot answer questions or clarify. This limitation must be considered when using the recorded or broadcast *Lecture*.

How-To

The Teacher's Role

Once it has been determined that the *Lecture* is the best Delivery Strategy for a particular segment of the *Unit Plan*, developing teams are encouraged to follow these steps for the most effective results:

- Preplan. While it is not necessary to write a verbatim script, the key points to be made should be listed and in the appropriate Organizational Pattern; that is,
  1. the general, overall structure is usually one of the following:
     a. main idea(s) developed by supporting details and examples
     b. supporting details and examples leading to the main idea(s)

  2. the specific, internal pattern [see chart on next page]

- Determine points where the audience will be involved, and label them on the outline or presentation plan.
- Limit each segment of the *Lecture* to 5–7 minutes for Grades 6 through 12 and 3–5 minutes for younger students; each segment should be punctuated with an activity to check for understanding. For example, ask various Levels of Questions. The total length of the *Lecture* should not exceed 30 minutes (or 20 for intermediate students).
- Include helpful Graphic Organizers or other visuals to clarify the information, particularly how it is internally structured.
- Include a written handout of supplemental material or a Note-taking format; this might also include a blank Graphic Organizer.

Familiar Organizational Patterns and Their Definitions	
Pattern	*Definition*
narrative	present the material as if it were a "story," complete with vocal inflections and anticipation
chronological sequence	present events in time-order sequence; embed in the context of other events (e.g., social, economic, political or military, scientific, etc.)
compare-contrast	present two or more homogeneous concepts (ideas, objects, people, events, etc.); draw parallel contrasts and full-developed comparisons
cause-effect	present events in the context of causes and effects—some of which may be multiple
persuasion	set forth a controversial issue; take a position (or present counter-positions equally); set forth support or evidence; acknowledge opposing points of view; discuss consequences of choices
problem-solution	pose a problem, quandary, or puzzlement; define it, pose plausible solutions, rule each out to get to the preferred one; provide the results
description	present a vivid description using sensory details and imagery; include figurative comparisons if it helps to clarify
how-to	present steps in sequential order; include any short-term or interim outcomes that are relevant to the final product

The Student's Role

One of the major tenets of Best Practices instruction is active student involvement. In our experience, the *Lecture* is most effective if the students have a role to play **before**, **during**, and **following** the presentation.

- **Before** the *Lecture*, determine what students already know; prepare them for what is to come, and help them anticipate the after-lecture activity. Sample prompts might include the following:
  - ◆ "Who has heard of ___ ?" (brainstorming)
  - ◆ "List three things that ____ ."
  - ◆ "Who has been to ____ ?"
  - ◆ "If ____ occurs, what might we predict will happen?"

- **During** the *Lecture*, check for understanding to be certain students are following along and comprehending what is being said or shown. The strategies in Table 7.1 may be helpful.
- **Following** the *Lecture*, check for understanding, but also ask students to synthesize what they've heard, verify or change their earlier predictions, apply what has been said, or expand it to other situations. The strategies in Table 7.1 may be helpful.

Table 7.1 is a list of specific prompts that do double duty to actively engage students but also to check for their understanding. All of them presuppose that students are Taking Notes. Some are more or less complex than others and are thus suitable for Differentiation. The list is divided into three levels: Comprehension, Application, and Evaluation or Extension. Each is adjustable for individual students, dyads or triads, or small groups.

Table 7.1   Comprehension, Application, and Evaluation Prompts for Lecture

Comprehension of the concept, skills, or information—as given

[in students' notes]
  a. *check off or underline or box the three main points that have been made*
  b. *highlight things that are confusing*
  c. *underline things you know now that you didn't know before*
  d. *supply three examples of _____ [what we've discussed]*

[in the margin of students' notes]
  e. *list three muddy points—what's confusing?*
  f. *summarize the information to this point*
  g. *add a note from your generation*
  h. *develop two **Level I** and three **Level II** Questions*
  i. *what does this remind you of?—what other thing have we studied that relates?*

[or elsewhere . . .]
  j. *write a Minute Paper that tells me (a) what stood out for you or (b) what's still confusing*
  k. *try solving this sample problem: [complete this analogy; draw this orbit, analyze this map, etc.]*
  1. *discuss with your peer partner why this might be true*
  m. *draw a graphic that compares these two ideas*
  n. *paraphrase the laws of _____*
  o. *if you were to teach this material to a younger child, what else would you need to know?*

Application of the concept, skills, or information given to a related but different situation

  a. *take the opposing point-of-view, and jot down your reasons [e.g., for voting "Guilty"]*
  b. *identify additional examples of this from your own life or other subjects*
  c. *solve this challenge-level problem: _____*
  d. *come up with a different answer, and show how you did it*
  e. *devise an alternate method to solve this problem (or resolve this dilemma)*
  f. *devise two Level III Questions for this material*
  g. *devise an alternate ending (what would have happened if _____)*

Evaluation of or Extension Beyond the concept, skills, or information given

  a. *with your team, prepare three positions from which to debate this issue, considering someone's perspective from the other side of your position.*
  b. *prepare a personal reaction to this issue; how would it impact you or those close to you?*
  c. *with your peer partner, identify what would have happened IF _____ had not occurred (e.g., the Invasion of Pearl Harbor; the discovery of radium; etc.)*
  d. *develop your own multistep problems for other students to solve*
  e. *in your group, evaluate these math problems in terms of—*
      1. *the operations used*
      2. *the correct order of operations*
      3. *the accuracy of the computation*
      4. *the correctness of the final answer*
  f. *apply the XYZ Scoring Rubric to this sample piece (an original composition, an Action Research design, an original science investigation)*
  g. *be the devil's advocate on this, and take exception to this generalization or rule; support your position, and anticipate the opposition to your position*
  h. *devise an alternate ending to the story; i.e., what would have happened if ___?*
      (for your scenario, be sure you indicate what other details would have had to change as well)

Cautionary Notes

The *Lecture* has fallen into disfavor, largely because it has been mishandled through the years. The following is a list of potential hazards that will compromise the effectiveness of a *Lecture*.

- The *Lecture* is too long; if it exceeds 10 minutes without checking for understanding—that is, engaging the students to be certain they comprehend—students are likely to become disengaged.
- The material is either disorganized or misorganized instead of being presented in a logical format that reflects its internal logic; for example, if the material compares two of something, the format should be a T-chart or a Venn diagram, **not** a linear listing of details.
- There are no concrete examples and/or no graphics or visuals to show relationships among the ideas. The *Lecture* lacks familiar examples, entertaining anecdotes, and/or humor to hold students' interests and make a more direct connection between their own lives or experiences and the material.
- The *Lecture* lacks enthusiasm, and it is delivered without genuine interest in the students or regard for the material.
- There is no role for the students to play during the *Lecture*; they are passively listening or taking notes.
- The students do not apply what they learn in the *Lecture*; the material is merely memorized for later regurgitation.

■ DEMONSTRATION

Definition

Demonstration is a performance or enactment that (a) shows students a **concrete illustration** of an otherwise abstract concept, or (b) **models a process**, skill, or procedure for students that they are expected to use or apply. Students who see and/or participate in the *Demonstration* are provided a direct experience with the concept and retain a sensory memory of the event. For the typical classroom, the keys to effective *Demonstration* are as follows:

- It must have an obvious relevance to the concept, idea, or principle from one or more *Performance Indicators* in the *Unit Plan*. Since the information is new to the students, the teacher must be prepared to check for understanding. This is not a broadcast approach.
- The results (including the processes and the final product) must be used by students to construct new meaning for themselves, but the teacher must be certain students understand what has occurred.
- All steps must be clearly visible and understandable to the students.

- Students must have a direct role to play (e.g., take notes, make drawings, replicate the demo itself).
- The *Demonstration* must be followed by a debriefing session, during which students and the teacher ask and attempt to determine *why*, *what-if*, and so on to clarify and then solidify understanding.

When to Use

The *Demonstration* is typically used when it is important for students to experience a concrete display of abstract concepts, ideas, or principles embedded within *Performance Indicators*. Such concepts can be more fully understood if they are physically represented or shown. In our experience, the *when to use* depends on the type of *Demonstration* to be done. The various types of *Demonstration* include the following:

- Students follow the teacher's lead and **participate with him or her** in the *Demonstration* (e.g., combining nonharmful substances to make a mixture).
- Students will *later replicate* the *Demonstration* (e.g., such as using a rubric to score one's own composition).
- Students serve as *objective observers*, watching (and listening to) the *Demonstration*, taking notes, making sketches, and otherwise recording information they will use to interpret what they see.
- Students serve as *critical observers* or evaluators of what they see (e.g., appraising the performance teams in a debate).

The key to all types of *Demonstration* is to leave students with a sensory memory that can be recalled as needed. The following are a few examples where one or more of the various types of *Demonstration* might be the appropriate strategy.

Science

- movement of warm- and cold-air masses in weather fronts (with clear plastic containers, water, ice cubes, food coloring, etc.)
- how light forms shadows (using flash lights, black and white paper, etc.)

Language Arts

- handwriting (letter formation and spacing)
- translating a prewrite diagram into a composition (using a wall chart or overhead)

Math

- computation with positive and negative integers using a thermometer to find the difference between warmest and coldest temperatures
- comparing the volumes of solids to derive formulas

Social Studies

- economic concepts such as supply and demand (using simulations or diagrams)
- using latitude and longitude to identify locations on a globe

How-To

The Teacher's Role

Once it has been determined that a *Demonstration* is the best Delivery Strategy for a particular segment of the *Unit Plan*—again, consistent with the *Performance Indicators*—teachers are encouraged to follow a planning sequence:

1. Decide what type of *Demonstration* would have the desired effect on students; what can they see and/or do to construct meaning for themselves?

2. Decide if students need a **Preview** activity. Do they already have enough background knowledge and prior experience to realize what they are seeing and/or doing, or do they need background information? For example, if the *Demonstration* is dissecting a beef heart, unless students understand the basic features and functions of the mammal heart and the unique features of a cow's heart, much of the *Demonstration* may get sidetracked with questions about "hearts" and "cow hearts compared with human hearts," to the extent that the core significance of the *Demonstration* is likely to be compromised. **If no**, proceed with planning the *Demonstration*. Don't waste the time and risk spoiling the effect with too much information, particularly if the *Demonstration* is to pique students' interest or curiosity. **If yes**, decide what students need to know, and plan for it. Just don't kill the thing with too much advance information.

3. Envision the **final product**. Define what students will produce to show they fully understood the *Demonstration* and have constructed their own meaning from it. This does not mean the completion of a worksheet, nor does it mean that every student is to turn out a product identical to everyone else's. The product should enable each student to construct his or her own meaning, within guidelines. It should be evaluated using a rubric, the criteria of which corresponds to the related *Performance Indicator(s)*. Remember, in constructing their own meaning, students' creativity and divergent thinking are important for ownership and internalization. After these 7 steps are examples with sample *products* added. They are written in *italics*. Also, note the boxed Learning Constructs.

4. Determine what students will do during the teacher's *Demonstration*; remember, these are data collecting strategies, and not final products, for example,
   ♦ Complete an observation guide.
   ♦ Make sketches.
   ♦ Take notes (in a prescribed format).
   ♦ Jot down questions.
   ♦ Copy or mimic teacher steps (if so directed).
   ♦ Answer teacher Questions (to ensure understanding and identify areas of confusion).

5. Plan a rough outline or basic scenario of the *Demonstration*, including key points where it is best to pause to check students' understanding. At these points, students should be asked general comprehension questions; invited to make predictions or hypotheses, including lots of *whys* and *why nots*; and urged to formulate questions of their own. The teacher should use (and post, if needed) key Vocabulary throughout the *Demonstration*, and remind students to record it in their notes and sketches.

6. Decide how students will be positioned (i.e., seated, standing); place all the materials and equipment needed near the *Demonstration* staging area; prepare any visuals, worksheets, and handouts.

7. Plan for the debrief, allowing sufficient time for it. This is the moment of truth: Did students get it? Remember, the newer the information provided is to the students, the more checking for understanding must be done by the teacher. Naturally, the teacher's questions will need to be less direct, but he or she must determine if the students have the information they will need to construct the product.

Science

- the movement of warm- and cold-air masses in weather fronts *student product*: *a bulleted list of details that describe the demonstration, including annotated sketches of the process, and three weather-related conclusion that can be drawn*
- *student product*: *sketches of the demonstration and a* Summary *that includes two facts demonstrated about the sun*

Language Arts

- handwriting (letter formation and spacing) *student product*: *the names of family members placed in the center of a page, surrounded by a* "picture frame" *decorated with all the letters of the alphabet—both large and small-case—correctly formed. (May be taken home to display)*
- prewrite for composition *student product*: *create an original* Graphic Organizer*, and then use it to write a descriptive essay on the best dessert imaginable*

Math

- computation with integers *student product*: *record temperatures for several days in different countries; create* Original Computation Problems *for classmates to solve*
- derive formula for volume *student product*: *make sketches of the demonstration; then use the given formulas for some of the containers (e.g., the cube) to* Predict *the formulas for the other containers (e.g., the pyramid); explain how this relates to storing leftovers*

Social Studies

- supply and demand *student product*: *a script that could be used on CNN or FOX news, using a particular product (e.g., an iPod, and Xbox)*

- latitude and longitude **student product**: *devise a series of Level I, II, and III* Questions *to check classmates' understanding*

Other sample products for Demonstrations *include the following:*

- solving similar but unfamiliar problems, including a Graphic Organizer of the steps taken to solve
- a *Demonstration* of their own to show a similar concept (or extend the original one)
- a Table or graph with interpretive statements that shows understanding of data collected and organized
- make predictions about what would happen if ___ [adjusting one or more variables]
- create a series of Analogies that compare the two items demonstrated

Note that a worksheet was not among the examples. Although a worksheet or structured Note-Taking format are excellent devices for collecting observation data, they do not typically demonstrate that a student can construct meaning.

The Student's Role

Even if the students will *not be asked to replicate* the *Demonstration*, they must be actively engaged in what goes on during the activity to collect the information they need to develop the product and construct the intended meaning for themselves. In particular, if they are to make predictions before the *Demonstration*, these should be written down for later reflection. If they will need to take notes, make this clear. The final activity of the *Demonstration* is for each student to complete the final product as directed.

Cautionary Notes

Demonstrations can be misleading or even disastrous if they are not carefully planned. However, even the most compelling *Demonstrations* will be ineffective if they are poorly planned. From our experience, demonstration errors that need not have occurred include:

- It was misaligned to the concepts, principles, or ideas intended by the *Performance Indicator(s)*; one of the most common misalignments is the cognitive demand. For example, when the indicator requires primary students to *"explain how a system of rules is necessary for an orderly society, including making and enforcing laws. . . ."* a misaligned *Demonstration* would be to conduct a courtroom simulation to put someone on trial for breaking a law. What *would* be appropriate would be to conduct a class activity without any rules, making sure there is at least one disagreement.
- It was developmentally too advanced or too immature (predictable) for the students; this flaw is best prevented when teachers know their students well and have a sense of what holds their attention.

Additionally, the effective use of the Pre-*Demonstration* activity will help fill any gaps in student readiness.

■ It could not be fully seen by all of the students.

■ The final product could not be compiled from the various notes, drawings, questions, observation guides, and so on that were collected by the students during the *Demonstration*.

■ The debrief was omitted; students were unsure what had happened exactly and even more uncertain what questions to ask.

A Word About Group Work and Mastery. Although *Demonstrations* are typically done for large groups, care must be taken that students are not overreliant on team members or even a partner to process the information. The more students rely on others, the less they demonstrate what they know on their own. Eventually, each student must demonstrate independent mastery of the concepts and ideas illustrated by the *Demonstration*. This is best accomplished by requiring all or a significant portion of the final product to be completed individually. A second method is to include on the *Unit* test at least one item requiring each student to develop an essay and/or diagram that applies the demonstration to an entirely new problem-solving situation.

GUIDED DISCUSSION   ■

Definition

Guided Discussion is not a free-for-all confab or general Q and A. It is the organized exchange of ideas within small groups of students about an issue having multiple and/or controversial perspectives. Each group is assigned one of the perspectives and asked to complete the same task as the other groups but from its own distinct perspective.

The key is that each group's output or decision reflects that group's assigned interpretation; their recommendation is judged or rated according to a rubric developed by the class.

Note: In contrast to free-form class discussion that often becomes a teacher-student exchange, and typically involving only the more vocal students, the *Guided Discussion* is carefully structured to involve all students. Moreover, it places the teacher outside the discussion in the role of facilitator, with students as the discussants. The *Guided Discussion* should not exceed two class periods; otherwise, students get too far off-track, bring other information to bear, and miss the focus point. Additional ideas, directions, and spin-offs identified during the *Guided Discussion* can and should be pursued as follow-up activities. These should be captured on wall-chart paper during the debrief and built into subsequent *Units.*

When to Use

The *Guided Discussion* is the Delivery Strategy of choice for students' deep-level consideration of key historic events, scientific controversies, current news items, or a significant act by an individual or group. But they must also be topics for which there are multiple perspectives and interpretations and not just one or two rather clear-cut points of view. The topics are items that students may take for granted, at first find mundane, or think totally unrelated to them. Bear in mind, the activity is to be a learning experience, not a venue for polarization and hurtful controversy. In addition, of course, the topics must be linked to one or more *Performance Indicators*. Topics that should be avoided are those with racial, political, sexual, or religious implications and which cannot be objectively discussed without casting a group of people or a set of beliefs in a negative light.

Among the reasons for selecting the *Guided Discussion* as compared to other Delivery Strategies are the following:

- For complex issues that students may have come to view as black and white, they must learn to identify and dignify alternate and equally viable points of view if they are to completely understand their own beliefs.
- To motivate students, pique their interest, and/or establish readiness for a larger research study. The *Guided Discussion* generates more questions than answers, but it allows students to approach the research from a sufficiently narrow focus, as compared to starting from scratch and having to narrow the topic.
- To feel the emotions of an interest group and to struggle with other interest groups to reach an equitable solution to a problem that affects them all will broaden students' horizons.

How-To

The Teacher's Role

When setting up the *Guided Discussion*, teachers find it works best to take the following steps:

1. Determine the topic of the *Guided Discussion* from the *Performance Indicators*; for example,
   - the United States' role in stabilizing Iraq
   - the future of the NASA space program
   - the deregulation of Cable TV
   - the preventable tragedy of Benedict Arnold
   - the role of the National Guard in the shootings at Kent State University
   - stem-cell research and genetic engineering
   - should _____ [character] ___ be placed on trial or excused as the victim of false arrest?
   - should all students be required to master Algebra before they are allowed to enter high school?
   - the voucher system as an alternative to mandatory public school attendance

2. Decide what multifaceted issue could be discussed by students; identify a problem that could be solved and the various points of view that could be applied. Below are two samples, one for intermediate and one for high school students.

♦ **Intermediate:** What do the numbers tell us about what REALLY happened on the *Titanic*? <u>Various Points of View for Groups:</u> (1) first class, (2) steerage, (3) crew, (4) owners [White Star Line]

♦ **Secondary:** What can be done about the school funding crisis in our state? <u>Various Points of View for Groups:</u> (1) the legislature, (2) citizens of wealthy districts, (3) citizens of poor small-sized districts, (4) citizens of urban districts, and (5) various school staff

3. Prepare factual background information to provide students adequate readiness for their discussion; for example,

♦ **Intermediate (Titanic):** basic number facts about the *Titanic*:
  ◊ *the number of passengers sailing*
  ◊ *the number and type of lifeboats on board*
  ◊ *the times each boat was launched*
  ◊ *the number and class of people in each boat*
  ◊ *the number and proportion of people saved: (1) men, (2) women, (3) children*

♦ **Secondary (School Funding):** What can be done about the school funding crisis in our state: the school funding history; the cause and effects of the current crisis; strengths of the current formula; weaknesses of the current formula; the number of required days; required services; curriculum requirements; and NCLB guidelines and mandates?

4. Design at least one prompt to guide the discussion, based on the *Performance Indicator(s)*; having multiple prompts is helpful if one proves too difficult or not sufficiently challenging. For example,

♦ **Intermediate:** What do the numbers tell us about what really happened on the *Titanic*?
  ◊ *Use the numerical data on the charts given to make a case that your group suffered greater loss and anguish than any of the other groups.*
  ◊ *What might have been done differently to prevent similar tragedies in the future?*

♦ **Secondary:** What can be done about the school funding crisis in our state?
  ◊ *What is a viable yet equitable solution to the school funding crisis?*
  ◊ *How can the public and nonpublic schools coexist as part of the solution?*

5. With the class, formulate a rubric to evaluate the viability of each recommendation or solution.

6. If students are not trained in group processes (i.e., acting as recorder, convener, process observer, etc.; taking turns speaking; actively listening to someone else), take time to address this, but use a practice prompt.

7. Since the *Guided Discussion* is a group activity, individual student mastery can be determined by any one or a combination of several methods:

♦ on the *Unit* Test, one or more extended response items asking students to
  ◊ *write a summary of the student's own group recommendation*

◊ *write a summary of the "jury's" decision about the recommendations*
◊ *use a graphic organizer to compare and contrast at least two recommendations*
◊ *answer Level II and III* Questions *about the various recommendations*
♦ as an authentic or performance assessment (*culminating* activity),
◊ *prepare an annotated* Graphic Organizer *that displays and compares all of the groups' recommendations*
◊ *prepare a Guided Discussion lesson, including a bulleted list of background information, at least three different perspectives, and a sample prompt*

The Student's Role

Since most students are accustomed to free-form discussion and the spontaneous give-and-take between and among students and between the teacher and students, they may need to be shown *how* to handle the guided discussion. In addition to the ground rules about the subject matter and the distinctive points of view, students learn to value multiple perspectives on the same issue. The following are key features of the student's involvement in the *Guided Discussion:*

1. Take Notes on the information provided; ask clarifying questions.

2. Student groups are as heterogeneous as possible; that is, mixed-ability, cross-gender, and culturally diverse.

3. Students hear and/or see the background information before they are assigned their perspectives or roles. The information is factual, free of bias or editorial comment.

4. Move quickly into assigned groups; [for each group], appoint a recorder, convener, and process observer to expedite the discussion process; help each other assume the role of the assigned interest group; seek clarification from the teacher.

5. Students must work with only the data provided; they may not obtain additional information to gain an advantage over the other groups. Later, there will be opportunity to broaden the discussion and consider additional data.

6. Students discuss the problem or issue from their assigned perspective, regardless of how they might feel personally, and prepare a formal response that contains their solution or recommendation, complete with a rationale. The responses will be rated according to a rubric as to the structure and quality of each.

7. Keep the rubric handy to ensure that the criteria for viable recommendations or solutions are considered.

8. As the group considers the issue and its particular perspective, the recorder should jot down all of the ideas, the convener should keep the group focused, and the process observer should monitor how the group functions. It is important that every group member participate.

9. [for older students] Anticipate the other groups' solutions and arguments; this provides each group a continual reality check and permits them to weigh their own position in relationship to the other groups.

10. Finalize the group's solution or recommendation for presentation to the other groups; select a group spokesperson.

11. Listen to each presentation, taking notes. At the conclusion, be prepared to share with the teacher and/or other class members the various methods and processes used by the group to devise its solution.

12. During the debrief, responses are compared and contrasted according to the rubric, and students share their perceptions about the issue and the activity. This is the perfect opportunity to ask students what would have been different had they known their assigned perspective or the prompt *before* hearing the background information.

13. To their amazement, students typically discover that there are usually multiple viable solutions to a problem and perspectives to an issue; they also realize, however, that viability is often relative to the interest groups involved.

Cautionary Notes

The *Guided Discussion* as outlined above will be most successful if:

- The issue to be discussed has several legitimate perspectives for the students.
- The teacher is knowledgeable about the issue or subject. While it is not necessary to be an expert, to attempt a *Guided Discussion* on a topic about which the teacher knows very little or has only sketchy information will compromise the activity. Not only will the background information be inadequate (or even inaccurate), it will be impossible to establish a rubric for viable recommendations.
- Every student participates and has a voice in formulating the group's position or recommendation.
- The groups force themselves to arrive at consensus but note areas of disagreement or confusion for a subsequent discussion.
- The groups listen to each other attentively, take notes, and ask each other pertinent questions.

INQUIRY, OR FORMULATING ■ AND TESTING HYPOTHESES

Definition

Inquiry is the process of asking questions about a mystery or puzzlement, followed by formulating hypotheses about what might help explain the quandary. In some cases, this questioning is followed by an actual experiment or activity to test one or more hypotheses in real time. In other cases, the Inquiry is limited to an informed discussion. *Inquiry* is also referred to as *Problem-Solving* and *Discovery*. For classroom use, there are two major types: Hypothetical and Real-Time

Both types of *Inquiry* require students to apply the same thoughtful and strategic procedure. During the inquiry process, students behave like scientists, investigating discrepant events and puzzlements, looking for reasonable solutions or explanations. Following the *Inquiry* process, a postinquiry debrief helps students reflect on what occurred. This is the time for students to pinpoint particularly successful strategies that can be repeated in subsequent inquiries, but they should also identify missteps to avoid the next time. The *Inquiry* process and its debrief are instructive, whether or not the student's hypothesis was correct.

Various Designs for Inquiry Lessons

If *Inquiry* is the Delivery Strategy chosen, teachers should select from among various designs the one(s) that would be most appropriate for the concepts being considered and the *Performance Indicator(s)* involved. We have identified and adapted these designs from the compilations of Best Practices by several noted researchers who based their work on such legends as John Dewey, Herbert Thelen, J. Richard Suchman, Hilda Taba, Jerome Bruner, and Byron Massialas and Benjamin Cox. The complete list of citations for these contributors are available from the authors upon request.

Below are six of the most popular *Inquiry* designs, three **Hypothetical** and three **Real Time**.

Hypothetical Designs

These are *Inquiries* that address discrepant events or quandaries that have already occurred. The object is for students to identify underlying causes and effects and to analyze the relationships among relevant factors. This done, they hypothesize alternative scenarios, or what ELSE might have been done, and examine the effect of changing one or more of the original variables. Following are examples of three hypothetical models: Systems Analysis, Historical Investigation, and Hypothetical Problem-Solving and Evaluating Options.

Systems Analysis. Students examine various kinds of systems to understand how each component functions alone and how they work together to achieve the system. Students predict the effect of altering one or more components, hypothesizing viable scenarios of the altered system. This is an especially important activity since in several states, the academic content standards require students to explain what happens to an entire system when one or more variables or features are changed. An example is the following:

"The Weeder Geese"
    For the second year in a row, nearly 80% of the Iowa corn farmers are facing possible ruin due to an overabundance of weeds. Last year they used several chemicals to kill the weeds, but these chemicals polluted nearly two thirds of the state's

> water supply and can no longer be used. There is neither the time nor the manpower available to pull all of the weeds by hand. In desperation, the group has just seen a video demonstration of Chinese Weeder Geese. A two-acre corn field was shown before and four days after 20 Weeder Geese were released, and all but a few weeds were gone. With harvest only a few months away, a decision must be made.

Historical Investigation. Students are presented with a historical or scientific event that has continued to be somewhat controversial. They obtain information about the situation (what is known and what is not known), propose viable alternative explanations about why it occurred and/or what might have been done differently, and decide on the most viable. They then weigh their alternative(s) against the constraints and conditions of the time and place to see if it is supported or refuted by other available evidence. This design is appropriate for *Performance Indicators* that ask students to analyze historic events to determine critical moments or turning points. The following is an example:

> "It's All in the Plan!"
> Students examine the facts behind tragedies due to architectural mistakes in design (e.g., the collapsed Silver Bridge, the collapsed walkway at the Kansas City Hyatt). Looking also at the various building codes enacted after the San Francisco earthquake of 1989, students decide what can be learned from architectural blueprints that might have prevented some structural tragedies and provide lessons to prevent subsequent disasters.

Hypothetical Problem-Solving and Evaluating Options. Students are presented with hypothetical situations (such as: "Who was the most influential rock group of the 90s?" or "What is a viable method to have ended World War II, other than the atom bomb?") and asked to pose viable options. If the process requires considering several equal options, students devise and use a rating system or set of evaluation criteria as a rubric to compare their ideas and arrive at the most objective decision possible. Typically, this design involves locating information to corroborate hunches and predictions, a skill that is the basis of several content standards and *Performance Indicators*. The following is an example:

> "The Speech Contest"
> Your school hosted the regional speaking competition to decide who would advance to the state championship. But a computer crash has prevented the compilation of the judges' scores, and all that remains are their handwritten notes. The final results cannot be posted until the ratings are sorted out. Unfortunately, each judge used his and her own wording, counting on the computer to make them uniform. Was there a winner? How can we tell?
> <u>Finalist No. 24:</u> good stage presence; did not get to the point soon enough, introduction too long; moderately strong external support; excellent examples; conclusion slightly off the mark; no sense of humor; delivery somewhat stiff; media well-done; language appropriate, mature

(Continued)

(Continued)

> Finalist No. 98: delivery natural, warm; way too many examples; fair external support; great intro, got straight to the point; language stiff, somewhat stilted; media hard to interpret; fair stage presence (taking hair off forehead); used quiet humor very well; logical conclusion
>
> Finalist No. 12: examples not all to the point; well-developed introduction; strong conclusion; delivery natural, sincere; excellent stage presence; humor verged on sarcasm; strong external support media very well-done (better examples than those given orally); some words were misused
>
> Finalist No. 217: nearly all good examples; slightly artificial delivery; got to point quickly, good introduction; excellent stage presence (reticent at first); language well-chosen; understated humor, but effective; media acceptable but not outstanding; strong conclusion; moderately strong external support

Real-Time Designs

In contrast to the Hypothetical Designs that address past events, Real-Time *Inquiries* involve students in solving actual problems. The object is for students to propose a solution or explanation and then test it as a scientist might or see what other questions it raised. Such *Inquiries* are well-suited to *Performance Indicators* that address the scientific method or action research.

Problem-Solving. Students are presented with a problem to solve, including constraints about materials they may use and conditions under which they must work. They first identify the underlying concepts involved and then the barriers and limitations to a solution. Next, they generate possible solutions, formulate hypotheses about how each solution might work, and test the most likely. Looking at the results, students distinguish hunches that were correct from those where they were mistaken. One of the Best Practices is the generation and testing of hypotheses, and this *Inquiry* design provides an opportunity for students to apply that practice. Two samples are provided.

1. **A Penny Saved!** Create a table to guide a student on a savings and expense plan that will yield $50,000, then $150,000, then $500,000, and so on, over time.

2. **Sooloo the Robot.** Sooloo was a robot who was learning to read. As he watched the boys and girls say their words and spell them and use them in writing, he thought it seemed easy. Sooloo was used to doing things in a hurry, so he grabbed all the words he could find and just dumped them all into his memory. But when he tried to do what he saw the children do, he became confused. He discovered that some words were things you do, or action words; some words were things or objects you could "hold in your hand," so to speak; and some words were feelings that were inside your head or your heart. He decided he had better sort the words into those three different sections of his memory. Can you help Sooloo solve his problem? (Adjust words for the developmental level of the students; some can be more than one category.)

| happy | afraid | clock | apple | hat | lonely | frog | angry |
| brick | skip | make | sad | pick | tell | hide | stretch |

Invention. Students use their knowledge about a concept to devise a new and more creative application. Based on the particular needs of the situation, students also devise a rubric or set of success criteria against which to judge their work. Below are two examples.

1. **Heart–Smart.** Devise a new set of cardiovascular exercises for people with specific disabilities or on special diets.

2. **Connotation-Denotation.** Even though words are merely inkstrokes on paper, they often convey a feeling or tone. Some are negative or critical (such as *skinny*) and others are positive or complimentary (such as *slender*). Still others are neutral; they can be either positive or negative, or neither (such as *thin*). The neutral sense of the word is its *denotation*, or dictionary definition. The feeling or attitude in a word is known as its *connotation*, either positive or negative. The difficulty is, without context, it is often difficult to tell which is which. Francine and Jorge have been asked to prepare a lesson for their group on connotation and denotation, and they have no idea how to begin. All they have is the following list of words, and the realization that they may not be consistent parts of speech.

courage	familiar	undecided	convince	visionary
inquiring	discreet	observe	intimidate	cost-conscious
miserly	secretive	covert	mellow	sycophant
reckless	wishy-washy	assertive	curious	persuade
loyal	monitor	unusual	weird	thrifty
ordinary	eccentric	uncertain	devotee	proven
aggressive	self-assured	suspicious	gutsy police	daydreamer

Experimental Inquiry. Students observe a discrepant event or something of interest or curiosity. They then apply rules and concepts they already know as the basis for making inquiries about or explaining the puzzlement. Where possible, they repeat the process or test the hypothesis in a different but related situation. Two examples follow.

1. **Is the Heat in the Sweater?** Young children assume that because blankets or sweaters keep them warm, there is actually heat in the objects themselves. What sort of demonstration can help them discover—without telling them—that this is not the case?

2. **The Six Coins.** It is possible to make each of the amounts listed with six coins. Record your answers on the chart.

50¢	25¢	10¢	5¢	1¢	Amount
					$1.30
					$1.51
					$ .42
					$ .95

When to Use

Inquiry is useful when students need to apply creative and critical thinking skills to solve real-time or immediate problems (e.g., why did the power go out?) or to identify viable reasons why a historic event occurred (e.g., how did they build the pyramids?). In addition, *Inquiry* is useful to give students practice at finding new associations within or applying fresh insights to existing ideas (e.g., how do symbols arouse deeper feelings than words?). Some teachers use *Inquiry* to drive detective work (e.g., What is the origin of the bathtub? What makes an airplane stay aloft? What country owns the North Pole? How can water move uphill, seemingly on its own?).

How-To

The Teacher's Role

Prior to the Inquiry Lesson. Students need an orientation to the *Inquiry* process, including the rationale behind the strategy and the acknowledgment that it will involve uncertainty and ambiguity. This is particularly important if students are accustomed to being given correct answers right away and seem to resist having to dig for information. The teacher must:

- Be certain students connect the *Inquiry* process with critical thinking, creativity, problem-solving, and the pursuit of alternative solutions. Help them value other students' thinking and honor valid uncertainty; reassure them that there is no such thing as failure, only a signal to try something else.
- Provide enough information and direction for students to proceed but not so much that it truncates the process and spoils the intrigue of discovery.
- Guide students to focus more on the process than getting a right answer.

During the Lesson. Most of the teacher's effort occurs prior to the *Inquiry* lesson to get it ready. During the lesson, the teacher's role is to facilitate the process, leading and prompting, without giving too much information.

- Carefully guide students to ask the proper Questions, focused on the activity and not too far afield (there is very little learning if students become silly or random).

- Record students' questions and Hypotheses, not only to provide a running record of progress but to guide the reflection process afterwards and identify points of uncertainty and confusion.
- Help students connect the *Inquiry* process to underlying content concepts and skills (this should occur during as well as following the activity). In addition to the Learning Constructs already listed, these connections may involve several others; for example, the Summary, various Vocabulary activities, developing and answering Questions, the use of Graphic Organizers to display; and any of the several was to express Similarities and Differences (e.g., Comparison, Critical Attribute, Metaphor, or Analogy).

Following the Lesson. To culminate the *Inquiry* process, a few minutes should be devoted to the debrief. The teacher's role during these crucial few minutes is to:

- Help students review the steps they took and what they might have done differently.
- Help students record in their journals or notebooks what they learned during the *Inquiry* activity and how they will be expected to apply it to other situations.

The Student's Role

In general, each *Inquiry* activity takes students through several steps, ones very similar to those used by professional researchers. In one form or another, students do the following:

- Identify the problem or discrepant event, reducing it to essential facts and removing nonessential details (students need to distinguish related from essential detail).
- Propose at least one Hypothesis for a solution (or probable cause-effect).
- Identify criteria for valid solution, including barriers to any of the proposed solutions.
- Try or test the most viable solution(s) (for **real time**, actually do the experiment; for **hypothetical**, talk through the relevant scenario, making sure to follow the steps above, and connect the dots).
- Provide valid support (proof, verification, corroboration) for the "favored" solution.

Cautionary Notes

As exciting and appealing as the *Inquiry* strategy has been for several decades, it can go horribly wrong if:

- Students are **not prepared for the *Inquiry* process**; that is, no orientation was provided.
- The **prompt is inappropriate for the age or experiential levels of the students**; that is, it is either too easy or too difficult.
- **Not enough direction is provided,** resulting in

◆ students going in several wrong directions that are more trial and error than organized inquiry; and/or

◆ students getting so far off-track as to become frustrated with the process and abandoning it; and/or

◆ the information suggested by the students does not get recorded, preventing a running record of the activity.

■ The **debrief is skipped** or mishandled, resulting in

◆ missing the opportunity to reflect on the process they followed, both as members of a team and as individuals;

◆ missing the chance to identify what went well and not as well, to replicate and to avoid next time; and

◆ missing how the *Inquiry* activities relate to a larger context and/or deep-level understanding of concepts and principles.

■ LEARNING CIRCLES

Definition

Learning Circles may be most recognizable to some readers as *Literature Circles*. The original intent was for students to take full responsibility for reading and analyzing a work of fiction. The amount of adult supervision was to be minimal to maximize student responsibility, cultivate self-management, and thus increase student enjoyment of the material. In most cases, the *Literature Circle* was not the only Language Arts activity in a course, but it was to be considered an important enhancement. It was thought that every student, regardless of ability and experience, would benefit from the interdependence of the group work and develop an authentic appreciation for literature.

In the *Instructional Design* process, we have adapted the *Literature Circle* to **all subject areas** and call it the *Learning Circle*. The more structured approaches borrow from the Cooperative Learning and Jigsaw techniques for group and intergroup learning. Depending on the *Performance Indicators*, the maturity levels of the students, and the nature of the material being studied, the *Circle* as a Delivery Strategy can be organized in any variety of formats, with varying degrees of student independence. The same core assumptions apply: choice, division of tasks, interdependence, self-direction, and accountability.

Learning Circles is a small-group independent reading strategy to help students take ownership of print and nonprint material and to be more comfortable in discussing it with peers. By being in charge of a reading task, it is hoped that students will feel more positive about reading, seeing, or hearing it and will take a more personal interest in determining its meaning and significance. The underlying premise of the *Circle* is that discussion and analysis of material in the informality and intimacy of a small group is less intimidating than with an entire class. But it also holds each student more directly accountable for making a personal investment in the material. In its **most highly developed form**, the student groups are totally responsible for the task of the *Circle*, including the selection of the book or material, the assignment of roles and responsibilities to each student, the preparation of a reading schedule, and the designation of a reporting format. In our experience, the *Circle* strategy has not been as widely accepted as it might be because many teachers mistakenly assume that students should be able to handle this maximum level of independence right away. When they cannot, and the activity is less than successful, teachers abandon it altogether. To prevent this hasty and premature rejection, we suggest various **lead-up versions** of the *Circle* to help students gradually prepare for the full-responsibility edition.

Key Decisions to Make

- **What is the Purpose of the material being read?** for example,
  - involvement with a **particular piece** and acquaintance with the author's message
  - in-depth consideration of a particular **genre** across several themes
  - in-depth consideration of a particular **theme** across several genres
  - to obtain basic, **foundational information** about a topic
  - to obtain enrichment or **extension information** about a topic
- **What is the theme (or guiding focus) of the task?** (i.e., How does it tie into the overall *Unit Plan* and the relevant *Performance Indicators*?)

For example, Grade 4 "Taking the Dare" (interdisciplinary Language Arts/Social Studies Unit on harvesting oil in the North Atlantic)

Language Arts *Performance Indicators*

[re:] . . . author's point of view . . . message

[re:] . . . central or controlling idea in nonfiction . . . supporting details

[re:] . . . use of technical vocabulary

[re:] . . . persuasive techniques used by an author . . . support in fact or precedence

Social Studies *Performance Indicators*

[re:] . . . how people have affected the physical environment . . .

[re:] . . . cooperative relations with other countries, for example, to explore and harvest resources in the North Atlantic

Texts for Circle Activity

- *Finding Oil in the North Atlantic, the Answer to the Fuel Shortage* by Edwina Norton, Exxon
- *Pirates for Oil in the North Atlantic* by Robert Kennedy, Jr., Americans to Preserve Mother Earth
- *Life on the Oil Rig* [transcripts and video clips from a National Geographic/ PBS documentary]

- **Will all students read the same or different material?**
  - Is it better that the entire class focus on a common document, with each group

◊ *examining a different aspect?*
◊ *examining the same aspects from different perspectives?*

♦ Is it better to use *several documents* to provide multiple "takes" or diverse points of view on the theme or topic?

♦ Is it important that a *central theme* or topic be the point of focus, or is it preferable to include *multiple themes*?

➥ **Will group tasks be prespecified, or left to the Circle's discretion; for example,**

♦ Will each student address a specific element? (e.g., *Fiction*: character, setting, conflict, style, message; *Nonfiction*: thesis ideas, developing detail, supporting evidence from primary and secondary sources, conclusions and generalizations)

♦ Will there be an agenda for each *Circle*?

♦ Is there a final product?

♦ Are there time lines and checkpoints?

♦ What are group tasks versus individual tasks?

➥ **How will the groups share their information with other groups?**

♦ Will there be Jigsaws?

♦ Will each group orally present its findings?

♦ Will each group prepare a written handout or monograph?

➥ **How will each member of the circle be accountable for the work?**

♦ Will each member be accountable for **a set** of features?

♦ Will each member be accountable for **all** the features?

♦ How will the Circle reflect on its own work?

When to Use

As a Delivery Strategy, the *Learning Circle* is useful at various points in a *Unit*, depending on what the *Circle* is to accomplish and how it connects to other *Unit* activities. If it is used early in the *Unit*, it is the primary method by which students get information to use for the rest of the *Unit*. If it occurs toward the end of the *Unit*, it is more like a capstone activity that may even be a part of the Culmination or a performance assessment.

By design, the *Circle* is not to be used as the only activity for the class. When students know they will have every class period to read for, say, two weeks, there is a tendency to dally a bit and not to make as good a use of the time. When the *Circle* activity is only a part of each class period or even every other day, other complementary activities (including monitoring) can be accomplished as well. Moreover, that arrangement helps students become accustomed to doing much of the reading on their own time.

The *when-to-use* is also a matter of the teacher's ultimate goal:

■ **For students to become facile** with the *Circles* method, sufficient to handle an entire activity with virtual independence by the end of the year, it should begin early in the school year and be used once each grading period. At first, it will be highly teacher-directed; but gradually, students will assume greater responsibility. Naturally (as is true of any strategy), care must be taken not to overuse the *Circles* strategy.

■ **For students to just experience** *Circles* (i.e., just for variety, or to give students a group experience), it need not begin right away. This delay may be particularly sensible if the students demonstrate very poor group-learning habits, resist the entire idea, or otherwise prove they will not benefit from the *Circles* approach. In such cases, it may be better to wait until later in the year when students are more mature and accustomed to self-direction.

How-To

The Teacher's Role

Like all Delivery Strategies, the success of the *Learning Circles* activity is largely contingent on thorough planning and preparation by the teacher. After that, the students do most of the work, and the teacher serves as a moderator and guide. Experience has shown that the following steps are essential.

- Prepare students for the *Circles* activity by explaining the rationale, the basic components, and the many options that can apply. Use the Key Decisions checklist shown earlier to plan for this.
- Depending on the maturity and self-directedness of the group and how well they handle independent work (which may differ even as the year wears on), the *Circle* activity will need to be more or less externally structured; that is,
  - For less mature students and those who are not self-directed, more structure is needed. Although each *Circle* will still make choices in how to proceed, these choices will be narrow, more focused, and involve fewer options;
  - For more mature and self-directed students, the teacher will provide only the basic guidelines, indicate the work to be done, and describe the basic parameters of the final product. But these students know they are accountable for specific accomplishments within prescribed time frames.
- Once the maturity decision is made, structure the activity as needed within the time frame of the *Unit* and in concert with the relevant *Performance Indicators*. Determine what grouping arrangement will best serve ALL students, keeping in mind that self-selection may work to the detriment of everyone concerned. Begin with the safest arrangements.
- Present guidelines to the group; review them carefully to be certain they are clear; they may need to be revisited a few times during the activity, especially the first time or two that students do a *Circle* activity.
- Monitor the group's work, including each student's effort, through
  - the notes they take (by the way, teachers should use sticky notes to provide feedback)
  - their *Circle* behaviors during class, including the feedback from Circle-Mates about individual contributions
- Be particularly alert and sensitive to students who are not keeping up with the reading or who are otherwise not benefiting from the experience. In deciding how to respond, distinguish the *won'ts* from the *can'ts*. The former are more of a discipline issue, whereas the latter are in legitimate need of academic intervention.

During the activity, use a concrete but private call-for-help such as a card bearing the letters SOS or SMS (Save My Ship) in bold capital letters, with space for the student's name and a date. Ask students to discretely leave such a card in a designated place, and then arrange to confer with him or her in a way that will not be embarrassing. These SMS students may need as little as some encouragement, or as much as direct intervention by the teacher. In some cases, they may need an alternate set of activities until they are ready to rejoin the Circle.

The Student's Role

Once the *Learning Circles* activity is underway, the students have the lion's share of responsibility for its success, a fact that they may not fully grasp at first. The following preparatory activities will serve them well.

- **Review** the guidelines for the *Circle* activity as set forth by the teacher; be clear on what choices need to be made and by when.
- **Follow directions** in setting up the *Circle* responsibilities and laying out the tasks to be done within the time frames specified; be certain what is due when, how the checkpoints along the way will work, and how the final product is to look.
- **Keep up.** And if not, notify the teacher immediately. Students must fully understand the importance of their responsibility both to *Circle* and to themselves. Indeed, they must also be fully aware of the consequences for failing to fulfill these responsibilities. Use the SMS cards as needed.

Cautionary Notes

The *Learning Circle* is most likely to be a successful Delivery Strategy if the following cautions are observed:

- Carefully plan a *Circle* activity that is appropriate to the *Performance Indicators* of the *Unit Plan* but also appropriate to the maturity levels of the students and the extent to which they have demonstrated self-direction and self-discipline.
- Be certain students are ready to take on the responsibilities of the *Circle* before beginning.
- Avoid overdoing the *Circle* method; use it strategically during the year.
- Help students feel secure and comfortable using the SMS card. Prepare a set of alternative or intervention activities to use with students who are not experiencing success with the Circle as it is structured.

■ SOCRATIC SEMINAR

Definition

The Socratic method of teaching, or teaching by asking students questions, dates as far back as 400 BC to its namesake, Socrates. It is the act of reflective thinking, prompted by probing, provocative questions. According to John Dewey, Socratic teaching relies on two basic elements: (a) doubt and (b) the act of searching to clarify ideas and details. In the Delivery Strategy called *Socratic Seminar*, students closely examine Rich Text, the most frequently cited examples of which are a piece of literature, an op-ed essay, a court transcript, a political cartoon, travel journals, tables of data, eyewitness accounts, the minutes of a Congressional hearing, a treaty, a work of art or music, the records of an experiment, and so on.

The activity consists of students seated in a circle responding to questions from the teacher and each other's questions about the Rich Text to clarify their understanding. Its core purpose is to provide students a risk-free opportunity to achieve a deep-level understanding of the material by answering questions. In so doing, each student's interpretation is extended, enriched by the diversity of perceptions offered by others. Each interpretive remark offered by a student must be based on details or features found in the Rich Text. The *Seminar* is not a forum for students to criticize the text or to offer personal opinions about its worth or merit. The *Seminar* ends with a follow-up activity assigned to be completed independently by each student. Typically a written product, the follow-up is an opportunity for students to construct their own meaning from the Rich Text, and this may include a personal reaction or critical analysis.

The keys to successful *Socratic Seminars* are as follows:

- All students must have read the text and prepared the ticket for admission.
- The number of Discussants is limited to 20 at one time; assign the additional students to act as Process Observers. (The Observers also complete the ticket for admission, as they may indeed rotate into the *Seminar*. At the conclusion of the *Seminar*, they are central to the debrief, and they will complete the follow-up assignment.)
- The selected text or object is rich with implications for reflection and analysis; students are intrigued and highly motivated to participate and anxious to weigh-in on the material. Students must be able to cite details or features from the Rich Text to support their interpretive remarks.
- Care is taken to confine the discourse to deep-level understanding and analysis of the Rich Text and not to allow the *Seminar* to lapse into critique or evaluation of the material.
- Discussants observe the rules of Socratic Etiquette; they listen to each other with courtesy and interest, respecting the diversity of perceptions, and honestly considering alternate interpretations.
- The follow-up activity asks students to construct their own meaning not only from the Rich Text itself but from the various questions and answers exchanged by the Discussants during the *Seminar*, all in direct relationship to one or more of the *Performance Indicators* in the *Unit*.

When to Use

The *Socratic Seminar* is used when students need to fully understand a complex and provocative text. It is also a means for students to interact with each other to construct meaning about a common experience. On one level, the *Socratic Seminar* involves deep-level interpretation of a written document, a work of art, or a transcript of historic significance. At another level, it involves students in thoughtful discourse about ethical ideas and moral dilemmas. Among topics frequently selected are the following:

- capital punishment
- genetic engineering
- censorship
- a symbolic poem
- a natural disaster
- conditions in elder care
- the prison system
- coming to grips with personal tragedy
- personal artistic expressions
- a biographical essay
- a thought-provoking song

- the military and do we need a draft
- the inequities in various economic systems
- the violation of individual rights
- research involving live animals
- a controversial legal ruling
- a painting or sculpture
- scandal in professional sports.

How-To

The Teacher's Role

Select Rich Text that is consistent with the theme and topic of the *Unit* and will help students master the designated *Performance Indicators*. Ideally, the text should be understandable by all students to provide the group with a common experience; the differentiation can occur in the follow-up assignment. Be certain that all students understand the procedure for the *Seminar*, including the role of the Discussants and the Process Observers.

That all students must complete the Ticket for Admission is concrete evidence that each student has read or observed the Rich Text and is prepared for the *Seminar*. For students with Special Needs, this "ticket" may be adapted or modified, and/or the students may be assisted in preparing it. Among the most popular Tickets for Admission are the following:

- a highlighted manuscript
- a Summary
- original Questions about details from the text
- an original chart or Graphic Organizer using details derived from the text
- several key Vocabulary words or phrases
- a series of Notes taken from the text

Arrange Discussants in a circle to provide every student equal status and to permit Discussants to see each other; use placards or name badges with first names, and instruct Discussants to refer to each other by name. Practice asking the teacher questions, and role-play how students should answer them; practice formulating and asking student-questions, including how to respond, using the rules of Socratic etiquette. Teacher should make sure students know they must support their remarks with details from the printed text or features from an object—whatever the Rich Text.

It is important that the Process Observers know their role as well. The teacher might model how they should record information and how they should share it during the debrief. The Process Observers also prepare a ticket for admission and complete the follow-up assignment.

For the *Seminar* itself, teachers are reminded to do the following:

- Open the *Seminar* with a thought-provoking question. For example, suppose the Rich Text is (a) a list of the names, occupations, and a brief background of the passengers aboard the *Mayflower* as she set sail from Plymouth, England, on September 6, 1620; and (b) a portion of the ship's log describing the voyage. The teacher might ask, "What sort of people do you think decided to take the voyage? What do you think motivated them? Let's take 10 minutes to describe them."

- Listen as Discussants respond to question with answers that reflect their ideas and understandings about the text, not their opinions. Each student should share his or her ideas, perhaps linking to the remarks just made by another student and extending that point, or suggesting a different line of thinking, but always supported in the text. Help students show that they value others' interpretations and take seriously alternative perceptions about the same details.

- As appropriate, prompt students to ask each other questions, including "How does my idea sound to you?" "Do you see gaps in my reasoning?" "Do you have different information?" "How did you arrive at that view?" A list of **Sample Appropriate Questions** appears in Table 7.2.

- Be sure students follow the rules of Socratic Etiquette, including the following:
  - Only one Discussant speaks at a time, but all Discussants are expected to speak.
  - Discussants do not cut each other off; they wait politely for a student to finish.
  - Discussants do not raise their hands to speak; they use body language to indicate they have something to say.
  - Discussants treat each other and their remarks with complete respect; the questions they ask, even when they disagree, demonstrate courtesy; for example,

    "I see what you mean, but another way to look at it might be. . . ."

    "I hadn't thought of it that way, but could this be another way to see it?"

    "Thanks, I missed that point."

    "I agree with your idea of ABC, but I also wonder about XYZ."

  - Process Observers also behave respectfully, and they do not directly acknowledge Discussants' remarks.
  - Discussants and Process Observers listen attentively to each speaker, observing appropriate body language, eye contact, and facial gestures.

- Periodically, insert a brief statement of summary, followed by an additional question. In the *Mayflower* scenario, the teacher might inject the following:

"It's clear that most of you think the majority of Mayflower passengers were trying to escape something in England rather than to find something in the New World. What sort of bonding do you think might have occurred on board ship as they became acquainted? The ship's log gives us a few hints, too."

- Limit the Seminar to 30 minutes; at the end, summarize the group's thinking. For the *Mayflower* activity, the students could have taken the *Seminar* in any one of several directions, but one example might be the "escape and redemption" theme. The teacher might summarize that direction as follows:

  "It seems as if the group feels that many of the passengers on the Mayflower were leaving England to escape either past crimes or a government that denied them the right to practice their faith. Many of you also feel that these passengers saw the New World as a chance for redemption. To start off fresh. It sounds as if you feel you know most of them fairly well."

- As the *Seminar* ends, the Process Observers and teacher lead the class in a debrief. The Discussants reflect on the *Seminar* experience, including their tickets for admission, the questions asked during the *Seminar*, the perceptions of fellow Discussants, and their own reflections about the text. They also make recommendations about what might make the next *Seminar* more successful. Students who acted as Process Observers provide feedback about how the Discussants exchanged information and reacted to each other.
- At the conclusion of the *Seminar*, make a follow-up assignment that asks students to extend their understanding about the Rich Text. This is typically a written assignment but varies in its length and formality. For the *Mayflower* scenario, this follow-up assignment might be appropriate:

  "As a follow-up, I'd like you to select one or two of the passengers who survived the trip, and prepare a travel journal of his or her 3 months at sea, including a scenario of his or her first few weeks ashore at Cape Cod."

The Student's Role

Once students are clear as to how the *Socratic Seminar* is to proceed, they need to be well-prepared to participate, whether as Discussants or Process Observers. They need to study or observe the Rich Text as thoroughly as possible, and each student needs to prepare his or her ticket for admission as assigned. If the Rich Text is a picture, sculpture, performance, or other nonprint medium, the "ticket" may be sketches, written reflections, or pertinent background information. Remember, any of the Learning Constructs mentioned previously may be used as "tickets." During the *Seminar*, students should focus on the guiding questions posed by the teacher, preparing an answer. In most cases, students will be expected to ask additional and pertinent questions of their classmates to seek clarification as shown in Table 7.2.

Table 7.2   Sample Questions to Be Asked by the Teacher and Students During the Socratic Seminar

1. Agree/Disagree
"Did anyone else have a similar reaction?"
"Who has a different take on that?"
"Would anyone like to take the opposite view?"
"What might BE the opposite view?"

2. Seek Clarification
"I'm not sure I understand what you mean."
"Tell me more about that."
"Do you see gaps in my reasoning?"
"Are you seeing something in the [text] that I missed?"

3. Ask for Support
"Can you give an example of what you mean?"
"Where in the [text] did you see that?"
"What would be a good reason for your idea?"
"What is some evidence for what you think?"

4. Cause and Effect
"Why do you think that happened?"
"How could that have been prevented?"
"Do you think it would happen that way again? Why or why not?"
"What might be some reasons people ___[behave a certain way]___?"
"What later events (effects) might be felt if this plays out as is?"
"What makes you think so?"

5. Compare/Contrast
"How are _____ and _____ alike? Different?"
"What is this similar to?"
"How does this differ from _____?"
"How does this [rich-text] remind you of _____?"
"What are some reasons this wouldn't [would] be a good idea?"
"You've identified reasons why this would work; are there reasons it would *not* work?"

6. Point of View/Perspective
"How might he or she have felt if the tables were turned, if some things were different?"
"What might he or she have been thinking when _____?"
"Suppose _____ had happened; would this still be true? Why or why not?"
"He or she might not like that, but can you think of who would?"
"Are there any *other* ways to interpret this?"
"Can anyone suggest another perspective?"
"Does anyone have a *different* set of conclusions?"
"Can anyone think of counterexamples?"

7. Personal Reaction, Response [*Not* Opinion]
"What are some things you wonder about?"
"What would you like to know more about?"
"What would YOU have done in this situation?"
"Has anything like this ever happened to YOU?"
"In what way is your situation alike or different from this one?"

It is especially important that students treat each other with courtesy, even if they disagree on an interpretive point. They are expected to respond to each other with affirming verbal and body language, including comments and questions that demonstrate respect for divergent thinking. Taking notes is an important part of the *Seminar* whether one is a Discussant or a Process Observer, since these will be essential to complete the follow-up assignment.

Cautionary Notes

Until and unless the *Socratic Seminar* becomes a familiar and frequently used Delivery Strategy, it may seem overwhelming. But enthusiasts urge teachers to be patient and not to give up on it, even if it is disappointing at first. In our experience, the *Socratic Seminar* is more likely to be **successful** if

- students are fully aware of the *Socratic Seminar* process and how it works;
- students see the Rich Text as pertinent, relevant, and worthy of discussion;

- the Rich Text reflects one or more *Performance Indicators*, and students can "see the point" of going through it;
- the opening questions (and those that follow) are provocative and inspire students to think on a deep-level about implications and interpretations;
- students' responses are grounded in the Rich Text itself, both during the Seminar and in the follow-up assignment; and
- students feel safe to express their interpretations and to raise questions that clarify and extend their understanding.

■ ACTION RESEARCH

Definition

Action Research is a real-time investigation of an actual hypothesis or hunch to determine its viability. The hypothesis may be offered as a possible explanation for a puzzlement, the solution to a problem, or the guiding question for an inquiry. Many state content standards for all four core subjects on one or both of two levels: (a) explicitly require students to formulate and test hypotheses; or (b) imply that students use *Action Research* to analyze a problem-solving situation, identify its determining variables, propose a *cause-effect* or *if-then* explanation, and locate corroborating information. Additionally, hypothesis testing is one of the Best Practices on most lists. The notion of real-time allows the study to be completed within a reasonable time frame so that its results can be useful for determining mastery of the related *Performance Indicators*.

If *Action Research* is the method chosen for students to demonstrate mastery of one or more *Performance Indicators*, the process must be completed by each student as an individual project. Moreover, each student must be able to explain every phase of the process from the preliminary idea through the final report, including any spin-off questions. Group research projects are useful for a myriad of other *Performance Indicators*, but as we describe *Action Research* here, it is the individual student project we have in mind.

Although an *Action Research* project is driven by the guiding hypothesis, its importance lies in the investigative process and the student's collection, compilation, analysis, and interpretation of information. Whether or not the guiding hypothesis is supported in the end is inconsequential, provided the investigation is done appropriately and students more fully understand the problem-solving process. In fact, and this parallels actual laboratory science, the majority of the projects will yield results that do not support the hypothesis. But students will use some of the language of research, including *hypothesis, null hypotheses, control group, target group, primary and secondary sources, observation, inference,* and *conclusion*.

Key Components

The research supports a variety of formats for *Action Research*, but the common features are as follows:

- ☛ That the topic can be studied in real-time and relates to one or more content standards (*Performance Indicators*)

- That the focus can be sufficiently narrowed to a reasonable hypothesis that can be proven or disproven
- That students will follow an approved Research Plan, with guiding questions, both primary and secondary references, the appropriate controls, the collection of sufficient data, and drawing viable conclusions

When to Use

Action Research is useful on two levels:

- as a delivery strategy to provide students with the information they need to master one or more *Performance Indicators*, and
- as an authentic or performance assessment that will demonstrate a student's mastery of one or more *Performance Indicator(s)*.

Whether it is used to provide information or as an assessment, the *Action Research* process is a protracted method that may take three or four weeks to complete, but it is not intended to be the sole teaching-learning activity for the duration. While the project is underway, other activities should continue. As with *Learning Circles*, we strongly urge teachers **not** to allow students to complete the entire project on class time. Students must learn to complete tasks that require a good deal of their work to be outside the classroom and to pace themselves across time, accomplishing the assigned tasks within designated time frames. Such learning habits as these are expectations from junior high through college, and students need opportunities to cultivate them in the intermediate grades. A sample three-week schedule for an *Action Research* project, with other activities interspersed, appears in Table 7.3.

Complement to Traditional Research

The *Action Research* process is best used to examine questions and puzzlements answerable with a real-time investigation that can be completed within three to four weeks. The *Action Research* process shares many of the features of the Traditional Research project. Both are driven by research questions, both include primary and secondary sources, and both are captured in a final report that includes data tables and charts, a personal reaction, and implications for further study. But they differ in that the major focus of *Action Research* is hands-on, real-time investigation with students looking at events as they unfold. The major focus of most traditional research projects is looking back at events after-the-fact, reviewing the research conducted by others, and presenting results as a historical rather than real-time investigation. But the two types of research complement each other very well, and both are essential for students to be fully proficient in the many investigative skills required of them to master content standards (or *Performance Indicators*) in all four core subject areas. They each play an important role in developing a student's skill and confidence in framing problems or puzzlements, observing relevant variables and conditions, and locating corroborative information.

Table 7.3   Sample Three-Week Schedule for Action Research

Week One					
Location	*Monday*	*Tuesday*	*Wednesday*	*Thursday*	*Friday*
In-Class Out-of-Class	Overview the Action Research Process (AR) Show students sample AR projects from prior years Set Expectations Share Scoring Rubric Discuss General Topics Question/Answer	Discuss the Research Plan Share Plan that goes with the sample AR project Explain the detail and terms of the Research Plan Discuss narrowing topic • Hypotheses • Research • Questions	Give students time to formulate their Research Plans, including data collection, sources, dates, etc. as per AR format Meet with each student to review and approve Plan as per guidelines [At the same time, other students rotate to media center to meet with the librarian and check Internet sites to be certain adequate Primary and Secondary sources are available for AR project]	Present note-taking strategies for secondary sources Review bibliography format Discuss and demonstrate data collection strategies for Primary sources	
	Review sample of completed project Select broad topic	Narrow own topic Identify Hypotheses, Research Questions	Finalize Action Research Plan as per format, including all dates and tasks	(Weekend) Assemble Secondary sources	

Week Two					
Location	*Monday*	*Tuesday*	*Wednesday*	*Thursday*	*Friday*
In-Class	Provide expository and persuasive writing workshop (circulate among students)	[Class time devoted to another *Unit* activity]	Conduct Progress Check for Action Research while other students proceed with other activity	[Class time devoted to another *Unit* activity]	[Class time devoted to another *Unit* activity]
Out-of-Class	• Conduct Primary research for AR project • Read Secondary Sources; take notes			Continue with Secondary Sources	

Week Three					
Location	*Monday*	*Tuesday*	*Wednesday*	*Thursday*	*Friday*
In-Class	Progress Check for Action Research; review final scoring rubric Students proceed with other *Unit* activity	[Class time devoted to another *Unit* activity]	[. . .other *Unit* activity] Teacher meets with students who have rough draft ready or who feel they need assistance	[. . .other *Unit* activity]	Action Research project displays, presentations
Out-of-Class	• Collect Primary Source data • Assemble data; prepare tables, etc.		• Finalize Action Research product		

How-To

The Teacher's Role

Although students have identified the steps in the Scientific Method for decades, the majority have not had the opportunity to conduct real-time research. Their customary laboratory activities are highly scripted and tightly controlled with predetermined steps to follow that lead to predictable outcomes. The *Action Research* process involves a bona fide investigation that may or may not yield predicted or even anticipated results. The teacher's role is coinvestigator and coach. Although each student conducts his or her own investigation, there are safeguards to make sure the studies are not superficial, wasteful, or dangerous. Each student's topic and Research Plan are approved by the teacher, and the teacher provides guidance and assistance along the way as needed. The following steps are those most commonly recommended for the teacher to facilitate successful *Action Research*:

- Introduce the *Action Research* strategy in developmentally appropriate language, including a compelling rationale and samples from prior years. Students who are unaccustomed to "working this hard" for an answer, especially when they may indeed discover a "nonanswer" and actually more questions, may be tough to convince.
- Show students how to identify topics of interest (relative to the *Performance Indicators* in the present *Unit*) that can be investigated. Have a few samples ready; for example,
  - ◆ Which snack crackers have more fat? Less fat?
  - ◆ Is there a predictive relationship between amount of time one studies and grades earned?
  - ◆ Do certain seeds grow better in some soil than others?

- ◆ What is the relationship between voting patterns in each precinct and the outcome of the elections?
- ◆ Does writing improve more after self-edit or peer-edit?
- Demonstrate how to narrow the focus to an hypothesis that will guide the inquiry; the hypothesis may be written in one of the two formats below (we will use the "relationship between time of study and grades earned" as the example):
  - ◆ a statement of fact written in the future or present tense: *"There is a positive relationship between the amount of time one prepares for tests and the score obtained"* (note: for older students, some teachers may encourage including the null hypothesis; that is, *"There is not a significant relationship between the amount of study time and a student's grades."*)
  - ◆ an *if-then* statement to imply causation; for example, "If one studies for tests (and other assignments), then he or she will get better scores."
- Show students how to devise research questions to guide the inquiry; for example:

  Guiding Question: What is the relationship between the amount of study time and grades earned?

  Research Questions:
  - ◆ Is there a difference in the study time needed for tests compared to daily assignments?
  - ◆ Are there various study techniques that work better than others?
  - ◆ Does it make a difference if the preparation is spaced out versus "crammed?"
  - ◆ Are there differences between the study patterns of boys and girls?
  - ◆ Are certain study techniques more successful than others for specific assignments?
- Explain how to identify the most likely Primary and Secondary sources of information to inform the study; for example,

  Primary [help students realize that these are data they collect]:
  - ◆ *interviews of target students* (e.g., asking how much time they spend in preparation, what types of study techniques they use, what are their levels of success)
  - ◆ *target-student study logs* (e.g., time spent on specific study tasks; time of day; time per subject each day)
  - ◆ *teacher interviews* (e.g., what study methods were suggested, how do suggested techniques vary by the task, is there a pattern in how students perform compared to their preparation)
  - ◆ *observations* (e.g., watch target students and control students during study halls, noting their behaviors and the extent of focus)

  Secondary:
  - ◆ *current research* (e.g., current research articles in popular magazines about learning and study habits, study time and grades earned)
  - ◆ *textbook references* (e.g., what the experts say about learning theory, research projects involving study techniques and academic success, differences in gender, age)

> ♦ *technical manuals* (e.g., how to study, including illustrations and directions; different suggestions for different subjects and the type of academic task)

- Demonstrate how to devise a Research Plan, including the following components:

1. **tasks**, for example,
   - ♦ determine what data to collect and the best technique
   - ♦ decide if and how control groups will work
   - ♦ determine how the data will be collected (including any permissions that are needed)
   - ♦ decide how the data will be organized
   - ♦ select what secondary sources will be referenced for corroborating information

2. **time frames for each task**

3. **the final product** for sharing or dissemination, for example,
   - ♦ tables of data
   - ♦ interpretive statements and conclusions drawn
   - ♦ implications for further study
   - ♦ bibliography of sources used
   - ♦ display:
     - ◊ *a conventional expository or persuasive "paper"*
     - ◊ *wall charts, a table display, PowerPoint, and so on*
     - ◊ *an oral presentation*

Exhibit 7.1, a sample research plan, appears at the end of the chapter.

The Student's Role

As with every Delivery Strategy, the sum and substance of the student's role in the *Action Research* method is planning and execution. But unlike some of the more familiar strategies, the idea of conducting real time, or live, research can be so daunting to students that they automatically assume they cannot make it work. Or, they fret about the possibility that their study will fail to prove anything. For most students, academic success is all about the right answer, and the idea that *process* and *discovery* are equally valuable is difficult for them to grasp. For this reason, we urge teachers to begin small and to exercise patience in helping students come to grips with the *Action Research* method. If enough teachers use it in a school, it won't take long for students, and parents/guardians, to develop a healthy respect for its potential.

Cautionary Notes

The most important caution to extend about *Action Research* is that students must be taught how to use it and to become comfortable with its uncertainties and the idea that failure (to prove a hypothesis) is actually success. To help students develop comfort with such a prospect, teachers must establish clear and simple ground-rules and walk students through their first few "investigations." To rush the process and/or to expect students to proceed independently too soon is to court disaster. And the problem with teachers doing it wrong is that students never get the opportunity to do it right.

■ ADVANCE ORGANIZER

Definition

The *Advance Organizer* is a Delivery Strategy that is used to introduce a concept or material. It serves to orient students to the topic using key concepts or ideas they already know to link to the new information. The *Organizer* functions cognitively to structure the material as it is presented, providing a kind of conceptual framework into which the learner will integrate the new information. It is **not** an overview or preview, but rather a verbal or visual guiding framework for the new material to be learned. For example, students' familiarity with soccer could be used as an *Advance Organizer* to study lacrosse, or a brief profile of several technology-based careers could be an *Advance Organizer* for a Technology Careers Fair, using the Commutative Property of Addition to help students understand how their multiplication facts work.

The *Advance Organizer* as a teaching strategy is credited to David Ausubel who began using the method in the 1960s. (Research citations are available from the authors upon request.) It is often referred to as the *hooks-and-loops* method of learning because it relies on our brain's effort to connect the unknown to something familiar. In this model, the *hooks* represent the structures or concepts that have been learned and hold a place in the brain, while the *loops* are the new information that comes into the brain and rests on a "hook." The key to using *Advance Organizers* is to make the connection between the new information and previous knowledge; it is a method of bridging and linking known information with new learning.

For maximum success, the following keys apply to the *Advance Organizer*:

- has an obvious relevance to the concept, idea, or principle from one or more *Performance Indicators*.
- provides a mental scaffolding to learn new information.
- allows students see that each lesson is not something completely new, but rather another form or use of a previously learned concept.
- can be used when complex concepts are to be introduced, but students have some of the fundamental pieces in their previous learning.
- can be a *statement*, a descriptive *paragraph*, a *question*, a *demonstration*, or even a *film*; it might be one sentence, or it might be an entire lesson that precedes the other lessons in a *Unit*; it might also be a Metaphor or Analogy.
- may take the form of a *dialogue* or *stories* and *anecdotes*, which may be memorable in their own right, but which also serve to relate the abstract material to a more or less familiar situation in the students' world.

When to Use

The *Advance Organizer* is helpful when concepts, ideas, or principles are highly abstract and difficult for students to understand, but which have a link or association with something they know from before. In addition, it is the strategy of choice when there is a need to bridge and link old information with something new.

How-To

The easiest way to understand the use of the *Advance Organizer* is to see several classroom examples. The teacher:

- shows visual representations of the theories of Democritus, Dalton, Thomson, Rutherford, and Bohr and relates their contributions to the development of Atomic Theory.
- has students bring in pictures that show the destruction caused by the 1989 San Francisco area earthquake before introducing earthquake waves and how they are measured. This could also be done with other natural catastrophes such as hurricanes and tsunamis.
- uses a Carl Sagan video about a scientific concept such as evolution before introducing Darwin's Theory of Evolution.
- shows a poster depicting many forms of energy and asks students to discuss and identify the examples of energy before introducing the students to a *Unit* on energy transformations.
- uses several different colored masses of clay that are cut apart, then joins the pieces together and rejoins them to form a different arrangement of the original mass to set the stage for studying The Law of Conservation of Matter.
- provides a Graphic Organizer that contains a visual clue about a complex relationship among many parts (e.g., charts, diagrams, oral presentations, or concept maps).
- asks students to compare and contrast the new content based on what they know (e.g., what can they tell about the color, shape, smell, feel, or taste).
- uses a parallel idea such as using baseball to teach cricket, or ping pong to teach tennis.
- gives scenarios and asks students to infer the rules based on their current knowledge; for example, give a diagram of a hockey rink to students with little or no knowledge of the game and ask them to infer the relationship between the various lines and some of the rules such as *icing* and *offside*.
- has students identify the characteristics of a known quantity (e.g., two-dimensional shapes) and then relate these to the new idea/concept of different types of geometric forms (e.g., three-dimensional objects) before discussing their individual likenesses and differences.
- shows a map of pre– and post–World War I Europe to set the stage for how borders changed, how ethnic groups relocated, and so on.
- uses a poignant or moving poem such as *Butterfly* to preview the study of the Holocaust.
- uses mitosis to connect the familiar to the new content of meiosis.
- uses a familiar metaphor such as the weather to preview a *Unit* on economic forecasting.
- reads a piece from O'Henry that shows irony and a piece from William Faulkner that does not and have students compare/contrast the two.

- uses a story about taking a jellyfish from the sea shore and putting it in a bucket of fresh water, or taking a pet frog for a swim in the ocean to precede a discussion of osmosis/diffusion.
- facilitates a brainstorm about facts and fallacies of inherited traits when beginning a study of genetics.

Cautionary Notes

Advance Organizers can be misleading or create confusion if
- they are misaligned to the concepts, principles, or ideas intended by the *Performance Indicator(s)*.
- they are developmentally too advanced or too immature for the students, or they are used for things that are already familiar to the students.
- the teacher has not thought through the *Advance Organizer* to ensure that it matches the concepts to follow.
- should *not* be a review of what was discussed in the last lesson unless there is a direct tie-in to the content that is coming.

■ SUMMARY

As the second of the two pillars that support the Best Practices methods and integrate them into the delivery and assessment of classroom instruction, the Delivery Strategies are structured to fit nicely into the Motivation and/or the Information quadrants of the *Unit Plan*. The important thing in using any Best Practice is to know which ones, and in what combination, best help students master the particular cluster of *Performance Indicators* on which each *Unit* is based.

Moreover, the activities that comprise these two quadrants are the INPUT side of the *Unit Plan* and must prepare students to demonstrate mastery in the OUTPUT side, or the Assessment and Culmination quadrants. To that end, teachers need to keep the two pillars in mind as they plan: (a) the **Learning Constructs**, or the tools used by students to process information; and (b) the **Delivery Strategies**, or the tools used by teachers to present the information.

Exhibit 7.1   A Sample Student Action Research Plan

Name: <u>Jamal Reynolds</u>   Course: <u>Biology</u>   Investigation Title: <u>*"Bacteria in Our Midst"*</u>

Time frame: *3 weeks*   Due: <u>*March 25*</u>

A.   Investigative Question(s): What is the purpose of your investigation?

If bacterial swabs are taken from various places and used to inoculate a Petri dish with a bacterial culture, can we observe and count bacterial colonies to find out where bacteria live and determine what kind of environmental conditions influence bacterial growth?

B.   Hypothesis

1. Based on Investigative Questions, written in the future tense

    The water fountain outside the gym will be more contaminated with bacteria than others because it is the most used, and it is the oldest in the building.

2. "If . . . then . . ." statement of Hypothesis

    If the water fountain outside the gym is older than others in the building and it is used the most often, then it most likely will be more contaminated with bacteria than the others.

C.   Research Questions

1. *How does the presence of bacteria in a water fountain relate to the frequency of its usage?*

2. *Do various types of bacteria show up in the same location or is it only one particular type?*

3. *Does the age, construction, and bowl composition of the water fountain make an impact on the presence of bacteria?*

4. *Does refrigeration (or not) have an impact on the presence of bacteria?*

D.   Schedule

Tasks	Time frame	Due Date
Establish schedule for trials; include— • *the locations of water fountains to be included* • *experimental: the gym, the office, the teachers' lounge* • *control: the 2nd floor hallway* • *the number of samples to be taken* • *a count of usage* • *the times when samples will be collected*	*homework assignment*	*March 3* *(two days and a weekend prior to the investigation)*
Collect primary data • *the collection of water samples* • *the culturing of samples taken* • *a count of the usage of each water fountain*	*2 weeks*	*After 10 days of testing; end March 18* *[continued]*
Locate corroborating information in secondary sources (e.g., possible identification of bacteria types via shape; color; texture; etc.); e.g., *"Bacteria: More Than Pathogens" by Trudy M. Wassenaar* *http://www.actionbioscience.org/biodiversity/wassenaar.html* *http://www.microbelibrary.org* *http://www.microbeworld.org/home.htm*	*7 days*	*March 20*
Organize and analyze data	*1 week*	*March 25 (1 week after testing ends)*
Prepare final product	*1 week*	*March 25*

(Continued)

Exhibit 7.1 (Continued)

E.   Procedure (numbered step-by-step instructions)

1. *Prepare 4 Petri dishes (3 trial, 1 control): turn them upside down and (using a marker) place initials, date, time, and sample location along the bottom <u>perimeter</u> of the dish — NOT in the middle.*

2. *Prepare water fountain sign-up charts for students to mark a tally each time they use it. Set charts up by class period to indicate time of day used.*

3. *At the trial (experimental) and control locations (outside the gym, the teachers' lounge, the office, and the 2nd floor fountain), swab the inside surface of each water fountain with a sterile Q-tip, being careful <u>not to touch</u> the ends of the Q-tip.* **Samples are taken on days 1, 3, 4, and 6.**

4. *Open the Petri dish (like Pac Man) and lightly rub the Q-tip across the agar in the dish. Tape the dish closed and draw what the dish looks like for Day 1. Place the Petri dish upside down on the tray.*

5. *Examine the Day 1 Petri dishes for all locations after 4 days. [Bearing in mind, the microbes are very small and may take a couple days to multiply enough to be visible on the dishes.] Record each observation in the Journal. On the upper half of each page, draw the appearance of each dish <u>daily</u>; on the lower half of each page, describe what was observed in that drawing, including color, shape, texture, the number of clusters growing, groupings, similarities, and differences. Record in a table (e.g., below) the number of clusters of bacteria that appear to be growing in each Petri dish.*

6. *After 4 days, compare the 4 dishes to determine which had the most growth. Day 1 sample is compared with Day 5; Day 3 with Day 7; Day 4 with Day 8, and Day 6 with Day 10.*

Table showing the **number of bacterial colonies** present for each location

Samples	Day 1 New	Day 2 X	Day 3 New	Day 4 New	Day 5 Old 1	Day 6 New	Day 7 Old 3	Day 8 Old 4	Day 9 X	Day 10 Old 6
Gym										
Teachers' Lounge										
Office										
(2nd floor) CONTROL										

F.   Identify the "Control" (conditions or materials that stay the same) for your experiment.

The control is the water fountain on the second floor. It is old, <u>unrefrigerated</u>, and the <u>same porcelain composition as the one by the gym</u>. It is in an out-of-the-way place, so it does not get very much use.

G.   Identify the "Variable" (conditions or materials that change) for your experiment.

One trial or experimental fountain is the water fountain by the gym because it gets <u>excessive use</u>. A second experimental fountain is by the teachers' lounge because it is <u>new and refrigerated</u>. The third experimental fountain is near the Office; it is old and porcelain and gets a moderate amount of use — similar to the one outside the gym.

Table showing the number of people using each water fountain.

Samples	Day 1	Day 2	Day 3	Day 4	Day 5	Day 6	Day 7	Day 8	Day 9	Day 10
Gym										
Teachers' Lounge										
Office										
(2nd floor) CONTROL										

H. **Attach Sample Data Sheets you will use to record your data (sketched, log, chart, etc.).**
[See previous charts.]

I. **Suggested ideas about how you might graph your data.**
Graph the days on the x-axis and the number of colonies of bacteria on the y-axis to show differences among the 4 water fountains. Use 4 different-colored lines.

Graph the days on the x-axis and the number of people using the water fountains on the y-axis to show differences among the 4 water fountains. Use 4 different-colored lines.

J. **How will you report the results?**

The water fountain by the gym	*The water fountain near the Office*
• **bacteria:** __ clusters and __ types	• **bacteria:** __ clusters and __ types
• **structure:** old, porcelain, not refrigerated	• **structure:** new, porcelain, not refrigerated
• **use:** __ times used during the two weeks	• **use:** __ times used during the two weeks
The water fountain outside the teachers' lounge	*The water fountain on the 2nd floor (CONTROL)*
• **bacteria:** __ clusters and __ types	• **bacteria:** __ clusters and __ types
• **structure:** new, metal, refrigerated	• **structure:** old, porcelain, not refrigerated
• **use:** __ times used during the two week	• **use:** __ times used during the two week

K. **What are ways you might present your results? (check those that apply)**
- ☐ wall charts
- ☐ drawings on the overhead
- ☑ PowerPoint
- ☐ conventional "paper"
- ☐ oral presentation with graphics

L. **Anticipate problems; what might compromise the study?**
1. Will <u>cleaning solutions</u> interfere with the bacteria count?
2. What if a fountain isn't used at all? Will it still have bacteria?
3. Will users <u>accurately chart</u> the number of times a fountain is used?

PART IV

Assessment

8

Unit Planning

Assessment and Culmination

INTRODUCTION ■

In Chapter 4, we introduced the *Unit Plan* format as the method used in the **Instructional Design** process to help teachers organize their delivery and assessment of classroom instruction. Chapter 5 was devoted to the INPUT portion of the *Unit Plan*: the *Motivation* and the *Information* quadrants. We included definitions, explanations, and several samples that teachers can use tomorrow. Since we use the Best Practices research to define the strategies that belong in the *Motivation* and *Information* sections of the *Unit Plan*, Chapters 6 and 7, respectively, were devoted to the two major Best Practice categories of (a) *Learning Constructs* (or

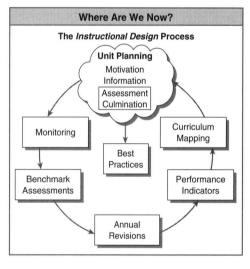

scaffolding techniques to help students construct meaning) and (b) *Delivery Strategies* (or methods used by the teacher to present the information needed by students to do this constructing). Several examples and clarifications were included in both chapters to help teachers visualize how they might use these Practices.

Performance Indicators	
————————	
————————	
Culmination	Motivation
Assessment	Information

This chapter addresses the OUTPUT section of the *Unit Plan*, or the *Assessment* and *Culmination* quadrants. These sections detail activities to determine each student's mastery of those *Performance Indicators* on which each *Unit* is built. To revisit the clock face metaphor, these two quadrants represent the space between 6:00 and 12:00, moving up the dial. *Assessments* are the abstract measures of OUTPUT, and the *Culmination* sets forth concrete measures, bringing us back full circle to where we began the *Unit* at the outset.

It was suggested in Chapter 4 that developing teams begin their *Unit Plans* with training in the "basics" of the rationale and format, from which they develop the first one or two *Plans* for the year. As training in the Best Practices proceeds (e.g., during each quarter to work on the *Plans* for the upcoming grading period), the teams will become increasingly skillful at inserting *Learning Constructs* and selecting the appropriate *Delivery Strategies*. Since the *Unit Plans* are piloted as they are developed, the teams get continual feedback from the Critical Friends network—those colleagues who are also piloting the *Plans*. As the *Unit Plans* are "green inked," they are actually backfilled with additional techniques and activities that make them even stronger and more responsive the next time they are taught. Special features such as Differentiation, Remediation, and Enrichment, or alternate materials are among those added as the pilot goes along, thus increasing the likelihood that every student will master each of the Performance Indicators. It is an embedded professional development process that continually refines and reshapes the culture of classroom instruction as it goes along.

■ ASSESSMENT

The *Assessment* quadrant of the *Unit Plan* features what are primarily traditional measures of student mastery, the best known of which is the old, familiar paper-pencil test. Less-often mentioned but equally viable are the teacher-observation checklist, pages from a journal or log, and selected homework assignments. Depending on the teacher and the *Unit*, these Assessments can be as follows:

♦ *Progressive.* Some Assessments develop continually throughout the *Unit* and are actually cumulative, picking up additional items—and developmental competence—as the *Unit* progresses. For example, a research project, journal pages, a growing bibliography, a collection of leaves, or the checklist of oral communication skills are not actually expected to be complete until the end of the *Unit*. However, students should be provided regular feedback along the way to guide their progress and help them self-correct.

♦ *Formative.* Some Assessments measure progress at intervals to help the teacher determine mastery thus far. These measures inform the teacher as to who needs what in terms of reteaching, remediation, or even enrichment. The current trendy term is *assessment for learning*.

♦ *Summative.* The final test does not occur until the end of the *Unit* when students are expected to know the material, and the class is ready to move on. This is considered the final or summative assessment, also known by its trendier term *assessment of learning*.

Located in the "6:00 to 9:00" portion of the *Unit Plan* clock face, the *Assessment* quadrant represents the region formed by the confluence of Abstract-Production. As such, *Assessments* require students to produce what they know but in the abstract or representational form. For example, on a Language Arts test, if a student can distinguish among story characters which one was the least likable, that is an abstract indicator that the student can distinguish likable from unlikable characters in general and identify which are which in a particular story. In Math, if a student can describe the effects of increasing some dimensions of a packing box on the number of Styrofoam peanuts it will take to fill it, this is a good abstract indication that he or she understands the concept of volume and its relationship to surface area. On a Science test, students who can explain and diagram how gasoline makes an engine run understand the concept of fuel combustion and energy. And in Social Studies, the student who can analyze a transcript of the Watergate hearings for evidence of cover-up has a good sense of the Nixon presidency and the abuse of power. In each case, the abstract *Assessment* is appropriate and adequate. It is not necessary for students to write a book to understand characterization, to physically measure and pack a box to demonstrate mastery of volume, to build a gasoline engine and point out its workings, nor to have been present at the Watergate hearings to realize its profound effect on the American presidency for all time. In *Assessments*, students are responding to prompts given by the teacher or text.

Structurally, the *Assessment* quadrant of the *Unit Plan* is convergent in that it has a rather narrow range of correct answers, enabling the teacher to quickly and objectively determine the student's level of understanding according to a predetermined answer key. Even the open-ended or constructed response items on a test, student journals, or observation checklists have a relatively narrow "window of correctness" or "limited stretch" to make the ratings less subjective.

In paper-pencil tests, the multiple-choice, true/false, matching, fill-in, and essay formats have remained largely unchanged over several decades, and they are as familiar to students as their own middle names. But prior to NCLB, teachers had virtual freedom to construct paper-pencil tests as they saw fit, to allow students as much or as little time to take them as the teacher deemed appropriate, and to alter or even drop specific items to meet the individual learning needs of their students. Classroom testing was more an afterthought than a conscious part of prior planning. But with NCLB, all that has changed, and for two very good reasons.

1. The High-Stakes Test. To prepare them for the rigorous state testing required of NCLB between Grades 3 and 8 (soon to be 12), students should be given paper-pencil test items that simulate the conditions for high-stakes testing. This includes four important stipulations. (a) At least portions of the tests should be timed to prevent students from being immobilized by "clock shock" when they encounter timed tests for the first time. (b) The tests should be identical (or standard) for all students who will not be exempt from other mitigating factors. Incidentally, the same teaching-learning accommodations that are made for students with Special Needs should also be made for classroom tests. (c) The objective items should be limited to multiple choice. While matching, true/false, and fill-in may be useful on worksheets, their limitations have excluded them from high-stakes tests. Thus, they should not be used on teacher-made tests. (d) In addition to the conventional multiple-choice items, these simulated high-stakes tests should also include some items that ask students to construct responses, both short answer and extended response. In some states, short answer includes the gridded response for math. Students must calculate an answer and grid the number onto their answer sheet. Exactly how to construct these tests will be discussed in more detail later in this chapter.

2.   A renewed interest in Valid Test Construction. Casting the NCLB spotlight over the classroom test has revealed that many are deeply flawed in terms of validity and reliability, both in content and structure. In content, many teacher-made and even published tests are incongruent with the intended outcomes of the Unit (i.e., standards or Performance Indicators), and many are asynchronous with the learning activities. In structure, many of these classroom tests fail to follow even the rudimentary principles of valid test development. For example, the multiple-choice stems are incomplete, the distractors are not parallel, and the student's errors do not reveal diagnostic information that is useful for remediation or advancement.

Some of the hottest commodities in the current school reform market are tests and test item banks. It appears that many districts are purchasing their tests, through either textbook publishers or companies whose sole function is to create and score tests. The *Assessment* component of the *Instructional Design* process includes the construction (or selection, if districts are purchasing tests or item banks) of valid, criterion-referenced test items that match the *Performance Indicators* being tested and are congruent with the learning activities of the *Unit*.

The Criteria for Assessment

The following row has been excerpted from Chapter 4 as Table 8.1 to synopsize the criteria for effective assessments and offer sample strategies. Explanations of each criterion will be provided, accompanied by illustrations from the **Africa** *Unit* from Chapter 5. For the reader's convenience, the Africa *Unit* has been reproduced in the next few pages.

They are traditional tests to determine mastery (paper-pencil or teacher observation).

The basic function of the *Assessments* in this quadrant is to determine student mastery on the abstract level. For the paper-pencil test, statisticians suggest providing students at least three, but ideally five, opportunities to demonstrate mastery. Some teachers translate this as "Oh, three multiple-choice items; that's easy!" But multiple choice may

Table 8.1   The Assessment Quadrant: Horizontal View

[criteria/definitions]			[samples]

Assessment (Abstract-Production)
■ traditional tests to determine mastery
 	
(paper-pencil or teacher observation); include
■ multiple-choice items (validly constructed; match the *Performance Indicators;* congruent with teaching-learning activities)
■ constructed response items
■ are *diagnostic* to identify needed intervention
■ are *selective* to infer mastery from a sampling
	Performance Indicators _____ _____ _____
	
	Culmination
	
	Assessment
		Motivation
		
		Information
			tests/quizzes that parallel high-stakes tests:
			■ multiple-choice items (with choices that are diagnostic upon analysis)
			■ short answer items that involve
			  ■ problem-finding, solving
			  ■ making inferences
			  ■ evaluating, making judgments
			  ■ explaining
			may also include observation checklists, journal entries, maps, data compilation, homework, etc.

not be the appropriate format to measure student mastery, and it may mean that students need three constructed responses (i.e., short answer or extended response). Or perhaps a combination of multiple choice and an extended response is best. The deciding factor for teachers must be what is congruent in structure and content with those *Performance Indicator(s)* it intends to assess. This applies as well to the other means of traditional assessments: the journal or log, the map, the observation checklist, or selected homework assignments. The difficulty with using intact publishers' tests or those that accompany the text is this congruence issue mentioned at the outset of this chapter. And nothing engenders the discouragement or kindles the anger of students (or adults) faster than to find items on a test that address material they never saw in class.

In the **Africa** *Unit*, the *Assessment* consists of several items. The *Unit* has been included as Table 8.2 and appears on the following pages.

1. students' journal entries, graded as per the directions provided at the outset of the *Unit*.

2. a map location test that expects students to locate countries, cities, landforms, bodies of water, longitude and latitude, and so on.

3. a paper-pencil test consisting of multiple-choice, extended response, and essay items, and including the students' own Levels I, II, and III questions.

4. a completed map of Africa (the one each student began during the pretest, including cities, landforms, highways, water, etc.)

Table 8.2   Best Practices Unit Plan

Unit Title: "Discovering Africa"	Course/Grade: Grade 6 Social Studies	Time frame: 4 weeks

Performance Indicators **or Learning Targets (shortened to make the sample easier to read)**

I A 9   Construct a multi-tiered time line to represent the development of a region politically, economically, culturally (class has begun a time line, beginning with *unit* 1, and they add to it as each unit progresses).

I F 2   Compare ancient civilizations (the Nile, Africa) re: government, religion, culture, language, etc.; construct a matrix.

II C 5   Analyze how world regions interact . . . diplomacy, treaties, alliances, military conflicts, trade . . . class structure, gender roles, beliefs/religion, traditions, language, agriculture, government, economic interests, etc. . . . present as a TV broadcast.

III A 12   Locate countries, cities, landforms, and bodies of water; use coordinates (latitude and longitude) to identify specific points.

III B 10   Interpret maps, charts, graphs to explain the distribution patterns of economic activity (e.g., mining, agriculture); use T-chart.

III C 7   List the positive and negative consequences of modifying the environment (e.g., dam-building, urbanization, education).

III D 2   Explain push-pull factors that cause people to migrate from one place to another, create a visual display, write an editorial.

IV A 8   Compare different regions in terms of geography, available resources, goods/services produced . . . interdependence, brochure.

V A 16   Create a graphic to show composition of a (country>state>city>town), explain sovereignty over country not geographically connected (i.e., mother country), border changes as a result of global events (e.g., war), interactions with neighbors.

VI A 6   Identify the characteristics . . . democracy, monarchy, dictatorship . . . re: citizens' rights (e.g., owning land); prepare a lesson.

(concrete)

Culmination (individual students)

1. Create an annotated map of Africa that displays various migration patterns from (a) outside-in (e.g., Europeans); (b) inside-out (e.g., the slave trade); and (c) from country to country within (e.g., famine, cultural ties, etc.); include physical changes (e.g., deforestation, border changes, desertification); specify the *who, what, when, where, why,* and *how* of key events

2. Write letters home (as if from the train) that describe major civic issues at each stop (e.g., voting rights, apartheid, etc.); explain how they impact life, and compare each stop to a similar region in the United States

3. Write a persuasive essay re: 4 environmental changes to modernize Africa (e.g., dam building, urbanization); follow established guidelines

4. Reflect on progress toward personal and content goals

Motivation

Have on wall (a) a giant outline map of Africa and (b) an empty matrix; these will be filled in with pertinent details as the unit progresses.

1. Students draw an outline map of Africa (kept in their notebooks); as a pretest, students fill in as much as they know (boarders of countries, cities, landforms, bodies of water); will add to

2. Brainstorm what students know about Africa re: geography, art, history, climate, politics, etc.; students pose 3 questions they have

3. Review the daily journal and note-taking formats; provide samples

4. Preview the Africa railroad trip; explain Culminating activities

5. Help students set personal and content goals; direct where to record the goals and how to self-monitor

Assessment

1. Journal entries, as per directions during *information*
2. Map location test: countries, cities, major landforms, bodies of water, longitude and latitude, etc.
3. Paper-pencil test (multiple choice, extended response, and essay; taken from students' own Levels I, II, and III questions)
4. Completed map of Africa (cities, landforms, water, etc.)
5. Compiled data charts (distances, precipitation, population, temperature, economic factors, etc.) ⇐ apply math skills

(T = Teacher; Ss = Students) Information

1. T tells Ss that Africa has two major regions: (a) Saharan and (b) Sub-Saharan; Ss predict likely attributes of each; in dyads, they verify or adjust their hunches with information from *directed* areas of the text; add information to the wall map.

2. T explains that the class will take a trip aboard the Cairo-to-Capetown railroad, stopping at Cairo, Nairobi, Livingstone, and Capetown; Ss will keep a travel journal, recording information they will need for the wall map, wall matrix, and their own maps and assignments. At each stop, the following will be addressed:
   a. notable landmarks
   b. significant historic and current events

(production) ... *(reception)*

(abstract)

Information, cont'd   Information, cont'd

(production)

    c. geographic and climactic information
    d. economic, political, cultural, social features

3. Students will chart distances between stops; record latitude and longitude; highest/ lowest points re: sea level; average temperature and precipitation; highs and lows of both; income and demographic rates; and apply math to notable features (e.g., the pyramids)

[Students will work in different dyads at each stop. When small group is used, this will be two dyads joined.]

4. Stop 1: Cairo, Egypt [Column 1 on wall chart]
    a. notable landmarks: the Nile, Pyramids, Sphinx, Cleopatra
    b. historic significance: the Nile Valley as birthplace of first humans (i.e., "Lucy," Dr. Leake)
    c. geographic and climactic features
    d. economic, political, cultural, social features

Ss take notes; work in small groups to develop Levels I, II, and III questions about the stop; each student adds detail to own map

T draws Ss together to decide what detail to add to the wall chart and the class map

5. Stop 2 : Nairobi, Kenya [Column 2 on wall chart]
    a. notable landmarks: the Serengeti, the Great Rift Valley
    b. historic significance: location of grand safaris (President Roosevelt, etc.); historic game preserve; US Embassy bombed in 1988 by Osama bin Laden
    c. geographic and climactic features
    d. economic, political, cultural, social features

Ss take notes; work in small groups to develop Levels I, II, and III questions about the stop; each student adds detail to own map

T draws Ss together to decide what detail to add to the wall chart and the class map

6. Stop 3: Livingstone, Zambia [Column 3 on wall chart]
    a. notable landmarks: Victoria Falls, museums, national park
    b. historic significance: site of first European explorer (David Livingstone)
    c. geographic and climactic features
    d. economic, political, cultural, social features

Ss take notes; work in small groups to develop Levels I, II, and III questions about the stop; each student adds detail to own map

T draws Ss together to decide what detail to add to the wall chart and the class map

7. Stop 4: Capetown, South Africa [Column 4 on wall chart]
    a. notable landmarks: diamond exports, Vasco DeGama; Cape of Good Hope; fine wines, exotic plant life
    b. historic significance
    c. geographic and climactic features
    d. economic, political, cultural, social features

Ss take notes; work in small groups to develop Levels I, II, and III questions about the stop; each student adds detail to own map

T draws Ss together to decide what detail to add to the wall chart and the class map

Side trips: T assigns small groups of students (different combinations than previously) each to take a "side trip."

Side trips to Morocco, the Congo, Liberia, Namibia, Madagascar, Mali, and Timbuktu. Groups locate the same information as was located for the group stops; each group enters info on wall map and wall chart [Columns 5-11]

8. T discusses push-pull factors that cause Africans to migrate; e.g., Europeans in, slaves out, migration across countries; Ss have guided discussion on how these impacted the continent; each small group prepares a summary of notes taken and discussion ideas
    a. In and Out of Africa:
       – slaves taken out
       – Europeans coming in
       – citizens leaving due to famine, wars, lack of jobs
    b. Within Africa:
       – famines, poverty, starvation
       – political unrest
       – natural disasters
       – economic shifts

9. Ss consider modernization efforts (e.g., mining for diamonds and gold; dam-building; energy-production and use; urban growth in major cities); in triads, Ss locate two articles describing the modernization efforts from different perspectives (e.g., positive, negative) re: impact on the country; triads share findings with class

10. T reviews with students how to develop a persuasive essay or speech (i.e., take a position, support it with evidence from viable sources, acknowledge alternate points of view); Ss practice reading sample persuasive essays to identify attributes, suggest improvements

11. Ss practice taking notes from sources and paraphrasing to prepare for Culminating activities, letters home; Ss cite sources accurately

12. T monitors student notebooks, journal entries (for letters home); questions developed; etc.; T meets with each student to discuss progress on unit goals—the Ss's individual goals as well as the unit goals

13. T lectures/explains the major economic factors of Africa:
    a. the "how" and "why" of trade and commerce *within* the 57 African countries (food, minerals, manufactured goods)
    b. the "how" and "why" of trade and commerce with other countries (i.e., exports: gold, diamonds, ivory, copper, etc.; imports: food, medicine, clothing, machinery, technology)
    c. interdependence
    d. lowest opportunity cost
    e. economic decisions involving trade-offs

14. T and Ss continually add to course time line, wall map of africa, and wall chart comparing regions and countries

Web sites:
http://www.EnchantedLearning.com/school/Africa/Africamaps.html

http://www.ahsd.25.k12.il.us/curriculum% 20info/africa/abutaf.html

(reception)

5. compiled data (charts and tables representing the data collected during the research activities, i.e., distances, elevations, precipitation, temperature, population, economic factors, or political developments)

A quick glance at the *Performance Indicators* and the teaching-learning activities in the **Africa** *Unit* will verify their alignment and the full congruence between them and the *Assessments* listed above. This is classic triangulation and the core logic that drives effective classroom instruction.

Multiple-choice items are validly constructed, match the *Performance Indicators*, and are congruent with the teaching-learning activities.

The test construction criteria used in the ***Instructional Design*** process are adapted from a program developed in the 1980s by testing specialists Dr. Barbara Chambers and Dr. Margaret Fleming, then working in the Cleveland Public Schools. Their program was validated and disseminated to school systems nationwide through ESEA's National Diffusion Network and later by McGraw-Hill. (Research citations are available from the authors upon request.) Their criteria for valid multiple-choice tests dovetail perfectly with more recent research on the construction of classroom tests and are as follows:

The Stem

- Should be **a complete thought** or sentence that gives direction as to where the item is headed. Students should not be forced to use the distractors to decide what the item is asking of them. A simple check is to cover the distractors, and the item should suddenly become a "short answer" prompt, stating clearly what sort of answer will be correct. In the sample provided (Table 8.3), the stem in the "Wrong" column

Table 8.3

Wrong	*Right*

Seahorses are
 	
   a. unusual in that they swim upright
   b. small fish with a head like a horse
   c. forced to eat frequently because of their very small stomachs
   d. the only animal where the male carries the fetus
	The feature about a seahorse that most notably distinguishes it from other animals is that the
	
	   a. backbone is actually made of muscle
	   b. female carries the eggs
	   c. male carries and delivers the unborn fetus
	   d. stomach is very small, requiring it to eat constantly

The stem gives no direction. It is impossible for the student to know where the question is headed.	

is incomplete and ambiguous. By contrast, the stem in the "Right" column more clearly articulates the purpose of the item: What feature of a seahorse most distinguishes it from every other animal?

- Should **reflect the core** concept of the *Performance Indicator(s)*, not the peripheral sidelights. For example, suppose the *Performance Indicator* asks students to "distinguish among the various persuasive techniques (or propaganda) used in advertising or political speeches to influence the opinions of the general population." The core concept of the *Indicator* is to recognize various methods used to persuade people to believe a certain way, leading them to vote or make purchases reflecting that belief. A more peripheral idea is the belief itself. The following passage below is typical of what students will see on high-stakes tests. It is an excerpt from a recent speech to the city council. "This country was founded on the principle of personal freedom. For you to tell us we cannot use cell phones while driving unless they are hands-free is a violation of our civil rights. We may as well live in a dictatorship." A sample multiple-choice question is provided in Table 8.4, showing both the wrong and the right way to construct multiple-choice distractors.

Table 8.4

Wrong	*Right*

The speaker wants the city council to
  a. resign
  b. back off passing laws dealing with cell phones
  c. give up requiring hands-free cell phone use in the car
  d. pass rules for hands-free use of cell phones
  e. outlaw the use of cell phones in the car
	The persuasive technique used by the speaker to influence the city council is best known as
	  a. name-calling
	  b. appeal to patriotism
	  c. bandwagon
	  d. stacking the deck
	  e. tradition

The Distractors

The design of the distractors is just as important as the stem. They should be as diagnostic as possible, indicating where students are confused or need further instruction (see Table 8.5). In our experience, very little thought is given to the choices, except to make sure the correct one is included. A sample multiple-choice question is provided in Table 8.4, showing both the wrong and the right way to construct multiple choice distractors.

- Should be **parallel** in structure.
- Should be listed in **ascending** or descending order (numeric or alphabetical); see the distractors in the "Right" column in Table 8.5.

This eliminates the teacher worrying about "which letter have I used the most?" and prevents students from wasting test time scanning for a pattern.

Table 8.5

Wrong	*Right*

Which of the following is an example of figurative language?
 	
  a. trees being described as having arms
 	
  b. don't cross that bridge until you come to it
 	
  c. a simile
 	
  d. the Kremlin reports an outbreak of . . .
	Which of the following is an example of figurative language?
	
	  a. breathing so hard, everyone could hear
	
	  b. getting caught up with housework
	
	  c. killing your enemy with kindness
	
	  d. trotting along the highway

- Should include **only one correct answer**; the distractors in the "Wrong" column in Table 8.5 include more than one correct answer.
- Should be **diagnostic** in that the wrong answers provide teachers with insight into what students may not understand. In Table 8.5, choices *a*, *b*, and *d* are literal, and choice *a* is a powerful sensory image but is not figurative. Choice *c* is merely a colloquial term, and *d* is the label given to that sort of movement.

These tests also contain Short-Answer and Extended Response items.

To counter critics' objection to using only multiple-choice items on high-stakes tests, developers of the high-stakes as well as published tests have begun to include constructed responses. In some states, there are both 2-point and 4-point items. From the research on testing (research citations are available from the authors upon request), we have attempted to extrapolate the criteria for valid prompts that ask students to construct a short or an extended answer.

Short Answer

These prompts are intended to elicit quick but substantive responses that demonstrate mastery of part or all of a *Performance Indicator*. Because the focus is on the substance of the answer rather than the structure, many short answer scoring rubrics don't require complete sentences, and in some cases, bullets are encouraged. These prompts are best understood by content examples, as shown in Table 8.6.

Table 8.6   Sample Short-Answer Prompts

Subject	2-Point Prompts	Performance Indicator (Abbreviated)
Math	Determine whether an estimate is reasonable; explain how you decided.	determine if an estimate is reasonable
Language Arts	Identify two examples of symbolism in the story.	symbolism to convey a message
Science	Which variable is experimental and which is the control?	distinguish experimental from control factors
Social Studies	Create a time line for the events described in this paragraph.	place events—in chronological sequence

Extended Response

As indicated by their name, these prompts require a more extensive and structured response. In contrast to the "short answer" items, they ask for the development of a complete thought or thesis idea relative to one or more of the *Performance Indicator(s)*. Complete sentences and correct grammar are expected, although in many state rubrics, they do not represent break points. The criteria for effective "extended response" items and the acceptable student answers are listed below.

Table 8.7   Sample Extended-Answer Prompts

Subject	4-Point Prompts	Performance Indicator (Abbreviated)
Math	Draw a shape on coordinate plane; make two transformations; describe how to go from the first position to the third without doing the second.	multiple transformations in a coordinate plane
Language Arts	[Quotation from selection] Explain how the author supports this sentiment in the rest of the selection. Support your answer with detail from the text.	author's message as captured in literal and inferential detail
Science	Compare and contrast plant and animal cells in terms of their structures; account for the difference in terms of the functions that they perform.	compare plant and animal cells in terms of their structures and the function of each
Social Studies	Analyze this section of map; what might it suggest about the entire region and the regions that surround it?	the interrelationship of climatic conditions, geographic features, and political boundaries

Prompts

- Should request a brief (one paragraph) but extended response; it is not, however, to be a full-length, multiparagraph essay, unless so indicated.
- Should specify the *organizational structure* and requirements of the response.

Responses

- Should use details from the passage or story to support the idea(s).
- Should identify specific details and, when more than one answer could be correct, include *might* or *may*.
- Should include the *why* of the student's thinking.

General Formats for Extended Response or Essay Items

Describe specific qualities, attributes

"Describe _____ [an object, process, event, image, reaction, etc.], including ___, ___, and ____." For example ,

- ◆ "Describe the three bears' cottage as Goldilocks found it, including the chairs, beds, and food."
- ◆ "Describe the opening ceremonies of the modern Olympic games, including the use of pageantry, international unity, and tradition."
- ◆ "Describe this Magnetic Resonance Image (MRI) of in vitro fertilization, including specific cell structures, the processes occurring, and how the probable gender of the zygote may be apparent."

Explain typically involves cause-effect

"Explain why [or how] _____ [an object, process, event, image, reaction, etc.] occurs [or what it is], including _____, _____, and _____ [☞ specific reasons, causes, steps, circumstances]." For example,

- ◆ "Explain why Little Red Riding Hood did not run away on seeing that her grandmother looked a bit unusual, including what fooled the girl and why she acted so bravely."
- ◆ "Explain the problem-solving strategy you used to discover which container had the most marbles, including how you made your estimate, how you checked your answer, and how the government could use the same strategy with our money."
- ◆ "Explain the contradiction of the Declaration of Independence, addressing how 'all men are created equal,' and yet many of the signers were slaveholders."

Compare-Contrast parallel similarities and differences

"Compare _____ [one person, place, event, behavior, object, idea, concept, etc.] with _____ [another . . .] in terms of _____, _____, and _____."

♦ **What:** qualities, attributes, characteristics
♦ **Who:** number, type of persons involved
♦ **Why:** causes, reasons, lead-up/surrounding circumstances
♦ **So What:** outcomes, results, applications, implications; for example,

◊ *"Compare the three houses constructed by the three little pigs in terms of their structures, the time required to build, and the end-results. How are they alike and different?"*

◊ *"Compare the triangle with the pyramid, the square with the cube, and the circle with the sphere; include likenesses and differences, and where each figure appears in the environment."*

◊ *"Compare and contrast three world religions—Islam, Judaism, and Christianity—in terms of how each was established; belief in a single, central figure; the role of women; and ancient versus modern practice."*

◊ *"Compare William Shakespeare's* Romeo and Juliet *with Leonard Bernstein's* West Side Story *in terms of character development, the role of family loyalty, the customs of society at the time, and the effect of the tragedies on those who remained."*

Procedure correct sequence of steps; involves technical understanding

"What procedure would be best to _____ [complete a process, solve a problem, create or construct an object, etc.]; optional: include _____, _____, and _____, [steps]." For example,

♦ "How would you make French toast? Start by walking into the kitchen and end with cleaning up. Include the ingredients and equipment needed and how you would go about the entire task."
♦ "Place the following numbers into a meaningful sequence to create a pattern, and explain how you decided: 20, 6, 22, 30, 2, 10, 26, 12."
♦ "How would you go about writing your autobiography? Include the steps you would take to preplan, draft, revise, and prepare the finished product."
♦ "What seemed to go wrong with this procedure (shown a picture or explanation of a failed procedure)? Explain the possible errors or missteps, and suggest a preferable alternative procedure."

Persuade

- logical (rather than emotional) reasoning
- acknowledgment of the opposition
- viable support from valid sources

"Prepare a position or argument about ___ [an issue or controversy], including clear and logical reasons why you feel as you do.

Acknowledge the opposing point(s) of view and address the objections involved." For example,

♦ "How do you think we should decide which field trip to take? We have discussed the zoo, the museum, and the archeology digs."
♦ "Should we require uniforms in this school? Why or why not?"
♦ "Should students be allowed to use calculators and keyboards in taking major exams? Why or why not?"
♦ "Was there an alternative to the bombing of Hiroshima to end World War II? Had you been advising the nation's leaders at the time, what would you have suggested?"

Critically Analyze

■ viable judgments based on valid criteria

"What is your opinion of _____ [a person, place, object, event, idea, concept, movement, etc.]? Include the criteria you used to make your judgment." For example,

♦ [May be an oral essay; criteria in *italics*] "What did you think of the speaker's presentation about being safe? How *clear* was his *explanation* of 'stranger-danger'? How *helpful* were his *examples*? Was there anything that you *did not like*? *Restate* his three rules to follow."
♦ "What is your opinion of the character's decision to resign? Include his motive, whether you found it plausible, how it will affect the rest of the story, and whether (and why) you feel the author should have done things differently."
♦ "What is your opinion of taxidermy? Indicate what you feel is the rationale for the practice (e.g., its contributions to science and history), and what are the major objections to it? Suggest how best to resolve the growing debate about whether to outlaw it."

Samples From the Africa Unit Plan

In the sample *Unit Plan* on **Africa**, the final or summative paper-pencil test includes both short answer and extended response items. It is understood that they will be developed according to criteria described earlier and be congruent with the *Performance Indicators* around which the *Unit* is constructed. Although this test is the final test, the same test-construction principles apply to interim or formative assessments. The amount of the content assessed is smaller, corresponding to the segment of the *Unit* being assessed. The extended response prompts for the summative test on the **Africa** *Unit* might be as follows:

Short Answer

■ What recent connection does Nairobi have with the United States?
■ What is significant about Livingstone to the British empire?
■ What are three modernization efforts in Africa presented by classmates?

Extended Response

- Describe the most notable landmarks on our stop in Cairo in terms of historic significance.
- Explain the push-pull factors that caused the migration patterns, including both in and out of Africa and within Africa.
- Compare and contrast two side trips presented by your classmates, including the name, location, physical features, notable facts, and importance to Africa.
- Critically analyze the internal economic situation in Africa among the 57 countries in terms of natural resources, manufacture, trade, and commerce, and propose a viable solution.

The Assessments are diagnostic to identify needed intervention.

The paper-pencil tests described above typically occur at the conclusion of the *Unit* and thus are considered summative measures of mastery. But since they identify not only what HAS been mastered but what has NOT YET been mastered, they also serve a diagnostic function to indicate where reteaching or intervention may be needed. In addition to the end of *Unit* tests, teachers are encouraged to give formative or interim tests along the way to monitor student progress and to identify areas that need retaught. If properly constructed, both formative and summative measures will provide the teacher, and student, with diagnostic feedback.

Notice in the **Africa** *Unit Plan*, the other assessments (in addition to the paper-pencil *Unit* test) also include this diagnostic feature. For the journal entries, the teacher will monitor these throughout the *Unit* and provide correcting feedback as needed. The map location test as well as the completed, notebook-sized map of Africa will yield a fairly transparent indication as to which students need to revisit the geographic detail addressed at each stop along the railway journey. The compiled data charts of distances, temperature, precipitation, population, economic factors, and so on will indicate a fairly complete sense of how well students can organize, display, and interpret data, and any mistakes will be easily spotted for correction.

The Assessments are selective to infer mastery.

Naturally, the *Assessments* cannot include 100% of the material addressed in the *Unit*. Such a test would be overwhelming in length and take half as much time to take as the *Unit* took to teach. And if such an inclusive test were given at the end of every *Unit*, the amount of class time available to actually teach would be eclipsed by the time devoted to testing. And that's before adding the time already taken out for high-stakes testing. Commercial test writers know that they must prioritize their test items to limit the length and intensity of a test to that which is reasonable, making the tests more representative than inclusive. For classroom tests, the teacher should construct or select key items that will represent mastery of the entire array of concepts, skills, and knowledge addressed in the *Unit*. For example,

- In Math, if students can select from among the line graph, bar graph, circle graph, or pictograph the most appropriate way to display a set of data, the teacher can reasonably infer that these same students also know *how* and *when* to construct the other three graphs as well.

■ In Language Arts, if a student can deconstruct one group of root words with affixes to locate Greek and Latin origins, it is reasonable to assume they can deconstruct others.

■ In Social Studies, if students can relate economic decline to population trends in one geographic region, it is likely they can do so for other regions.

■ In Science, students who can distinguish physical from chemical changes on one list can probably do so with other lists.

The idea is that if the *Assessment* is validly constructed, the scores on one test—or observation checklist or journal entry, and so on—will predict or imply a similar level of success with other parallel items on subsequent measures. A measure of every single skill or item of knowledge is unnecessary, even if it were possible.

Meta-Analysis

As they develop formative and summative assessments for each *Unit Plan*—including paper-pencil tests, journals, and so on—developers are encouraged to plan time for students and the teacher to thoughtfully review the results as a *meta-analysis*. This will give students an opportunity to review their graded materials to see both their mistakes and their successes and to reflect on any patterns that may help them on subsequent tests, journal entries, and other *Assessment* activities. This important step in a student's academic progress requires that teachers provide substantive and timely feedback on students' work to reinforce what they are doing well and to give them direction for improvement and growth. The meta-analysis activity also links directly with the students' review of their own personal and academic goals, both along the way and at the end of the *Unit*.

But the meta-analysis is equally instructive for teachers, particularly teams who work as professional focus groups or even the Critical Friends network. From the earliest days of developing initial *Unit Plans*, teachers are encouraged to examine their paper-pencil tests against the criteria for valid test construction. After they have considered the proper way to construct valid tests that truly and fairly measure the *Performance Indicators*, developers and their colleagues are far more confident about making sure their *Assessments* are also congruent with the Delivery Strategies and Learning Constructs used. And with the pilot of the *Units* and the collection of "green ink," the overall quality of each *Unit*—both the delivery strategies and the *Assessments*—will be considerably richer and stronger.

Begin at the Primary Level

In our experience, many primary teachers consider the discussions about paper-pencil tests irrelevant to them. But we disagree and try to help them see how important it is to begin the process early. Even very young children can learn to select items or pictures from among options and to explain why they did not choose the others. Moreover, primary students should learn to respond to questions by drawing pictures and diagrams and to orally explain their thinking. As soon as possible, they must learn to represent their thoughts in writing, even if it's nonsense or scribble early on. It makes the association for them that what they write is an important way to express themselves. They should also learn to operate within basic time limits, to check their work, and to examine their work after the fact to consider what they might do differently next time. These are all lead-up skills to prepare them not only for paper-pencil classroom tests but for the high-stakes assessments that will so heavily affect them.

CULMINATION   ■

The final quadrant of the *Unit Plan*, *Culmination*, also deals with assessment. Located in the Concrete-Production portion of the clock face, these measures are defined as *authentic* or *performance* assessments. Not so long ago, learning outcomes that couldn't be placed on a traditional paper-pencil test weren't considered a worthy measure of academic success. There was a thinly veiled bias against "performance assessments," acceptable, perhaps, for the *vocational* or *performing* areas but certainly intolerable for academia. Thankfully, educators have outgrown that foolishness, and the authentic or performance assessment has achieved the respect it deserves in determining academic mastery. Although we know there are subtle distinctions between the "authentic" and "performance" assessment, for convenience, we will use the terms interchangeably.

Authentic or performance assessments ask students to complete holistic, real-life tasks such as writing an original short story or poem, constructing a working model, negotiating a treaty, devising story problems, creating a business plan to produce widgets, conducting an original experiment, collecting data and placing them into interpretive tables, or performing a dance or dramatization. While these products are creative and expected to be fairly divergent, they are not without form or structure. They are circumscribed by a set of guidelines based on the *Performance Indicators* they are intended to measure. These holistic, divergent assessments contrast with the more discrete and convergent tasks contained in the traditional paper-pencil measures of the *Assessment* quadrant, which are abstract demonstrations of mastery.

As has been suggested throughout this book, the most valid approaches to determining student mastery include an appropriate balance of paper-pencil tests and authentic assessments. And although there is some overlap between the two types of measurement, a few important distinctions exist. These are shown in Table 8.8.

If students are to own the content or skills embedded in the standards (or *Indicators*), they can call them to mind and apply them without prompting by a teacher or a text. Only this level of mastery makes students fully equipped for success in the adult world. While most students are accustomed to the traditional tests, journals, checklists, and other abstract measures that are at home in the *Assessment* quadrant, the idea of independently completing holistic tasks and constructing products as a summative *Assessment* of mastery may be relatively unfamiliar, even in progressive districts. But the strategic inclusion of Best Practices in their *Motivation* and *Information* activities prepares teachers and students for the successful accomplishment of the *Culminating* activities.

Two Difficulties

From the outset, there are two difficulties for some teachers to over-come: (a) the use of groups working on *Culminating* activities, since that's what's always been done, and (b) the feeling that such capstone or end-of-*Unit* tasks should be more about enjoyment and celebration than academics. Both issues are important considerations in the development of every *Unit Plan* and can make the difference between success and failure.

Table 8.8   Comparison of Assessments With Culminating Activities

Assessments are . . .	*Culminating activities are . . .*
(1) selective and representative, measuring key items addressed in the *Unit* which *imply* a wider mastery; students respond to these items in ways that mimic or closely parallel classroom practice	(1) holistic projects or tasks providing *direct* measures of mastery; students apply skills and concepts learned during the *Unit* to solve problems, complete projects, create original products beyond those done in the classroom
(2) both *formative* and *summative;* the formative measures check for understanding during the *Unit*; the summative measures (aka the Unit Test) determine mastery at the end of the *Unit*	(2) more *summative* than formative; they are intended to show independent mastery of the *Performance Indicators* and the ability to apply what was learned in a different context
(3) teacher-developed prompts with exact (or limited range of acceptable) answer(s) that correspond to a scoring key; extended responses may be creative but are still fairly convergent, and the "product" is typically paper-pencil (although observation works well, too!)	(3) student-constructed products with a wide range of options to complete and more than one right "answer"—albeit within guidelines; evaluated with a rubric that reflects the *Performance Indicators* being assessed and typically result in a concrete display or product
(4) designed to approximate high-stakes testing (e.g., Iowa, SAT, tests used for NCLB) by including multiple-choice and extended response items and by being timed	(4) designed to approximate real-life situations (i.e., entire problems to solve, products to develop, processes to complete, etc.), including more flexible time frames

The "Group" Thing

When first introduced to the idea of *Culminating* activities, some teachers have a tendency to see them as not much different from what they've always done with groups. And although many *Culminating* activities we've seen are accomplished in groups, for a single student to be given credit for independent mastery of the *Performance Indicator(s)* involved, he or she must develop the final product—or whatever the requirement of "mastery"—independently.

For example, the *Culminating* activity might involve a team of students creating an original dramatic production, but each student must be able to demonstrate those portions of the production corresponding to the *Performance Indicator(s)* involved, for example, the development of the plot line, the characterization, and the technical aspects of the production. Or if the class prepares and delivers a debate, at least two teams will be involved (pro and con). But if each student is to be given credit for mastering indicators relative to preparing a position or rebuttal, he or she must demonstrate those skills independent of the other students. It may be that each student researches one aspect of an argument or counterargument, organizes it, and prepares that part of the delivery outline. Or each student may be asked to summarize and/or critically analyze the opposition's entire argument.

What makes a group activity a *Culminating Assessment* is that each student shows his or her independent mastery of the skills, concepts, or knowledge involved. Otherwise, these group tasks are perfectly viable activities, but not measures of mastery. The cautionary note here is to avoid spending too much class time on the group activity at the expense of new learning or the measure of mastery. Taking too long on even the most exciting and motivating *Culmination* will come at the price of some students disconnecting and others deliberately stringing things out. In studies we have conducted involving parents/guardians and class projects, an overwhelming majority of parents say (and this is paraphrased), "Yes, we understand the need for these big projects such as the ___ [big project] ___, but frankly, after seven weeks we were all sick of it, and our child had to sit through six other student presentations of the same thing."

The Nonacademic, "Celebration" Thing

To tie off a *Unit*, many participants think it appropriate and just to reward students with a fun or frivolous activity. In our years of experience, we have encountered an amazing array of such nonacademic ideas; they include the following: (a) making a coat of arms, (b) creating an imaginary animal, (c) performing in a talent show, (d) designing a new planet, (e) holding a festival of some sort (with no academic anchors), (f) having a guest speaker (with no connection to *Performance Indicators*), and (g) going on a field trip (without any academic accountability).

To be clear, we're not killjoys who begrudge students having an enjoyable or celebratory experience. But since there is so little instructional time in the first place, we worry when considerable class time is spent on activities for which there is little or no academic payoff. Our suggestion is to include these celebratory and nonacademic activities at a time beyond the school day. Or if they must be done on class time, they should be limited to one class period (or a full day, max) and be in addition to more substantive tasks that actually measure student mastery. And the truth is, we've seen teachers do so many exciting and engaging *Culminating* activities that are academically focused, many of which are included in the pages that follow, that we are confident participants need not select either frivolous or boring tasks for this quadrant.

The Criteria for *Culminating* Activities

The Culmination row has been excerpted from Chapter 4 (Table 8.9) as a synthesis of the criteria for effective *Culminating* activities as well as a few sample strategies. Following the row is an explanation of each criteria, with detail from the **Africa** *Unit* to illustrate.

Table 8.9 The Culmination Quadrant: Horizontal View

Culmination (Concrete—Production)	Performance Indicators		writing an original piece of literature or a composition

Culmination (Concrete—Production) are holistic, life-related tasks extending beyond the classroom draw together the *Unit* learning experiences allow students options for completing these tasks help students measure their own goals scored with a rubric based on the *Performance Indicators*	*Performance Indicators* _____ _____ _____		writing an original piece of literature or a composition devising a treaty or a contract between two parties collecting, displaying, and analyzing data designing and conducting an original experiment analyzing error patterns in a series of "solved" problems developing original problems to solve preparing a script for a TV talk show or newscast formulating arguments; etc.
	Culmination	Motivation	
	Assessment	Information	

The Criteria for Effective *Culminations*

Are holistic, life-related tasks extending beyond the classroom.

In contrast to the abstract or indirect measures in the *Assessment* quadrant, the *Culminations* are the concrete or direct measures. One teacher put it aptly by saying, "So in Assessment, students describe how the mousetrap might be built and how it could function, or malfunction. But in Culmination, they build the mousetrap, right?" The idea is that even though the authentic or performance task is the *Culmination* of the *Unit* in reference, the tasks are transferable and generalizable to other *Units* and to life.

In the **Africa** *Unit*, students have three Culminating activities:

1. They create their own annotated map of Africa that contains the major landforms, cities, bodies of water, and landmarks—recorded during the various stops along the railway—but also features the various migration patterns (outside-in, inside-out, and within). The annotations (presented as little boxes or flags) specify the *who*, *what*, *when*, *where*, *why*, and *how* of key events in each pattern.

   Note: This is one of those "progressive" measures alluded to earlier that begins at the outset of the *Unit* and continues through the end, symbolic of the railway journey itself, since its features are completed in greater detail with each stop. What is especially significant about the annotated map is that (like the large wall map that is fleshed-in by the class as the *Unit* goes along) it remains a constant in the student's mind as well as a prominent image in his and her notebook. This technique is particularly effective in helping students create a lasting memory of a continent that may be relatively unfamiliar and obscure to them. Within reason (mindful of time-and-energy efficiency), students add their own personal touch to the maps, giving them creative and artistic interpretations.

2. They write letters home (as if from the train) that describe major civic issues at each stop, for example, voting rights, apartheid, education, and so on; explain how these issues affect the lives of the citizens; and compare each stop to a similar region in the United States.

   Note: This, too, is a progressive assessment, being completed in increments throughout the *Unit.* As with the map of Africa, each student's progress can be monitored as the journey proceeds. Not only does this measure the students' comprehension and perceptual insights into the social studies content (i.e., their knowledge of culture as a sense of people, events, and place, both in Africa and in the parallel stop in the United States), it also strengthens their journaling and letter-writing skills. Here again, the students are encouraged to be creative (but not at the expense of accuracy), and the importance of the individual voice of each cannot be overstated.

3. They write a persuasive essay addressing four environmental changes to modernize Africa (e.g., dam-building, urbanization, health education) and appeal to the African authorities to handle these changes responsibly in ways that will be helpful to the citizens without harming the beauty of the country or upsetting peoples' lives. Follow the guidelines for persuasive writing (i.e., take a position, provide a rationale, include supporting evidence, etc.).

   Note: Unlike the previous two activities (which are progressive and completed cumulatively as the *Unit* proceeds), this one is an on-demand piece. That is, it is not prepared ahead of time but written during class. Some teachers may permit students to use their notes to complete the essay. Others may prefer that the work be done from memory, particularly since the teacher will have previewed the activity during the *Motivation* section of the *Unit*, and students will be reminded to prepare for it throughout the *Unit* as they take notes.

Naturally, one of the concerns that arises is "If students are permitted to do any of this outside of class, they'll either do each other's work, or they'll get help from family members." So the perceptive teacher sets things up so that the important work is done in class, or at least the work that will count toward mastery is done in class. Another concern is "Won't that take a huge amount of class time?" And our answer is to refer to the **Africa** *Unit*; most of the work is done as the students go along as part of class work.

   Note: This doesn't contradict our earlier advice not to allow students to complete all of their Learning Circle or Action Research work during class. Those were Information quadrant activities; these are assessments of mastery.

   Part of the process of selecting *Culminating* activities is to be careful not to choose those where students don't do their own work or ones that take more time to complete than the returns would justify. With all due respect to the profession we dearly love, there is simply no training regimen for the two major muscles in the teacher's anatomy: (a) knowing their own students very well and (b) common sense.

Draw together the *Unit* learning experiences.

One of the major functions of the *Culminating* activity is to physically and psychologically (as well as pedagogically) draw the *Unit Plan* together. As strange as that may sound, we feel that after three or four weeks of activity on a theme or topic, students need to feel a sense of closure, that they have completed something and reached a milestone of some sort. After all, during *Motivation*, the teacher previewed these *Culminating* activities, and from Day 1, each *Unit* activity was designed to move students to this point. Granted, not every single *Unit* activity or even every *Performance Indicator* will reappear in a *Culminating* task, but their effects will be apparent. Put another way, the student will be unable to complete the *Culminating* tasks without at least a basic mastery of all the *Performance Indicators*.

In the **Africa** *Unit*, the map brings together all the geographic, cultural, economic, and political considerations discussed throughout the *Unit*, including key people, movements, changes, and the all-important motives and results. The letters home verify each student's recognition, understanding, and appreciation of his and her stops along the way and, more important, ensure deep-level comprehension through accurate comparisons with similar places in the United States. The persuasive essay gives every student a forum to sound off about the effect of modernization in an informed, thoughtful way. The compelling need to help people who lack adequate food and shelter, medical care, and gainful employment must be balanced with respect for the environment, local control, and the endemic suspicion of things modern. Each student's reflection on his and her academic and personal goals is an authentic opportunity to give voice to accomplishments, frustrations, and continued needs.

In addition to each student's independent mastery, these activities also reveal the various collaborative networks established among students. They further provide an opportunity for classmates to exchange their questions and ideas about Africa and to learn from each other as they go along.

Allow students options for completing these tasks.

One basic tenet of constructivism is that students be provided options for completing their tasks and/or be permitted to choose from among various alternatives the one that best reflects their own particular interpretation. We encourage teachers to include options for students throughout the *Unit Plan*, but this is especially important in the *Culmination* quadrant. Since the intent is that each student be accountable for his and her own learning, part of that responsibility should lie in deciding how best to organize, complete, and present the process or product. This latitude becomes especially important during the debrief, when students reflect on the project and decide what choices turned out to be more or less effective.

When students themselves design and complete the task, the reflection takes on a more personal, inside-out tone than the more detached, outside-in tone when the task was designed by someone else. It's like a vacation, for example, when the traveler designs the itinerary, and everything occurs as he or she planned. Because the traveler is more personally invested in the arrangements, he or she tends to work harder at making the best of each event and making the trip a success. In contrast, when the traveler is forced to follow an itinerary planned by someone else, every inconvenience and mishap becomes an excuse not to enjoy the trip. The whining actually takes precedence over the sites to be seen and events to enjoy.

In the classroom parallel, students who respond to the teacher's design rather than their own can fall back on the excuse, "I didn't understand what I was to do" and waste their academic energies criticizing the prompt rather than attempting to address it. Unchecked, this pattern of behavior persists into adulthood and leads to predictable failures in relationships as well as academic success.

In the **Africa** *Unit*, students have all sorts of options for presentation of their products, providing the information they include is accurate and complete. They can personalize their maps of Africa and can use their creativity to decide how to display the annotations. Their letters home can be creative in terms of style and voice, they select the key issues about which to write, and they select the parallel spot in the United States to compare with each African stop. Their persuasive essays require them to observe the conventions of the persuasive essay but allow them considerable flexibility in deciding which environmental changes for modernization to include.

Help students measure their own goals.

In the discussion of *Motivation* in Chapter 5, considerable space was devoted to the Best Practice of student goal setting. This is at least one part of the *Unit* over which each student has full control. Some teachers even allow students to give themselves a letter grade or rubric score for making progress toward their goals. Student goal setting is one extremely direct way for students to see the cause-effect relationship between how they behave, or choices they make, and their academic and personal success. Each student decides how he or she will work at the goals, how to measure them, and then whether and how much progress has been made on each goal by the end of the *Unit*. Teachers should help students establish one or two Content Goals and at least one Personal Goal using the preassessment data as well as other information pertinent to that student.

Two important requirements of student goal setting should be clarified. First, students should monitor their own progress on each goal throughout the *Unit* and that teachers periodically review this information to provide students with encouraging and substantive feedback. Second, teachers should include time during the *Culmination* of the *Unit* to review with each student the status of his and her goals as the *Unit* winds down. This telegraphs to students that the teacher holds the goals in high regard and sees them as worthy of class time.

It must be remembered that the important point of goal-setting is not so much that each goal is accomplished as that progress has been made—the needle has moved—and that the student realizes how that came about. If, as a student, I can associate "the things I do" with some measure of academic and personal success, I can feel empowered and confident of ultimate success. Could a *Unit* end any better?

In the **Africa** *Unit*, time is set aside during the *Motivation* activities for students to set goals and during the *Culmination* to reflect on what levels of progress were made toward their accomplishment. If teachers expect students to take their goals seriously, time and opportunity must be provided to revisit the goals and reflect on the progress made. Even more important, the teacher must give dignity to the goals and work them into the evaluation of the *Culminating* activities.

Are scored with a rubric based on the *Performance Indicators.*

In the 1980s gallery of the school reform hall of fame, next to the displays of "constructivist learning" and "performance assessment" is the bust of "Rubric." Two decades ago, the use of rubrics took the assessment world by storm as the antidote to measuring all things academic with the traditional paper-pencil test. It was somehow ordained that anyone who was anyone in education should henceforth establish a checklist of criteria (or rubric) for learning products. As is often the case with trendy ideas, the rubric had really existed in education for quite some time. Indeed, vocational education had been using rubrics for years to evaluate everything from the lowly tool box made in shop class or the apron sewn in home economics through the replica of a Duncan Phyffe china cupboard or a rack of authentic period costumes sewn for the school production of *Phantom of the Opera.*

We confess that in earlier years, we attempted to provide extensive training to teachers in how to develop effective rubrics. We brought dozens of samples to the workshop and thought teachers would surely find one that suited them for each *Culminating* activity, adapt it, and attach it to the *Unit Plan.* But that approach was tantamount to offering drinks of water at a fire hydrant. Teachers were simply overwhelmed; there were too many choices and not enough guidance on how to select. Having learned our lesson, we now approach the issue of rubrics far more strategically . . . and successfully. First, we encourage schools (if not districts) to adopt a consistent set of baseline rubrics for writing, speaking, and listening, all of which proceed developmentally across the grades. But for other tasks and projects unique to the *Unit Plan,* we suggest that teachers design rubrics that correspond to the *Performance Indicators* involved.

Many teachers have been using rubrics for years and with considerable success and can quickly adapt the process to the tasks included in each *Unit Plan.* Other teachers really struggle. When we compare the *Unit Plans* where the rubrics seem to be working with those where they are not, four major questions arise:

1. Have the appropriate criteria been identified for the product? That is, do the criteria reflect the *Performance Indicators* on which the *Unit* is based?

2. Has the appropriate type of rubric been selected, holistic or analytical? Is a single score adequate, or should multiple scores be provided? Teachers who are making rubrics work for them are using rubrics that fit their *Unit Plans,* not ones they found in a book of rubrics or rubrics.com and have attempted to retrofit.

3. Is there a district (or schoolwide) baseline rubric for common core tasks such as written products, speaking, or listening? If so, is it consistent and developmentally cumulative across grade levels? And do teachers then add specific criteria appropriate to a particular project, such as a critique or autobiography?

4. If there is not a consistent district (or schoolwide) baseline rubric for the core areas of writing, speaking, or listening, what is the net effect of each teacher devising his or her own, irrespective of other subjects or adjacent grade levels?

So, rather than assume the rubrics currently being used are effective or ineffective, we ask teachers to examine them for (a) their congruence with the *Performance Indicators* and (b) whether they are the correct type in terms of one holistic score or multiple scores. The third and fourth issues, pertinent to the use of a consistent, developmental baseline rubric, added-to with criteria unique to the special project, tend to be far more political than pedagogical. This can be a major stumbling block. But our experience has shown that without these developmentally consistent baseline rubrics as the foundation, projects that do involve writing, speaking, and/or listening become moving targets for students. And without this foundation to anchor the additional unique criteria of the special project or task, students are forced to guess at what is expected.

The Products

The centerpiece of the *Culminating* activities is the product. And for many teachers, that is also the most difficult part to conceptualize as an independent task. But on the other hand, there are some teachers who begin planning their *Units* by identifying the *Culminating* activity first and working backwards. The four most important features of the product are as follows: (a) that it reflect at least one of the *Performance Indicator(s)* in the *Unit*, (b) that it assess an individual student's mastery (it may be a group activity), (c) that it be prepared-for during the *Unit* (i.e., via the Motivation and Information activities), and (d) that the evaluation criteria are derived from the indicator(s).

Table 8.10 shows a small sampling of the products we have seen used successfully over the years. To the discriminating eye, many of them look like products that could also be used with *Assessments*. And they are. What makes them *Culminating* activities rather than *Assessments* is their position in the *Unit Plan* and their purpose. If they represent the discrete and convergent response to a teacher's prompt, they are more at home on a paper-pencil test, and there will typically be few options for "correctness." If they are the holistic, self-contained product that reflects independent mastery, and there are any number of options to be "correct," they are likely to be *Culminations*.

Structurally, the *Culminating* activities are more divergent than their *Assessment* counterparts. They are set up as a prompt or set of basic directions that specify the overall task(s) and include basic guidelines for the final product. But remember, these *Culminating* measures of mastery are intended to be flexible and to require the students themselves to plan the task, execute the plan, and create the final product. Three samples from each of the four core subjects are listed below.

Math

Elementary. Prepare an expense sheet showing dollars, expenses, subtractions, carrying balances forward, and so on, using figures supplied by the

Table 8.10 Sample Products for Authentic or Performance Assessments

Oral	Written		Pictorial	Construction
conversation	add a chapter to . . .	log entries	blueprint	board game
debate (position)	analogies	math formula	brochure	cartouche
demonstration	annotations for . . .	metaphors	cartoon	class museum
dialogue	autobiography	movie poster	charts	computer program
dramatization	book jacket	movie script	comic strip	display
historic profile	book review	movie story board	demonstration	game
interview	biography	myth	drawings	musical instrument
lesson (taught)	brochure	notes taken from . . .	flow chart	puppets
monologue	by-laws	personal narrative	graphic organizer	scale model
newscast	constitution	persuasive essay	graphics	scientific experiment
(talking head)	critique	poem	map	sculpture
panel discussion	dedication speech	predictions	mural	terrarium
poem	descriptive essay	procedure (how-to)	painting	3-D relief map
predictions	diary	proposal	pictograph	totem pole
public service	editorial	questions	poster	working model
announcement	eulogy	research report		
questions	expository essay	rubric		
re-enactment	fable	summary		
resident expert on. . . .	folk tale	survey		
role-play	hypothesis	tables		
speech	job application	time line		
summary	job description	treaty		
talk show	letters			
video				

teacher (hint: the teacher should create three or four scenarios, place them in a hat, and draw one per student).

Intermediate. Design a blueprint for the redecoration of the den (include the flooring: carpeting, tile; include the walls: wallpaper, border, paint; allow for doors, windows, and other unusual features); use correct scale, include XYZ type shapes, and show proportions (option: may also include costs and a virtual three-dimensional view of the proposed product).

High School. Devise a rubric to analyze a variety of problem situations involving measurement computation (e.g., volume, area, rate, money, distance) to discover possible errors in (a) labeling, (b) conversions, (c) accuracy of computation, (d) viability of estimate, (e) accuracy of measurement, and (f) the viability of the solution; show samples to illustrate each possible error.

Language Arts

Elementary. Compose a letter to (e.g., a hotel manager) (making a request, lodging a complaint, telling about an unusual experience, etc.); use a rubric to develop (and to evaluate).

Intermediate. Write an original poem that features figurative language (as per the *Performance Indicators* in the *Unit*; e.g., similes, metaphors, onomatopoeia, personification); use a "poetry rubric" to guide the development and to evaluate, for example, (a) conventions of poetry type, (b) poetic devices/format (rhythm, rhyme scheme, etc.), (c) imagery (including figurative language), (d) consistent voice, and (e) mechanics (grammar, punctuation, spelling; specific syntax rules).

High School. Write an original persuasive piece (e.g., a campaign speech, a letter to the editor, an argument to jury) that follows the conventions of persuasive writing and those of grammar and mechanics; that is,

- *Idea Development* (a) takes a clear position or argument that responds to assigned prompt, (b) develops the position or argument with logic and clarity, (c) uses at least three sources of external support, (d) acknowledges alternate points of view and explains why these are not viable, and (e) uses mature, appropriate language.
- *Organization* (a) uses an effective introduction (sets forth the argument), (b) body develops argument or position with supporting ideas, and (c) conclusion ties off argument or position (e.g., summarizes, asks a pertinent question).

Social Studies

Elementary. Interview a relative about a family (cultural) tradition, transcribe the interview, and make personal comments (oral and/or written reflections) about how these traditions affect contemporary life.

Intermediate. Compare two or three provinces (states, countries) in the same geographic region with regard to specific factors as per *Performance*

Indicators (e.g., climate, topography, political structure and prominent issues, social-cultural characteristics, economic base); include a description of relationships between (among) them; and use at least three media (i.e., writing, pictures, graphics) to prepare final product. (Note: while this would also make a great oral presentation, it is every bit as effective submitted as a project.)

High School. Analyze some actual and some online examples of African American, Native American, and Latino art, music, literature, and popular media to discover unique characteristics; describe specific aspects of our contemporary American society that reflect each of these perspectives and debunk common stereotypes; and display as a graphic organizer.

Science

Elementary. Conduct an original (but guided) experiment with regard to (*Unit* topic), record observations, make inferences and predictions, test the predictions, and note results.

Intermediate. Create a realistic representation (e.g., an annotated model, a picture, or a poster) of how an imaginary canyon developed in your back yard; include both (a) slow-moving changes on the earth's surface (e.g., erosion, weathering, mountain building, deposition) and (b) rapid processes (e.g., volcanic eruptions, landslides, earthquakes); explain the progression of the changes and how they resulted in the canyon and its features.

High School. Create a time line that demonstrates the development of an earlier theory (e.g., continental drift, the greenhouse effect) into a current theory (e.g., global warming, plate tectonics, etc.) by plotting the development or use of various technologies (e.g., submersibles, satellite imaging, advances in photography) to account for the changes; use yarn, for example, to include descriptive (explanatory) annotations.

Scoring Rubrics

There are dozens of Web sites and software packages that offer sample rubrics for scoring all sorts of projects from writing pieces through the design and execution of an original science experiment. The first step to designing the appropriate rubric to score *Culminating* activities is to pull the criteria from the *Performance Indicators*. The following are four content examples of *Culminating* activities to illustrate how this is done. Each presupposes the use of a consistent baseline rubric for the core areas of writing, speaking, and listening.

- **Math:** Devise a personal budget that illustrates a small income and living expenses and includes a savings program.
  Criteria: format, expenses versus income, comparing budgets, accurate computation of all pertinent data, and drawing valid inferences.

- **Science:** Design an experiment to determine if certain breads grow different kinds of mold.

Criteria: a viable hypothesis; controls for variables such as light, moisture, and so on; notes taken; diagrams or drawings; and valid conclusions; use baseline writing rubric, with the addition of the above criteria for the write-up.

- **English:** (Mythology *Unit*) Write an original myth, and present it to classmates.
  Criteria: the conventions of the myth as a genre (e.g., character[s]; the challenge or difficulty; setting; plot events, including the development and resolution of the conflicts; moral or lesson); baseline writing rubric (e.g., organization, language, voice, mechanics); speaking rubric (e.g., articulation, language, eye contact, body language and gestures, visual aids); and listening rubric (e.g., capture main ideas, tone).

- **Social Studies:** Engage in a debate on the electoral college.
  Criteria: (a) the conventions of Debate (e.g., identification of the argument; definition of pro and con positions; the preparation of viable arguments, supported with primary and secondary evidence); (b) baseline speaking rubric, with the addition of special delivery methods for the debate, for example, the initial presentation, the rebuttal, and the final summation; and (c) the preparation of both the *pro* and *con* arguments, including ___, __, and ___ (content as per the ideas discussed during class).

The second step is to decide whether to use a **holistic** rubric (one score, combining all of the criteria) or an **analytical** rubric (several scores, each representing one of the criteria). Convincing arguments can be made for either type, but the analytical rubric offers more granular results in that it considers each component of the finished product as a separate entity. Moreover, if a baseline rubric does exist, and the special criteria for the task are added, the results are more easily disaggregated. The analytic rubric also doubles as a checklist for proceeding with the task.

The third step is to decide on the **numeric values** to be used. Of course, if a baseline rubric does exist, and the teacher is building onto it, the same (or complementary) numeric values should apply. But if a rubric is being designed, the simplest approach is to use an *either-or* (0 or 1) to designate the requirement was met or it was not, period. More elaborate rubrics use a continuum or range of numeric values to reflect shades or degrees of the required criteria. If that is the approach, we recommend using an even number such as 2, 4, or 6 to prevent the temptation to mark the middle rate, which is in limbo between positive and negative. Whether they choose the holistic (one value) or analytic (separate values) rubric, teachers should always create several concrete models or scenarios, each of which reflect the various possible scores and combinations. This way, there is a definite distinction between a 3 and a 4 in one particular criteria (analytical) or the one score (holistic). The majority of mishaps we've seen in the use of rubrics are the inability of teachers to define exactly what is meant by any of the numeric values, particularly in comparison to the one just above or below it.

■ SUMMARY

The OUTPUT side of the *Unit Plan*, the Assessment and Culmination quadrants, is the payoff for all of the hard work and effort that has gone into the design and delivery of the *Unit*. For many developing teams, the OUTPUT side is the best place to begin planning, and then work backwards to devise those *Motivation* and *Information* activities most likely to yield the intended results. There is still much debate about the extent of Differentiation that should be provided in the OUPUT quadrants for children with Special Needs. Some feel strongly that the requirements should be adjusted to the developmental and academic levels of each child to ensure at least some degree of success. Others hold fast that this is the "soft bigotry" of watered-down expectations and insist that every student can pass the *Assessments* and accomplish the *Culminating* tasks if given enough time and the appropriate instruction. The 2008 election and the fate of NCLB will cast a defining light on this argument, at least politically. But pedagogically, the educators in each district and individual school must decide *now* what is best to do.

PART V

Capacity-Building

9

Capacity-Building to Integrate Classroom Reform Into the Deep Culture of Each School

INTRODUCTION ■

In our many years of experience working with school reform, by far the greatest disappointment has been to watch an impressive array of reforms accomplished during a project, only to see things revert to prior practice once the project is completed. In every case, the single most common factor was the lack of capacity within the staff to sustain the reforms. In effect, the reforms were never integrated into the deep culture of the school or district as the way "business was done" as part of the daily routine. In case after case, we have observed (a) the meager use of diagnostic data to plan classroom instruction, (b) a shortage of leadership among the teaching staff,

(c) serious disconnects between the reform activities and the roles and responsibilities of the principals, and (d) a lack of "community" among the teachers, where each functions in virtual isolation from the other, and/or (e) lack of data management system to monitor student progress.

This final chapter takes an in-depth look at the steps a district should take to make the enacted reforms an integral part of the district culture and the way its schools do business each day. Perhaps even more important is how to make certain the reforms can withstand the continual challenge of external pressures (such as NCLB and public scrutiny) and the internal tensions of funding shortages, staff turnover, political in-fighting, and evolving student needs. The assimilation of a new curricular and instructional program into the district and school infrastructure is an enormous and complex undertaking. And we realize that trying to address it in one chapter cannot possibly do it justice. But we have also learned several lessons about how to launch a capacity-building effort in a district that is serious about ensuring the survival of its enacted reforms.

In our opinion, deep-level integration comes through **capacity-building** on the following fronts:

♦ **Benchmarking:** the assessment of academic progress at strategic intervals from outside the classroom on a district-level or schoolwide perspective; these include paper-pencil measures, the mastery of *Performance Indicators*, and the effective use of high-stakes test results.

♦ **How Data Should Be Used by Teachers and Administrators:** not as mere rhetoric but as actual practice in each school; principals and staff closely examine testing reports to identify each student's strengths and weaknesses to provide the most appropriate instruction, predicated on a data management system that makes useful and timely data available to teachers, students, and parents/guardians; training and support are sufficient for all stakeholders to access and use the data to more efficiently plan instruction and monitor student performance.

♦ **Building Leadership Teams:** a cross-section of teachers, professional support staff, and building administrators who plan, implement, and monitor the reform efforts; they work with all staff (divided into cohorts) to communicate project activities, provide support and encouragement, and to elicit continuous feedback.

♦ **Administrative Stewardship:** specific training and implementation activities to help central office and building-level administrators assume their respective roles and responsibilities to facilitate and sustain the enacted reforms.

♦ **Collaborative Observation:** a four-part process to help teachers and administrators work in collaborative pairs to analyze specific teaching strategies and their effect on student performance; the process uses each of the course tools and procedures from *Instructional Design* and provides the means to fully integrate them into each classroom and to help every teacher successfully implement the enacted reforms.

A complete list of the supporting research for these capacity-building processes is detailed in the References section. A set of annotated references to works cited is available from the authors on request.

And Don't Forget the Data Management System

With the considerable data requirements imposed by NCLB have come another indicator of a district's effectiveness: its ability to gather, process, organize, and use student performance data. Not five years ago, such records were kept manually, but with so many advances in user-friendly and affordable technology, most of the obstacles to maintaining accurate, timely, and accessible student performance data have all but disappeared.

Guidelines

A few suggestions are offered to guide the establishment of an effective data management system. Look for a system that will integrate all student performance information—demographics, achievement, discipline, attendance, and so on—to provide a continuous and current look at student achievement and all of the factors that may affect it. Once a system has been found that meets a majority of the conditions above and those in the following bullets, install it on a pilot-only basis.

- Establish the student data base, including demographics, attendance, discipline, and various measures of academic achievement; involve all staff who will be responsible for keeping it current and accurate; and provide adequate training to data management support and administrative staff.
- Integrate detailed information from high-stakes tests with the results of district Benchmark assessments and classroom mastery of the *Performance Indicators*; these comprise a profile of the academic status of each student, of NCLB subgroups, and of entire cohorts of students.
- Provide training to teachers and building administrators in the functions they are to perform, and arrange time and opportunity for teachers to input student mastery information (and principals to access it) from anywhere in school or home; most systems now provide parents/guardians read-only access to their students' information to keep them fully vested in the educational process.
- Enable useful reports to be easily generated by and for all stakeholders; teachers need classroom summaries, individual student reports, and needs-group summaries; parents/guardians need cumulative records for only their children; district-level administrators need summaries of discipline, attendance, and achievement by subject area and grade level, all of which are disaggregated by NCLB subgroup; and principals need similar reports for their own schools.

These few suggestions should trigger others that are unique to each district. The best-case scenario is for the provider to allow the district to pilot the system on a limited basis to make sure it works before making a major investment in a districtwide installation. There are a number of horror stories from districts who "bought the sales pitch and a glitzy demo," only to find themselves stuck with an unworkable, inflexible system that did not meet their needs.

If student performance data are to be continuously monitored and legitimately used to inform the district's strategic planning as well as to affect what happens in each classroom, the following must occur. The district must find an efficient and workable data management system, provide the infrastructure to use it effectively and keep it maintained, and garner a sufficient level of commitment and trust among stakeholders. Like every other information enterprise, capacity-building in school districts must begin and continue with good data management.

■ BENCHMARKING

The typical meaning of Benchmark assessment is a single test. But in the *Instructional Design* process, Benchmarking is multifactored, using several different but complementary measures of student performance to determine student mastery at a given point in time. In this section, we will examine several such measures that, taken together, represent how well each student is mastering the required content. The most common types of benchmarking include: The Benchmark Tests, Classroom Mastery of Performance Indicators, and Standardized or High-Stakes Tests. Figure 9.1 shows how these several measures can work together in a school, once curricular and instructional reforms have been implemented. As illustrated, each measure should become part of the ongoing, systemic routine throughout the district. Note that the **icons** in the text below reference the corresponding sections in Figure 9.1. These icons include 📄 for diagnostic and mastery tests, ▦ for quarterly or year-end Benchmark tests, and 📊 for high-stakes tests.

The Customary Benchmark Tests

Typically, Benchmark assessments are paper-pencil tests that consist of multiple-choice items and open-ended prompts that require students to provide constructed responses similar to the high-stakes tests students will take for NCLB. These tests measure those grade level and subject standards (or, in this case, *Performance Indicators*) that students were to have mastered up to the point of the test. It is essential that the tests be carefully secured and coordinated by the district using a highly controlled testing situation. This ensures a level of equity, fairness, and consistency that validates the results. There are any number of variations in Benchmark testing; some of the most popular are listed in this chapter.

The Diagnostic and Mastery Test [📄]

This is the familiar pre- and post- or bookend method. The test is based on the highest priority standards (known as Power Standards or Essential Learnings, or the *Performance Indicators)* and identifies each student's

Figure 9.1 Year-Long Benchmarking

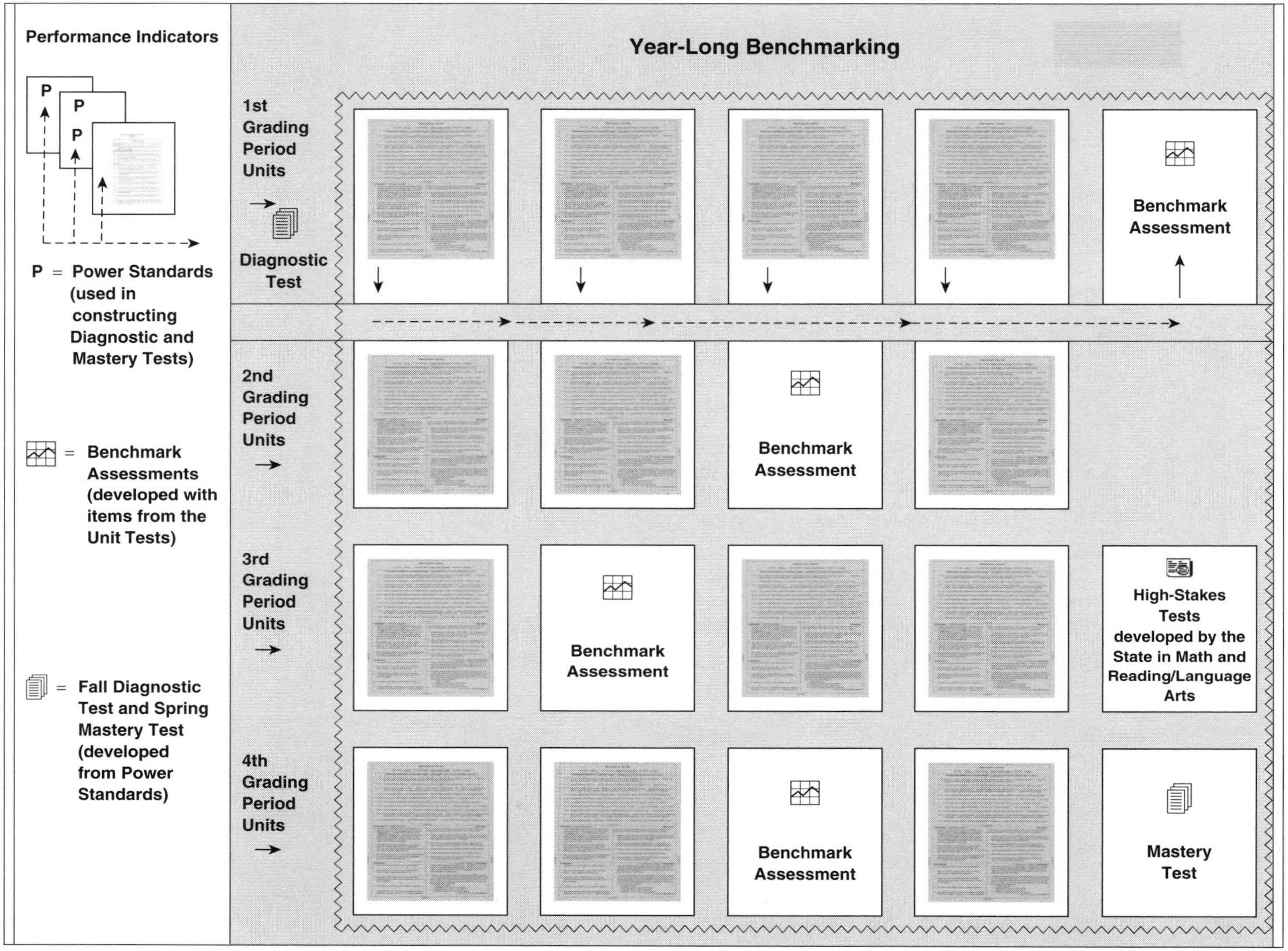

entry-level or readiness for the upcoming school year. A parallel Mastery test given at the end of the year determines the extent to which each student has mastered the designated *Performance Indicators* and reveals the precise amount of growth for each student (and groups of students) across the school year.

The Quarterly Assessment [▦]

The Quarterly Assessments measure those *Performance Indicators* that students should have mastered during the grading period, and reveal specific targets for intervention. The quarterly approach ensures a prudent consistency in the curriculum and helps teachers remain focused. It is the method of choice in many urban districts, since students frequently move around among schools. Critics of the quarterly method feel it is too inflexible, too frequent, and promotes teaching for the test.

The Mid-Year and Year-End Assessment [▦]

The Mid-year/Year-end assessment determines mastery for the first semester and then the second semester. In a year-long course, the mid-year results may also provide diagnostic information for the second half of the year.

Development of Benchmark Tests

Just who should develop the Benchmark tests is always an issue. A commercial off-the-shelf test rarely matches the local district curriculum, and while some publishers will customize the tests, this is extremely costly and inflexible to the changing needs of the district and its students. The downside of this costly, albeit customized, approach is that the test—and not the *Performance Indicators*—drives the curriculum. More emphasis is placed on students' test scores than how well they master the *Performance Indicators*.

Another approach is for teachers to devise the Benchmark tests themselves. While this is certainly less expensive and provides unlimited flexibility, unless the tests are validly constructed and care is taken to ensure consistency in test administration and quality control, the results are suspect and rarely useful. Districts who create their own tests can get bogged down with the overwhelming logistical burdens of preparing valid tests and keeping them current, copying and distribution, grading, and preparing the reports. And atop all this, security is next to impossible with so many people having access to the tests.

Many districts are purchasing tests from companies who claim that their tests are aligned to a given state's standards. Some are computerized and taken online; some are even individualized to the student's level of mastery. These vendors guarantee a quick turnaround in reporting the data back to teachers. This approach is only worth the investment if teachers use the data to inform their instruction.

In our experience, the most successful Benchmark tests are those that are developed by a team of district staff, assisted by consultants with considerable training and experience in test construction. The items should be criterion referenced to the district's own *Performance Indicators* and include items developed and used by teachers, providing they are validly constructed and reveal diagnostic information about student mastery. Most important, even small districts can maintain security if the tests are kept off-site and parallel forms are used.

Classroom Mastery of *Performance Indicators*

The second component of the Benchmarking process occurs in each classroom. It's the determination by teachers of whether each student has mastered the *Performance Indicators*. Typically, this determination is made at the end of each *Unit*. But when students fail to master one or more indicators by the end of any one *Unit*, intervention is provided to give them additional opportunities to demonstrate mastery. Depending on the *Unit* plan, mastery may be measured on a paper-pencil test, a performance assessment, or ideally a combination of both. Some *Performance Indicators* appear in multiple *Units* at different points during the year. How well students master the Board-adopted *Performance Indicators* is as important a part of their academic success as their scores on the high-stakes tests. With an efficient and effective data management system, teachers enter "mastery" or "nonmastery," and a report is compiled each grading period (or quarter) that accompanies the grade card to keep parents/guardians well-informed as to their students' current academic mastery.

Standardized or High-Stakes Tests [🖼]

The longest-standing and still the most trusted and frequently used indication of student achievement is the high-stakes test. Since the first standardized tests were published in the nineteenth century, schools in the United States have used them to determine how well their students were performing academically in comparison to the rest of the state and the country. And as long as the schools in America seemed to be graduating enough capable students to run the country, it wasn't a major concern that a third to half the students really weren't scoring very well. In those days, the standardized test merely classified and labeled students according to their academic and vocational potential. It didn't seem to trouble anyone that a huge segment of the student population left school without the skills needed to earn a living.

With the twentieth century came unprecedented federal legislation mandating that students of every race, economic status, and handicapping condition be provided the same quality of education as the children of privilege. Standardized testing took on new meaning. Instead of merely categorizing students, it was designed to identify learning strengths and weaknesses and to signal the need for rigorous intervention programs.

With NCLB has come an entirely new focus on the group achievement test and an entirely new era of accountability for student achievement. No longer can districts decide what grade levels, subjects, and students to test; this has been decided for them. In addition, how the data are analyzed and reported is a decision made outside of the local school district. The test results are disaggregated by subgroup, showing comparisons between and among them: (a) Special Needs students and non-Special Needs students, (b) socioeconomically disadvantaged and non-socioeconomically disadvantaged students, (c) comparisons among ethnic groups, and (d) students who are English Language Learners compared to those who are English speaking. Each of these subgroups must make what has become known as Adequate Yearly Progress (AYP), or proportionately the same rate of growth. AYP is statistically determined for each state (and district) using a formula provided by the U.S. Department of Education. The consequences of any subgroup's continued failure to meet AYP are dire for the school or district as a whole. Parents/guardians may take their children to private tutors at the district's expense, and ultimately, the state may close a school, reconstitute it, or take over the operation.

One of the major shortcomings of the high-stakes tests is, of course, the reports. There is little flexibility in the types of reports provided by the publisher; most reports are limited to "strand" scores such as Measurement in Math. But wherever possible, districts are urged to request reports that not only give scores but the skills and concepts behind the scores—what it is that each student can and cannot do, not merely what numerical score he or she obtained. In most states, this level of granularity is not possible, and the reports sent to schools are not only inadequate diagnostically, but they arrive too late to help the current group of students.

■ HOW DATA SHOULD BE USED BY TEACHERS AND ADMINISTRATORS

In developing their capacity to maintain curricular and instructional reforms, districts must include strategic plans to collect and continually use student performance data to make decisions. To this end, the importance of the data management system, with timely and easy access by stakeholders, cannot be overstated. The student data base must contain each child's demographic information as well as attendance, disciplinary records, and Benchmark measures of academic achievement.

Paper-Pencil Benchmark Test Data

For the **paper-pencil Benchmark tests**—be they Diagnostic/Mastery, Quarterly, or Mid-year/Year-end—the results should be part of the file for each student. For each teacher, the results should be compiled and printed as Individual Student Reports, Class Summaries, Grade-Level Summaries, and Disaggregations for AYP subgroups. Because the tests are measures of the *Performance Indicators*, teachers can use the results to plan daily instruction providing for Differentiation, remediation, and enrichment. In addition, Individual Student Reports are ideal for arent/guardian and student conferences. For principals, the subject-area and grade-level summaries should also be disaggregated by NCLB subgroup to help principals target specific skill areas that continue to be problematic across grade levels. In addition, principals can see if there are patterns or trends in discipline and attendance that may affect student achievement and whether there are any particular subgroups that are particularly affected. This wide-angle view of student performance is essential if the principal is to effectively monitor the performance of the students, meet with teachers to discuss results and their impact on classroom instruction, and determine areas for professional development. It is in the interpretation of these reports that the issue of trust and the responsible use of the data come into play.

Performance Indicator Data

Once mastery data are "keyed in" for the *Performance Indicators,* reports should be generated for teachers to use in conferencing with students and their parents/guardians as well as in classroom summaries to plan more strategically. The truth is that despite repeated interventions and reteaching, there will always be some students who simply do not master 100% of the *Performance Indicators* in a given subject for a particular year. But the documentation of several opportunities for mastery and multiple interventions helps the school and the district honor its accountability to every student. And if the curriculum is truly standards-based, students will have additional opportunities to master parallel indicators in subsequent grade levels.

High-Stakes Data

For the **high-stakes NCLB tests**, most districts administer the tests in the spring, and the results are received as the school year is ending. As indicated earlier, the reports may not be tremendously helpful unless the following can be obtained:

◆ Lists of the skills and concepts tested, so that teachers can connect these with the *Performance Indicators* and when they are being taught. Naturally, the test company will have used the state content standards, which connect to the *Performance Indicators,* but teachers need to hone in on the cognitive demand of the skills and concepts tested, in relationship to the corresponding content.

◆ Class summaries of results, in addition to building and district summaries that include disaggregations by the NCLB subgroups.

Teachers can analyze the results from the prior year from both the curricular and the instructional perspectives with an eye toward planning the subsequent year. From a curriculum and instruction perspective, Grade 4 teachers could analyze the data for the students coming out of Grade 3. This would allow the Grade 4 teachers to grasp where their incoming students are strong or weak in the prerequisite skills for fourth grade. Secondly, the Grade 3 teachers would analyze the same group's data to identify where they need to do a better job of instruction for the Grade 3 students. In both analyses, the decisions about curriculum and instruction would focus on (a) realigning the *Curriculum Map* to place *Performance Indicators* in the appropriate sequence to address the greatest needs; (b) adjusting instruction in terms of the time of year as well as the amount of time devoted to certain concepts; and (c) determining what instructional strategies, experiences, and materials used to teach certain concepts did and did not work for students. In addition, there may be areas where teachers need professional development to fully address the academic content standards and teach to the level of cognitive demand required. Using the high-stakes data to make decisions about professional development will allow teachers to participate in growth opportunities that will yield the greatest gains in student achievement.

Teachers should examine the results in order by percentage of mastery: i.e. concepts mastered by 80% of the students first, 41–79% second, and less than 40% third. Since teachers know their students, they can determine where there are anomalies in the data and identify instances in which even the best students failed to demonstrate mastery of certain concepts or struggling students "got lucky" with several guesses at difficult concepts. At any rate, teachers can use the data to begin planning for Differentiated instruction to address individual and small group needs, rather than trying to address all weaknesses as a whole class.

For the concepts not mastered, teachers should look at their *Performance Indicators, Curriculum Maps,* and *Unit Plans* to determine where, when, and how specific enabling concepts and skills are taught. The Grade 4 teachers can see how to remediate missing skills and concepts as well as enrich those concepts and skills where students are already proficient. Grade 3 teachers can examine the troublesome *Performance Indicators* in the context of their *Curriculum Map* and *Units.* They may decide to reorder their *Maps* and *Units* to ensure that they are allowing students adequate opportunity to master certain skills and concepts. Not getting to the *Unit* that deals with probability (for example) for several years in a row is simply not acceptable; students need to have this learning experience each year, or the holes in the curriculum are too much for any one grade level to make up.

A Quick Note About Value-Added Analysis

One of the most often-cited criticisms of NCLB is that it expects all students to achieve the same level of academic success, including students who face barriers over which the school has no control. These barriers include educational disabilities, socioeconomic disadvantage, students who are English-language learners, and those who are members of an ethnic group. These are the basis of AYP determination for the NCLB disaggregation. By simply looking at year-end test scores and comparing one year's results to the next year's results, NCLB fails to account for how gain may have been made by individual students and subgroups during the course of the year. This flaw provides states and districts with perverse incentives to "game the system" by any one of the following misguided tactics: (a) Exclude students who might bring down the overall scores. (b) Spend disproportionate amounts of intervention time tutoring "bubble students," that large majority who nearly pass but not quite, to prepare them to pass the next test in hopes of raising the district's overall score enough to keep it out of academic trouble. (c) Set academic standards low to reduce the number of schools failing under the law. (d) Report group scores that mask individual needs within the group.

With so much riding on the NCLB test scores, it is understandable that districts feel trapped. While some states have threatened to boycott the

NCLB law by refusing any federal money or bringing suit against the U.S. Department of Education, other states are considering the use of various growth models, the most popular of which is Value-Added. A complete set of annotated reference cites for the Value-Added research is available from the authors on request.

Applying the Value-Added analysis to student test scores enables a district to determine each student's progress from one year to the next as the measure of growth accrued to his or her educational account as a function of attending one year of school. It allows the state or district to report not only the extent to which each school has been successful in achieving state and district standards but also the rate of growth among individual students and subgroups from one year to the next. Each student serves as his or her own control group, and each student's performance at the end of one year is compared with his or her score from the year before, not to a group of students. The statistical methods employed in the Value-Added analysis adjust for the influence of nonschool variables such as socioeconomic status, English language difficulties, and educational disability. Each student can be followed across the years to carefully monitor his or her individual growth and provide intervention as needed on a more focused and timely basis. Value-Added allows for the use of incomplete data as well so that even if a student missed parts of a year, his or her other data can be compiled. Finally, Value-Added analyses identify what failures and successes have occurred during, say, the two years of the reform project, giving staff a starting point for decision making.

Value-Added shows how such a growth model can help districts reap a far more bountiful harvest from their reform efforts than is available to them with summary scores and group averages. The use of individual scores offers a level of granularity and precision not otherwise possible; conventional group scores obscure the precise needs and strengths of individual students. We encourage districts to use their high-stakes test results as one of several measures to determine the effect of their reform efforts. The application of a growth model such as Value-Added will greatly enhance their ability to do so, providing the motive is to strengthen classroom instruction on behalf of students, and not to place blame.

BUILDING LEADERSHIP TEAMS ■

Who Are They *Really*?

What makes any multistep approach to school reform so difficult is that every step should be first. And one such step that should have been taken well ahead of any reform initiative is the establishment of the Building Leadership Team. If districts (or buildings) omit this important aspect of the reform process, nothing else they do will matter much, and trying to retrofit it after the fact is like attempting to put a foundation under a house after it's built. The 1980s concept of shared leadership, teacher empowerment, or collaborative decision-making may have morphed into the trendy professional learning community, but the core principle remains unchanged: Teachers must be substantively involved in planning, implementation, and the continuous appraisal of the reform initiatives if they are to succeed. Any skeptics need only to examine a school where such a Team has been overlooked.

For maximum effectiveness, the Leadership Team should consist of staff who are highly respected by and can speak for a grade level, subject area, and/or specialty (e.g., guidance, technology, media). This is not the place for the struggler, nor for the disgruntled and pessimistic teacher whose agenda is primarily self-serving. The Leadership Team should be a microcosm of the staff, including a cross-section of experience levels, genders, ethnicities, and political agendas.

The Function of the Building Leadership Team

Initially, the Building Leadership Team will use the analysis of the school's current status as the "team-building" experience and review the school Profile, or other compilation of entry-level data. In so doing, they analyze (a) the current level of student achievement as reflected by high-stakes test scores and various other district benchmarks; (b) stakeholders' perceptions about the school's effectiveness and the extent to which respondents feel they are an integral part of what goes on; (c) the school's current reform initiatives and how well each is working; (d) current professional development practices, including how professional development is planned, who attends, and how it is determined whether each practice has had any effect on student performance.

We suggest that the Building Leadership Team meet for 20 to 30 clock hours to review the Profile material and to prepare the Action Plan. It is during this organizational phase that the Team is provided training in adult communication strategies such as the role of the Leadership Team vis-à-vis the building principal, trust-building, setting and prioritizing goals, problem-finding and problem-solving, consensus building, team versus individual norms, conferencing techniques, and group decision making. One personalization strategy that has worked very well in our experience is for each Team member to assume direct responsibility for a small cohort of teachers. For already busy people, this limits what may seem a daunting task and makes it more doable; it facilitates quick and focused communication, prevents mix-ups about who was to communicate with whom, and prevents the deadly and all too frequent "leaving someone out of the loop."

The Leadership Team will draft a multiyear *Action Plan* that will guide the entire reform effort. These Action Plans typically focus on academic priorities in one or more subjects and specify reform initiatives in standards-based curriculum and the use of Best Practices to deliver and assess classroom instruction. But most Action Plans also include such related priorities as discipline, communication, and parent/guardian-community relations, things that have been called correlates of student achievement. The typical Action Plan format sets forth specific performance goals, strategies and activities to attain them, detailing who is responsible for doing what, the time frames for each strategy, interim check points to monitor progress, and the criteria for the successful achievement of each performance goal. When using the *Instructional Design* process, the strategies are to identify *Performance Indicators*, devise *Curriculum Maps*, develop *Unit Plans*, and establish a series of valid formative and summative assessments to measure student mastery. Benchmarking and data management typically find their way into most Action Plans as well. One important point that cannot be overlooked is that in many schools, there is already in place some sort of Continuous Improvement Plan or School Reform Plan as a result of a state department mandate or the requirements of a grant. We strongly recommend that this existing Plan be the basis for the *Instructional Design* Action Plan and that the components be dovetailed into it. Nothing is more aggravating to a staff than to be told their previous work is no longer relevant and that they must begin again.

The Building Leadership Team should share the Plan, along with the backup data from the Profile that led them to it, with the remainder of the staff. During this sharing, the Team receives feedback about the Action Plan from the staff as well as suggestions for further consideration. This is a most critical juncture in the reform process in that the *Instructional Design* Action Plan must appear as a seamless and integral part of the overall Continuous Improvement Plan (or whatever the existing document is called). If there is no such prior Plan, the Action Plan must be robust and inclusive enough to carry the school's entire reform initiative. Either way, throughout the reform effort, Team members will use the Action Plan to communicate with staff members about the reform activities, address their questions and concerns, and encourage their feedback.

During the quarterly meetings, each Team member shares current developments and perceptions from his and her cohort meetings, particularly how students are progressing and how well the data management system is working. These meetings are particularly useful for discussing "green ink" edits and recommended adjustments to the course tools and logistical procedures. The Team should be certain that everyone is conveying the same information to the staff. Throughout the discourse, it must be remembered that the building principal is ultimately responsible for the operation of the school and is legally accountable for decisions that are made. But it is nonetheless important that Team members keep a read on staff perceptions about the work being asked of them and discover any concerns and disconnects that must be addressed. If teachers are to feel ownership in the reforms, and if each is to assume his or her rightful accountability for the success of the reform effort, the collective voice of the staff must be considered in the decision-making process. Rather than diminish the principal's power, this shared governance actually increases and deepens it. The Leadership Team can help the staff realize how and why decisions are made and act as a buffer to support the principal in the face of judgments that are tough or unpopular, though necessary.

Throughout the *Instructional Design* Process, the Team will continue to function, typically meeting quarterly and at the end of the year. They are active during the development of the various curriculum and instructional components, perhaps as members of one or more developing Teams who devise the *Performance Indicators*, *Curriculum Maps*, *Unit Plans*, *data management*, *Benchmark Assessments*, and so on. They share what is developed with their staff cohorts and/or grade level teams, and they are the catalysts for the Critical Friends network. It is the Building Leadership Team who maintains the Big Picture of the entire reform process; they design the scope of the work, set time lines for the various pieces, and make decisions for the overall good of all stakeholders in the process.

During the course of most multiyear school reform projects, superintendents typically change at least once, curriculum directors come and go, and principals leave and/or are reassigned. In our experience, the constant is the teaching staff. Successful, responsive Building Leadership Teams typically survive leadership changes remarkably well and can sustain the reforms, regardless of what happens at the administrative level.

It is suggested that as the year draws to a close, the Building Leadership Team should collect the "green ink" and other staff feedback to recommend revisions in the course tools for the next school year. In addition, the Team should examine student performance data using authentic data analysis techniques to identify specific patterns and trends of academic growth as well as areas of weakness. Based on all of the results and activities of the school year, the Team should review the original Action Plan to determine what, if any, adjustments are needed. Where possible, this year-end review should occur as a retreat that will not only celebrate the completion of a successful reform year, but provide a soothing and unhurried atmosphere in which to reflect on preparations for the year to come.

■ ADMINISTRATIVE STEWARDSHIP

Among the tiresome catchphrases that make everyone's eyes roll about school reform is that the principal is to be the instructional leader of the school. What we find so disturbing is that when the reform discussions finally get to the administrative team, principals look at us as if we should not expect them to "take on" one more thing. In study after study, students from schools where the principal took an active role in the teaching-learning process outscored students from schools where the principal had little to do with what happens in classrooms. With so much compelling evidence, the importance of the administrator's role simply cannot be denied.

We stick to our belief that the principal is the instructional "leader of leaders." That is, he or she must establish an environment in the school that supports (no, requires) teachers to be accountable for doing all they can to help every student succeed. Because the principal is legally accountable for the operation of the school and invested with the responsibility to supervise and evaluate teachers in the performance of their classroom duties, he or she operates from <u>position</u> power. But that's certainly not the power that makes enacted reforms a success. The <u>authentic</u> power comes from and within the staff, from being challenged by the principal to get involved in the development of the *Performance Indicators* and then using them to guide instruction, to rely on the *Curriculum Map* to structure the school year and conference with parents/guardians, and to use the Best Practices and materials set forth in the *Unit Plans* to deliver and assess classroom instruction. With the support of the Building Leadership Team, the reform-minded principal has articulated to the faculty what he or she believes constitutes high-quality instruction and what practices and procedures are expected of every teacher. These principals leave no doubt they expect the work to be done. But they also "go first" to model those attributes they expect and to provide the support each teacher needs to attain those high standards of performance; this includes release time, clerical help, professional development, and substantive feedback about the quality of their work.

The result of creating this high-powered "leader of leaders" is that the tools and procedures of the enacted reforms soak into the school's deep culture and become integral to the daily routines and operations of the entire building. When the reforms have been totally integrated, they are "the way business is done here," and no one would consider behaving otherwise. Although the Building Leadership Team is a vital part of this integration, it is the oversight and stewardship of the building principal that surrounds and anchors the effort. Only the principal can adjust the infrastructure—including the budget, the schedule, and the assignment of students—in ways that will accommodate and support the new practices and procedures. And it is also the principal who shields the effort from the various external and internal pressures that would compromise its effect.

If this is what's needed, why don't all principals take up the challenge and just do it? The research backs up what years of observation have shown: that this level of stewardship is not included in most principal preparation programs. Specifically, the requirements of licensure include degrees and work experience, and within the degree programs, course requirements are more about organizational skills, logistics, and personnel. A very small proportion is devoted to courses in teaching and learning, with practically no emphasis on the use of data to make instructional decisions. With school reform encompassing the entire district and changing the way classroom instruction is delivered and assessed, it is impossible for building principals and central office staff to oversee and facilitate this new process without additional training. And from this reality, we devised the Stewardship training and implementation process.

The Changing Role of the Building Administrator

To implement the *Instructional Design* process, principals and curriculum staff should reconsider what they do in their respective positions. They can no longer send teachers off to learn about new teaching-learning practices and allow them to implement these new practices if they so choose. The professional development provided to teachers must be directly related to the Action Plan; the enacted reform practices, procedures, and course tools must become a regular part of each teacher's daily routine. Moreover, the principal must be familiar with and supportive of these reforms, providing the facilitation and supervision needed to put them in place.

A few principals in our experience have relied on the central office curriculum person to explain the new processes to teachers, provide them the course tools they need, and observe the new curriculum and instructional practices at work. In this scenario, the principal is virtually disconnected from the reform process. He or she may pop into a meeting, grab a bagel, say a few encouraging words, and then disappear to do the "real work" of being the principal. Later in the year, this same principal performs the official obligatory teacher evaluation but without a single reference to the new instructional reforms. Unless the principal understands the reforms and works to make them an integral part of the system, including them in the evaluation process, the principal sends the message that he/she doesn't understand how the reforms are to play out, nor that the reforms are important.

In the current era of accountability, with NCLB, every principal has been thrust into the foreground of responsibility for making sure each teacher is Highly Qualified—not only on paper but in actual classroom practice—and for making sure that each subgroup of students achieves AYP. Not only are many principals woefully underprepared to assume this level of responsibility, but a disproportionate number of teachers are skeptical that their particular principals are capable of meeting the challenge.

The Stewardship Training

To devise the kinds of training needed by principals and central office administrators, we drew on two of the most widely used sources of principal competencies for the twenty-first century: (a) the Interstate School Leaders License Consortium (ISLLC) standards promulgated by the Council of Chief State School Officers in 2003 and (b) the taxonomy of school reform responsibilities for principals, codeveloped by Doug Reeves and the National Association of Secondary School Principals (NASSP) in 2004. From these seminal criteria and performance checklists, we derived the Stewardship training and authentic implementation activities. They consist of simulations, discussions, and reviews of literature to help accomplish the following:

- Assess one's own leadership style and take steps to move from an authoritative or laissez-faire style to a collaborative facilitator of continuous school improvement.
- Accept the challenge of working in an era of fewer resources but greater accountability; formulate a personal-professional working philosophy of distributed leadership and commitment to the school as a professional learning community; include measures for self-checking and self-correcting.
- Destabilize the school organization and infrastructure to allow for change to occur and be sustained, but not to disrupt the fundamental stability of the building.
- Increase contact with and involvement of parent/guardian and community representatives; formulate a schedule for communicating information to and getting feedback from them (e.g., a school Web site, newsletter, phone calls, committee meetings), particularly about the reform process and how it is unfolding.
- Work with the superintendent to rewrite job descriptions to include roles and responsibilities that are necessary to facilitate, sustain, and continuously monitor the enacted reform initiatives throughout the school (see Superintendent section later in this chapter).
- Evaluate one's own use of time over the past six months; determine the relative proportion of time spent on each major duty area across a week, noting in particular what proportion of time was spent on classroom-related tasks; plan to reapportion the schedule to accomplish job targets dealing with the enacted reforms and spend the majority of time dealing with academic issues.
- Know the fundamental tenets of the *Instructional Design* processes, including the following: (a) *Performance Indicators* as the district's official achievement target; (b) *Curriculum Maps* as the year-long overview or syllabus of each grade-level course (subject); (c) *Unit Plans* that set

forth the delivery and assessment strategies based on the Best Practices research and including alternatives for differentiation; (d) Multifactored Benchmarking of student performance and the continual use of data to plan, adjust, and evaluate classroom instruction.

- Assume a role of authentic involvement with the **Instructional Design** process, including the following: (a) Serve on one or more work teams to devise the *Performance Indicators*, *Curriculum Maps*, and *Unit Plans*; (b) Work as part of the Building Leadership Team to communicate the work in progress to other staff; facilitate the Critical Friends process in circulating drafts; (c) Facilitate and attend grade level (department/subject) team meetings as a participant; (d) Coordinate (but not dominate) Building Leadership Team meetings to review progress of reform initiatives; (e) Collect, analyze, interpret, and communicate student performance data; (f) Use the Collaborative Observation Process (described at the end of this chapter) to assist teachers in their implementation of the reform procedures and course tools; (g) Present at least quarterly progress reports at the Superintendent's cabinet meetings, and coordinate with teachers and students the school's annual report to the Board.

Teachers "Who Just Don't Get It"

Unfortunately, a few teachers do not behave like leaders. We cluster them into three groups: (a) the *nasties* who have earned their reputations by being negative and uncooperative about anything new; (b) the *skeptics* who are those who feel they have "been there, done that" and "this too shall pass"; and (c) the *passive resisters*, those who pretend to go along but are quietly subverting the entire process. Although they are in the minority, these folks must understand that life as they knew it is over, and that the reforms are here to stay. Moreover, the process is never finished; it evolves as the needs of the students change. But the good news is that the majority of teachers *are* "leaders" and are eager to do the right things, if they know what the right things are and receive adequate support to be successful. Indeed, this is the group who feels that the principal needs to address the resisting teachers described above who have not been held accountable in prior reform efforts. In nearly every district, there is an unspoken understanding that principals avoid certain staff, circling around them, while holding others accountable. Effective teachers are weary of this double standard and want their colleagues to be brought to task for their behavior. The important point is that the culture of the school should be defined by the "leaders" and not the others; if these "nonleaders" will not change, they must be removed.

Stewardship in the Use of Data

In addition to the delivery of classroom instruction, the reform-minded principal takes an active role in the interpretation and analysis of student performance data. Helping teachers use these data to make adjustments in their teaching-learning practices based on students' strengths and weaknesses gives the principal a badge of competence that engenders the respect of the most skeptical teachers. By the way, this does not mean using student performance data to threaten, embarrass, or intimidate teachers, such as the insensitive stunt of posting test scores on the hallway bulletin board. Such flagrant misuse of data (thankfully, by only a minority of principals) is an unbelievable abuse of power and one of those "intolerable acts" that diminishes the entire profession.

The Importance of the Superintendent

Although the primary target audiences of the Stewardship activity are the principals and the central office staff, it is the Superintendent who will determine the success or failure of the process. If principals are convinced that they are accountable to attend the training, and legitimately involve themselves in the various development and training activities of the *Instructional Design* process, it will happen. If there is the slightest equivocation or ambiguity on the part of the Superintendent, the entire effort will be compromised. Admittedly, there is considerable angst and much resistance at first. These have not been the customary duties and responsibilities of most principals. And resistant principals are extremely adept at avoidance, forgetfulness, feigning confusion, and misplacing directives. We all know the type who cherish their favorite duties and skillfully use them to keep from having to do the jobs they dislike.

But even the most stubborn traditionalist can be helped to see the light once the training and the actual implementation begin. It is recommended that, at the very least, the Superintendent agree to the following for all building principals and central office staff who deal with curriculum, instruction, assessment, and the management of student performance data:

- Require their participation in the Stewardship training and the completion of all assignments as directed.
- Rewrite each administrative job description to specify duties and responsibilities pursuant to the curricular and instructional reform process; these will include (a) working with designated Building Leadership Teams; (b) the compilation of entry-level and exit Profiles; (c) the development, pilot, and implementation of course tools; (d) the facilitation of and attendance at Grade-Level (or department) meetings to discuss the progress of the reform initiatives; (e) the compilation of student performance data to communicate with parents/guardians; and (f) training, facilitation, and the direct use of the Collaborative Observation process.
- Include in the annual performance review the level of involvement and successful completion of all duties and responsibilities set forth in the job description, focusing particularly on those associated with the curricular and instructional reform process.
- Stewardship of the reform process should be a condition of initial and continued employment for every administrator who deals in any way with curriculum, instruction, assessment, or the management of instructional data. Granted, the old adage about "leading a horse to water" tends to insert itself in the minds of the teachers when they think about their principals being required to take an active role in Instructional Design. But if the Superintendent can be emphatic about the above conditions, it will at least "salt the oats."

COLLABORATIVE OBSERVATION ■

Despite the flurry of school reform activity since 1983, many of the recognized leaders in the movement feel its net effect on student performance has been negligible. Since 1985, we have completed hundreds of observations, and in many of these classrooms, the only way to know whether it is 1975, 1985, 1995, or 2005 is the haircuts and the style of clothing. If change is to occur in schools, it must be one classroom at a time. Early in our work with *Instructional Design*, we realized that some sort of process would be needed to ensure that what happens in classrooms reflects the curricular and instructional reforms embodied in the course tools. If these are to become systemic, teachers must use them on a daily basis and receive feedback about the effect of these efforts with students.

Philosophical Base

When districts have undertaken the *Instructional Design* Process, it is important to have a system to support teachers as they develop and implement new instructional practices in each classroom. Collaborative networks or peer partnerships are the cornerstone of professionalism. Through these partnerships, teachers form a community of learners who openly and constructively provide each other feedback about classroom instruction. They share a common philosophy about the direct connection between teacher behavior and student response. Furthermore, they believe that professional growth occurs from within and is not imposed from without, despite the authority of the negotiated agreement or principal's role as evaluator. To make the point more clearly, Collaborative Observation is purposely distinguished from evaluation. As partners learn to trust each other, there is a greater inclination for each to take growth risks in his or her classroom. Because they share a mutual interest in each other's success, the process is nonthreatening. The strategies they try are collaboratively devised, and they are convinced that the changes will yield positive results for students. There is an atmosphere of encouragement and support for each other as new strategies are attempted to improve the quality of the teaching. Each teacher has areas of strength and needs for growth and is confident that the partner can be a catalyst for positive change. Visiting others' classrooms decreases the isolation typically felt by many teachers. Sometimes in the process, the observer notes a strategy or activity for use in his or her own classroom. *Collaborative Observation* implies a shared responsibility among those involved for the professional welfare of the entire group. Talking about instruction from a nonevaluative perspective inspires teachers to think about what they do and how they might do it differently.

Districts who have participated in the *Instructional Design* process will have already developed peer partnerships during the development of the *Performance Indicators*, the *Curriculum Maps*, and the *Unit Plans*. Through their Critical Friends networks, they will have piloted these course tools. As they continually monitor student performance and use the data to more precisely pinpoint student needs, all staff are invested in determining the effect of their teaching strategies on student achievement.

The Collaborative Observation process works on two levels. One is *conceptual* in that we join *Instructional Design* as the axis of school reform with *Collaborative Observation* as a proven method to leverage and sustain teacher growth and renewal. The second is *structural* in that it is guided by a four-part process through which the conceptual link becomes an operational reality. The four parts of the process are summarized below, including the protocol for each.

♦ **The Preobservation Conference** serves three important purposes. First, rapport and trust are established through a dialogue about instruction. Second, the observer becomes familiar with the lesson and understands what the teacher intends to accomplish. In a larger context, he or she sees how this lesson fits into the total *Unit*. Third, the teacher is provided a rare opportunity to talk about what he or she does in planning instruction, and the mental run-through of the lesson is like a reflection in advance. It bears repeating that the Preobservation Conference is a face-to-face interview between the observer and teacher. The observer records the teacher's responses as he or she talks. The teacher should be familiar with the form, but it should be made clear that there is no need to complete it prior to the Conference. It is the dialogue during the Conference that helps build the rapport and trust of a peer partnership. Figure 9.2 represents the protocol for the Preobservation Conference. The questions included on the form reflect Best Practices advocated in the school reform literature.

♦ **The In-Class Data Collection and Lesson Analyses** are structured formats for collecting key details about the lesson—teacher behaviors and how students responded—in a scripting format. The analysis is an objective connection between the teacher's behavior and its effect on students. Analysis statements describe the actions and are void of "value" words (e.g., excellent way to . . .; I like the discussion technique of . . . ; enthusiastic about . . .). Each analysis statement is carefully placed beside the segment of script to which it refers. The analysis sections are the references to the Best Practices that characterize the **Instructional Design** process. Figure 9.3 shows the protocol for the observation and analysis.

♦ **The Postobservation Conference** is a conversation between the teacher and observer to debrief on the lesson, and a specific form is completed by the observer. Prior to the actual Post Conference, this serves as the planning guide for the conversation. The items listed on this planning form are grounded in the data collected during the Preobservation Conference and the classroom observation and analysis. Figure 9.4 shows the protocol for the Postobservation Conference.

♦ **The Growth Plan** is the culmination of the Postobservation Conference. It is collaboratively developed by the teacher and observer to set forth a target area or two for growth with the strategies to accomplish and the accompanying success criteria. While many growth plans may focus on classroom management, most reflect the curricular and instructional reforms enacted. In the case of **Instructional Design**, they would reflect attention to the *Performance Indicators* and/or the use of the Best Practices to deliver and assess classroom instruction. Figure 9.5 shows the Growth Plan format.

Figure 9.2   The Preobservation Conference Form

The Preobservation Conference

Observer _____

Teacher Observed _____   Conference Date/Time _____

Subject _____   Grade _____   Observation Date/Time _____

PART I: THE UNIT PLAN

1. What is the title of the **UNIT**?   2. How much time do you spend on this **UNIT**?

    _____   _____

3. What *Performance Indicators* are assessed in this **UNIT**? (on the form, several lines are provided)

4. How are these *Performance Indicators* related to content and objectives in other subject areas?

5. How will/did you introduce or MOTIVATE students for the **UNIT**?

6. What CONTENT/CONCEPTS/SKILLS are taught and WITH WHAT METHODS so students can master the *Performance Indicators* for this **UNIT**?

7. How will you ASSESS what students have learned in the **UNIT**?

8. What AUTHENTIC/REAL-LIFE APPLICATIONS will students do to demonstrate ownership/mastery of the *Performance Indicators* for this **UNIT**?

PART II: THE LESSON TO BE OBSERVED

9. Where does the **LESSON** to be observed fit into the total **UNIT**?

10. Which *Performance Indicators* are being specifically addressed in the **LESSON** to be observed?

11. Outline the **LESSON** I will see; give approximate time frames, what you will do, what the students will do, and the type of grouping arrangement you plan to use. (Note: be sure the teacher outlines specific content/skills/concepts to be addressed in the **LESSON**.)

Time	What the Teacher Will Do	What Students Will Do	Grouping/Setting
	(etc.)		

12.   What specific areas of the **LESSON** do you want me to observe?

Figure 9.3   A Sample Script and Lesson Analysis

Lesson Description			Lesson Analysis	
Time	Teacher Behavior	Student Behavior/Response	Strengths	Concerns/Questions
8:05	Aztecs—American Indian Race Reviewed words from Nawatal that are still used today		Relating Aztec vocabulary to modern language provides real-life context for students	
	City Life: City named Tan_; built on Lake __ How many people did Cortez have? Close, 600	Students give correct response as a group Chris: 500!		Level of question prompted recall type of response; did not ask students to do critical thinking
	Religion Prisoners Sacrifice: What if they sacrificed and they had an eclipse? Then came the plumed serpent… Why did Montezuma fear him? What else? Was he driving a Chevrolet?	Chris: they didn't sacrifice enough Pete: Quetaequala(SP); fair skinned (laughter); riding a horse (several say)	Level of question prompted student to extend knowledge Use of humor gets students' attention	
8:13	T showed article from magazine; held up pictures for class to see Pyramids What is outstanding about their pyramids? Asked: How big were the pyramids? They were 20 stories.	John: they had no machines to move the rocks No response		T did not build on higher order student response; did not elaborate or extend with another question; this may send the message that factual responses are what is sought
8:20	They had schools; outstanding s's became priests; average students were in houses of youth; most of us are average, a few would be priests.			What message may be conveyed to students about their ability with this statement?

Figure 9.4   The Postobservation Conference Format

PLANNING THE POSTOBSERVATION CONFERENCE

1. **Positive points to be reinforced:** (be sure to write as teacher behavior/impact on students with documentation in the script).

2. **Questions or concerns to be addressed:** (be sure to write as teacher behavior/impact on students with documentation in the script).

3. **Areas from the Preobservation Conference** needing <u>clarification</u>, including <u>feedback</u> on areas-teacher asked you to observe.

4. **Outcomes for the Conference;** when the process is completed, what behaviors would you like to see incorporated into the Action Plan as behaviors to add or delete from one's teaching repertoire?

5. **Alternatives:** what other activities, strategies, or techniques might also be effective for teaching a lesson such as this? (Often, a teacher will ask an observer about other ways to accomplish the task; it is good to have thought about this in advance of the conference.)

Figure 9.5   Sample Growth Plan

Area of Focus	Specific Strategies (begin with a verb)	Criteria for Success	Time Frame	Role of Support Staff
Higher level questions	1. Classify test and quiz questions as to level of difficulty: Level 1: factual recall or memory; Level 2: inferential or implied level; Level 3: divergent or hypothetical; have students think of higher-order applications and what-if 2. Devise at least 5 level 2 questions and 2 level 3 questions for each class discussion; write them in advance; begin a file to encourage repeated use, etc.	1. students value high-level questions and see a reason to listen to each other's responses 2. students learn to extend each other's responses and connect them to each other	Next *Unit*	Ms. ___ will work with me to develop higher-level questions for the next *Unit;* after that, I will develop the questions on my own and share them with Ms. ___ for feedback. I will observe Mr. ___ teaching to note how he uses higher-level questions in his class discussions.

Note: Each of these four steps and the components of each protocol are fully documented in the research literature available from the authors upon request.

What Makes the Collaborative Process Work?

By asking appropriately structured questions, the partners enable each other to reflect about their teaching behaviors and how students responded. Partners verbalize and rephrase what happened in a descriptive, not prescriptive way and make interpretations, not evaluative judgments. When the outcomes of the lesson match or exceed the intents, the process enables the partners to identify how specific activities or strategies had such a positive effect on students and how they can be repeated for a similar effect. When the effect on students is not what was intended, the process provides for the joint analysis of what occurred. There are times when even though an activity did not work as designed, the result achieved the desired purpose. When the result is disappointing, both teachers become action researchers, as they hypothesize why this might have happened, propose a corrective course of action with specific strategies, and determine the impact on students. The net effect is that every teacher can grow and become more proficient, and weaker practices can be made stronger or replaced through instructional discussions.

Through reflective dialogue, successful practices are reinforced or enhanced and inspire the confidence to broaden one's professional repertoire. The development of a Plan is not only for the struggling teacher. Growth Plans benefit all teachers to expand their skills from the strugglers, to the mediocre teachers who have not grown much lately, to the master teacher who is always looking for ways to improve his or her performance.

Using Collaborative Observation to Monitor *Instructional Design*

With the installation of specific reform tools and procedures, the classroom becomes the focus for the reform. Using a *Collaborative Observation* process gives districts the means to continually monitor these reform initiatives while nurturing a culture of collegial growth. For education to be authentically reformed, one of the core values that must be significantly recast is the onus of responsibility for success. In the past, the primary responsibility for this ambiguous "value" seemed to fall within the principal's job description. More recent research clearly supports that the accountability for school outcomes must be shared by the entire staff. Since the responsibility for implementation of instructional reforms lies with the classroom teacher, the major accountability for monitoring the reform rests there as well. Our experience has shown that teachers who participate in *Collaborative Observation* and sincerely follow the Growth Plans developed with their partners are better prepared for formal observations related to contract status. In our opinion, the *Collaborative Observation* process is the ideal tool for helping teachers assume their shared accountability and responsibility for improving classroom instruction. Each teacher wants to know "how I am doing" with a new technique, and each of us needs encouragement to continue trying when our efforts fall short.

A Structured Program: But Not Evaluation

It cannot be overstated that *Collaborative Observation* is nonevaluative. All observations are kept separate from the evaluation process.

The principal is part of the *Collaborative Observation* the team, and when the principal participates in *Collaborative Observation*, the observations done are kept separate from the formal evaluation process.

SUMMARY ■

If the reforms that a staff has worked so hard to accomplish are to survive and yield significant and lasting gains in student performance, the changes must become fully integrated into each school's deep culture. They must become the way business is done there every day. To make this a reality, the administrative and teaching staff must begin developing the capacity to sustain their reforms from the very outset of the project. This includes the continual use of data to provide more effective classroom instruction and to inform the district's strategic planning, the development and support of teacher-leaders to help implement the reforms throughout the building, the direct involvement and accountability of each district administrator in the reform process, and the use of Collaborative Observation to help teachers and administrators work as partners in the implementation of the specific course tools and processes in each classroom. Figure 9.6 represents these capacity-building elements for accomplishing the goal of improved student achievement.

Figure 9.6   Capacity-Building at a Glance

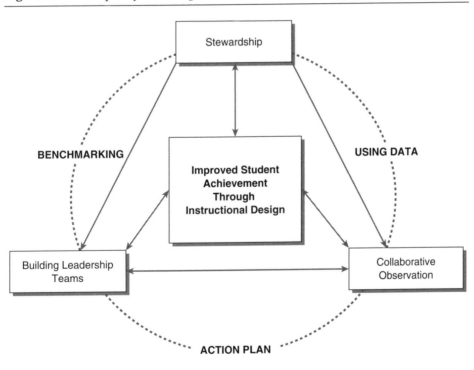

Appendix A

Ohio Summary of Results

Thirteen of the districts who have implemented the Instructional Design Process are from Ohio (5 rural, 5 suburban, and 3 urban). Over three to five years, their students have experienced academic success, as shown in the following tables. The sources of these data were the Ohio Achievement Tests and Proficiency Tests taken from Ohio's District Report Card each year of a district's involvement through 2004–05. The Math and Reading charts below show the average "start" percentage of students passing a test and the "end" percentage of students passing a test for each type of district.

AVERAGE GROWTH MADE

District Type and Number of Districts	Grade 4 Percentage Passing		Change	Grade 6 Percentage Passing		Change	Grade 9 Percentage Passing		Change
MATH	Start	End		Start	End		Start	End	
RURAL (5)	50.2	77.6	+27.4	70.6	65.4	−5.2	83.6	93.8	+10.2
SUBURBAN (5)	63.6	72.5	+8.9	69.8	67.4	−2.4	80.2	84.8	+4.6
URBAN (3)	31.5	42.7	+11.2	42.5	43.3	+0.8	44.3	60.7	+16.4
TOTAL COMBINED	**56.3**	**67.6**	**+11.3**	**63.8**	**61.1**	**−2.7**	**67.1**	**75.8**	**+8.7**

District Type and Number of Districts	Grade 4 Percentage Passing		Change	Grade 6 Percentage Passing		Change	Grade 9 Percentage Passing		Change
READING	Start	End		Start	End		Start	End	
RURAL (5)	63.0	84.4	+21.4	74.0	77.2	+3.2	97.5	98.6	+1.1
SUBURBAN (5)	53.4	76.7	+23.3	69.2	72.0	+2.8	95.2	95.5	+0.2
URBAN (3)	41.9	53.9	+12.0	35.1	48.1	+13	71.7	83.2	+11.5
TOTAL COMBINED	**59.5**	**74.4**	**+14.9**	**64.7**	**68.5**	**+3.8**	**83.4**	**86.5**	**+3.1**

Rural Districts showed an increase on 22 of 30 tests (73%) and a decrease on 8 of 30 (27%).

Suburban Districts showed an increase on 18 of 28 tests (64%) and a decrease on 10 of 28 (36%).

Urban Districts showed an increase on 16 of 18 tests (89%) and a decrease on 2 of 18 (11%).

Combined, the 13 districts showed an increase in the number of students passing on 56 of the 76 tests (74%) and a decrease on 20 of the 76 (26%).

In addition to the above grade-level data, cohort comparisons were also made. In the 13 districts, it was possible to follow cohorts of students across 2, 3, and 4 years of test results. In Math, there were 76 such cohorts, and in Reading, 102. The following tables reflect the changes in the percentage of students passing in these cohorts during the project year.

COHORT RESULTS FOR MATHEMATICS (Change in the percentage of students passing in a cohort)			
Change in scores ⇓	RURAL (20 cohorts)	SUBURBAN (34 cohorts)	URBAN (22 cohorts)
INCREASED	65%	70%	82%
REMAINED CONSTANT (Within 2 Percentage Points)	15%	15%	—
DECREASED	20%	15%	18%

COHORT RESULTS FOR READING (Change in the percentage of students passing in a cohort)			
Change in scores ⇓	RURAL (30 cohorts)	SUBURBAN (44 cohorts)	URBAN (28 cohorts)
INCREASED	73%	68%	88%
REMAINED CONSTANT (Within 2 Percentage Points)	10%	14%	<3%
DECREASED	17%	18%	11%

In both Math and Reading, the percentage of increase for urban schools is proportionately higher than the other two populations, but consideration must be given to the fact that a much lower percentage of urban students were passing both tests at the outset.

One district in New Jersey is in its 5th year of the Process. The data in the following table were taken from the state reports based on the grade-level tests administered. The following table shows these results.

New Jersey Test Results: Percentage of Students Passing

TEST	SUBJECT	PRIOR TO PROJECT OR FIRST TEST POINT	END OF 2005–06 SCHOOL YEAR	GROWTH IN % PASSING
Grade 3 NJ ASK	Math 2001–02	56.3%	83.3%	+27
	Language Arts 2001–02	66.9%	81.6%	+14.7
Grade 4 NJ ASK	Math 2004–05	74.4%	78.3%	+3.9
	Language Arts 2004–05	76.1%	76.3%	+.2
Grade 5 NJ ASK	Math	First Test Point Was 2005–06	79.6%	NA
	Language Arts	First Test Point Was 2005–06	84%	NA
Grade 6 NJ ASK	Math	First Test Point Was 2005–06	68.1%	NA
	Language Arts	First Test Point Was 2005–06	69.5%	NA
Grade 7 NJ ASK	Math	First Test Point Was 2005–06	67.1%	NA
	Language Arts	First Test Point Was 2005–06	80.8%	NA
Grade 8 GEPA	Math 2003–04	49.4%	64.6%	+15.2
	Language Arts 2003–04	63.5%	72%	+8.5

Scores improved in all six test points where there were baseline data and end-of-third-year data. The range of growth was from less than 1% increase in students passing to 27% increase in the number of students passing a given test. The mean growth was 6.95 percentage points.

Appendix B

River Bend
Local Schools

MATH PERFORMANCE OUTCOMES for 2004–2005

Performance Outcomes: A "T" Means Mastery at That Grade Level	Pre-K	K	1	2	3	4	5	6	7	Pre-Alg	Alg I	Comprehensive Math I	Comprehensive Math II	Geo	Hon Geo	Alg II	Hon Alg II	Pre-Calc	Hon Pre-calc	Calc	AP Calc
I. Number/Number Sense and Operations																					
A. Number/Number Systems																					
28. Recognize and classify numbers as even or odd (e.g., divide a set of objects into 2 sets; are there leftovers – odd and same size sets – even) [NS.2.1.2; NS Benchmarks: B; Math Processes: A, F]				✓																	
29. Use the mathematical language and symbols < (less than), > (more than), = (equal to), ≤ (less than or equal to, at most), ≥ (greater than or equal to, at least) to compare numbers and sets of data in problem situations [NS.3.1.3; NS Benchmarks: A; Math Processes: J]					✓																
[money] 30. Identify a penny, nickel, dime, and quarter and recognize that coins have different values (e.g., match coins to pictures) [NS.PK.1.12]	✓																				
31. Verbally identify a penny, nickel, and dime; state the value of each coin [NS.K.1.9; NS Benchmarks: D; Math Processes: A, B]		✓																			

Performance Outcomes: A "T" Means Mastery at That Grade Level	Pre-K	K	1	2	3	4	5	6	7	Pre-Alg	Alg I	Comprehensive Math I	Comprehensive Math II	Geo	Hon Geo	Alg II	Hon Alg II	Pre-Calc	Hon Pre-calc	Calc	AP Cal
37. Write, represent, compare (< and >), and order whole numbers between 1 and 999 in multiple ways using place value concepts (i.e., 10 can mean 10 ones or a single entry of 1 ten); write up to 3-digit numbers in expanded form (i.e., 243 = 2 hundreds, 4 tens, and 3 ones, or 24 tens and 3 ones, or 2 hundreds and 43 ones) [NS.2.1.1; NS Benchmarks: A; Math Processes: F]				✓																	
II. MEASUREMENT																					
B. Measurement Techniques/Tools																					
13. Estimate and confirm the weight of given objects using nonstandard units [M.1.2.4; M.1.2.1; M Benchmarks: A, C; Math Processes: D]			✓																		
14. Choose appropriate nonstandard and standard units to estimate and weigh various objects (both metric and U.S. Customary grams/ounces and pounds) [M.2.2.1; M.2.2.3; M.2.2.5; M Benchmarks: A, B, C, D, E; Math Processes: C, D]				✓																	
15. Identify and select appropriate unit of measurement to determine weight in both U.S. Customary and Metric systems; measure weight to the nearest ¼ and ½ unit [M.3.2.1; M.3.2.5; M Benchmarks: A, C, D; Math Processes: F, G]					✓																

Appendix C

Various Methods to Determine Mastery of *Performance Indicators*

Note: A performance assessment may not necessarily be the most appropriate method to measure a *Performance Indicator*; we have included one with each sample indicator just to illustrate the possibilities.

Explanatory Key

(a) Sample Performance Indicators	(b) Teacher Observation	(c) Paper-Pencil Test	(d) Student Logs / Journals	(e) Performance Assessment and Scoring Rubrics
Sample indicators (*PIs*) are offered to help illustrate the assessment method. For each indicator, a code is included that identifies it by subject and grade level.	For some *PIs*, the teacher's observation is *one* of and/or at times the *best* method to determine mastery.	Although the most familiar, the "test" is not always the most valid way to assess mastery.	Not a new concept, but using it to record products for mastery may be; the key is to prespecify mastery criteria.	Holistic or authentic tasks that require students to demonstrate independent mastery of one or more *PIs* to successfully complete; the scoring rubric uses criteria from the *PIs* themselves.

Methods to Determine Mastery

(a) Sample Performance Indicators	(b) Teacher Observation	(c) Paper-Pencil Test, Student Logs	(d) Student Logs or Journals	(e) *Performance Assessment and Scoring Rubrics (criteria ✓ derived from the Performance Indicators)
Identify own name in print, name the letters in first name, and name several other upper and lower case letters in the context of posters and the collages made by peers (PreK LA).	Ask each child.			Collage of words that identifies the selected letters ✓ includes own name ✓ uses words with letters (letter reversals are acceptable at this level)
Contrast how families lived in the past with the present; use given photographs, letters, books, and artifacts to identify clues from the past about school, clothing, earning a living, housing, transportation, and communication; use a Venn Diagram or T-chart to compare then with now (Grade 1 Social Studies).	Observe each child examining the materials.		Venn Diagram or T-chart that compares the 2 time periods.	Pull one or more artifacts from the past out of a hat; give a Brief Talk re: how each was used then, and compare how they are used today; include ✓ description/explanation ✓ context in daily life ✓ comparison to modern counterpart

(Continued)

(a) Sample Performance Indicators	(b) Teacher Observation	(c) Paper-Pencil Test, Student Logs	(d) Student Logs or Journals	(e) *Performance Assessment and Scoring Rubrics (criteria ✓ derived from the Performance Indicators)
Compare and contrast the different activities (e.g., food-getting, skin cover, movement, reproduction of Ohio's common animals during the four seasons), and create a four-column table to display your findings. (Grade 2 Science)	Observe students completing laboratory experiments.	Multiple-Choice and Extended Response (brief essays)	Lab Write-Ups	Poster featuring the table; must include ✓ food-getting ✓ body covering ✓ movement etc.
Count money and make change for single and multiple purchases using coins and bills to ten dollars; make purchases at class department store or restaurant, and draw pictures to represent the money in the transactions, including the change involved. Grade 3 Math	Observe each child handling money.	Multiple-Choice and Short Answer	drawings in Math Log	Make purchases in a School Store with play money; then— ✓ prepare a receipt of items purchased ✓ indicate total spent ✓ show change, if any
Distinguish between earth's renewable and nonrenewable resources; explain that nonrenewable resources (e.g., coal, oil, minerals) are limited but can be extended (though not indefinitely) by reducing, reusing, and recycling; prepare a conservation pamphlet to distribute in the community. (Grade 5 Science)		M-C; Short Answer; and Extended Response (brief essays)	annotated drawings	Conservation Pamphlet; includes ✓ introduction ✓ definition, examples of renewable ✓ ... nonrenewable ✓ distinction between . . . ✓ ideas for reducing, reusing, recycling
Analyze a variety of real-life problems involving rational numbers (i.e., percentages, whole numbers with exponents, and decimals), some of which contain problem-solving errors; use the algebraic order of operations, including parentheses; make			sample problems accompanied by flow chart of procedures	Explanation of the work done for each problem ✓ number each step ✓ identify each step, including procedure and numbers used in problems with errors

(a) Sample Performance Indicators	(b) Teacher Observation	(c) Paper-Pencil Test, Student Logs	(d) Student Logs or Journals	(e) * Performance Assessment and Scoring Rubrics (criteria ✓ derived from the Performance Indicators)
an estimation as to whether the answer provided is logical, and verify the work with a calculator; for the problems with errors, provide a written explanation of the errors made and what should have been done; for the problems without errors, explain the process followed. (Grade 7 Math)				✓ indicate the error ✓ determine how it might have occurred ✓ rework to show correction ✓ write an explanation to the person about the work
Analyze characteristics of traditional, market, command, and mixed economies with regard to private property, freedom of enterprise, competition and consumer choice, and the role of government; include specific countries to illustrate; prepare a brief lesson to teach younger students. (Grade 9 Social Studies)		M-C for definitions and examples		Lesson Plan must include . . . ✓ definitions of . . . ✓ comparisons among . . ✓ the role of government ✓ countries who . . . . etc.
Write a persuasive composition about a contemporary issue that (a) articulates a clear position, (b) uses rhetorical devices and viable persuasive techniques to convince the reader, (c) supports the position with valid evidence and/or data from at least two external sources, and (d) objectively acknowledges the counterargument(s); observe the Prewriting requirements and Writing Conventions set forth in the district Writing Rubric; prepare as a "talking head" segment on CNN or Fox News. (Grade 11 Language Arts)	Brainstorm about the issue and narrow focus. Meet one-on-one to approve work plan and sources of support.		written Prewrites first drafts and edits successive revisions	Final Script for the "Talking Head" ✓ articulates a clear position ✓ uses the conventions of persuasion ✓ uses effective rhetorical devices ✓ uses valid evidence to support ✓ acknowledges counter-argument ✓ uses Writing Process and Mechanics as per district checklist etc.

Selected References

Adler, M., E. Rougle, et al. (2004). "Closing the gap between concept and practice: Toward a more dialogic discussion in the language arts classroom." *Journal of Adolescent & Adult Literacy, 47*(4), 312-322.

Ainsworth, L. (2003). *Power standards: Identifying the standards that matter the most.* Denver, CO: Advanced Learning Centers.

Airasian, P. (2000). *Assessment in the classroom: A concise approach 2nd ed.* Boston, MA: McGraw-Hill Higher Education.

Allen, L. (2004). "From votes to dialogues: Clarifying the role of teachers' voices in school renewal." *Phi Delta Kappan, 86*(4), 318-321.

Ancess, J. (2004). "Snapshots of meaning-making classrooms." *Educational Leadership, 62*(1), 36-40.

Anderson, R. (1995). "Curriculum reform: Dilemmas and promise." *Phi Delta Kappan, 77*(1), 33-36.

Applebee, A., J. Langer, et al. (2003). "Discussion-based approaches to developing and understanding: Classroom instruction and student performance in middle and high school English." *American Educational Research Journal, 40*(3), 685-730.

Areglado, R. (2005). "Perspectives on the principalship." *Principal, 84*(5), 40.

Atherton, J. S. (2003). *Learning and teaching: Advance organizers.* Online. UK. Retrieved June 2004 from http://146.227.1.20/~jamesa//teaching/adavance_organisers: htm

Audette, A. (2004). "Lesson study: Teachers learning together." *New England Reading Association Journal, 40*(2), 31-34.

Ausubel, D. P. (1960). The use of advance organizers in the learning and retention of meaningful verbal material. *Journal of Educational Psychology, 51,* 267-272.

Ausubel, D. (1968). *Educational psychology: A cognitive view.* New York: Holt, Rinehart & Winston.

Baker, W., M. Lang, et al. (2002). "Classroom management for successful student inquiry." *Clearing House, 75*(5), 248-252.

Barber, M., & M. Fullan (2005). "Tri-level development: Putting systems thinking into action." *Education Week, 24*(25), 32-34.

Baxendell, B. (2003). "Consistent, coherent, creative: The 3 C's of graphic organizers." *Teaching Exceptional Children, 35*(3), 46-53.

Beers, K. (2003). *When kids can't read: What teachers can do.* Portsmouth, NH: Heinemann.

Bell, L. I. (2003). "Strategies that close the gap." *Educational Leadership, 60*(4), 32-34.

Bell, R., L. Smetana, et al. (2005). "Simplifying inquiry instruction." *The Science Teacher, 72*(7), 30-33.

Bernauer, J. (2002). "Five keys to unlock continuous school improvement." *Kappa Delta Pi Record, 38*(2), 89-92.

Bernhardt, V. (2002). *The school portfolio toolkit: A planning, implementation, and evaluation guide for continuous school improvement.* Larchmont, NY: Eye On Education.

Berry, B., D. Johnson, et al. (2005). "The power of teacher leadership." *Educational Leadership, 62*(5), 56-60.

Blachowicz, C., & P. Fisher (2002). *Teaching vocabulary in all classrooms 2nd ed.* Upper Saddle River, NJ: Merrill Prentice Hall.

Black, P., & D. William (1998). "Inside the black box: Raising standards through classroom assessment." *Phi Delta Kappan, 80*(2), 139-148.

Bloom, B., J. T. Hartings, et al. (1971). *Handbook on formative and summative evaluation of student learning.* New York: McGraw-Hill.

Bloom, B. S. (1956). *Taxonomy of educational objectives: The classification of educational goals: Handbook 1: Cognitive domain.* New York: David Company, Inc.

Boardman Moen, C. (May, 2005). "Literature circles revisited: Learning from experience." *Book Links:* 52-53.

Bonstingl, J. J. (1992). *Schools of quality.* Alexandria, VA: Association for Supervision and Curriculum Development.

Box, J., & D. Little (2003). "Cooperative small-group instruction combined with advance organizers and their relationship to self-concept and social studies achievement of elementary students." *Journal of Instructional Psychology, 30*(4), 285-287.

Brandt, R. (2003). "Will the real standards-based education please stand up?" *Leadership, 32*(3), 16-20.

Brooks, J. G. (2002). *Schooling for life: Reclaiming the essence of learning.* Alexandria, VA: Association for Supervision and Curriculum Development.

Brooks, J. G. (2004). "To see beyond the lesson: Why we must make meaning making the core of teaching." *Educational Leadership, 62*(1), 8-13.

Brooks, J. G., & M. G. Brooks (1993/1999). *In search of understanding: The case for constructivist classrooms.* Alexandria, VA: Association for Supervision and Curriculum Development.

Broward County Public Schools (August, 2003). "District benchmark assessment 2003–2004: Introduction to district benchmark assessments." *Broward County Public Schools Research, Evaluation, Assessment, and Boundaries.*

Bruner, J. (1966). *Toward a theory of instruction.* Cambridge, MA: Harvard University Press.

Bruner, J. (1973). *Going beyond the information given.* New York: Norton.

Bryant, D., & M. Driscoll (1998). *Exploring classroom assessment in mathematics.* Alexandria, VA: Association for Supervision and Curriculum Development, with National Council of Teachers of Mathematics.

Buckley, G., N. Bain, et al. (2004). "Adding an 'active learning' component to a large lecture course." *Journal of Geography, 103*(6), 231-237.

Caine, G., & R. Caine (1991). *Making connections: Teaching and the human brain.* Alexandria, VA: Association for Supervision and Curriculum Development.

Carey, K. (2004). "The real value of teachers: Using new information about teacher effectiveness to close the achievement gap." *Thinking K-16, 8*(1), 3-42.

Carpenter, T., E. Fennema, et al. (1999). *Children's mathematics: Cognitively guided instruction.* Portsmouth, NH: Heinemann.

Cetron, M., & K. Cetron (2003/2004). "A forecast for schools." *Educational Leadership: 61*(4), 22-29.

Chappuis, J. (2005). "Helping students understand assessment." *Educational Leadership, 63*(3), 39-43.

Chappuis, S., R. J. Stiggins, et al. (2004). *Assessment for learning: An action guide for school leaders.* Portland, OR: Assessment Training Institute.

Chen, P., & D. McGrath (2004/2005). "Visualize, visualize, visualize: designing projects for higher-order thinking." *Learning & Leading With Technology, 32*(4), 54-57.

Chrisman, V. (2005). "How schools sustain success." *Educational Leadership, 62*(5), 16-20.

Collins, J. (2001). *Good to great.* New York: Harper Collins.

Cooper, S. (2003). "Some lecturing dos and don'ts." *The Journal of Continuing Education in Nursing, 34*(3), 99-100.

Costa, A. (1985). *Developing minds: A resource book for teaching thinking.* Alexandria, VA:x Association for Supervision and Curriculum Development.

Costa, A., & B. Kallick (2004). "Launching self-directed learners." *Educational Leadership, 62*(1), 51-55.

Daniels, H., & M. Bizar (2005). *Teaching the best practice way: Methods that matter.* Portland, ME: Stenhouse.

Danielson, C. (1996). *Enhancing professional practice: A framework for teaching.* Alexandria, VA: Association for Supervision and Curriculum Development.

Danielson, C. (2002). *Enhancing student achievement: A framework for school improvement.* Alexandria, VA: Association for Supervision and Curriculum Development.

Darling-Hammond, L. (2000). "Teaching quality and student achievement: A review of state policy evidence." Center for the Study of Teaching and Policy, University of Washington.

Davis, B. (1997). "Listening for differences: An evolving concept of mathematics teaching." *Journal for Research in Mathematics Education, 28*(3), 355-376.

Dewey, J. (1933). *How we think: A restatement of the relation of reflective thinking to the educative process.* Boston, MA: Henry Holt.

Drury, D., & H. Doran (2003). "The value of value-added analysis." *Policy Research Brief: Examining Key Education Issues, 3*(1), 1-4, National School Boards Association.

DuFour, R. (2003). "Central office support for learning communities." *School Administrator, 60*(5), 16-17.

DuFour, R. (2004). "What is a professional learning community?" *Educational Leadership, 61*(8), 6-11.

Dunn, R., & S. Griggs (1988). *Learning styles: Quiet revolution in American secondary schools.* Reston, VA: National Association of Secondary School Principals.

Eisner, E. (2004). "Preparing for today and tomorrow." *Educational Leadership, 61*(4), 6-10.

Elmore, R. (2003). "A plea for strong practice." *Educational Leadership, 61*(3), 6-10.

Falk, B. (2002). "Standards-based reforms: Problems and possibilities." *Phi Delta Kappan, 83*(8), 612-620.

Findley, N. (2002). "In their own ways." *Educational Leadership, 60*(1), 60-63.

Fiore, D. (2004). *Introduction to educational administration: Standards, theories, and practice.* Eye On Education.

Fleming, M., & B. Chambers (1983). Teacher-made tests: Windows on the classroom. *Testing in the schools: New directions for testing and measurement.* W. E. Hathaway. San Francisco, CA: Jossey-Bass. *19*: 29-38.

Foote, C., P. Vermette, et al. (2001). *Constructivist strategies: Meeting standards and engaging adolescent minds.* Eye On Education.

Fullan, M. (2002a). "Moral purpose writ large." *School Administrator, 59*(8), 14-16.

Fullan, M. (2002b). "Leadership and sustainability." *Principal Leadership, 3*(4), 14-17.

Fullan, M., A. Bertani, et al. (2004). "New lessons for districtwide reform." *Educational Leadership, 61*(7), 42-46.

Fulton, K. P. (2003). "Redesigning schools to meet 21st century learning needs." *T.H.E Journal, 30*(9), 30-32, 34, 36.

Gardner, H. (1983). *Frames of mind: The theory of multiple intelligences.* Basic Books: Harper-Collins.

Greenleaf, C., R. Schoenbach, et al. (2001). "Apprenticing adolescent readers to academic literacy." *Harvard Educational Review, 71*(7), 79-129.

Gregorc, A. (1984). *Gregorc Style Delineator: Developmental Technical and Administration Manual.* Columbia, CT: Gregorc Associates, Inc.

Grove, K. (2002). "The invisible role of the central office." *Educational Leadership, 59*(8), 45-47.

Harvey, S., & A. Goudvis (2002). *Strategies that work: Teaching comprehension to enhance understanding.* York: Stenhouse.

Hawbaker, B., M. Balong, et al. (2001). "Building a strong BASE of support for all students through coplanning." *The Council for Exceptional Children, 33*(4), 24-30.

Herman, J. L., & E. L. Baker (2005). "Making benchmark testing work." *Educational Leadership, 63*(3), 48-55.

Hershberg, T., V. Adams Simon, et al. (2004). "The revelations of value-added: An assessment model that measures student growth in ways that NCLB fails to do." *School Administrator, 61*(11), 10-14.

Hess, F. M. (2003). "The case for being mean." *Educational Leadership, 61*(3), 22-26.

Hiebert, J., R. Gallimore, et al. (2003). "The new heroes of teaching." *Education Week, 23*(10), 42, 56.

Hirsh, S. (2001). "We're growing and changing." *Journal of Staff Development, 22*(3), 10-17.

Hurley, V., R. Greenblatt, et al. (2003). "Learning conversations: Transforming supervision." *Principal Leadership (middle-school ed.) 3*(9), 31-36.

Hyerle, D. (1996). *Visual tools for constructing knowledge.* Alexandria, VA: Association for Supervision and Curriculum Development.

Interstate School Leaders License Consortium. (2003). "Standards for school leaders." Washington, DC: *Council of Chief State School Officers.*

Irvin, L., & D. White (2004). "Keys to effective leadership." *Principal Leadership (high school ed.), 4*(6), 20-24.

Jacobs, H. H. (1989). *Interdisciplinary curriculum: Design and implementation.* Alexandria, VA: Association for Supervision and Curriculum Development.

Jacobs, H. H. (1997). *Mapping the big picture.* Alexandria, VA: Association for Supervision and Curriculum Development.

Jacobs, H. H. (2000). "Upgrading the K-12 journey through curriculum mapping." *Knowledge Quest, 29*(2), 25-29.

Jacobs, H. H. (2001). "New trends in curriculum: An interview with Heidi Hayes Jacobs." *NAIS Independent School Magazine: Curriculum Conundrum,* 18-22.

Jacobs, H. H. (2004). *Getting results with curriculum mapping.* Alexandria, VA: Association for Supervision and Curriculum Development.

Jacobson, L. (March 2, 2005). "Book spells out 'core curriculum' for teacher training." *Education Week, 24*(25), 10.

Jenkins, J., M. Stein, et al. (1984). "Learning vocabulary through reading." *American Educational Research Journal 21:* 767-787.

Jennings, J. (August 17, 2003). "Keeping score: Tests are vital but will not fix education alone." *Chattanooga Times.*

Jerald, C. (2003). "Beyond the rock and the hard place." *Educational Leadership, 61*(3), 12-16.

Joyce, B., & B. Showers (2002). *Student achievement through staff development.* Alexandria, VA: Association for Supervision and Curriculum Development.

Kane, M., & N. Khattri (1995). "Assessment reform: A work in progress." *Phi Delta Kappan, 77*(1), 30-32.

Kennedy Manzo, K. (January 12, 2005). "NRC publishes follow-up on student learning." *Education Week, 24*(18), 11. [Ms. Manzo cites comments made by Suzanne Donovan and John Bransford of the National Research Council].

Kilpatrick, J., W. G. Martin, et al., Eds. (2003). *A research companion to principles and standards for school mathematics.* Reston, VA: The National Council of Teachers of Mathematics.

Kim, A.-H., S. Vaughn, et al. (2004). "Graphic organizers and their effects on the reading comprehension of students with LD: A synthesis of research." *Journal of Learning Disabilities, 37*(2), 105-118.

Kolb, D. A., & R. Fry (1975). "Toward an applied theory of experiential learning." *Theories of Group Process.* C. Cooper (ed). London: John Wiley Publishing.

Koppang, A. (2004). "Curriculum mapping: Building collaboration and communication." *Intervention in School and Clinic, 39*(3), 154-161.

LaBeau, B., & P. Morehead (2004). "Successful curriculum mapping: Fostering smooth technology integration." *Learning & Leading With Technology, 32*(4), 12–17.

Leahy, S., C. Lyon, et al. (2005). "Classroom assessment: Minute by minute, day by day." *Educational Leadership, 63*(3), 19-24.

Lewin, K., Ed. (1951). *Field theory in social science.* New York: Harper & Row.

Liben, D., & M. Liben (2005). "Learning to read in order to learn." *Phi Delta Kappan, 86*(5), 401-406.

Lin, C.-H. (2004). "Literature circles." *Teacher Librarian, 31*(3), 23-25.

Love, N. (2002). *Using data to get results: A practical guide for school improvement in mathematics and science.* Christopher-Gordon.

Manouchehri, A., & D. Lapp (2003). "Unveiling student understanding: The role of questioning in instruction." *Mathematics Teacher, 96*(8), 562-566.

Manthey, G. (2003). "Answering the question: Are we there yet?" *Leadership, 32*(3), 11.

Marzano, R. (2002). "Standardized curriculum." *Principal, 81*(3), 6-9.

Marzano, R. (2003a). *What works in schools: Translating research into action.* Alexandria, VA: Association for Supervision and Curriculum Development.

Marzano, R. (2003b). "Using data: Two wrongs and a right." *Educational Leadership, 60*(5), 56-60.

Marzano, R. (September 13, 2004). "Why is there a need for these standards?" from *Windows* on ASCD Website.

Marzano, R., & J. Marzano (2003). "The key to classroom management." *Educational Leadership, 61*(1), 6-12.

Marzano, R., D. Pickering, et al. (2001). *Classroom instruction that works: Research-based strategies for increasing student achievement.* Alexandria, VA: Association for Supervision and Curriculum Development.

Massialas, B., & B. Cox (1966). *Inquiry in social studies.* New York: McGraw-Hill.

McCarthy, B. (1990). "Using the 4MAT system to bring learning styles to schools." *Educational Leadership, 48*(2), 31-37.

McDonald, J. P. (1999). "Redesigning curriculum: New conceptions and tools." *Peabody Journal of Education, 74*(1), 12-28.

McNameed, G., & J. -Q. Chen (2005). "Dissolving the line between assessment and teaching." *Educational Leadership, 63*(3), 72-77.

McTighe, J., & K. O'Connor (2005). "Seven practices for effective learning." *Educational Leadership, 63*(3), 10-17.

McTighe, J., E. Seif, et al. (2004). "You can teach for meaning." *Educational Leadership, 62*(1), 26-30.

McTighe, J., & R. S. Thomas (2003). "Backward design for forward action." *Educational Leadership, 60*(5), 52-55.

Memory, D., C. Yoder, et al. (2004). "Creating thinking and inquiry tasks that reflect the concerns and interests of adolescents." *The Social Studies, 95*(4), 147-154.

Miller, A. (2001). "Finding time and support for instructional leadership." *Principal Leadership (high school ed.), 2*(4), 29-33.

Mills, M. (2001). Ensuring the viability of curriculum mapping in a school improvement plan. ERIC document #ED 460 141.

Mizell, M. H. (2003). "Facilitator: 10, refreshments: 8, evaluation: 0." *Journal of Staff Development, 24*(4), 10-13.

Mizell, M. H. (2004). "From muck to mountaintop." *Journal of Law in Education, 33*(2), 261-273.

Moon, T., C. Brighton, et al. (2005). "Development of authentic assessments for the middle school." *Journal of Secondary Gifted Education, 16*(2/3), 119-133.

Moon, J., & L. Schulman (1995). *Finding the connections: Linking assessment, instruction, and curriculum in elementary mathematics.* Portsmouth, NH: Heinemann.

Morgan, R., J. Whorton, et al. (2000). "A comparison of short-term and long-term retention: lecture combined with discussion versus cooperative learning." *Journal of Instructional Psychology, 30*(1), 53-58.

Moulds, P. (2003/04). "Rich tasks." *Educational Leadership, 61*(4), 75-78.

National Research Council. (1999). *Uncommon measures: Equivalence and linkage among educational tests.* Washington, DC.

Nicholson, M. (January 24, 2006). Proposal to USDE to use value-added as component of AYP. Columbus, Ohio: Battelle For Kids.

Niguidula, D. (2005). "Documenting learning with digital portfolios." *Educational Leadership, 63*(3), 44-47.

O'Connell, S. (2000). *Introduction to problem solving: Strategies for the elementary math classroom.* Portsmouth, NH: Heinemann.

Olson, L. (October 5, 2005). Classroom assessments stir growing global interest. *Education Week, 25*(6), 8. [Reports comments made by Dylan William, James Popham, and Richard Stiggins at Organization for Economic Cooperation and Development meeting, September 12–15, 2005.]

Olson, L. (October 19, 2005). "Purpose of testing needs to shift experts say." *Education Week, 25*(8), 7. [Reports comments made by C. Danielson, K. Langraf, S. Navarro, J. Pellegrino, and L. Shepard at ETS 2005 Invitational Conference, October 10–11, 2005.]

Olson, L. (November 30, 2005). "Benchmark assessments offer regular checkups on student achievement." *Education Week, 25*(13), 13-14.

Patterson, D., & C. Rolheiser (2004). "Creating a culture of change." *Journal of Staff Development, 25*(2), 1-4.

Piaget (1952). *The origins of intelligence in children.* New York: International University Press.

Popham, W. J. (2001). *The truth about testing: An educator's call to action.* Alexandria, VA: Association for Supervision and Curriculum Development.

Postrech, R. (April 30, 1998). *Methods and materials: Discussion forum.* Online document retrieved June 2004 from Postrechr@alpha.montclair.edu

Quinn, T. (2002). "Redefining leadership in the standards era." *Principal, 82*(1), 16-20.

Reeves, D. (2000a). "Finishing the race." *Thrust for Educational Leadership, 29*(5), 26-29.

Reeves, D. (2000b). "Standards are not enough: Essential transformations for school success." *NASSP Bulletin, 84*(620), 5-19.

Reeves, D. (2001a). "If you hate standards, learn to love the bellcurve." *Education Week, 20*(39), 38-52.

Reeves, D. (2001b). "Leave me alone and let me teach!" *School Administrator, 58*(111), 36.

Reeves, D. (2002). *Making standards work: How to implement standards-based assessments in the classroom, school and district.* Advanced Learning Press.

Reeves, D. (2003). "Standards are not anti-child." *Educational Leadership, 32*(3), 19.

Reeves, D. (2004a). *Accountability for learning: How teachers and school leaders can take charge.* Alexandria, VA: Association for Supervision and Curriculum Development.

Reeves, D. (2004b). *Assessing educational leaders.* Thousand Oaks, CA: Corwin Press, National Academy of Secondary School Principals.

Reeves, D. (2005). "Constructive alternative in a destructive debate." *Principal Leadership, 5*(7), 38-43.

Renzulli, J., M. Gentry, et al. (2004). "A time and a place for authentic learning." *Educational Leadership, 62*(1), 73-77.

Rettig, M., L. McCullough, et al. (2003). "A blueprint for increasing student achievement." *Educational Leadership, 61*(3), 71-76.

Richland, L., K. Holyoak, et al. (2004). "Analogy use in eighth-grade mathematics classrooms." *Cognition and Instruction, 22*(1), 37-60.

Rock, T., & C. Wilson (2005). "Improving teaching through lesson study." *Teacher Education Quarterly, 32*(1), 77-92.

Roth-McDuffie, A., & T. Young (2003). "Promoting mathematical discourse through children's literature." *Teaching Children Mathematics, 9*(7), 385-389.

Ruebling, C., S. Stow, et al. (2004). "Instructional leadership: An essential ingredient for improving student learning." *The Educational Forum, 68*(3), 243-253.

Rupley, W., J. Logan, et al. (1999). "Vocabulary instruction in a balanced reading program." *The Reading Teacher, 52*, 336-346.

Sagor, R., & J. Cox (2004). *At-risk students: Reaching and teaching them.* Larchmont, NY: Eye On Education.

Sanders, W. L. (2005). "A summary of conclusions drawn from longitudinal analyses of student achievement data over the past 22 years (1982-2004)." Governors Education Symposium, Asheville, NC (June 10-13).

Schloemer, G. R., & J. Johnson (2003). *Closing the achievement gaps: Toward high achievement for all students.* Columbus, OH: State of Ohio Board of Education Task Force.

Schmidt, W. (2004). "A vision for mathematics." *Educational Leadership, 61*(5), 6-11.

Schmoker, M. (1999). *Results: The key to continuous school improvement.* Alexandria, VA: Association for Supervision and Curriculum Development.

Schmoker, M. (2001). *Results fieldbook: Practical strategies from dramatically improved schools.* Alexandria, VA: Association for Supervision and Curriculum Development.

Schmoker, M. (2004). "Tipping point: From feckless reform to substantive instructional improvement." *Phi Delta Kappan, 85*(6), 424-432.

Senge, P. (1990). *The fifth discipline: The art and practice of the learning organization.* New York: Doubleday.

Senge, P., N. Cambron-McCabe, et al. (2000). *Schools that learn: A fifth discipline fieldbook for educators, parents, and everyone who cares about education.* New York: Doubleday.

Sharkey, N., & R. Murnane (2003). "Learning from student assessment results." *Educational Leadership, 61*(3), 77-81.

Shepard, L. (2005). "Linking formative assessment to scaffolding." *Educational Leadership, 63*(3), 66-71.

Siegler, R. (2003). "Implications of cognitive science research for mathematics education." *A research companion to principles and standards for school mathematics.* J. Kilpatrick, W. G. Martin, & D. Schifter (eds). Reston, VA: The National Council of Teachers of Mathematics.

Smith, T., & L. Desimone (2003). "Do changes in patterns of participation in teachers' professional development reflect the goals of standards-based reform?" *Educational Horizons, 81*(3), 119-129.

Stahl, S., & M. Fairbanks (1986). "The effects of vocabulary instruction: A model-based meta-analysis." *Review of Educational Research 56*: 72-110.

Stanford, P., & S. Reeves (2005). "Assessment that drives instruction." *Teaching Exceptional Children, 37*(4), 18-22.

Sternberg, R. J. (1977). *Intelligence, information processing and analogical reasoning: The componential analysis of human abilities.* Hillsdale, NJ: Erlbaum.

Sternberg, R. J. (1990). "Thinking styles: Keys to understanding student performance." *Phi Delta Kappan, 71*(5), 366-371.

Sternberg, R. J., & E. L. Grigorenko (2004). "Successful intelligence in the classroom." *Theory into Practice, 43*(4), 274-280.

Stien, D., & P. Beed (2004). "Bridging the gap between fiction and nonfiction in the literature circle setting." *The Reading Teacher, 57*(6), 510-518.

Stiggins, R., J. Arter, et al. (2004). *Classroom assessment for student learning: Doing it right, using it well.* Portland, OR: Assessment Training Institute.

Stripling, B. (2003). "Fostering literacy and inquiry." *SLJ/Learning Quarterly, 49*(9), 5-7.

Strong, R., H. Silver, et al. (2001). *Teaching what matters most: Standards and strategies for raising student achievement.* Alexandria, VA: Association for Supervision and Curriculum Development.

Strong, R., H. Silver, et al. (2003). "Boredom and its opposite." *Educational Leadership, 61*(1), 24-29.

Stronge, J., P. Tucker, et al. (2004). *Handbook for qualities of effective teachers.* Alexandria, VA: Association for Supervision and Curriculum Development.

Suchman, R. J. (1962). "The elementary school training program in scientific inquiry." Report to the U.S. Office of Education, Project Title VII. Urbana: University of Illinois.

Sutton, J., & A. Kreuger, Eds. (2002). *EDThoughts: What we know about mathematics teaching and learning.* Aurora, CO: Mid-continent Research for Education and Learning.

Taba, H. (1962). *Curriculum development: Theory and practice.* New York: Harcourt Brace and World.

Taba, H. (1966). *Teaching strategies and cognitive functioning in elementary school children.* San Francisco.

Texas Education Agency (2002). *Research-based content area reading instruction.*

Thelen, H. (1960). *Education and the human quest.* New York: Harper and Row.

Thorndike, E. L. (1928). *Adult Learning.* New York: Macmillan.

Thorndike, E. L. (1932). *The fundamentals of learning.* New York: Teachers College Press.

Thornton, B., G. Peltier, et al. (2004). "Systems thinking: A skill to improve student achievement." *Clearing House, 77*(5), 222-227.

Tomlinson, C. A. (1999a). *The differentiated classroom: Responding to the needs of all learners.* Alexandria, VA: Association for Supervision and Curriculum Development.

Tomlinson, C. A. (1999b). "Mapping a route toward differentiated instruction." *Educational Leadership, 57*(1), 12-16.

Tomlinson, C. A. (2000). "Reconcilable differences: Standards-based teaching and differentiation." *Educational Leadership, 58*(1), 6-11.

Tomlinson, C. A. (2001). *How to differentiate instruction in mixed-ability classrooms.* Alexandria, VA: Association for Supervision and Curriculum Development.

Tomlinson, C. A. (2004). "Sharing responsibility for differentiating instruction." *Roeper Review, 26* (4), 188.

Tyler, R. (1950). *Basic principles of curriculum and instruction.* Chicago: University of Chicago Press.

Udelhofen, S. (2005). *Keys to curriculum mapping: Strategies and tools to make it work.* Thousand Oaks, CA: Corwin Press.

Vacca, R., & J. Vacca (2004). *Content area reading 8th ed.* Boston, MA: Allyn & Bacon.

VanSciver, J. H. (2004). "Challenging students to achieve." *Principal Leadership, 88* (638), 39-42.

Wagner, T. (1998). "From compliance to collaboration: Four leadership qualities needed to change schools." *Education Week, 17*(2), 36-40.

Wagner, T. (2003). "Reinventing America's schools." *Phi Delta Kappan, 84*(9), 665-668.

Walker, S. (2003). "What more can you ask? Artmaking and inquiry." *Art Education, 56*(5), 6-12.

Waters, J. T., R. Marzano, et al. (2004). "Leadership that sparks learning." *Educational Leadership, 61*(7), 48-51.

Weiss, I., & J. Pasley (2004). "What is high-quality instruction?" *Educational Leadership, 61*(5), 24-28.

Wenglinsky, H. (2004). "Facts or critical thinking skills? What NAEP results say." *Educational Leadership, 62*(1), 32-35.

Wies Long, T., & M. Gove (2003). "How engagement strategies and literature circles promote critical response in a fourth-grade, urban classroom." *The Reading Teacher, 57*(4), 350-361.

Wilen, W. (2002). "Conducting effective issue based discussions in social studies classrooms." *International Journal of Social Studies Education, 18*(1), 99-110.

Wood, C. (2002). "Changing the pace of school: Slowing down the day to improve the quality of learning." *Phi Delta Kappan, 83*(7), 545-550.

Wood, K. (2001). *Literacy strategies across the subject areas.* Boston, MA: Allyn & Bacon.

Wormeli, R. (2005). "Busting myths about differentiated instruction." *Principal Leadership, 5*(7), 28-33.

Yendol-Hoppey, D., & K. Tilford (2004). "Does anyone care about elementary social studies? Dilemmas of teaching elementary social studies methods within a high stakes testing context." *Social Studies Review.* Online article find-articles.com.

Zemelman, S., H. Daniels, & A. Hyde (1993). *Best practice: New standards for teaching and learning in America's schools.* Portsmouth, NH: Heinemann.

Zemelman, S., H. Daniels, & A. Hyde (1998). *Best practice: New standards for teaching and learning in America's schools (second ed.).* Portsmouth, NH: Heinemann.

Zull, J. E. (2004). "The art of changing the brain." *Educational Leadership, 62*(1), 68-7.

Index

CORWIN PRESS

The Corwin Press logo—a raven striding across an open book—represents the union of courage and learning. Corwin Press is committed to improving education for all learners by publishing books and other professional development resources for those serving the field of PreK–12 education. By providing practical, hands-on materials, Corwin Press continues to carry out the promise of its motto: **"Helping Educators Do Their Work Better."**